THESE SCATTERED ISLES

OTHER BOOKS BY KÓSTAS MAVRÍKIS

Cartographers and Engravers of the Northern Sporades
Alónnisos in the 17th and 18th Centuries
The Folklore and Crafts of Alónnisos (in preparation)

THESE SCATTERED ISLES

Alónnisos and the Lesser Northern Sporades

Kóstas Mavríkis

edited and translated
with additional research
by

Anthony Hirst

Oxford Maritime Research

Original Greek edition, *Anō magnētōn nēsoi*,
published by Kóstas Mavríkis in Alonnisos;
printed by Editions Lychnia, Sons of Th. Vgontzas Partnership,
Leophoros Athinon & Odhos Markoni, Athens

Second English edition, 2010.
First and second English editions published by:
Oxford Maritime Research
Unit 7, 127 West Central, Milton Park,
Abingdon, Oxfordshire OX14 4SA

British Library Cataloguing in Publication Data

A catalogue record of this book is available from the British Library.

ISBN: 978-0-9566181-1-5

Editing and design by
Martin Noble Editorial
Iffley, Oxford, UK
www.copyedit.co.uk

Second English edition
printed and bound in Great Britain by
Lightning Source UK Ltd,
Chapter House, Pitfield, Kiln Farm,
Milton Keynes MK11 3LW

CONTENTS

This book is dedicated
to the memory
of Debby Fischer

BIOGRAPHICAL NOTE ON THE AUTHOR

KÓSTAS MAVRÍKIS was born on 3 June 1968 at Stení Vála, Alónnisos, where he now runs the Íkaros Supermarket and a cafe. He is married to Angéla Agállou, and they have three children. He is the founder of the Mavríkis Museum, and his ambition is to enrich and extend its collections. This is his second book. His first was *Cartographers and Engravers of the Northern Sporades*, a dual-language publication in Greek and English, based in part on his own collection of old maps; and his third (in Greek only) is *Alónnisos in the 17th and 18th Centuries.* He is now working on a fourth book on the folklore and crafts of Alónnisos.

Figure 0.1 Stení Vála, 1952. *Courtesy of Valándis Vláikos.*

AUTHOR'S PREFACE TO THE GREEK EDITION

FOR THOSE of you who may be interested in the best-known islands of the Northern Sporades, Skópelos and Skiáthos, there are many guidebooks and historical documents, as well as a number of studies by contemporary authors. But very little has been written about Alónnisos – the island where I grew up and where I still live – and even less about the uninhabited islands to the north and east of it. Apart from two historical booklets for tourists, one by X. Athanasíou (1965) and another by A. Sampsón (1973), nothing has been published in recent decades. Having noticed this gap, I determined to fill it as best I could.

Since childhood I have had a great desire to learn who inhabited these islands at various times in the past, what culture they developed, and what writings and archaeological remains they left behind. Filled with enthusiasm, I began to collect objects belonging to people of earlier periods, I searched through books, Greek and foreign, and every day I found something that threw new light on the past. The difficulties were many. First of all, there were very few earlier studies I could turn to for help. Most of the relevant texts were written either in ancient Greek or in foreign languages that needed translating – and until last year my basic occupation was that of fisherman. I felt I was facing a very high mountain, which, given the state of my knowledge, it was going to be almost impossible for me to get over. After a while, with the generous help of many friends, I confronted the problem and began the writing of this book. I gave up many times, feeling that I wasn't capable of transferring to paper all the things that I had learned. But each time, thanks to the urging of friends and the encouragement of my wife, I did eventually resume the task. Finally, after many delays and the passage of two more years, the manuscript was ready for publication.

Alónnisos and the lesser Northern Sporades, with the landscape changing dramatically from island to island, have always delighted visitors, who come to explore and admire the peaceful countryside, the strange geological forms and the visible remains of the past. I have travelled around these islands in the company of people who live or used to live here, and taken photographs of all the traces of ancient habitation I could find, some so impressive and magnificent that they have given rise to legends or become the focus of traditions. I have consulted the writings of Greek and foreign scholars, geographers and travellers, and tried to sort out the various names that the islands have been given at different times. Because of the many alternatives and the imprecision of the ancient geographers, the names have got mixed up over the centuries. Piecing together legends, archaeological evidence and historical accounts and documents, I have tried to give a multifaceted image of the islands of Alónnisos, Peristéra, Kirá Panayá, Yoúra, Pipéri, Psathoúra and Skántzoura.

The sea around these islands is almost as interesting as the islands themselves, for thousands of ships of all periods lie on the sea bed, and together constitute perhaps the most important concentration of wrecks in the world, not only because their sheer number but also because of their significance and the great antiquity of some of them. From the time men first set out to sail the seas with primitive log boats to the present day with its high-technology ships, these islands have served as important junction, stopping place and refuge, but the swift currents and submerged rocks are also an ever-present danger to the unwary or unlucky sailor.

These wrecks have for the most part been preserved from human greed and natural disasters, and still wait in the solitude of the deep to deliver their secrets. When I first encountered some of them in their virgin state, I was overcome by an emotion so powerful that I lost all sense of my body and its movements. When I recovered from the first shock of contact the unanswerable questions begin to emerge: What were theses ships? Where were they going? What dreadful fate had brought them there? The same questions will arise for the local student and the foreign reader. I have done what I can to provide some answers.

All this endeavour emerges from my love and respect for Alónnisos, its marvellous uninhabited islands, and its people.

My warmest thanks to all those who contributed unselfishly and with great enthusiasm towards the publication of this book. I hope that my efforts will not be judged too harshly, for I am not a historian, merely a lover of antiquity devoted to the Northern Sporades.

Stení Vála, Alónnisos, 1995–97
Kóstas D. Mavríkis

Figure 0.2 Kóstas and Angéla Mavríkis with their youngest daughter Nína on a boat travelling between Peristéra and Stení Vála.

AUTHOR'S PREFACE TO THE ENGLISH EDITION

I WAS SURPRISED, delighted and deeply moved when I received the late Debby Fischer's generous proposal to commission an English translation of my book.

Surprised ... because I never thought that a book that was written purely out of love for my island, and by one who is not a historian, would merit presentation to the discerning English-speaking public. Delighted ... to think that the history of the place where I was born and grew up would emerge from obscurity, for now every visitor, and anyone interested in Alónnisos, will have the chance to become acquainted with its long history— its heroes and the events of its troubled past. And deeply moved ... as much by the realisation that there are such people as Debby Fischer who are devoted to the island and willing and eager to offer their support, as by the recognition of all the labour, my wife's as well as mine, that went into the writing of this book.

I hope in the pages that follow that I shall be able to entice my readers into the past, and to help those who may already appreciate the great beauty of Alónnisos to discover another aspect of the island, as I myself did in the course of researching this book. I came to realise the historical significance of my island; and I was inspired to create a museum, as another way of bringing our rich cultural heritage to light. Only those who come to Alónnisos will fully understand my feelings; and I am sure that those who do come to the island will fall under its spell.

Kóstas Mavríkis, Stení Vála, 2010

TRANSLATOR'S ACKNOWLEDGMENTS

Many people were consulted during the lengthy process of producing the English version of this book. I would particularly like to thank Philip Carabott, a historian of Modern Greece, for reading the chapters on the post-Byzantine history of the islands and saving us from a number of errors (any remaining errors are entirely the responsibility of the author and translator). Dr Carabott was pleasantly surprised to learn new things about the exploits of his grandfather, who appears in this book as Captain Yánnis Karabótsos (pp. 240 and 277). The Appendix is largely made up of quotations from the writings of foreigner visitors to the islands, three of them German. It did not seem right to translate these passages from the Greek without reference to the original German, and I am very grateful to Brigit Newcombe who provided me with English translations of the passages from Ross (1851) and Philippson (1901); and to Andy Smith who provided English translations of the passages from Fiedler (1841). Finally I would like to thank the author, Kóstas Mavríkis, for patiently answering my questions during many afternoons in Sténi Vála.

Anthony Hirst, London, 2010

TRANSLATOR'S INTRODUCTION

Greek Words and Names

THIS BOOK contains many hundreds of ancient, Byzantine and modern Greek personal names and place-names, and the translation employs three different systems for the representation of Greek words. Two of these systems play a relatively minor part and are restricted to ancient Greek words and names. For modern personal and place-names and other modern Greek words a phonetic system of transcription has been employed, so that the reader who does not know Greek can gain at least an approximate idea of how the words are pronounced. This system, in which acute accents indicate the position of the stress in words of more than one syllable, is set out in the form of a table on page xxiv. The system is not applied to place-names that have a well established and familiar English form. Thus the reader will find, to give only a few examples, 'Athens' not 'Athína', 'Thessalonica' not 'Thessaloníki', 'Thessaly' not 'Thessalía', and 'Crete' not 'Kríti'. Nor have the names of members of the Greece's (foreign) royal families been transliterated from Greek, since these are familiar in their original, non-Greek forms. The reader will find 'King Otto' not 'Óthonas' and 'Queen Frederica' not 'Fridheríki'.

Transliterated modern Greek proper names are not italicised, though other modern Greek words and phrases are.

Ancient place-names, the names of figures from Greek mythology and ancient Greek history, and the names of ancient Greek authors all have their established English forms, based for the most part on Latin. These are the forms that will generally be found in writing in English about ancient Greece (though there is now a movement to replace the Latinised forms by a more direct representation of the Greek); and it is these Latinised forms (in some cases anglicised beyond the Latin) that are used in this translation. In the case of ancient place-names, these are printed in small capitals, following an initial normal capital. The ancient place-names, 'SCIATHOS' and 'HALONNESOS', represent the same two Greek words as the phonetically transcribed modern names 'Skiáthos' and 'Alónnisos', words whose spelling in Greek has not changed in more than two and a half millennia.

However, while the island of Skiáthos retains its ancient name, the island known today as Alónnisos, as the reader will quickly discover in the first chapter of this book, is not ancient HALONNESOS. There is no consensus among scholars as to which island is the HALONNESOS referred to by several ancient authors. Kóstas Mavríkis presents several different views, and concludes that the most likely candidate is the island immediately to the north of Alónnisos, Kirá Panayá. In some cases names have been modified over time. The modern town of Chalkídha occupies the same position on the southwest coast of the island of Évvia at the point where it almost touches the mainland, as did the ancient town of CHALCIS. The coincidence of modern and ancient place-names, or the distinctions between them, are important parts of the argument in several chapters of this book, and for this reason I have taken advantage of the existence in English of an established system of representing ancient place-names to create, with the additional use of small capitals for the ancient names, a clearer differentiation between them than was possible in the original Greek text. Small capitals are always used for ancient place-names even where Mavríkis is quoting other authors, ancient or modern.

No distinction is made between ancient and modern names for the major geographical divisions of mainland Greece (Attica, Macedonia, the Peloponnese, Thessaly, Thrace, etc.) or the names of groups of islands (the Cyclades, the Northern Sporades) for all of which established English forms exist and are employed throughout this book regardless of the historical period in question.

In the case of ancient personal names the familiar Latinised or anglicised forms are again used, but without small capitals, since there are no modern equivalents from which they need to be distinguished.

In the very few cases where ancient Greek words other than proper names have to be represented, or where the actual spelling or etymology of an ancient name is in question, I have used yet another system, again well established in scholarly works in English, in which each Greek letter is consistently represented by a single distinct letter (or a distinct combination of two letters) of the Latin alphabet. Greek accents are not represented, but the macron (a horizontal line over the letter) is used to distinguish long ***ē*** (*ēta*) and long ***ō*** (*ōmega*) from short ***e*** (*epsilon*) and short ***o*** (*omicron*), and ***h*** is used to represent an initial aspirate, indicated only by a diacritical mark in Greek. In this system Alónnisos /HALONNESOS appears as ***Halonnēsos***. Here, as in the body of the book, ancient Greek words and names that are transliterated in this way, rather than represented by the conventional Latinised equivalents, are printed in ***italic sans serif type***.

Byzantine names raise the question of where the boundary between ancient and modern Greek should be drawn. In general – and it is mainly a question of the personal names of saints and monks, or the names of churches and place names that remain current today – I have treated them as modern Greek and transliterated phonetically. The only exceptions are the names of Byzantine emperors and the names of icon types, which I have treated like ancient names, using the established English forms. Thus the reader will find 'St Athanásios' not 'Athanasius', but 'the Emperor Nicephorus Phocas' not 'Nikifóros Fokás'.

'Áyos' and 'Ayía' (both meaning 'Saint' or 'Holy', masculine and feminine respectively) are retained only for the names of churches, which are treated as modern place-names, and for villages or other localities named after saints. Thus the large modern church in the centre of the old village of Alónnisos is referred to as 'Áyos Nikólaos'. If the saint to whom it is dedicated were mentioned, it would be as 'St Nikólaos', but the icon of St Nikólaos in the old Naós tou Christoú (Church of Christ) in the same village is referred to as 'a St Nicholas'. Icon types have well established English names in art-historical discourse, and others would seem unnecessarily unfamiliar if transliterated ('an Áyos Ioánnis Pródhromos' instead of 'a John the Baptist', for example).

This threefold system for representing Greek names may seem a little complicated when described, but it is hoped that it will in practice make the book easier to read, and create fewer problems than the systematic application of a single system of transcription to all Greek names regardless of period. The visitor to Greece is likely to meet with or hear of people with names such as Afrodhíti, Odhisséfs and Pinelópi, and these names are indeed the same, when written in Greek, as those of the goddess Aphrodite, the Homeric hero Odysseus and his wife Penelope. But it would be as unhelpful to speak of present-day inhabitants of Greece as being called Aphrodite, Odysseus and Penelope as it would be confusing to speak, in English, of the mythological characters as Afrodhíti, Odhisséfs, and Pinelópi.

The Transcription of Modern Greek

The system for transliterating ancient Greek referred to above gives an accurate representation of the spelling of Greek words. The system used in this book for representing modern Greek is not, strictly speaking, a system of transliteration at all, since it does not operate letter by letter and, consequently, does not reflect the way Greek words are spelt. Its purpose is, rather, to provide a reasonably accurate indication of the way the Greek words sound. It uses 23 letters of the English alphabet. The letters **j**, **q** and **w** are not used at all, and **c**, **h** and **u** have no independent values, being used only in the combinations **ch**, **dh**, **th** and **ou**. These four combinations and the twenty letters used independently represent the nineteen basic consonantal sounds and the five vowel sounds of spoken modern Greek. (The letter **x** does not really represent a distinct sound, since it combines the values of **k** and **s**. It is retained because it represents a distinct letter of the Greek alphabet and to substitute **ks** would be to depart further than necessary from Greek spelling.) The combinations **ng** and **ps** (though the latter represents a single Greek letter) are not distinct sounds, since they combine the values of **n** and **g,** and **p** and **s,** respectively. They are included in Table 0.1 simply because they are liable to be mispronounced in certain positions.

Double consonants are employed where they occur in Greek (as in 'Aló**nn**isos'), but they do not affect pronunciation. Except from the combination **ou**, when two or three vowels occur together they do not combine but each represents a separate syllable. When an unstressed **i** precedes another vowel it tends to approximate to **y** (this will come naturally to English speakers), but still remains distinct from the following vowel.

Turkish Names

There are a number of Turkish place-names and a few Turkish personal names and other Turkish words in this book. In the original these are either transliterated into Greek or given in Greek forms that may differ considerably from the Turkish. In order that the reader may identify Turkish place-names on a modern map of Turkey they are given in the proper Turkish spelling (though in some cases the Greek, or common English forms are given as well). Turkish words and names are all printed in sans serif type: Çeşme, Mustafa Kemal.

Table 0.1 Phonetic representation of modern Greek

Letters used	***Approximate phonetic values***
a	between the short **a** in f**a**t and the long **a** in f**a**ther
b	as **b** in **b**et
ch	guttural as in Scottish lo**ch** or German i**ch**, Ba**ch** etc.
d	as **d** in **d**og or han**d**
dh	as **th** in **th**is or fa**th**er (contrast **th** below)
e	always short as in p**e**t
f	as **f** in i**f** or **ff** in o**ff**, never as **f** in o**f**
g	always hard like the first **g** in **g**arage, but more guttural, never soft like the second **g** in gara**g**e
i	as **ee** in m**ee**t
k	as **c** in **c**at or **k** in **k**itten
l	as **l** in **l**et
m	as **m** in **m**et
n	as **n** in **n**et
ng	always as **ng** in a**ng**er, never as in ha**ng**er or da**ng**er
o	always short as **o** in p**o**t
ou	as **oo** in m**oo**n
p	as **p** in **p**et
ps	as **ps** in la**ps**e: the **p** is always sounded, even at the beginning of a word, never silent like the **p** in **p**sychology
r	as in English but slightly rolled and always sounded: never merely a vowel-modifier like the **r** in pa**r**t
s	as **s** in **s**it or **ss** in pa**ss**, like **s** in ha**s** only before **m** and **v**
t	as **t** in **t**in
th	as **th** in **th**in or pa**th**, never as in **th**is or la**th**e (contrast **dh** above)
tz	like **dz** in a**dz**e or **ds** in goo**ds**
v	as **v** in **v**an or e**v**er
x	as **cs** in politi**cs** or **x** in a**x**es, even at the beginning of a word: never modified to a z-sound like the **x** in **x**ylophone
y	always like **y** in **y**et, even in the middle of a word: never merely a vowel-modifier like **y** in gre**y** or pla**y**er
z	as **z** in **z**ebra

The Turkish alphabet uses 22 of the letters in the English alphabet (omitting **q**, **w** and **x**) and creates five additional letters by adding diacritical marks (**ç**, **ğ**, **ö**, **ş**, and **ü**) and a sixth by having an undotted as well as a dotted form of **i** (**ı**). Diacritical marks, including the dot on the **i** are always retained on capitals (**Ç**, **Ğ**, **İ**, **Ö**, **Ş**, **Ü**). The approximate phonetic values of the six pairs of letters distinguished only by the presence or absence of diacritic marks are given in Table 0.2. Other letters are pronounced more or less as in English (**a** and **e** are always short, and **f** always as in **if**, never as in **of**; **j** as **s** in plea**s**ure; **y** may be consonantal as in **y**et, but is also a vowel modifier: **ay** is pronounced as **y** in fl**y**, **ey** as in gr**ey**, **oy** as in b**oy**).

Table 0.2 Letters of the Turkish alphabet that differ from the English

c C	as **j** in **j**et or **g** in **g**in
ç Ç	as **ch** in **ch**in
g G	always hard as **g** in **g**un
ğ Ğ	lengthens the preceding vowel
ı I	similar to **u** in b**u**tter or the second **a** in aval**a**nche
i İ	as **i** in s**i**n or **ee** in s**ee**n
o O	as **o** in h**o**t
ö Ö	as German **ö**, or French **oeu** in **oeu**vre (similar to **er** in n**er**ve)
s S	as **s** in **s**ign
ş Ş	as **sh** in **sh**ine
u U	as **oo** in c**oo**k or **u** in p**u**ll
ü Ü	as German **ü**, or French **u** in t**u** (similar to **u** in imm**u**ne)

BIOGRAPHICAL NOTE ON THE TRANSLATOR

Anthony Hirst was until recently a lecturer in Byzantine and Modern Greek in the Institute of Byzantine Studies at Queen's University Belfast. He remains Director of the international Byzantine Greek Summer School at Queen's University and is also Academic Director of the Durrell School of Corfu. He is the author of *God and the Poetic Ego* (2004), a study of the use and abuse of biblical and liturgical language in the work of three modern Greek poets; he edited (with Michael Silk) *Alexandria, Real and Imagined* (2004), and also edited the Greek text for C.P. Cavafy, *The Collected Poems* in the Oxford World's Classics series (2007). He has translated volumes of poetry by Cavafy and Vrettákos (the latter with Kathryn Baird) to be published in the series, Library of Modern Greek Classic Authors.

NOTE ON THE ALÓNNISOS PHOTO-MUSEUM PROJECT

THE MAVRÍKIS family and the Fischer family have initiated the Alónnisos Photo-Museum Project (http://www.alonissosmuseum.com) to create a picture archive of Alónnisos, its people, and its visitors. We are enormously grateful to all those who have already contributed to the archive so generously.

For the English edition of this book we have taken the opportunity to showcase a small sample of the first images to illustrate the history. Eventually the whole archive will be available to view online.

We aim to collect as many pictures as possible for the archive, and for this purpose quality is not an issue. If you have any images you would like to contribute, please visit:

http://www.alonissosmuseum.com/pages/Museum-Friends.html

Figure 0.3 Vótsi, 1969. *Courtesy of Fótis Tzortzátos.*

LIST OF FIGURES, TABLES & MAPS

Figures

Tables

Maps

Modern Maps

Historical Maps

MODERN MAPS

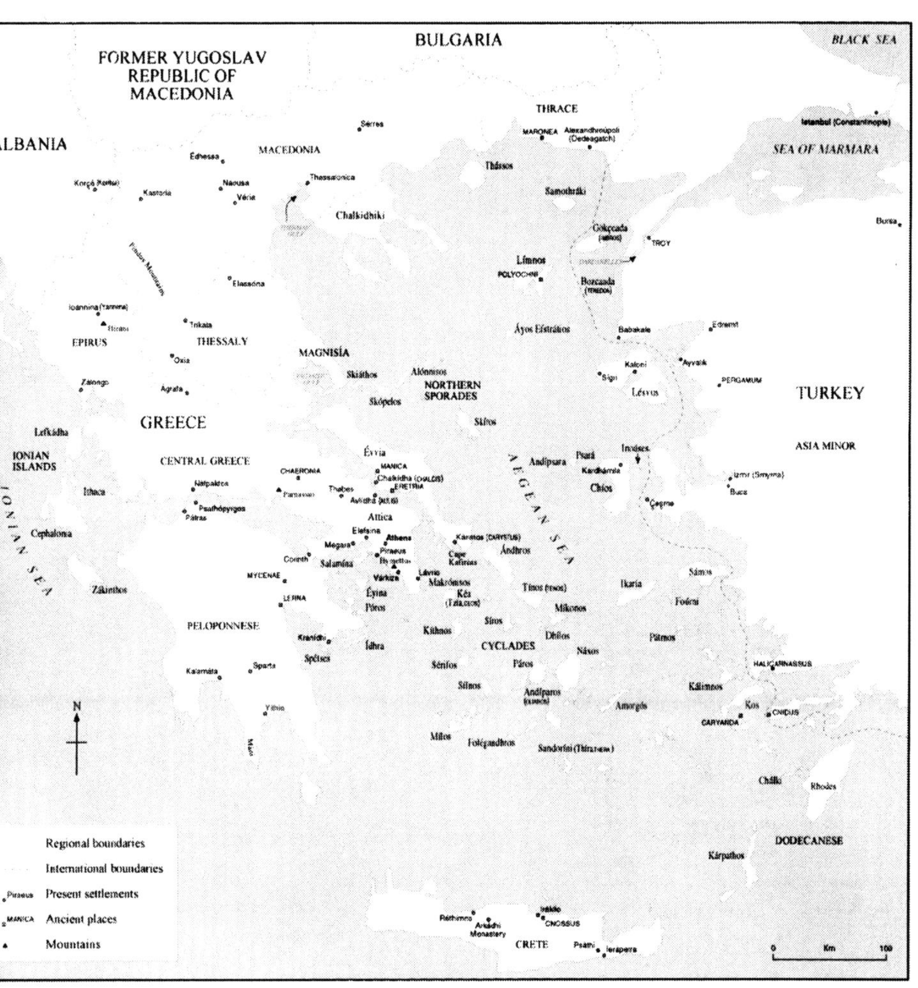

Map 1 Greece and its neighbours. *Drawn by Susie Jones.*

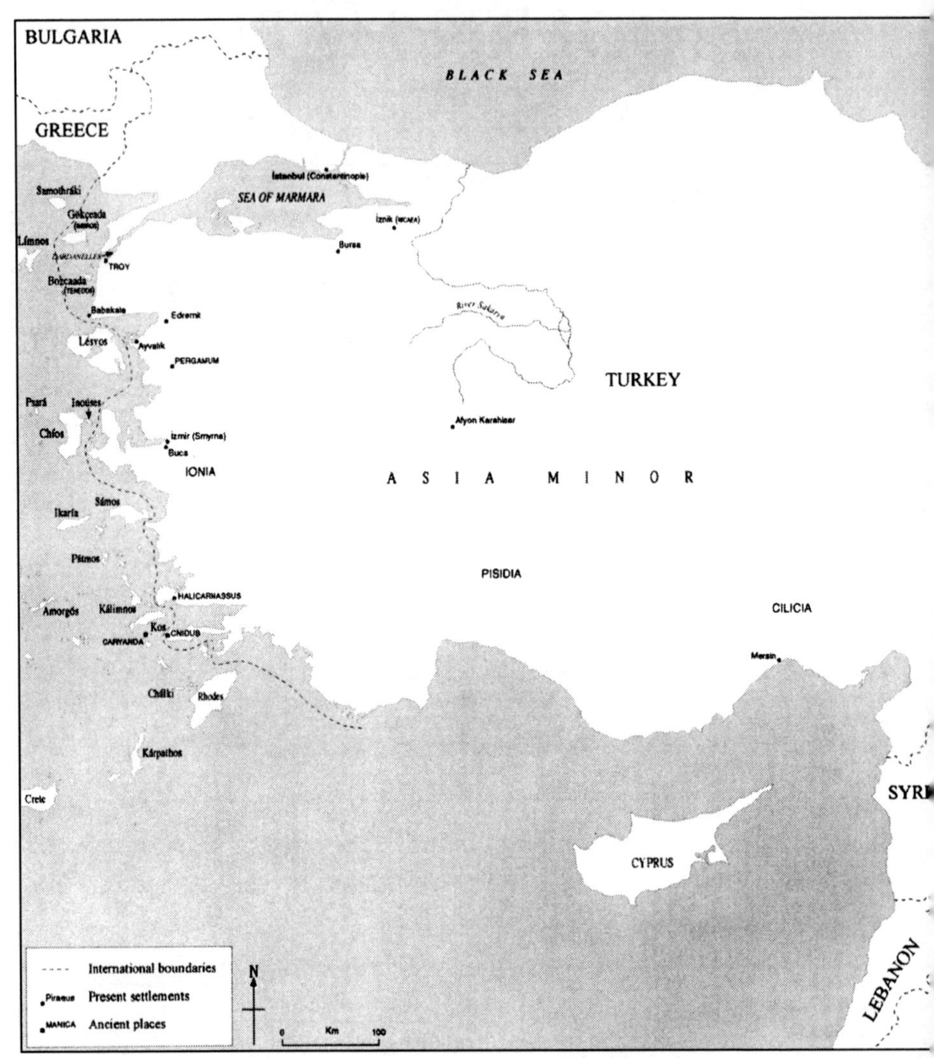

Map 2 Western Turkey. *Drawn by Susie Jones*

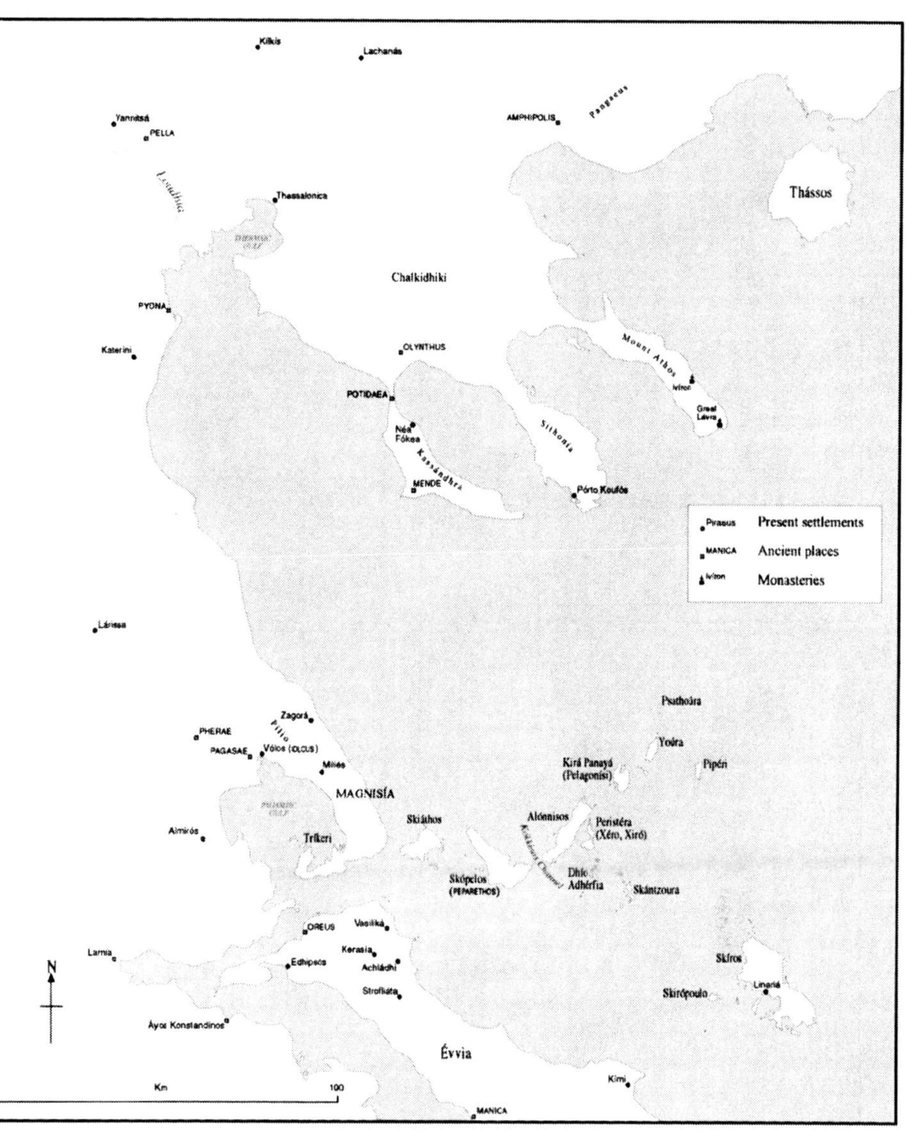

Map 3 The northwestern Aegean. *Drawn by Susie Jones.*

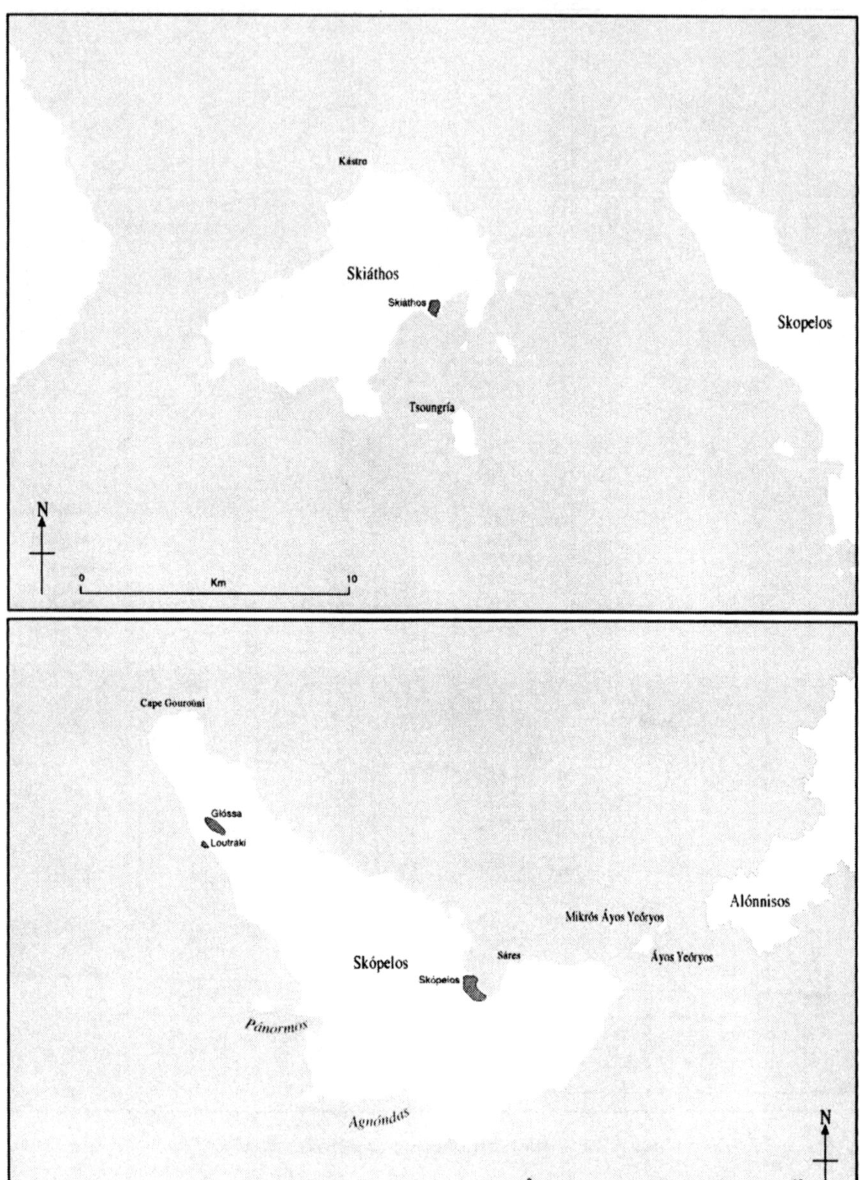

Map 4 *Top*: Skiáthos; *bottom*: Skópelos. *Drawn by Susie Jones.*

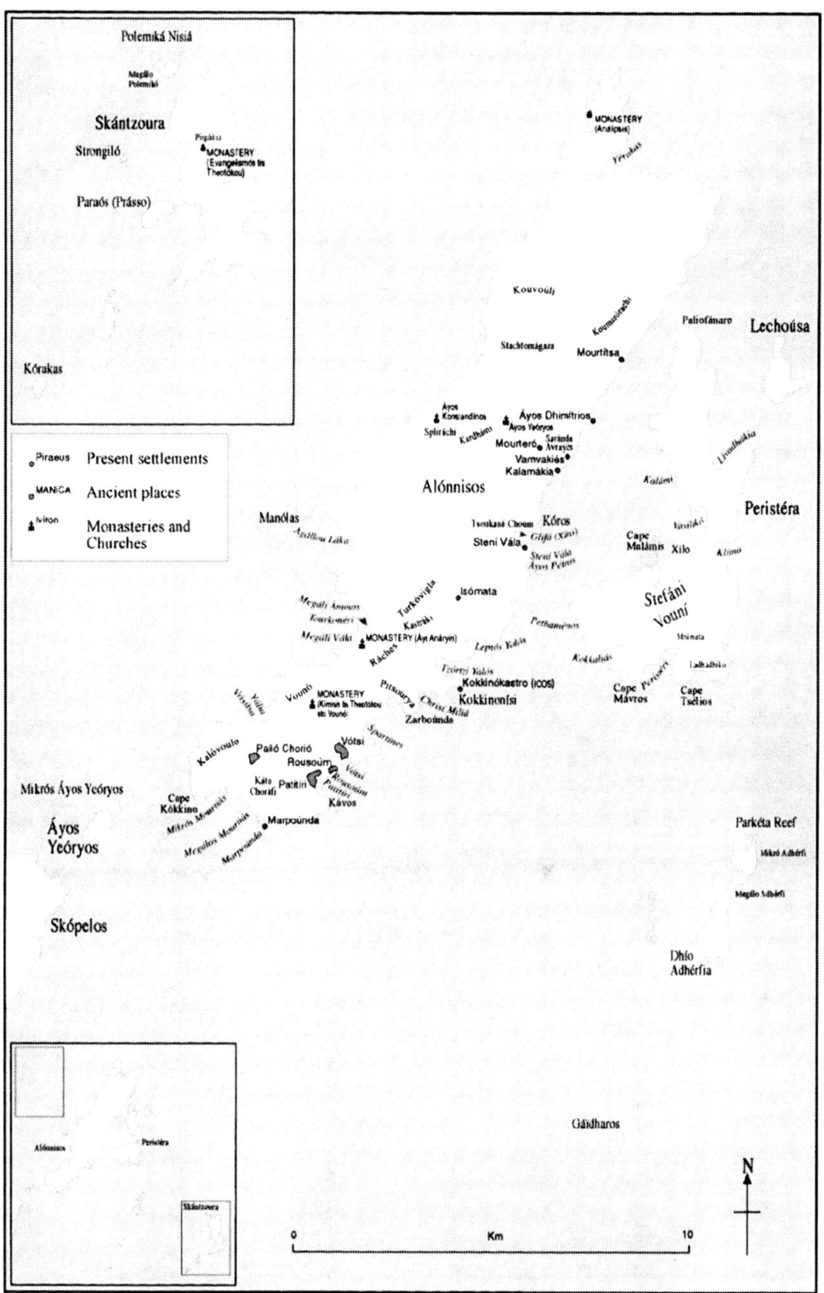

Map 5 Alónnisos and Peristéra. *Drawn by Susie Jones.*

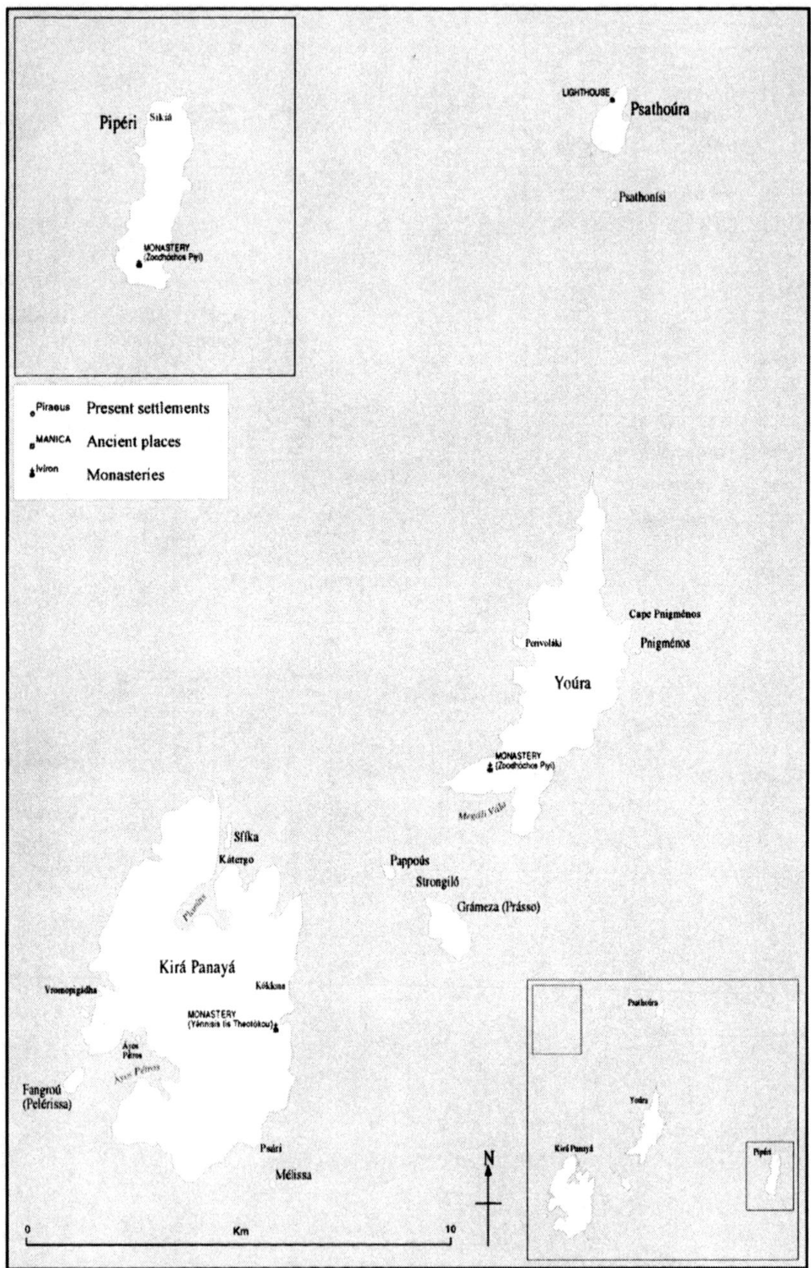

Map 6 The lesser Northern Sporades. *Drawn by Susie Jones.*

THE ISLANDS

Figure 1.1 The lateen-rigged boat of Bárba Kóstas Agállou, Peristéra, 1973. *Courtesy of Nikólaos Agállou.*

ALÓNNISOS, Peristéra, Lechoúsa, Kirá Panayá, Grámeza, Pappoús, Yoúra, Psathoúra, Pipéri, Dhío Adhérfia and Skántzoura constitute a unique complex of islands in the central Aegean, at latitude 38° 45′–39° 45′ north, and longitude 23° 30′–24° 50′ east. Each island has its own characteristic charm and offers its own particular delights to the visitor.

Between Alónnisos and Peristéra a great 'lake' has formed with sheltered harbours and clean beaches. Kirá Panayá and Skántzoura with their fertile soil, their imposing monasteries and natural refuges, offer a feeling of security; on Yoúra, considered the wildest island of the archipelago, the scenery is breathtaking. On Psathoúra, whose tropical landscape is unique in the Mediterranean, you feel totally alone, as though you had landed on some desert island; while on remote Pipéri you think you may be disturbing the peace of some ascetic. This pleasing picture is completed by the rocky islets that surround the larger islands like moons around their planets.

Figure 1.2 Fishing in the Northern Sporades, 1957. *Courtesy of Holger Reichhart.*

Ownership of the islands is rather complex. Alónnisos has been a part of the Greek state since 1830, as have all the other islands of the group. The Northern Sporades were among the first groups of islands to be included under the terms of the London Protocol of 1830, when an independent Greek state was formed from former Ottoman provinces, following the destruction of the Ottoman and Egyptian fleets in Navarino harbour in 1827. The Municipality of Alónnisos is responsible for the administration of the islands of Peristéra, Dhío Adhérfia and Lechoúsa; while Skántzoura, Grámeza, Pappoús and Kirá Panayá belong to the monastery of the Great Lávra on Mount Athos, which leases them to private individuals. Pipéri is owned by the Lemonís family from Skópelos. Yoúra was once offered to the King of Greece for the excellent hunting of wild goats it offered. The king, however, coming by ship to view the island and seeing its wild mountainous terrain, declined the offer, and since then Yoúra has belonged to the Greek state. It is now administered by the Forestry Department of Skópelos. Psathoúra is a special case: one part is privately owned by people from Alónnisos, another belongs to the Municipality of Skópelos, while the area around the lighthouse belongs to the Greek Navy.

The flora and fauna of these islands are truly amazing. On and around the islands live many rare and almost extinct species of animals, including the Mediterranean monk seal (*Monachus monachus*), the Aegean gull (*Larus audouinii*), the wild goat of Yoúra (*Capra aegagrus*, known locally as the *kri-kri*), the striped dolphin (*Stenella coeruleoalba*) and the sperm-whale (*Physeter catodon*). The flora too is exceptional, with mosses and wild flowers, a wide variety of tree species, and an impressive range of rock plants. The underwater flora is equally abundant, with endless submarine meadows and with forests of seagrass (*Posidonia oceanica*). With a mean annual temperature of 17 °C, the climate is favourable to a wide variety of plant and animal species. Recognition of the richness of local natural life led to the creation by presidential decree of the National Marine Park of Alónnisos Northern Sporades in May 1992.[1] Table 1.1 gives the size of each of the islands described in this book. It includes all the islands and rocky islets over a certain size. There are hundreds of other smaller rocky islets or isolated rocks, which are not included because of their limited interest.

Table 1.1 The size of the islands

Island	***Surface area (km^2)***	***Coastline (km)***
Alónnisos	65.090	79.110
Dhío Adhérfia: Megálo Adhérfi	1.050	6.250
Mikró Adhérfi	0.400	3.200
Fangroú	0.178	1.698
Grámeza	0.844	4.449
Kasídhi	0.008	0.356
Kórakas	0.120	1.557
Kirá Panayá	24.970	40.790
Lachanoú	0.049	0.939
Lechoúsa	0.620	4.560
Mélissa	0.004	0.272
Nisáki Pnigménou	0.012	0.475
Nisiá Polemiká	0.115	1.503
Pappoús	0.080	1.267
Peristéra	14.510	36.260
Pipéri	4.160	12.920
Prásso	0.264	2.773
Psathonísi	0.021	0.596
Psathoúra	0.771	4.330
Sfíka	0.055	1.204
Skántzoura	6.320	21.580
Yoúra	11.180	28.250

Source: Electronic archive of the Hydrographic Service of the Greek Navy.

The inhabitants of our islands are generally hospitable and hard-working with a strong sense of family ties. The influx of summer tourists, outnumbering the local population, has done little to change our social relations, or our manners and customs. The inhabitants of Alónnisos are involved mainly in tourism, fishing and stock breeding; and to a lesser extent in construction work, agriculture and resin tapping. The other islands in the group were gradually abandoned as their inhabitants moved to Alónnisos, which is the centre for all activities, providing primary and secondary schools and a hospital. Patitíri serves as the capital for all the islands. The municipal offices and the market are located there. Other settlements on Alónnisos include Palió Chorió, Vótsi, Rousoúm, Stení Vála, and Kalamákia. The rest of the islands are uninhabited except for a few herdsmen on Kirá Panayá, Peristéra and Skántzoura. In recent years one or two monks have also returned to Kirá Panayá.

The highest point in the island group is the summit of the mountainous mass of Yoúra at 516 m above sea level, followed by Kouvoúli, a peak on Alónnisos, at 476 m. There are two important areas of winter marshland, one at Áyos Dhimítrios and the other at Paliofánaro on Peristéra, and both attract migrating birds. Caves are found on all the islands, but above all on Yoúra and Pipéri, where underwater caves with their phosphorescent organisms amaze the visitor.

Note

1. *Fíllo Efimerídhas Kivérnisis* (Government Gazette) 519/92.

Figure 1.3 Fishing boats at Kirá Panayá, 1971. *Courtesy of Fótis Tzortzátos.*

Figure 1.4 The warden K. Kiriazís collecting a *kri-kri* (wild goat) killed by hunters.

Figure 1.5 Children on a donkey in Palió Chorió. *Courtesy of K. Efstathíou.*

Figure 1.6 View of Patitíri, 1952. *Courtesy of the Ziméris Archive.*

Figure 1.7 Yeóryos Malamaténios ploughing on Pipéri.

2

THE NAMES OF THE ISLANDS

IN ANCIENT texts the Northern Sporades appear as *Magnētōn nēsoi*, the 'islands of the Magnetans' (or Magnesians),[1] that is, the inhabitants of the region of Magnesia, which lies close by on the mainland. But the name in common use at the time of the 1821 Revolution was Dhemonónisi, 'Demon Islands'. They were given this name because in those days they were a refuge for pirates. For the same reason they were also referred to as the *Kleptofoleé*, 'Thieves' Dens', while to the Turks they were known as Şeytan Adaları, 'Satan's Islands'.

2.1 Alónnisos

Figure 2.1 Palió Chorió, 1960. *Courtesy of Athanásios Páppos.*

The name Alónnisos was given to our island, rather carelessly and quite erroneously, by a decree of the Ministry of the Interior in 1836. We should remember, of course, the chaotic state of affairs that prevailed during those years of reorganisation. The post-revolutionary government, having other urgent matters to attend to, gave second place to the question of exact nomenclature. Before its official 'baptism' as Alónnisos, the island had appeared in documents of the revolutionary period, and also in the London Protocol of 1830, as Iliodhrómia.

Figure 2.2 Bárba Panaís, Stení Vála, Alónnisos, 1978.
Courtesy of M. and D. Papavasilíou.

During the period of Turkish rule Alónnisos was often referred to by foreign travellers and cartographers by the strange name of 'Dromo' or 'Dromos', from *dhrómos*, which in modern Greek means 'road'. It may have got this name originally from the tomb of Peleus, which, according to the testimony of ancient authors, was situated on the island. A certain Molenas[2] invited Peleus, the father of Achilles, to spend his old age on the island we now call Alónnisos. After Peleus' death Molenas, following the Mycenaean custom, built an imposing tomb to honour him. Mycenaean royal tombs always had a *dromos*, that is to say, an impressive stone-paved approach road.[3] If the tradition is reliable, the imposing character of this tomb and its *dromos* gave the island its name.

Alónnisos also appears as Achilleodhrómios, Chiliodhrómia, Liadhrómia and Dhiádhromos ('Passageway').[4] All these names suggest some connection with the demigod and hero, Achilles, or his father's tomb. But there are many who dispute the correctness of this derivation and maintain instead that these names reflect the island's geographical position. In every period Alónnisos has been at the centre of all the Aegean sea routes, at the meeting point, that is, of 'a thousand roads', or *chílii dhrómi* in Greek. Hence the name Chiliodhrómia, which could have been corrupted to Achilleodhrómios ('Achilles' road') or Iliodhrómios ('Sun's road'), and shortened to Liadhrómia or Dhrómos.

However, the name given to the island by all the writers and geographers of the pre-classical, classical, Hellenistic and Roman periods is *Ikos* (ICOS in its Latin form).[5] This is a pre-Hellenic name, like many other names beginning with 'I', such as *Ikaros* (Icarus), *Ilisos* (the river ILISSUS), etc. Usually the pre-Hellenic peoples named places after their founder, some famous warrior or chieftain, who in the case of Alónnisos appears to have been called *Ikos*.

Scholars have always disagreed, as we shall see, about the identity and position of ancient HALONNESOS. There can be little doubt, though, that our island, the present-day Alónnisos, is the ancient ICOS. The geographer of antiquity, Strabo, informs us that:

> off the country of the Magnetans lie numerous islands, but the only notable ones are SCIATHOS, PEPARETHOS, ICOS, and also HALONNESOS and SCYROS, all having cities of the same name.[6]

We see that he places the ancient ICOS after SCIATHOS and PEPARETHOS (modern Skiáthos and Skópelos) in the position of present-day Alónnisos. Another piece of evidence which leads us to a secure identification of the island is an inscription discovered by Yeóryos and Chrístos Athanasíou. At Tsoukaliás these two archaeologists found an inscribed amphora handle from a local workshop. In the clay of the handle the word ΙΚΙΩΝ (*Ikiōn*) had been impressed. Coins with this same inscription have also been found on the island.[7]

Two German scholars and geographers, Ludwig Ross and Carl Fredrich, came to the island at different times (Ross in 1841, Fredrich in 1905), and after careful research identified it with ICOS. But Ross and Fredrich both made the same unfortunate mistake about HALONNESOS, identifying it as the present-day Áyos Efstrátios, which lies to the south of Límnos and is not one of the Northern Sporades.[8] Below we shall see that historical evidence indicates that this cannot be the case.

2.2 Kirá Panayá, or Pelagonísi, the Ancient HALONNESOS

The next island in the chain after Alónnisos is Kirá Panayá, which owes its modern name to the fact that since Byzantine times it has belonged to Mount Athos. According to Athonite tradition, all the outlying monastic possessions are dedicated to the Mother of God, as is the peninsula of Athos itself (and this is one reason why no other women are admitted to the Holy Mountain). Kirá Panayá is one of the titles of the Virgin Mary, and in relatively recent times the monks gave this name to the island itself.

Figure 2.3 Easter celebrations at the monastery, Kirá Panayá, 1952.

After persistent searching through many ancient sources as well as making some local investigations, I have reached the conclusion that the HALONNESOS of the ancients is the island we today call Kirá Panayá. It is evident from surviving texts that there was a bitter struggle between the Athenians and the Macedonians over the island they called HALONNESOS. In the 4th century BC the Macedonians began to expand as a naval power, while the Athenians were determined to hold on to the influence they had until then exercised in the northern Aegean region.

What both sides wanted above all was a naval station in the centre of the north Aegean, and both saw HALONNESOS as the ideal place. It was well provided with springs for the supply of water, and had an abundance of natural foodstuffs; above all, its forest offered wood for shipbuilding. Topographically Kirá Panayá is certainly well suited to be a naval base, since it has two secure harbours, one at Áyos Pétros in the south, the other at Planítis in the north. Even today these natural harbours are considered the best in the northern Aegean. There is no other island in the region so well provided with harbours. Indeed, we encounter steep rocky shores throughout most of the islands in the group.

Figure 2.4 Olive press at the monastery, Kirá Panayá. *Courtesy of Anthony Hirst.*

Figure 2.5 Fishermen relaxing on Kirá Panayá, 1950.

On Kirá Panayá there are the remains of two castles: the watch tower of Tzavétis which commands the central part of the island, and a larger castle on the east side of the bay of Planítis. The latter is very extensive and overlooks the whole of the bay, and stands, surely, on the site of the ancient city of HALONNESOS to which Strabo refers.

In the surrounding area there are clear traces left by men of the classical and Hellenistic periods, including pottery and the remains of buildings. The strongest argument for identifying Kirá Panayá with HALONNESOS rests on the etymological connection between the ancient Greek name HALONNESOS and Pelagonísi, the Byzantine name of Kirá Panayá. The name *Halonnēsos* is made up of two ancient Greek words, *hals (halos* in the genitive), which means 'sea', and *nēsos* ('island'),[9] and thus means 'island in the sea'.

Admittedly this seems a rather empty meaning since all islands are islands in the sea. But something that is not obvious to us must have prompted the pre-Hellenic inhabitants of the island to give it this name. Since we do not know what prompted them, naturally we cannot understand their reasoning. It was common in later periods to take the ancient place-names seriously and devise new names with a similar meaning. Bewildered, unable to fathom the mystery of its meaning, the Byzantines followed this practice, and called the island Pelagonísi. Thus today we have two names: one ancient Greek, HALONNESOS, which means 'island in the sea', and one Byzantine, Pelagonísi, which has the same meaning, since *pélagos*, like *hals*, means 'sea', and *nisí* is a modern variant of *nēsos*.

In an official document of AD 993, recording the purchase of the island by St Athanásios the Athonite, it is named Yimnopelayísion, a variant form of Yimnopelagonísi ('barren island in the sea'). Many foreign travellers, including

Porcacchi (1572), Gastaldi (1575), Mallet (1683) and Choiseul-Gouffier (1782), called it 'Pelagnisis'. The variant 'Pelegisa' appears in a portolan chart of the Aegean dated 1664 and was also used by Lapie (1838), while Dapper (1703) and Van der Aa (1729) actually refer to this island as 'Alonesus', thus identifying it with ancient HALONNESOS.[10]

2.3 Yoúra

The island of Yoúra is probably the GERONTIA of the ancients.[11] (We shall give below some evidence for the alternative view that it could be the ancient HALONNESOS.) According to Chrístos Athanasíou, the name Yoúra comes from the ancient word *gualon* or *guaron* (*l* and *r* are often interchangeable in Greek) which means 'cavern' or 'hollow'.[12] It is a most suitable name, since it reflects the topography of the island, the steep mountainous terrain that favours the development of caves (an environment perfectly suited to the rare wild goats found there).

The numerous caves were often utilised by the inhabitants and may have prompted them to give the island the name Yoúra. A variant name, 'Jura', is applied to the island by Mercator (1590), and 'Joura' by Lapie, but the island is referred to by its present name of Yoúra, spelt 'Iura', in the charts and descriptions of many other foreigners, including Gastaldi, Lauremberg (1638), Visscher (1682), Mallet, Da Vignola (1685), Boschini (1658) and Delisle (1733); and Yoúra is the name that was officially given to the island in 1836.

Figure 2.6 The *kri-kri* of Yoúra, a breed of goats found nowhere else in the world. *Courtesy of Thomas Vestrum.*

In the writings of many travellers, Yoúra is described as the 'Isle du Diable' ('Devil's Isle'), because it is so jagged, rocky and precipitous that it strikes fear into anyone who thinks of setting foot on it. Among those who were sufficiently impressed by its wildness to give the island such a bloodcurdling name are d'Anville (1756) and Choiseul-Gouffier. In antiquity, according to Ioánnis M. Skavéntzos (a scholar from Skópelos), Yoúra and Psathoúra were known collectively as HALONNESOS:

> There are no grounds whatever for the islands of Kirá Panayá and Xéro [Peristéra] to lay claim to either of the ancient names ICOS and HALONNESOS. Kirá Panayá was certainly a part of the territory of the Magnetans, but it does not offer any signs of either ancient or more recent habitation. But Yoúra and Psathoúra, though they are considered of less importance than Kirá Panayá, show evidence of many settlement sites. Close to Psathoúra in the direction of Yoúra there are the submerged remains of a city that was destroyed by a volcanic eruption.[13]

Figure 2.7 The first two regular ferry boats serving Alónnisos, 1967, *Kíknos* (*Swan*) and *Thira. Courtesy of Athanásios Páppos.*

2.4 Psathoúra

Psathoúra is the most northerly of all the islands of the group. Its name comes, as we shall see in more detail below, from the fact that it resembles a rush mat (*psátha* in Greek) lying on the sea. Close to this island, as Skavéntzos noted, there are ruins of sunken buildings. From my personal investigations I have come to the conclusion that this island may well be the ancient CHRYSE. As a place-name, CHRYSE ('Golden') was given to cities that either possessed gold mines or had some connection with 'Golden Athena', such as a temple dedicated to her. Let us see what the great geographer of antiquity, Pausanias, has to tell us about it:

> The following incident proves the might of fortune to be greater and more marvellous than is shown by the disasters and prosperity of cities. No long sail from LEMNOS was once an island CHRYSE, where it is said, Philoctetes met with his accident from the water-snake. But the waves utterly overwhelmed it, and CHRYSE sank and disappeared in the depths. [. . .] So temporary and utterly weak are the fortunes of men.[14]

Let us turn now to the Homeric epics and other ancient writings to learn more of the island of CHRYSE and Philoctetes. When Jason stopped at CHRYSE (the first port of call in his voyage from ancient IOLCUS in Magnesia) he erected an altar in honour of Athena, who bears the epithet ***chrysē***. At this altar the most ancient of all seafarers sought the help of the goddess in his difficult quest for the Golden Fleece in the rich lands around the Black Sea. There are many other references in Homer (900/700 BC), while Sophocles, in his tragedy *Philoctetes* (409 BC), describes in the greatest detail the dramatic story that unfolded on the island of CHRYSE.[15] The story runs as follows.

The leaders of the Trojan expedition received an oracle to the effect that if they wanted to seize TROY, they must first find the buried temple of Athena (buried probably by an earthquake) and offer a sacrifice there. Only Philoctetes knew where to find the hidden temple, and he showed it to the commanders of the waiting Greek fleet. For this he was punished by the Goddess with the bite of a guardian snake. The wound festered and would not heal, and the Greeks, unable to bear either the smell of the wound or Philoctetes' cries, abandoned him on the island of LEMNOS for the duration of the war. Philoctetes was continually tormented by frightful pains, and his sufferings ended only after a new oracle declared that the Greeks would not take TROY without the weapons of Heracles, which were in the possession of the wounded Philoctetes. Neoptolemus undertook to obtain the weapons and sailed to LEMNOS with Odysseus. Neoptolemus gained possession of Philoctetes' bow by deception, but was overcome by remorse and would have given it back but for the intervention of Odysseus. After further discussion he did return it, but Heracles himself then appeared and commanded Philoctetes to go to TROY and assist in its final defeat.

The reasons for connecting Psathoúra with ancient CHRYSE are as follows. First, it is on the route of both the Argonauts and the Trojan expedition. Secondly, Psathoúra is volcanic. (Its tropical beaches, its dark colour and its low elevation – it rises to only 14 m above sea level – remind one of the volcanic islands of Polynesia.) Thirdly, I think it not unlikely that the buildings submerged beneath the sea are a temple complex. Neither the size of the island nor its exposure to the winds would have favoured habitation and the growth of settlements.

Psathoúra is referred to as 'Arsura' by Gastaldi, Mercator, Lauremberg, Boschini, Visscher, Dapper, Da Vignola, Coronelli (1696) and Bauprand (1716). The Portolan Chart of the Aegean and Mallet add the initial consonant L and name the island 'Larsura'. It is also given two other rather strange names: 'Larzar' by Robijn (1683), and 'Isle Plane' ('flat island') by Roux (1764) and Lapie.

Another attested view, which seems, however, not to have convinced many, is that Psathoúra is the ancient HALONNESOS. This view was put forward by Ioánnis Sarrís in an article entitled 'Which is the Ancient HALONNESOS?' He rejects the hypotheses of other researchers (to which we need not refer here) as to which island is the HALONNESOS of the ancients, and puts forward a forceful argument which deserves to be noted. Sarrís agrees in part with Skavéntzos, but acknowledges only Psathoúra as the island in question. He writes as follows:

> This island is scarcely 2 sq. km. in extent. Next to it there is an even smaller island called Psathonísi, separated from Psathoúra by a channel with a maximum depth of 7 m. Geologically both islands are composed of hard

igneous rocks, which provide the inhabitants of Iliodhrómia with millstones and grindstones. The small size of Psathoúra is not necessarily an obstacle to accepting its identification with ancient HALONNESOS, since DELOS, which is also very small, was, in ancient times, the most important of the Cyclades. At least three arguments lead to the conclusion that Psathoúra is the ancient HALONNESOS.

(1) This island occupies a strategic position: as the most northerly of the Northern Sporades, it lies closer to Macedonia than any of the others. For Philip II of Macedon, who was planning to seize the Northern Sporades as part of the gradual encirclement of ATHENS by a network of fortified bases, the obvious course would be to begin by seizing the nearest of these islands. HALONNESOS [i.e. Psathoúra] would serve him as a naval station between Macedonia and OREUS [in Évvia] which he had recently captured (343 BC). To this day, ships sailing around Évvia bound for Thessalonica pass by this island; this could explain the existence there of pirates in the time of Philip II. Today a lighthouse on the island serves passing ships, but apart from the lighthouse keeper only a few shepherd families live there.

Figure 2.8 The lighthouse keeper, Psathoúra, 1958.

(2) Psathoúra is truly a *halonnēsos* [an 'island in the sea'], that is to say, it is a low-lying island, barely 10 m above sea level on the west, which during storms appears to be largely submerged by the waves [...]. Furthermore, the modern names Psathoúra and Psathonísi also signify that it is low-lying, like a 'rush mat' (*psátha* in Greek) in the midst of the sea. There are many similar place-names with the same significance, such as Psátha (near Mégara), Psathópyrgos (on the Gulf of Corinth), Psathákia

> (near Yíthion in the Peloponnese) and Psáthi (near Ierápetra in Crete). As the ancient name HALONNESOS and the modern name Psathoúra both allude to the form of the island, they also distinguish it from those nearby, which, being high and mountainous, present a very different aspect. Indeed, the two nearest islands, Yoúra and Pipéri are particularly high and inaccessible.
>
> (3) According to the testimony of Strabo, HALONNESOS had a city, and among all these islands it is only here on Psathoúra that there exist the remains of a city,[16] for the most part under water today. The sponge divers of the Dodecanese who explore the Aegean sea bed, speak with astonishment of the submerged ruins between Psathoúra and Psathonísi, reporting walls of houses with the lower parts of door and window openings. It seems, then, that a part of the island that was once dry land has been transformed into a shallow sea bed. None of the chroniclers tell us when this city was drowned, nor is this submerged city known to the scientific world. It is only among the sponge divers and the inhabitants of Chiliodhrómia that it has always been well known, as has that other submerged city in the shallows of Cháros, in the area of Xéres ['Reefs'], twelve nautical miles east of Límnos. [. . .] It is evident that in ancient times HALONNESOS [i.e. Psathoúra] had a greater surface area than today, and was joined to Psathonísi. Between them a small bay, which admittedly can no longer be clearly made out, would have served as the harbour of the city.[17]

Sarrís concludes by referring to the sequence of the names of the islands in Strabo[18] (see above), but this serves equally well, if not better, as an argument for identifying ancient HALONNESOS with Kirá Panayá.

2.5 Pipéri

With all the confusion of names among the numerous small islands that make up the lesser Northern Sporades, it is very difficult to sort out which ancient names belong where. By a process of elimination we would have to attach the ancient name IRESIA to modern Pipéri. The name Pipéri is adopted by all the travellers of the medieval and later periods. There are two schools of thought about the origin of this unusual name, but neither is altogether persuasive.

The first, which has wide support, is that the name refers to the shape of the island, which resembles a large peppercorn (*pipéri* is Greek for pepper). Ludwig Ross, in his account of his voyage to the island with King Otto, takes this view, and observes that other rocky islands have been given this name for the same reason. The alternative explanation of the name is that the terrain of the island is such as to make it inaccessible to sailors: it offers no anchorage and no shelter from the sun, and therefore burns like pepper those who venture there.

The island is called 'Piper' by Gastaldi and Mercator in the 16th century; and the same in the 17th century by Boschini, Robijn and Coronelli. In the 18th century it is referred to as 'Pipéri' by d'Anville, but more often as 'Piper', as, for example, by Seller (1675) and Van der Aa, while in a monastic document of the 1830s it is erroneously given the name Pepárithos (that is, PEPARETHOS, the ancient name of Skópelos).

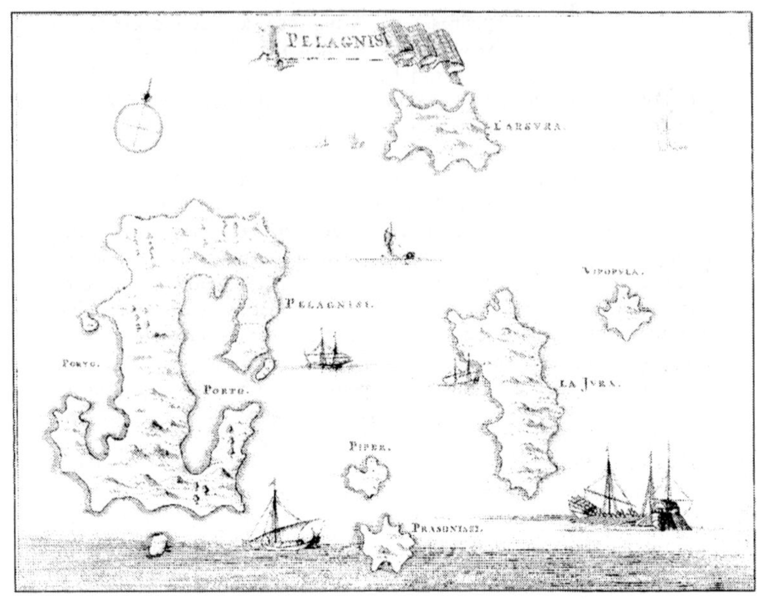

Map 7 Dapper, 1688 (Kirá Panayá, Yoúra, Psathoúra and Pipéri).
Source: *Kóstas and Angéla Mavríkis' collection of old maps.*

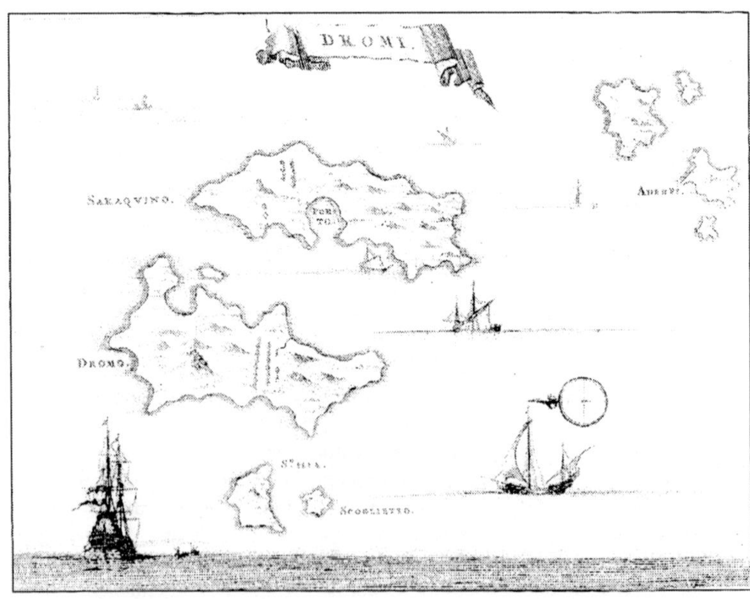

Map 8 Dapper, 1688 (Alónnisos, Peristéra and Dhío Adhérfia).
Source: *Kóstas and Angéla Mavríkis' collection of old maps.*

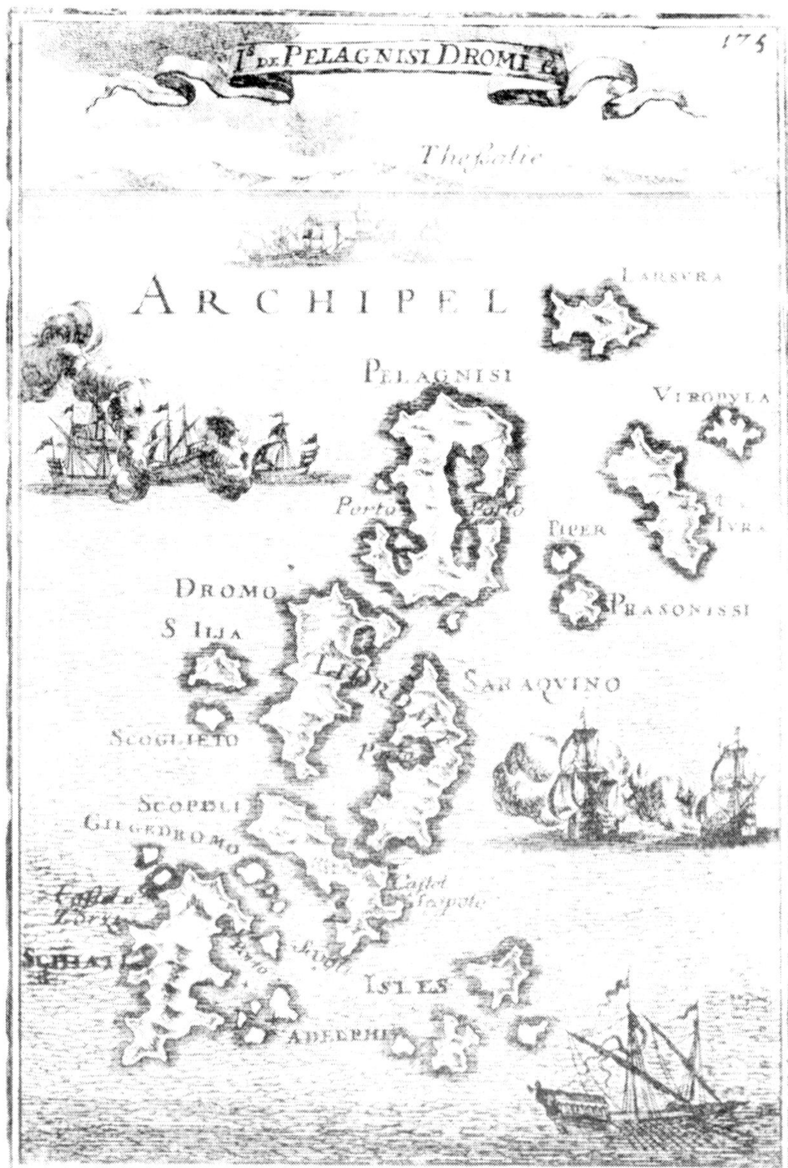

Map 9 Mallet, 1683 (Archipelago of the Northern Sporades).
Source: *Kóstas and Angéla Mavríkis' collection of old maps.*

Figure 2.9 Transporting pine logs, Pipéri, 1957. *Courtesy of Holger Reichhart.*

2.6 Peristéra or Xéro

Peristéra is considered by many to be ancient EUONYMOS or even HALONNESOS. The former identification is defended by Chrístos Athanasíou on the grounds that *euonumos*, literally 'well named', is also a classical euphemism for 'on the left' (the side associated with things of ill omen) and Peristéra is to the left of HALONNESOS (i.e. Kirá Panayá). Lolling (1848–1894), a German archaeologist and author of geographical works, is one of those who assign the ancient name HALONNESOS to Peristéra.[19] This view is shared by Iákovos Rangavís who says of 'Sarakíno or Peristéra' that 'this island is often inundated by sea water, and this, it seems, gave rise to the ancient name HALONNESOS'.[20]

Another notable cartographer, Van der Aa, confused by the sheer number of our islands, referred to this island as both 'Peparethus' (PEPARETHOS) and 'Saraquino', but the first of these names is securely identified with modern Skópelos. In medieval and later times Peristéra is sometimes referred to either as 'Peristéri', as in the Portolan Chart of the Aegean dated 1664, and in Lapie – though Lapie also calls it 'Sarakino' – or 'Peristéra' as in Benoist (1827), but more often by some variant of the Greek name Sarakíno: 'Saraquino' in Gastaldi, Mercator, Boschini, Mallet, Coronelli and d'Anville, and 'Serakino' in Delisle.

In Greek, *peristéri* and *peristéra* both mean 'dove', and the name reflects the strange shape of the island. If you climb to the summit you get the impression that you are about to fly off on the back of an enormous dove. As regards the other name, Sarakíno, there is a tradition that seems to have a sound historical basis. At the beginning of the 10th century the power of the Byzantine Empire began its gradual decline. The shores of the Mediterranean had always favoured the growth of piracy, and the Aegean now saw the merciless plundering of both mainland shores and islands by various pirate clans.

In 904 Thessalonica was suddenly overwhelmed by Saracen pirates based in Crete. 'Saracens' (*Sarakiní* in Greek) was the name given by Christians to Arab pirates, and chiefly to those who conquered North Africa and established themselves there. In 823 they had captured Iráklio in Crete and made it the principal base for their piratical expeditions. The looting of Thessalonica was one of the more daring plans of these unscrupulous people. Having seized not only goods but also inhabitants of the city as living merchandise, they departed as quickly as they could, to avoid Byzantine reprisals.

On their return journey they encountered bad weather and sought refuge at Peristéra, anchoring their fleet in the harbour now known as Vasilikós. The holds of the ships were full of captives from Thessalonica (men, women and children), destined for the slave markets of the Barbary Coast, white flesh being a valuable commodity among the dark-skinned Arabs of North Africa. The few local inhabitants secretly observed this unknown fleet anchored in their sheltered harbour, and the weeping and groaning of the slaves chilled their blood. As soon as the weather improved, the pirates set off for their southern havens, but the visit of the Saracen fleet made such an impression on the simple inhabitants of Peristéra that they named their great harbour Sarakíno.

Figure 2.10 An Easter gathering, Peristéra, 1952. *Courtesy of E. and D. Dhiómas.*

Figure 2.11 Vasilikós, Peristéra, 1966. *Courtesy of Marína and Panayótis Diniakós.*

Figure 2.12 The harbour at Vasilikós.

Figure 2.13 An old anchor pulled up by a drift net and brought to Vasilikós on Peristéra.

Figure 2.14 Fishermen on Skántzoura, 1957. *Courtesy of Holger Reichhart.*

The story does not end here, though. The Byzantines were outraged at this atrocious crime and did not forget it. In 961 a Byzantine fleet set out from Constantinople intent on driving the Saracens out of Crete, in revenge for the earlier humiliation at Thessalonica.

The Emperor Nicephorus Phocas himself was in command of the fleet, which was held up for several days in the very same harbour at Peristéra that had sheltered the Saracens. (Nicephorus Phocas' expedition took place in winter, and at Skíros he was again delayed for several days by adverse weather.) The inhabitants of Peristéra were amazed when they learned that the emperor himself was aboard one of the Byzantine vessels.

So momentous was this event for the islanders that they renamed the harbour Vasilikós ('Imperial'). This name has endured to this day, as has Sarakíno, a reminder of a horrifying but at the same time significant event. The name Vasilikós has, however, largely replaced the earlier name, though Sarakíno, as we have seen, has sometimes been used of the island itself.

Figure 2.15 Kóstas and Máchi Agállou, Peristéra, 1951. *Courtesy of E. and D. Dhiómas* .

In 1836 the Greek government officially named the island Peristéra. But the name most frequently used today among the inhabitants of Alónnisos is Xéro (meaning 'dry'). This name reflects the conditions on the island, which is almost entirely without water.

2.7 Skántzoura

Figure 2.16 The monastery on Skántzoura in 1963. Some of the first tourists to visit the islands.

Skántzoura is situated between Skíros and Alónnisos. Its ancient name was probably SCANDIRA, which we find in Pliny,[21] though Pomponius Mela (AD 44) refers to it as SCANDILE: 'in the Aegean sea near Thrace are THASOS, IMBROS, SAMOTHRACE, SCANDILE, POLYAEGOS, SCIATHOS, HALONNESOS and [. . .] LEMNOS'.[22] Bursian, in his two-volume *Geography of Greece*, makes an unconvincing attempt to identify Skántzoura with ancient HALONNESOS.[23] In a document on Mount Athos, dated 1815, which concerns the building of the monastery on the island (which we shall examine later), the island is referred to as Skántzoura, as it is by Lapie, though he spells it 'Scantsoura'.

A number of variant forms of the name were recorded by earlier foreign travellers and cartographers. It appears as 'Scandola' in the Portolan Chart of the Aegean of 1664, but 'Scanda', used by Mercator, Boschini, Visscher, Coronelli and many others, is more common, though it is called 'Scangero' by d'Anville and Choiseul-Gouffier. Other strange names that appear include 'Standa' in Gastaldi, and 'Schasoli' in Delisle.

Skántzoura is surrounded by a large number of smaller islands. Among these are the three islands to the northwest known collectively as the Polemiká Nisiá or 'Military Islands'. They take their name from their orderly geographical arrangement: looking at them one is reminded of a row of battlements. Kórakas ('Crow') and Stróngilo ('Circular') reflect the shapes of the islands that bear these names. There is also Paraós, which, since it is the closest to Skántzoura, is considered a geographical 'adopted son' (*parayós* in Greek, contracted to *paraós*). Another small island, Kiriákos, is named after a man who was shipwrecked there.

Now that we have considered all the larger islands, we must not neglect to mention some of the smaller ones. These islets, so far devoid of archaeological interest, remain as eternal geographical monuments in this much disturbed region. Their few square metres of soil have been trodden by human beings of all periods. Vessels of every kind have passed their shores, from primitive dugout canoes to pirate galleys, from Byzantine warships to the fast-sailing brigs of the Revolution. Among these islets are Manólas, Dhío Adhérfia, Lechoúsa, Grámeza and Pappoús.

2.8 Manólas

In the 19th century our islands were home to many pirates, including one called Manólas. According to the tradition this Manólas, after looting a neighbouring monastery, fled back to his retreat on the west of Alónnisos to nurse a wound he had received in a skirmish. The folk tradition expects those who violate holy places to be punished, and in this case relates that the wound never healed. Manólas was buried by his men on the islet that had been his hideout and which now bears his name.

2.9 Dhío Adhérfia

According to a fable related by Papadhiamándis, the Northern Sporades are the product of the sport of two giants who threw rocks of enormous size into the sea. Falling one on top of another, these rocks formed the islands.[24] It seems that in the case of the Dhío Adhérfia ('Two Brothers'), the giants' 'pebbles' fell so neatly that they formed two twin mountains.

Whoever sees the 'Two Brothers' from the distance gets a strange sense of nature's creative genius. This name was probably given to the islands in antiquity, for the ancient Greeks were always inspired in their choice of place names. The earliest written evidence is in maps of the medieval period, where the islands already have the name by which they are known today.

2.10 Lechoúsa

There have always been pirates in this region, and many place names are derived from the names or exploits of pirates. Lechoúsa was formerly known as Likórema, 'Wolf-Gorge'. The island is certainly big enough for a secret refuge, and has a gorge with a cave at its head. (As recently as the Second World War, Greek partisans sought refuge on this island and were secretly transferred from there to the Middle East.) The gorge must once have been chosen as a hideout by pirates, whose savagery prompted the local people to speak of them as wolves.

The modern name, Lechoúsa, is taken from the cape of the same name on Peristéra which it faces. *Lechoúsa* is a Greek term for a woman who has just given birth, and it is also applied to animals. Cape Lechoúsa is the most well-watered part of Peristéra, and goats who have just delivered their kids go there to drink, to replace the fluid they have lost in giving birth.

2.11 Grámeza, or Prásso

Grámeza, a steep barren island, stands to the east of all the other Northern Sporades, and to this it owes its name. In the language of sailors, the verb *grammízo* means 'chart a voyage'. By corruption of *grammízo*, we get the name Grámeza; this name is appropriate, since once past Grámeza one can set a course to the west coast of Asia Minor, or the Dardanelles. Another possible explanation of the name is that, though small, the island has many steep cliffs (*gremí* in Greek). Its alternative name is Prásso or Prasilídha, from the wild leeks (*prássi*) that grow there in abundance.[25]

2.12 Pappoús

Pappoús is a small island between Yoúra and Kirá Panayá. Like the latter it is dedicated to the Most Holy Mother of God, since it too belongs to Mount Athos; but its name, Pappoús ('Grandfather'), refers to St Athanásios, the founder of the Athonite community on the island. In the last years of his life St Athanásios was addressed as 'Grandfather' as a mark of respect, even by older Athonite monks. This small island reflects the character and achievements of St Athanásios at the monastery of the Great Lávra on Athos.

Thanks to his energy, his Byzantine talent for organisation and his deep faith, he succeeded in creating a large Christian community in a short space of time and in a confined area, but on such a firm basis that it is still flourishing today. Similarly, the small island of Pappoús through its stoical determination succeeded in becoming so self-sufficient and so well organised that it was regarded as unique among Greek islands and a model for imitation.

2.13 Other Smaller Islands

There are many other rocky islets in the Northern Sporades, several of which owe their name to their shape, including Mélissa ('Bee'), Amóni ('Anvil'), Gáidharos

('Donkey') and Kórakas ('Crow'). Others, such as Fangroú and Óstria, take their name from their situation. Fangroú was given its name by fishermen because it lies in a fishing ground rich in sea-bream, which are called *fangriá* in Greek; while the islet of Óstria is particularly exposed to the south wind, known as the *óstria* in the lingo of Greek sailors.

Nisáki Pnigménou ('Isle of the Drowned Man') is so named because at the beginning of the 20th century, when the timber on nearby Yoúra was being felled by merchants from the island of Sálamis near Athens, a body was washed up on the shore there.

Notes

1. The title of the original Greek edition of this book is the classical Greek phrase, *Anō magnētōn nēsoi*, 'The Upper [*or* Northern] Islands of the Magnetans'. [Translator]
2. Molenas seems to be unknown in ancient Greek mythological literature. In the main mythological tradition Peleus became an immortal and as such would have had no grave. [Translator]
3. The basic meaning of *dromos* in ancient Greek is 'course' or 'track' for racing, but it was also used of ceremonial approach roads. [Translator]
4. Dhiádhromos: this form may have arisen as the result of a misreading of, or an early printer's error for, Liádhromos (or even Liadhrómia, with the ending adjusted to produce a recognisable word). In Greek, capital *delta* (Δ, here transliterated as Dh) is very similar to capital *lambda* (Λ, transliterated L) and their interchange is a common error in older printing. [Translator]
5. Throughout this book ancient place-names are given in their Latinised forms and printed in small capitals (see p. xvi). [Translator]
6. Strabo, *Geographus* 9.5.16. Translation from Jones (1917–32), vol. 4, p. 427.
7. See pp. 128, 130.
8. See Ross (1851); and Fredrich (1906).
9. Athanasíou (1964).
10. The specific geographical or cartographical publications referred to here and throughout this chapter are identified in the Bibliography.
11. Some authorities identify GERONTIA with Pipéri, others with a small island in the bay of Vólos. [Translator]
12. Athanasíou (1964).
13. Skavéntzos (1854).
14. Pausanias, *Periegeta* 8.33.4. Translation from Jones (1918–35), vol. 4, p. 69.
15. See also Philostratus Junior (4th century AD), who says Philoctetes was of noble birth (*Imagines* 17). Translation from Fairbanks (1931), p. 365.
16. This is far from being the case as the reader will discover. Though writing in 1925, Sarrís seems unaware of the remains of a city at Kokkinókastro on Alónnisos described by Fiedler in the mid 19th century (see pp. 444–51). [Translator]
17. Sarrís (1925), pp. 219–21.
18. Sarrís (1925), p. 222.
19. Lolling (1889).
20. Rangavís (1853–54), vol. 3, p. 57.
21. Pliny, *Naturalis historia* 4.12.72. Translation from Rackham, Jones & Eichholz (1938–63), vol. 2, pp. 171–3.
22. Mela, *Chorographia* 2.106. Translation from Rohmer (1998), p. 97.
23. Bursian (1862–72), vol. 2.
24. Papadhiamándis (1981–88), vol. 3, p. 285. Aléxandhros Papadhiamándis (1851–1911) was a prolific and popular writer of short stories. He lived in Skiáthos and many of his stories

reflect life in the Northern Sporades in the late 19th and early 20th centuries. The fable of the giants forms an interlude in one of them. For a selection of his stories in English see Papadiamantis (1987). [Translator]

25. Prásso is also the name of a smaller island off the west coast of Skántzoura, and this is the one which appears under this name in Table 1.1 on p. 37. [Translator]

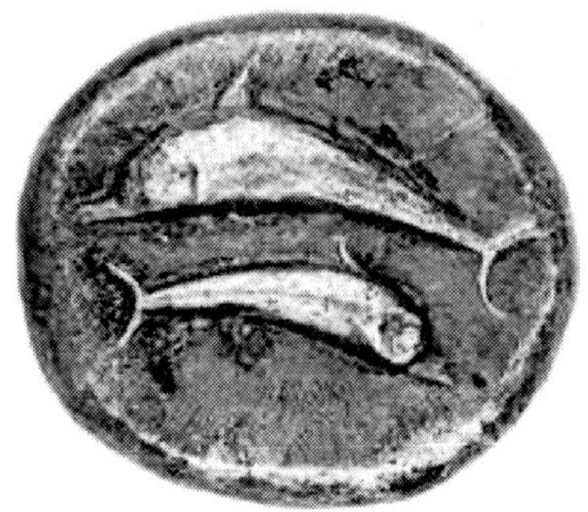

Figure 2.17 Fishermen at Vótsi. *Courtesy of Thomas Vestrum.*

Figure 2.18 A sponge diver processing sponges, Yoúra. *Courtesy of Thomas Vestrum.*

Figure 2.19 Aerial view of Palió Chorió from a helicopter (a). *Courtesy of Thomas Vestrum.*

Figure 2.20 Palió Chorió. *Courtesy of Thomas Vestrum.*

Figure 2.21 Aerial view of Palió Chorió from a helicopter (b). *Courtesy of Thomas Vestrum.*

Figure 2.22 Aerial view of Palió Chorió from a helicopter (c). *Courtesy of Thomas Vestrum.*

3

ORIGINS OF THE FAMILIES OF ALONNISOS AND THE GROWTH OF THE POPULATION

IN 1538 the notorious pirate, Barbarossa, enslaved or slaughtered most of the inhabitants of Alónnisos and burned the island from end to end. The attack must have been sudden, unexpected and from all quarters at once, for the inhabitants did not have time to seek refuge. The few who did manage to hide, and thus survive, left the island for fear of further attacks, fleeing to the nearby shores of Thessaly and Évvia. The island remained desolate for a while and was not repopulated until the end of the 16th century.

The Tsoukanás, Gioulís, Anagnóstou, Kónstas, Efstathíou and Malamaténios families were among the first to return to Alónnisos, or to establish themselves here for the first time, after this depopulation. Among the oldest, too, must have been the Tzórtzis family, whose name indicates their Venetian origin and points back to the period of Venetian rule. Later the population was diversified by refugees who came to Alónnisos from various regions, to escape the Turkish sword.

First were the revolutionaries from the Epirus who, hunted by the ruthless Ali Paşa, found refuge in our islands. Later there were other revolutionary movements like those in Thessaly and Macedonia. After the failure of the latter, many of the revolutionaries came to our islands with their families. Even so, by 1821 the population of Alónnisos and the lesser Northern Sporades still amounted to barely 300 persons. This was due mainly to the relentless piracy. There was a further influx in the 1820s, during the early stages of the Greek War of Independence, when the Turks ravaged the mainly Greek town of Aïvalí (in Turkish Ayvalık) on the coast of Asia Minor, and Omer Bey of Káristos in Évvia ravaged that island, while Abdul Abut, the Paşa of Thessalonica, laid waste Chalkidhikí, the three-fingered peninsula southeast of Thessalonica, and later besieged and destroyed Náousa, to the northwest. Refugees from all these places were made welcome in the Northern Sporades. The greatest burden fell on Skíros, Skiáthos and Skópelos which had the capacity to feed them. There were, however, so many refugees that, inevitably, a considerable number of them came to Alónnisos.

The Athanasíou family, driven out of Epirus, went to Kerasiá in Évvia, but one branch later moved to Alónnisos. The Kaloyánnis family came here from the Yánnina area, fleeing from Ali Paşa. The Vláikos family were a noble Greek family of Rumanian extraction who came to Greece to join their compatriots. They settled in Évvia where they still live, but some of them have moved to our island. The Alexíou family are also from Évvia, as are the Piliótis family, named after the village of Pílio in Évvia from which they came. The Kiriazís family came from Píli in Évvia; the Phloroús from Kranídhi in the Peloponnese. The Diniakós family came from the island of Tínos; and the Karamanlís from Aïvalí. The Karakatsánis family came from Évvia and later introduced the Vouyouklís family, whose roots are in Thessalonica, to the island when they adopted a boy of that name. Similarly the Triandafillou family owes its presence on the island to an act of adoption by members of the Paraskevás family who came from Macedonia. In the case of the adoption of a member of the Athanasíou family by one Ioánnis Chrístou in 1839, the deed of adoption has survived and reads as follows:

> This day, Thursday the 28th of October in the year one thousand eight hundred and thirty-nine, the wife of Andhréas Yeoryíou Athanasíou having died, I, the undersigned Ioánnis Chrístou, have taken his younger child to be my son, and in witness thereto I make this affidavit. Wherefore from today and henceforth if I, namely Ioánnis Christou, should revoke my decision to take this child and make him my child, I shall pay five hundred (500) drachmas each year. If on the other hand the child's actual father should revoke his decision he likewise shall pay the aforesaid sum of 500 drachmas each year.

There are two distinct families on our island with the name Kastánis and the members of one family are in general much taller than the members of the other. The taller ones come for Achládhi in Évvia, while the stockier people named Kastánis, who are also found on Skópelos, are all descended from a certain Turk who killed his wife and her lover and took to sea to avoid arrest. His course brought him to Alónnisos. The hospitable islanders received him gladly and had him baptised, and his godfather gave him the surname Kastánis.

Figure 3.1 Boats belonging to the Alexíou and Tsoukanás families.
Courtesy of Ioánnis Alexíou.

The Agállou family are from Náousa and a branch of the family lived for a while in Tríkeri near Vólos, but have recently returned to Alónnisos. The Papavasilíou are one of the older families, but not indigenous. They came to Alónnisos after 1821, when Ménges Papavasilíou, who had fought in the Revolution, decided to settle here permanently. The Frantzéskos family are of Rumanian origin, and take their name from a Rumanian called Francescu who came to live in Skópelos, where he raised a family. However, he divorced his wife and remarried in Alónnisos. Later he abandoned his second family and went to Chalkidhikí where all trace of him was lost.

The Tzanís family came from Vasiliká in Évvia, the Strouflíótis family from Strofliáta, also in Évvia. The Dhrosákis family come from further afield, from Réthimno in Crete. After the destruction of the Arkádhi monastery during the 1866 Cretan uprising,[1] two of the Dhrosákis men left Crete to avoid the brutality of the Turks. One embarked for Alónnisos where he became the head of a large family, while the other sought refuge in Eastern Thrace (the European part of Turkey).

In more recent times there has been an increase in the amount of commerce between Alónnisos and the surrounding regions. The beauty of the Alonnisiot women, economic circumstances and the development of the island have brought a number of new names to Alónnisos. Between 1900 and 1940 various families arrived here from other islands: the Malathrítis and Mavríkis families from Ikaría, the Karoútsos family from Foúrni, the Mikoniátis family from Míkonos, and the Aryiríou and Páppos families from Skópelos; and in the same period the Papachrístou family arrived from Oxiá near Tríkala, in western Thessaly.

Since the time of the reconstruction after the 1965 earthquake the mosaic of our island families has been considerably enriched.[2] A number of soldiers from all parts of Greece who came with the engineering corps to work on reconstruction married local women. From then on, as the population continued to grow, the catalogue of new surnames that appeared in our island has developed into a lengthy one, and many of the names are of Western European origin.[3]

Tables 3.1 and 3.2 present information collated from various sources[4] about the growth of the population of our islands from 1821 to 1981. From 1821 until 1852 the population of Alónnisos remained stable. Piracy and remoteness were the two principal factors that discouraged people from settling in Alónnisos and the surrounding smaller islands.

After 1852, the Aegean gradually became more secure, and the systematic development of shipping was a stimulus to many inhabitants of Évvia to move permanently to Alónnisos. Between 1852 and 1981, Alónnisos was one of the island regions with the highest rate of population growth. Among the islands that formed part of the original Kingdom of Greece (1830), only Sálamis, with an increase of 775%, surpassed Alónnisos, where the rate was 404%. Next came Évvia with an increase of 193%

Figure 3.2 Celebration in Paliochorafína, 1963. *Courtesy of E. and D. Dhiómas.*

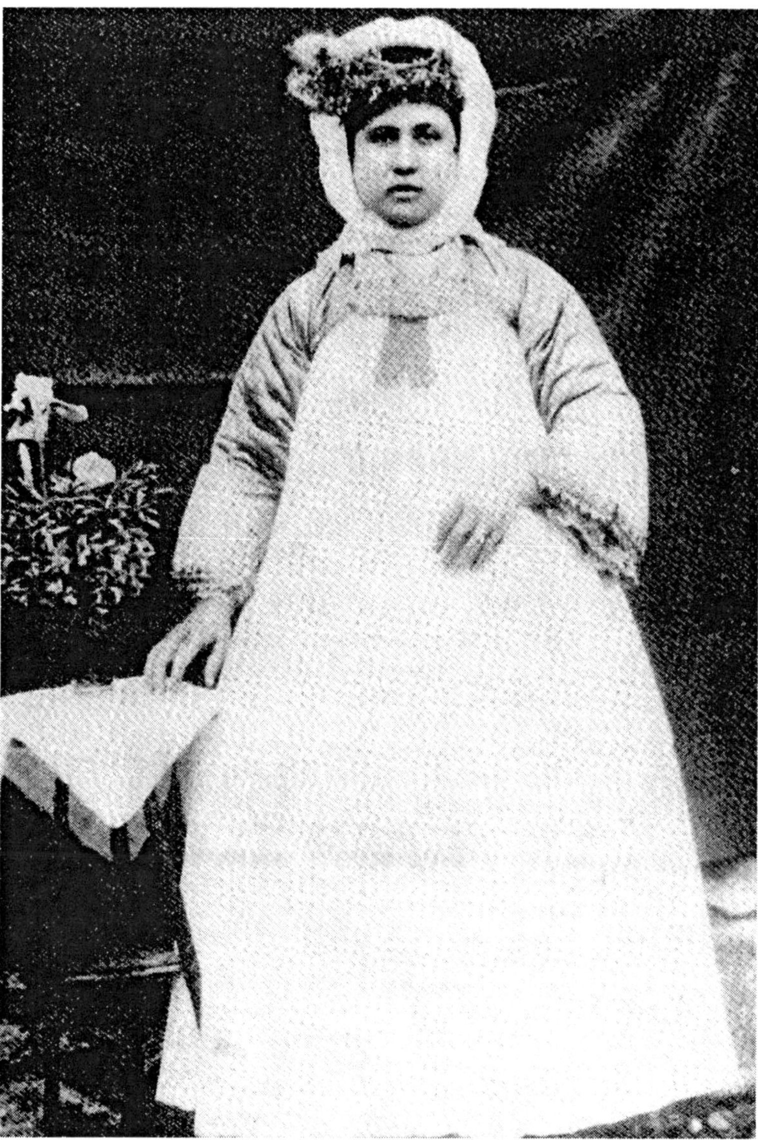

Figure 3.3 Eléni from the Alexíou family on her wedding day just before the Second World War.

Figure 3.4 Girls from Alónnisos in traditional costumes.

Figure 3.5 An Alónissos family photographed in the village square.

By contrast, though, the population of the smaller islands in the Northern Sporades has declined dramatically in recent years. In 1961 there were 159 people living on seven of these islands, while by 1981 only four were still inhabited by a total of 26 people. Kirá Panayá and Skántzoura are fertile islands but they are monastic property and house-building is not permitted. The lighthouse on Psathoúra has been automated and lighthouse keepers and their families no longer need to live there. The number of inhabitants of Peristéra declined significantly because of the lack of a school.

Table 3.1 Population of Alónnisos, 1821–1981

Year	*Population*		*Year*	*Population*		*Year*	*Populaton*
1821	300		1855	487		1928	1,005
1848	312		1856	311		1940	1,334
1849	315		1861	303		1951	1,341
1850	312		1870	360		1961	1,308
1851	315		1879	400		1971	1,426
1852	317		1889	498		1981	1,528
1853	488		1907	689			
1854	483		1920	779			

On Alónnisos we have seen Palió Chorió, Mourteró and Isómata largely abandoned, and most of the population concentrated in Vótsi and Patitíri. This is related to the rise in tourism. At the same time the village of Stení Vála was created and has grown dramatically. When my grandfather, Kóstas Mavríkis, a personal friend of the famous George Zorbás (the model for Aléxis Zorbás in *Zorba the Greek*), went to Stení Vála after the Second World War, he encountered a barren place with nothing but rocks and lentisk trees. Nevertheless he bought the whole area for 40,000 *okádhes* (51.2 tonnes) of charcoal, and undertook the necessary preparations for its development. Later other families came and now, sixty-five years later, it has become a small village.

In the last two decades many foreigners have discovered the exceptional beauty of the settlements at Palió Chorió and Mourteró and have begun to buy or build houses there. These two villages have come to life again, if only in the summer season. The tendency to decentralise led to the resettlement of other islands by local people, who exploit the land for tourism. The abandonment of Palió Chorió was due to the earthquake of 1965 and the erection of new housing close to the sea at Patitíri. In 1978 the junior school (*Dhimotikó*) was transferred to Patitíri and the other amenities followed. Those few people who would have liked to remain in Palió Chorió were obliged to move to Patitíri and many sold their houses for the price of a loaf of bread.

In 1961 Kirá Panayá had a population of 69. This was because the monastery of the Great Lávra was exploiting the island's holm-oak forest for charcoal production. Many people from Alónnisos were employed in woodcutting. At that time there were very limited opportunities for employment, and some people also took up resin tapping. On both Kirá Panayá and Skántzoura there were monks and farming families who lived an interdependent existence. On Yoúra from 1952 to 1995 there were always two wardens in residence, together with their families, whose job was to protect the rare breed of wild goats that live on the island. On Psathoúra the population consisted of the lighthouse keepers and their families.

Table 3.2 Population of Alónnisos and the other islands, 1940–1981

Island or settlement	*1896*	*1940*	*1951*	*1961*	*1971*	*1981*
Alónnisos						
Isómata			66			
Marpoúnda						4
Mourteró		114	24			
Palió Chorió		770	617	491	347	26
Patitíri		225	304	366	599	957
Stení Vála					116	86
Vótsi		225	240	451	364	455
Yérakas			90			
Total (Alónnisos)		1334	1341	1308	1426	1528
Other islands						
Dhío Adhérfia				1		
Kirá Panayá	16	8	20	69	14	7
Peristéra		21	53	66	23	15
Pipéri			14	11		
Psathoúra	14	4	7	6	5	2
Skántzoura		19	11	5	1	
Yoúra	13			1	2	2
Total (other islands)		52	105	159	45	26
OVERALL TOTAL		1386	1446	1467	1471	1554

Note: 1896 figures for Kirá Panayá, Psathoúra and Yoúra have been added for comparison.

Most surprisingly, the 1961 census shows that there was a single person living in isolation on Dhío Adhérfia. This was a herdsman who lived there for several years and survived despite the large numbers of poisonous snakes that make human habitation of the islands well-nigh impossible. His home was a small cabin built by the *kinótita* of Alónnisos.[5]

Notes

1. The monks and revolutionaries defending the Arkádhi monastery blew it up rather than surrender to the Turks. [Translator].
2. For details of the earthquake see pp. 296–304.
3. It is worth noting in this context that certain Christian names for women still current on the island today, such as Sinióra, Muresó and Sirainó, go back to the periods of Venetian or Frankish rule.
4. Greek Government (1992), Yangákis (1989), Philippson (1901).
5. Although Alónnisos had been a *dhímos* since 1830, in 1925 it was redefined as a *kinótita* (community). In 1994 it was once more recognised as a *dhímos*, and special local elections were held here, since they were not due generally in Greece at that time. [Author]

The *kinótita* and the *dhímos* are the smallest units of subdivision of local administration in Greece. *Kinótita* and *dhímos* can refer either to the administrative body, or to the geographical area it covers, or to the inhabitants of that area, according to context. Greece is divided into 52 *nomí*, roughly equivalent to English counties. Each *nomós* is divided into regions known as *eparchíes*, and each *eparchía* is made up of a number of *dhími* (often translated 'municipalities' and typically but not necessarily consisting of or centred on a town of some size) and *kinótites* (rural 'communities'). Alónnisos is in the *eparchía* of Skópelos, which is part of the *nomós* of Magnesía. [Translator]

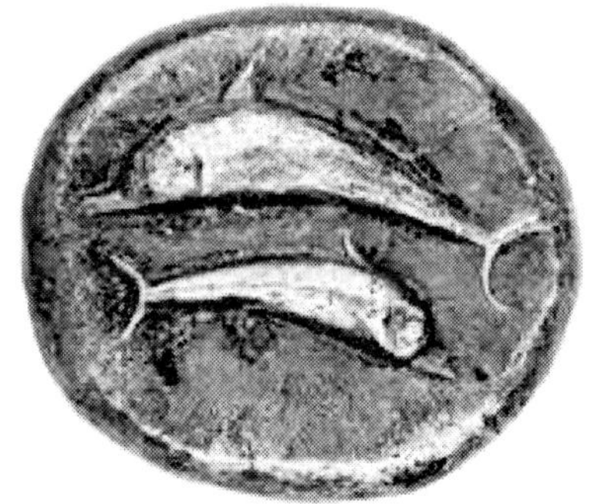

Figure 3.6 Threshing, Palío Chorió, 1965. *Courtesy of Marína and Panayótis Diniakós.*

Figure 3.7 The harvest, Palío Chorió, 1930. *Courtesy of Angelikí Floroús.*

Figure 3.8 Turning the soil in a vineyard, Palío Chorió, 1933. *Courtesy of Angelikí Floroús.*

Figure 3.9 Women in an alleyway, Palió Chorió, 1959. *Courtesy of M. and I. Besínis.*

Figure 3.10 A family group, Patitíri, 1949.

Figure 3.11 The Tzórtzis family at Áyos Pétros, Kirá Panayá, 1977.

Figure 3.12 Family boat outing, Alónnisos, 1961. *Courtesy of M and I. Besinis.*

Figure 3.13 Traditional costume, Alónnisos, 1959.
Courtesy of Marína and Panayótis Diniakós.

Figure 3.14 Traditional costume, Palío Chorió.
Courtesy of Valándis Vláikos.

Figure 3.15 Traditional costume:
(a) Unidentified location on Alónnisos (left). *Courtesy of Kóstas and Karen Kaloyánnis.*
(b) In Palió Chorió, 1969 (right).

Figure 3.16 Restoring a boat, Alónnisos, 1957. *Courtesy of Holger Reichhart.*

Figure 3.17 Travelling on the *Paschális*, 1957. The sign reads 'Coffee Lemonade'.
Courtesy of Holger Richhart.

Figure 3.18 Fishing with lamps, 1957 (a). *Courtesy of Holger Reichhart.*

Figure 3.19 Fishing with lamps, 1957 (b). *Courtesy of Holger Reichhart.*

Figure 3.20 The caïque of Stamátis Floroús, Patitíri, 1936.
Courtesy of Michális and Evanthía Vláikos.

Figure 3.21 View of the waterfront at Patitíri, 1967. *Courtesy of Athanásios Páppos.*

Figure 3.22 Stení Vála, 1952. *Courtesy of Valándis Vláikos.*

Figure 3.23 Partial view of Patitíri from the sea, 1952. *Courtesy of the Ziméris Archive.*

Figure 3.24 A woman from Alónnisos at the tiller.

4

THE ISLANDS IN THE STONE AGE

MANY MILLIONS of years ago the region of the Northern Sporades, like the rest of Greece, was covered by the sea. The sea-bed went through many changes, which I shall now discuss.

4.1 The Geological Origins of Our Islands

More than 180 million years ago two great cracks appeared: one where the Píndhos mountains, the spine of mainland Greece, now stand; the other in the Ionian Sea, on the west side of Greece. These two great 'ditches' were gradually filled with the shells of marine organisms, mixed with erosion debris carried down from submerged mountain ranges. This gradual silting up of the 'ditches' continued for about 150 million years until, in the Oligocene epoch, tectonic movements caused the deposits in the 'Píndhos ditch' to fold and rise, forming the Píndhos range. Some millions of years later, at the beginning of the Miocene epoch, the 'Ionian ditch' rose in the same way, forming western Greece and the Ionian Islands. In the meantime, and closer to the Northern Sporades, about 140 million years ago at the beginning of the Cretaceous Period, the Pelagonian mountain range emerged from the waves. Extending southwards from northern Macedonia, it included eastern Thessaly, some of the Northern Sporades, parts of Évvia and Attica, and the Cyclades.

These large-scale changes, together with other smaller ones, were responsible for producing the Aegean landmass known to geologists as the *Aigaiis*. By about 25 million years ago, the *Aigaiis* was a continuous mass of land covering all of present-day Greece as well as Asia Minor (western Turkey) and the whole of what is now the Aegean Sea. But the earth was experiencing convulsions. Millions of years passed and many transformations occurred in the region of the *Aigaiis*. Mountains emerged and sank, lakes formed, and new sea ways opened as the Mediterranean gradually penetrated the interior of the *Aigaiis*. About 18 million years ago, in the Miocene epoch, a vast lake covered the Northern Sporades, Central Thessaly and northeastern Évvia.

As the ages passed, the geological changes continued. Some time between 12 and 6 million years ago, during the Pliocene, the ribbon of land that would later constitute the archipelago of the Northern Sporades began to rise, dividing the large lake into two smaller lakes, one to the north and one to the east of the Sporades.

Figure 4.1 Geological phenomena, Yoúra.

4.2 The First Traces of Man

By the end of the Pliocene epoch, about 2 million years ago, the general lines of the morphology of Greece had been determined. Minor transformations took place during the Pleistocene epoch (2 million to 10,500 years ago). The Pleistocene is the transitional epoch of the Ice Ages, when man first appeared in the Aegean region. During the recurrent glacial periods, the intense cold resulted in a lowering of the sea level by 100–200 metres. At these times, the larger islands of the Northern

Sporades were joined to the rest of Thessaly, forming a peninsula. This did not include the more northerly islands of the archipelago (Kirá Panayá, Yoúra, Psathoúra and Pipéri) that together formed a separate island. Later the sea made inroads, transforming the peninsula and this northern island into the smaller islands we know today. Another characteristic of the Pleistocene epoch is the growth of trees, chiefly pines. In warm interglacial periods tropical vegetation developed, and in colder glacial periods vegetation characteristic of the steppe or tundra.[1]

When the waters froze and the sea level fell, great herds of animals, including large mammals, found their way to Alónnisos. They were concentrated chiefly in an expansive valley which is now the straits between Peristéra and Alónnisos, and there they found food and refuge. It was natural that a region with such rich food supplies should attract the human beings of that period. Alónnisos Man (100,000 BC) could easily find shelter and food in the surrounding mountainous terrain, and obtain skins and bone tools from his hunting in the valley.

From the limestone rock of our islands he was able to fashion his tools and weapons. Close to the routes followed by game he would set up temporary encampments, where he would cut up the animals he killed, work their skins and make his bone tools. Then he would transport parts of the animals to his hearth, including the brain for his primitive rites, and the furs for winter. Because of the land bridge to the mainland he could, if necessary, cover great distances in pursuit of game. With the caves of the Northern Sporades as his permanent residence, he managed to survive the harsh conditions of the last Ice Age (70,000–10,500 years ago).

An important role in the next stage of the history of our human ancestors in this region was played by an animal found in abundance here. To be specific, the palaeontologist's mattock has uncovered in a cave in a neighbouring region (just south of Thessaly, near Ágrafa in Central Greece) bones of the cave bear (*Ursus spelaeus*). The cave bear was the divine gift that saved human beings in those difficult frozen winters. It was easy to track down in the caves and even easier to kill if it was hibernating. Thus men acquired abundant supplies of meat, large warm furs for their clothing, fat for the fire and bones for their tools.

But what sort of men flourished at this period? The king of these far-distant millennia was Neanderthal man. This upright, if somewhat stooped, precursor of modern man left clear traces at several places in the Northern Sporades, notably at Kokkinókastro on Alónnisos. He was a hunter who lived in caves and used fire as a means of defence against wild beasts. His tools show a certain degree of inventiveness in their construction. He hunted the larger animals with traps, and for the smaller he used his spear.

In temporary encampments he skinned and cut up the animals before transporting them to his hearth. In such camps it was also his custom to quarry stone cores and to make primitive stone tools, which he perfected with the passing of the centuries. Unfortunately, however, the dominance of *Homo neanderthalensis* in the Northern Sporades, as in other regions, was relatively short-lived. Unable to adapt to the changing requirements of the times, he was inevitably displaced by *Homo sapiens*.

Homo sapiens was the more intelligent type of man, who came from the east and made his own mark in the historical record in Alónnisos and the nearby islands.

The blade was his basic weapon. Once he had displaced his backward predecessor, *Homo sapiens* held sway in our region and took the first steps towards civilisation. His chief technological achievement was the blade, a revolutionary invention for that time, which allowed him to make great strides in his intellectual and social development. Natural conditions helped him to a very considerable extent. The climate improved, but this very improvement produced new difficulties in the finding of food, for, as the ice melted, the larger animals moved towards the colder north; only the small and swift-footed remained behind.

Homo sapiens was then obliged to consider how he could survive and began to intervene in nature. He no longer seized game directly from the environment, but started to domesticate animals; gradually he learned to cultivate the earth and eventually to fish. He acquired a partial control over nature and thus secured the necessities for his sustenance. He no longer lived with the need for constant hunting and had more free time at his disposal. This gave him the opportunity to redeploy his energies, investing them in the development of his intellectual faculties. His restless, inventive spirit found various different outlets: religion, burial rites, pottery, cave painting, the perfecting of weapons, and new means of communication.

In the Upper Palaeolithic (33,000–10,500 years ago), when the spirit of *Homo sapiens* broke free and created a culture that was the forerunner of the cultures of the historical period. A basic factor in this development was the stabilisation of the climate at the end of the Palaeolithic Period (about 8,500 BC). Man was liberated from his continual struggle with unstable climatic conditions and began to travel. From then until today, journeys and migrations have played a fundamental role in the development of culture.

4.3 The First Local Culture of Alónnisos

In 1969–70, the distinguished prehistorian and archaeologist Dhimítrios Theocháris, excavating at Kokkinonísi, the island in the bay of Kokkinókastro on Alónnisos, brought to light an encampment of the type described above, belonging to the Middle Palaeolithic (300,000–33,000 years ago). In his excavations Theocháris found large quantities of the fossilised bones of the animals killed by the Neander-thal hunters of Alónnisos. These included animals related to modern deer, horses, cattle and gazelles, and even a form of rhinoceros. This list gives a good idea of the kind of animals who lived on our soil and of the dietary customs of our local ancestors. In the same excavation were found flakes of hard limestone. From the quantity of game animals we surmise that the stone tools, which our ancestors made by striking flakes from the core, were effective and well crafted for their period.[3]

Theocháris' discoveries are considered of great significance, for Alónnisos is the only place in the entire Aegean where these earliest signs of mankind have so far been found. This is a straightforward result of research, but one which should, nevertheless, makes us proud, not only because we live in a place whose history began 100,000 years ago, but also because there is a continuity of development from those remote ancestors to today. We are fortunate to live in a place with a history so ancient that only a few regions of Greece and some regions of China can compete with it. Kokkinonísi is still being excavated today by specialist archaeologists, but their findings have not yet been published. Further systematic excavation needs to be done, both here and at other sites on Alónnisos if we are to know more of the men of this obscure period.

There is another site with a mass of 'Palaeolithic refuse', investigated more recently than Kokkinonísi, at Tsoukaná Choúni, the valley behind the bay known as Glifá or Xéro, immediately to the north of Stení Vála. There, at approximately the same height above sea level as at Kokkinonísi, large quantities of limestone flakes[4] from the working of tools and weapons were found.

This position, on the side of the valley, would have been ideal for a temporary encampment. The Alonnisiot hunters could wait there patiently for the herds to pass, fashioning their stone weapons and tools. Indeed the visitor today can see the results of this activity: an abundance of small and occasionally some large pieces of hard metamorphic limestone, which have stubbornly endured the passage of the centuries, as they have in other places on our island and on Peristéra. Let us hope that in the future the archaeologist's spade will bring to light other temporary or permanent encampments which have not been destroyed by floods, earthquakes or volcanic eruptions; and that these will provide us with new information about the development of our region.

4.4 The Middle Palaeolithic on Peristéra

At Vasilikós on Peristéra there is a site that shows evidence of continual habitation from the Middle Palaeolithic to the present. One can clearly make out the place where the hunter of the Palaeolithic Period stopped to skin his game and repair or make his stone weapons. As yet, there has been no research excavation and thus we have no evidence of bones. Tools, however, are found in abundance.

The wasteful methods of the men of the Middle Palaeolithic Period are clearly evident. Having collected their raw materials, the pebbles or large stones that were plentiful in the surrounding mountains, they brought them to their workshop, which also served as an abattoir, and there they worked them. From a large stone core they might make a very small stone tool, to be used as a knife, a needle or a pin. The flakes from their work remained where they fell and can still be seen today.

As I have already mentioned, the straits between Alónnisos and Peristéra were at that time a great valley. Men either came on hunting trips from their permanent homes in Magnisía, or else established permanent dwellings around the valley, which was rich in game. This latter custom was very widespread. Ancestral man, that is to say, first chose his hunting ground, and the place that he would use as his abattoir and workshop for stone tool making, and then built his permanent dwelling place nearby, but higher up, in the hills. (Three such sites have now been located: two on Alónnisos and one on Peristéra.) His home was a rock shelter. A tall rock, of the kind plentiful in Peristéra, would be utilised as one side of the house. This type of dwelling is still found today. There are a number of cabins at Vouní, on the hill known as Stefáni in the southern part of Peristéra, where one wall of the house is solid rock. Primitive man would probably not have built a house, but erected a tent made of skins against the rock, angled to take maximum advantage of the sunlight.

The archaeological site on Peristéra has not yet been investigated. It is a virgin Palaeolithic abattoir in a remote place far from the destructive hand of modern man. I came across it quite by chance in the course of a ramble. I immediately brought it to the attention of officials of the Athanasákio Archaeological Museum in Vólos (where Theocháris was Director), which is considered a model museum in Greece. They showed intense interest, and I hope that the necessary investigations will eventually take place. There are, however, insufficient archaeological personnel to cover the area. The limited number of archaeologists working in the region have certainly made superhuman and praiseworthy efforts. The present archaeological team continues the work with the same enthusiasm as Theocháris and Chourmouziádhis (who succeeded him at the Athanasákio Museum).

4.5 The Mesolithic Period (8000–7000 BC)

Figure 4.2 Mesolithic bone tools from the excavation of the Cave of the Cyclops, Yoúra.

The traces that men of the Mesolithic Period have left on our islands call into question many of the current theories about this little known epoch. Adhamándios Sampsón has produced a number of a valuable works that provide information on many cultural and archaeological subjects relating to our islands (see the Bibliography). Even more important, though, are his activities as an excavator. In 1993, as *Éforos* for Antiquities[5] and leader of a research team, he went to Yoúra to excavate the cave that is known to the inhabitants of Alónnisos as the 'Cave of the Cyclops'. Yoúra is the wildest and most rugged island in the Aegean. The mission was difficult because of the terrain and the remoteness of the island and the consequent supply problem. The results, however, amply repaid the efforts made by Sampsón and his team. The investigation was recognised as one of the most important currently in progress in Europe, and the team returned to Yoúra in 1994 and again in 1995, when many other important discoveries were made.[6]

The archaeologists were able to throw new light on the obscure Mesolithic period. Among other artifacts, they brought to the surface several dozen bone fishing hooks. The length of the hooks varied from 7 cm for smaller fish to 16 cm for larger ones. This range of hook sizes is still found in fishing tackle shops today. For very large fish an elongated spike with a line attached to its centre point was used. The fish would swallow the baited spike lengthways, and would then be caught by a tug on the line which would turn the spike the other way across its stomach. The line would have been made from plant fibres or horsehair. Such devices were still in use on Alónnisos in the 1930s. The fact that the hooks were found among thousands of bones from fish of all sizes leads us to the conclusion that we are dealing with highly skilled fishermen who were using methods that were distinctly innovative for their era. Many of the kinds of fish they caught – tuna for example – are still found today several miles out to sea. This suggests that these far distant ancestors of ours new how to sail and could even cover considerable distances. But how? What kind of boats did they have in those days?

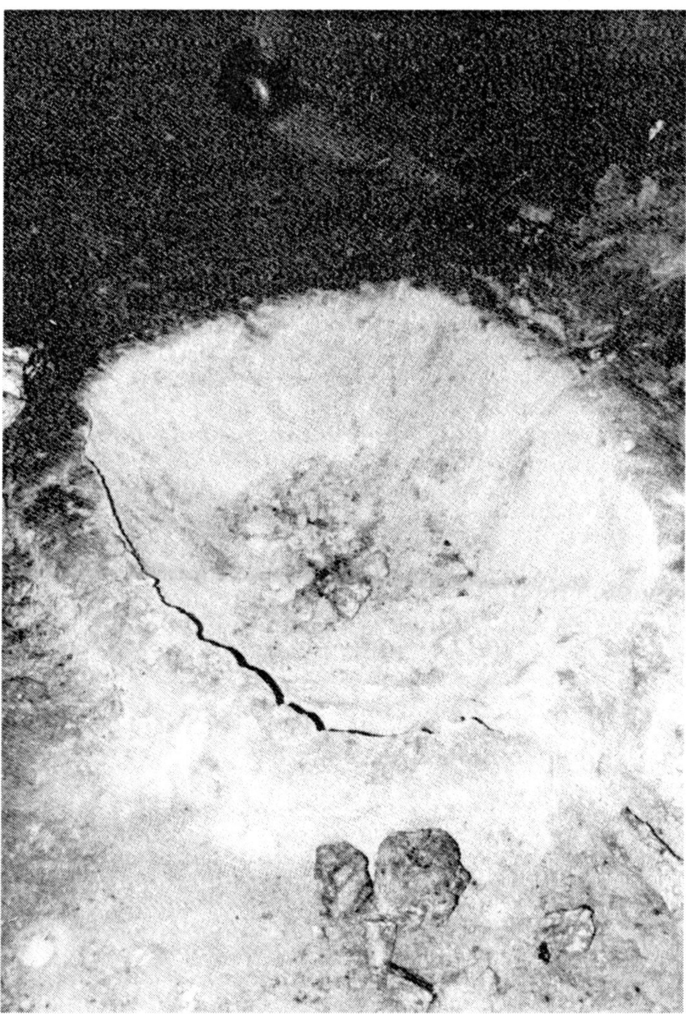

Figure 4.3 Basin for water collection, Yoúra.

They would surely have bound reeds (papyrus) together to make substantial boats suitable for covering the kind of distance that could be rowed in a day. In the evening they would have dragged the boat ashore to dry out before continuing the next day. Such a boat could carry about four oarsmen and a small amount of cargo (see Figure 4.11, p. 112).[7] With craft of this kind the prehistoric fishermen of Yoúra could have fished and travelled.

It is at this period that we see the first evidence of trade. As techniques of boat-building and navigation developed and fishing skills were perfected, the fisherman of that epoch would have been able to exchange his surplus fish for other goods. In the caves that served him as temporary camps, once he had gutted and cut up the fish, he could preserve and store them for his own use or for trade.

In the same period a 'technological development' involving obsidian can be observed. For there to be trade in obsidian as well as fish, Mesolithic man must have made the difficult passage south to Mílos, the source of this hard glasslike substance. These journeys would have given him the opportunity to appropriate the skills and knowledge of his fellow men, and to develop new techniques of stone-carving, pottery- and jewellery-making, and cooking, which improved his way of life, and left many objects for us to find, including stone and bone tools, beads from necklaces, bone needles, ear-rings and various kinds of seashells. The bones of a seal were also found, indicating that man was making at least limited use of the subcutaneous fat of this creature to help him survive.

But the most radical and important discovery was that of the bones of goats, which the excavators uncovered in a context dated to about 8000 BC. Until then the prevailing view had been that the domestication of goats began only in the Neolithic Period, and at a later date in Greece than in the Middle East. The archaeologists believed that the domestication of goats and their rearing in flocks originated in more evolved cultures and only gradually spread to our region. The discoveries on Yoúra, however, indicate that this view is not sustainable. The indigenous culture of our islands was well advanced in the Mesolithic Period. It was not brought here from Asia Minor, but developed alongside the culture of the East, and was closely linked to the developments of the immediately following and revolutionary (in terms of prehistory) Neolithic Period. In the upper levels of the excavation the gradual development of the cave dwellers of Yoúra can be observed. In the levels belonging to the Middle Neolithic (5000–4000 BC) and Upper Neolithic (4000–2800 BC) fine examples of pottery have come to light.

4.6 The Neolithic Period (7000–2750 BC)

It was in the Neolithic Period that man first discovered the secret properties of clay and began to make pottery. At first his creations were crude and thick and of a purely utilitarian nature. Later, though, when his interventions in nature had secured for him a relatively comfortable life, he was able to devote a great deal of time to artistic pursuits. The restless spirit of the Neolithic inhabitants of our islands, whose horizons were broadened by journeys to Asia Minor and Thessaly, created a style of pottery whose fine decoration was unique. It is a style developed only by the potters of the Northern Sporades, though it shows clear influences from the mainland shores to east and west. On their clay vessels they began to incise patterns probably derived from the knitted and woven fabrics of the day. These were then coloured white on a background of dark red. This technique persisted into the Upper Neolithic, and we have some splendid examples from this later period, found at Áyos Pétros on Kirá Panayá.

4.7 The Neolithic Settlement at Áyos Pétros, Kirá Panayá

In the large natural harbour on the south side of Kirá Panayá, there is a small island called Áyos Pétros where traces of Neolithic habitation are evident on the surface. Dhimítrios Theocháris investigated this site during three seasons, 1969–71 while the nearby Byzantine wreck was being raised by Kritzás,[8] who also helped Theocháris with the excavation of the island. The excavation at Áyos Pétros was resumed by Níkos Efstratíou in 1981.[9] Theocháris and Efstratíou brought to light considerable quantities of pottery, figurines, bone needles and obsidian tools. The pottery was very similar to that found in the cave on Yoúra. Most of it was thick-walled and monochrome.

There were, though, other vessels with applied (not incised) basket-weave decoration influenced by the Thessalian style (see Figure 4.10, p. 111). The colour was the same as examples from Yoúra. The figurines that were found in the same spot show the desire of local craftsmen to progress beyond a rudimentary style, using incised lines to indicate hair and attempting to give some life to these inert clay forms. The bone needles point to sewing and the working of skins. Chiefly, though, it is in the painting of pottery that we must acknowledge a remarkable and meticulous art that we do not meet with even today.

The presence of obsidian again shows that the men of this epoch had developed stone-working to a high level and were involved in sea trade. Finely worked tools with a polished surface were found, as well as flakes of obsidian which, after further working, were used as sickles. The great number of these finds confirms a continuous exchange of products. With the small boats of that time, the sailors of Kirá Panayá travelled as far as Mílos, and perhaps further. Mílos (as there was no other source) was in those days the centre for the extraction of the hard glasslike material known as obsidian, and there they would barter their own products (crops, meat and dairy products, fish) for unworked blocks of this black glass.

Many scholars believe that the primary sea routes of the Neolithic Period converged on Mílos, from the Peloponnese, from Lávrio in Attica and the nearby island of Kéa, and from TROY, via Límnos, Skíros and northern Évvia. But they have all neglected the island of Kirá Panayá, which offered safe harbours, fresh water, provisions and opportunities for trade, and was frequently used as a port of call. This island in the Northern Sporades with its geographical advantages was rich in trade goods and also functioned as a centre for cultural exchange.

The settlement at Áyos Pétros must have consisted of some 25–40 houses with a population of the order of 100–200 individuals. It is an unfortunate fact that the lea level in those days was about five metres lower than it is today, and many buildings, as well as much other historical evidence, have been lost in the sea. The basic difference between Áyos Pétros and Yoúra is that the former was a permanent settlement, the latter only a place of refuge.

Figure 4.4 Neolithic head from Áyos Pétros, Kirá Panayá.
Source: A History of the Greek Nation, published by Ekdhotikí Athinón A.E. 1970.

Figure 4.5 Another Neolithic head from Áyos Pétros, Kirá Panayá. *Source*: *as for Figure 4.4.*

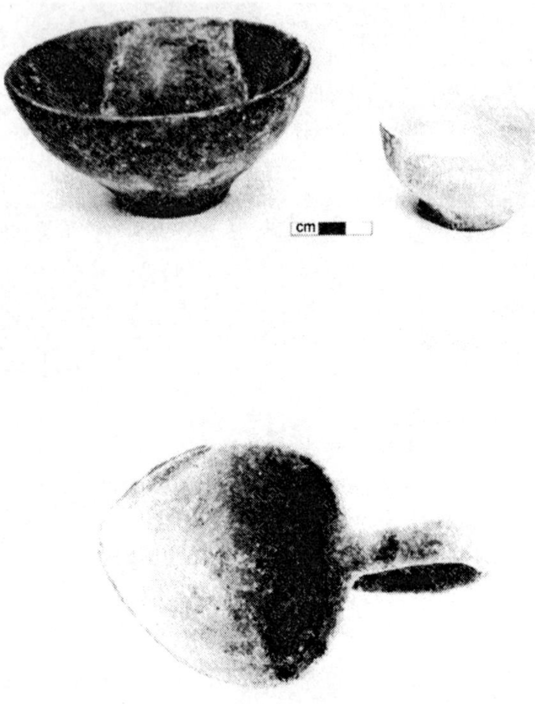

Figure 4.6 Vessels from Áyos Pétros on Kirá Panayá.

Figure 4.7 Bone needles. From the book *Áyos Pétros* by N. Efstratíou.

Both Theocháris and Efstathíou conclude that Áyos Pétros is one of the oldest settlements so far discovered and investigated in the Aegean. It belongs to the Middle Neolithic Period and was occupied in the late sixth and early fifth millennium BC. It has been shown that the Northern Sporades enjoyed economic autonomy. Their technological developments were not transplanted from the east, and the area produced fine examples of local culture, with distinct characteristics.

Figure 4.8 Cult figure from Kirá Panayá. From *Áyos Pétros* by N. Efstratíou.

Figure 4.9 Various tools from the settlement at Áyos Pétros.
From *Áyos Pétros* by N. Efstratíou.

Figure 4.10 Basket-weave decorated pottery. From the book *Áyos Pétros* by N. Efstratíou.

4.8 The Neolithic on Peristéra and Other Islands

In the Vasilikós area of Peristéra there are traces of human activity in all phases of the Neolithic. Among artefacts made of obsidian we can observe both the crude techniques of the early Neolithic as well as the faultless fine work of the later. The density of finds is not great, and this suggests that we are not dealing with a permanent settlement but a temporary camp. At various other locations on the island there have been isolated discoveries of Neolithic tools, and at Mnímata in the southern part there is more extensive evidence of habitation. Peristéra is an island with much to offer the archaeologist and it requires more thorough investigation.

There are indications of Neolithic habitation, still awaiting excavation, on other islands in the Northern Sporades. Obsidian tools and/or sherds of pottery from the Neolithic Period have been found at Áyos Ioánnis, Kastráki and the tiny islet in the bay of Glifá on Alónnisos, on the small island of Kórakas to the south of Skántzoura, and on Grámeza. Our islands were at the centre of the Neolithic triangle formed by Thessaly, Skíros and Límnos. The ceaseless trade between these three important centres must have been supported by small seaboard settlements that served as ports of call. And many of these were, surely, located on the remote islands of our archipelago, whose position and morphology favoured the development of villages. Let us hope that future generations will uncover the habitation sites of our Neolithic ancestors and learn more about this distant epoch.

Figure 4.11 Transport of obsidian by papyrus boat.
From the Institute for the Conservation of the Naval Tradition.

Notes

1. For more information about the geological formation and early prehistory of Greece see (in English) Hourmouziadis, Asimakopoulou-Atzaka & Makrís (1982), vol. 1, pp. 18–25.
2. The Palaeolithic (or Old Stone Age) is the first of the *cultural* periods distinguished by archaeologists. The *geological* eras, periods and epochs are part of a different system of classification. [Translator]
3. Theocháris (1970b).
4. The stone cores used here came from Spartínes, several kilometres down the coast, beyond Kokkinókastro.
5. An *éforos* is the director of a regional archaeological service. [Translator]
6. See Nikitídhis (1995) and Karkatzélou (1995).
7. Boats of this type are called *papiréles* (papyrus boats). The illustration of the boat (Figure 4.11, above) and the details of its capabilities are from the *Institoúto tis Prostasías tis Naftikís Parádhosis* (Institute for the Conservation of the Naval Tradition).
8. Theocháris (1970a) and Nikonános (1972). For an account of the Byzantine wreck at Áyos Pétros, see pp. 396–401.
9. Efstratíou (1985).

5

FROM THE DAWN OF HISTORY TO THE ARCHAIC PERIOD

BECAUSE OF the scarcity of documentary and monumental evidence, much about the deep past of our islands still remains uncertain. There are many theories, particularly about who the inhabitants of these islands were in the period. It has been established that some branch of the Indo-European race came from the east and either amalgamated with the indigenous population, or else displaced them. The former is more likely, since, in most cases, when the Indo-European race spread its tentacles it came into peaceful contact with the local population.

5.1 Bronze Age (2750–1100 BC)

From the scant evidence (tombs, stonework), it appears that those who first came to Alónnisos and the neighbouring islands were Pelasgians – a name applied by ancient Greek writers to a prehistoric people whose traces were found in Greek lands. Though the Pelasgians are historically attested, there are many different views about their origins.[1] What is most likely is that Dolopians, one of the 'purer' Pelasgian tribes, and a culturally more developed group, inhabited the whole Northern Sporades archipelago. Taking advantage of their geographical location, they devoted themselves to piracy. The Dolopians were among the first to involve themselves in this most ancient profession.

The Dolopians of ICOS, seduced by the prospect of easy gain, began to make systematic raids; and, though they operated in a period notorious for its anarchy, their name became a byword for piracy. From Cyprus and other places they began to import copper, while the trade in obsidian continued; but since they were firmly established at the crossroads of the Northern Sporades, the Dolopians preferred to obtain their material goods through plunder rather than trade.

That our island was first conquered by Pelasgians is evident from the following:

1. The name ICOS is Pre-Hellenic as we have already seen (see p. 45).
2. There are Cyclopean walls all over the island. The Pelasgians, including the Dolopians, are characterised as builders of Cyclopean walls. One can see such

walls on the hills at Kastráki in the centre of the island and near the church of Áyos Ioánnis just outside Palió Chorió. Visiting Kastráki, one cannot fail to be impressed by the massive size of the stone blocks from which the earliest wall is constructed. A careful examination of the hill reveals how these huge blocks were quarried and worked. One is overcome by awe when one considers how the craftsmen of those days quarried and cut the stones with the limited means at their disposal, and how they transported them over the steep and stony ground of the hill. Here Philostratus can enlighten us. In his *Heroicus* he says that the Pelasgians were much taller than was normal. Perhaps their unusually large bodies would have helped them to work with such large stones.

3. The tall skeletons, found in recent times in various parts of the island by Alonnisiot vine growers, are a further indication that the island was once inhabited by long-bodied Pre-Hellenic people of Pelasgian origin. In the immediate post-war period, when the local people were digging all over Alónnisos to plant new vineyards in a concerted effort to develop wine production, the discovery of ancient tombs was a common occurrence. One grave containing an unusually large skeleton was found at that time by a farmer in the area where the new settlement in Patitíri, built after the 1965 earthquake, stands today. Naturally this grave aroused considerable interest among the local people, not because of the grave goods – which scarcely interested them at all – but because of the giant skeleton. According to those who saw it, this skeleton was twice normal size. Similar cases had been reported before in other places, but unfortunately no evidence remains today. In those days people were not much concerned with archaeological matters, having more serious problems to contend with, including hunger, unemployment and the Civil War. Anthropological studies may help us to understand many things about our Pre-Hellenic forbears.

4. Another fact that bears witness to the existence of the 'Dolopians of ICOS' is the demonstrable presence of Dolopians on nearby Skíros. The Dolopians remained there for about 2500 years. It is thought that some pirates belonging to the Dolopian race still remained on Skíros when Cimon of ATHENS arrived in 468 BC to eliminate all the pirate bases in the Sporades. The pirates were either killed or enslaved. It is certain, however, that, in addition to piracy, the Dolopians of our islands were involved in agriculture and stock rearing. It is probable that before 468 BC the islands had maintained political autonomy as much because of their distance from the Greek mainland as because of the slow development of sea trade.

The Pelasgians were dominant in our region throughout the Early and Middle Bronze Age, that is, from 2800 to 1600 BC. The ensuing period, the Late Bronze Age (1600–1100 BC) is one of great historical confusion. Did the Minoan from the island of Crete colonise the island, or did the Dolopians remain in possession? There is written evidence, admittedly rather late (2nd century BC), that tells us that the Cretans who had colonised Skópelos spread to Alónnisos. In his *Periegesis*, Scymnus of CHIOS names SCYROS, PEPARETHOS and SCIATHOS as islands that are close to CARYSTUS in Évvia, and adds:

> of these islands, the Cretans who once came from CNOSSUS with Staphylus colonised PEPARETHOS and also ICOS, the island that lies next to it, while Pelasgians who came from Thrace colonised SCYROS and SCIATHOS[2]

The information that Scymnus gives is not necessarily correct. He may have been writing mythology rather than history; and several scholars, including Chrístos Athanasíou, have rejected the theory of a non-Hellenic Cretan colonisation. Their view is supported by the fact that up till now no trace of a Minoan presence has appeared in the archaeological record.

The Minoans were a Bronze Age non-Hellenic civilisation dating from approximately 2000 to 1400 BC, centred on the island of Crete. Perhaps in the past some Minoan tomb was found, but no information of any such discovery has come down to us.

Logically, though, Alónnisos must have been visited by the energetic Cretan race, who had developed such a high level of culture. Neighbouring PEPARETHOS (Skópelos) was inhabited by Cretans with their hero Staphylus as leader. Alónnisos, as a natural extension of Skópelos, was surely acquired for its fertile soil, to increase the power and wealth of their king. In antiquity our island was renowned for the quality of its wine and olive oil, as Ovid attests in the case of neighbouring PEPARETHOS (Skópelos):

> But OLIAROS and DIDYME, TENOS, ANDROS, GYAROS and PEPARETHOS, rich in glossy olives, gave no help to the Cretan fleet.[3]

The initiation into the secrets of oil and wine production must be connected with the expertise of the Minoans, with which we are all familiar.

The probable date of arrival of this energetic seafaring people is the 16th century BC. Unfortunately, the characteristic of the Greek race from its earliest origins until today is that, once it has achieved a high level of culture which is the envy of the world, it is immediately divided by internal disputes and enmity. It was such a conflict between Cretan kings that prompted the Cretan expansion beyond their island throughout the entire Aegean.

The islands beyond Skópelos, which it appears that they conquered without difficulty, would have been a basic key to their northward expansion. The earlier inhabitants were not driven out and there must have been peaceful coexistence between Cretans and Dolopians.

The Dolopians were at a lower cultural level than the Cretans and would, surely, have accepted with enthusiasm their new neighbours and the innovations in metalworking, farming and navigation that they brought with them. The Cretans no doubt took advantage of the lower cultural level of the Dolopians to take over the organisation of trade and thus become the dominant class in these islands. The Minoans constructed no fortifications, because they were undisputed masters of the sea and had no fear of attack from any quarter. For a long time no enemies appeared on the horizon, and they lived in peace.

Around 1500 BC, a wave of refugees began to pour out of Crete and strengthened the Minoan centres throughout the Aegean. This exodus followed the earthquakes that struck their capital, destroyed their palaces and houses and transformed their social organisation. Similar events were repeated after the eruption of the volcano on THERA (Santorini) From this point on Minoan civilisation was in decline and the Minoans were eventually subjugated by the people of ancient Greece, the Achaeans.

The city that the Cretans established on Alónnisos must have been located at Kokkinókastro. The Cretans usually built their cities by the sea. The deep bay to the north, now known as Tzórtzi Yalós (Tzórtzis' Beach), offered a sheltered harbour where many ships could anchor. The Kokkinókastro–Tzórtzi Yalós area is fairly centrally placed and could have constituted a military base for the control of the whole island state.

The farmsteads of the Dolopians would have been scattered throughout the hinterland. Life went on smoothly with this social structure in Alónnisos and the surrounding smaller islands, but across the water on the Thessalian mainland dramatic changes were taking place.

The Achaeans, the creators of the Mycenaean civilisation, were one of many Indo-European tribes whose migrations brought them to Greece. When they arrived, they quickly subdued the Pre-Hellenic population. They were better armed and they used horses in battle. At that time most parts of Greece were, like Alónnisos, under the influence of Minoan culture. The Achaeans adopted Minoan culture, adding their own distinctive elements to it, so that Mycenaean and Minoan culture have much in common.

The name 'Mycenaean' was applied to the culture by modern historians after the excavation, in the 19th century, of the ancient citadel of MYCENAE in the Peloponnese. Closer to the Sporades, the cities of IOLCUS (on the site of the modern Vólos) and PAGASAE were established on the bay of Vólos (the Pagasitic Gulf), and were among the largest cities of that period.

From being herdsmen and farmers the Achaeans became craftsmen, sailors and merchants on the Minoan model. They built fleets and their merchandise was distributed throughout the Mediterranean. Our islands were essential as supply and trading bases, and provided safe harbours. The power of the Achaeans had never been greater.

As Mycenaean culture developed in Alónnisos it gave a new impetus to social life. The cultivation of vines and olives became more systematic. Wine and oil were the principal exports. Defensive walls of the Mycenaean type were built. The dead were buried in tholos tombs,[4] whose grave goods bear witness to the Mycenaeans' skill in metalworking, ceramics and sculpture.

Examples of tombs of this kind have been found in various places on Alónnisos, but, sadly, they have been pillaged and destroyed. At the time they were discovered, there was no interest locally in archaeology, and farmers used the stones to build their terraces.

There were two Mycenaean cities on Alónnisos. Kokkinókastro was the port and trading centre, but there was another city close to where Palió Chorió now stands. Its probable site was on the hill of Áyos Ioánnis, also known as Rachokokkaliá. All the island's most fertile and cultivable land is close to this hilltop site, which would have been very convenient for access to the fields.

Towards the end of the 13th century BC, Mycenaean civilisation reached the height of its power; and myth and legend tell us that it was at that particular point that the Trojan War broke out. The Greek fleet passed through the Sporades archipelago en route for LEMNOS. But not only that, for our islands were the umbilical cord for the whole expedition. From TROY, via LEMNOS, the Achaean ships came to ICOS bringing news of the campaign. They then continued on to IOLCUS, where they took on supplies, weapons and soldiers before returning, by the same route, to the rigours of the twelve-year war. Despite the vital importance of the route between TROY and IOLCUS, nowhere in the *Iliad* does Homer refer to ancient ICOS.

The Trojan War provided opportunities for certain non-Achaean tribes. Because of the demands of the war, the Achaeans handed over a part of their trading activities and agricultural production to other, friendly peoples. It appears that one such foreign merchant, Molenas, from the tribe of the Abantes, exploited the Trojan War and the key position of Alónnisos and became very powerful economically. It is unlikely that Molenas would have been of noble birth, but in my view he was probably a resourceful merchant who rose to prominence.

According to tradition, Molenas invited Peleus, the father of the demigod Achilles, to spend his old age with him: 'He came in winter to the island of ICOS, and, having been received into the house of a certain Abantus named Molenas, he ended his life there.'[5] From this one might expect that an impressive royal tomb appropriate to Peleus would have been built on Alónnisos. It may be that the tholos tomb and the road leading to it gave rise to the later name of the island Achilleodhrómios, corrupted to Chiliodhrómia.[6] It is perhaps the only reference to a possibly historical event on the island in this period.

Similar testimony is given by Antipater of SIDON, in a sepulchral epigram on Homer, in which the speaker is the island of IOS, where Antipater believed Homer to be buried. The epigram concludes with a comparative reference to Peleus ('the spouse of Thetis'):

> If thou marvellest that I who am so small cover so great a man, know that the spouse of Thetis likewise lies in ICOS that hath but a few clods of earth.[7]

Where then might Peleus' splendid tomb be found? There are three views as to its possible fate:

1. That it exists somewhere in the bowels of Alónnisos, patiently awaiting archaeological excavation.

2. That it was robbed in antiquity or in more recent times.

3. That the contents were transferred elsewhere in ancient times. It was a common practice in antiquity to transfer the bones, weapons and grave goods of demigods and heroes to leading cities of the day. One known case is that of Cimon, the Athenian general, who removed the bones and weapons of Theseus when he opened his tomb in nearby SCYROS. According to the tradition, even 800 years after the death of Theseus the people of SCYROS were not willing that his bones be removed and refused to tell Cimon where the tomb was. One day, when he had almost given up hope, Cimon saw an eagle persistently

scratching with its beak and claws at a small mound. It was there that Theseus was buried.[8]

There are no other recorded references to this period, though there is no shortage of myths. Most important among these is the myth of Philoctetes which refers to the island of CHRYSE, which may well be present-day Psathoúra.[9] Another myth, associated with many islands where large caves are encountered, is that of the Cyclops. The cave on Yoúra, given its position in the Aegean, has a good claim to be connected with the home of the Cyclops. According to local tradition it was on Yoúra that Odysseus was imprisoned by the Cyclops and from which he eventually made his cunning escape. In recent times this tradition has been exploited to attract tourists. The bones of some donkey which, some years ago, sought refuge in the cave and died just inside the entrance, have become known as the bones of the Cyclops; and a rock in the sea near the cave has become the rock that the angry giant hurled down at Odysseus' ship.

In the 12th century BC, in the aftermath, perhaps, of the Trojan War of legend, great changes were seen in Greek lands. A new tribe, the Dorians, coming down from the north, exploited the confusion. Their arrival was responsible for the decline of Mycenaean culture, and ushered in a new epoch. The Dorians were an important new element that contributed to the ethnological make-up of the Greek people.

5.2 The Dark Age of Antiquity (11th–9th Centuries BC)

Invading from the north with iron weapons and a great passion for war, the Dorians easily destroyed the Achaean strongholds and became the dominant force in Greece in the 11th century BC. With the defeat of the Achaeans, however, the development of art and writing was interrupted, and dominance in trade passed from the Greeks to the Phoenicians. Piracy reappeared and stopped communications between the islands. Only in agriculture was progress made, through the introduction of iron tools. The decorated pottery of the period is known as Geometric, since its decoration consisted largely of austere geometric patterns. Along with the great mixture of tribes and races that had already passed over her land, Alónnisos received the Dorians. As a result there was a cultural regression after the extraordinary achievements of the Mycenaean period, and the forgotten Dolopians of ICOS seized the opportunity to resume their piratical activities.

In the Aegean generally very few examples of Geometric pottery have been found, and on Alónnisos we can be proud of the Geometric cemetery at Áyos Konstandínos, about halfway up the west side of the island, where signs of ancient habitation, terraces now largely buried in the soil, can also be seen. Shortly before the Second World War, a local herdsman noticed a strange depression in the ground close to his sheepfold. He began to dig and found a rich grave with gold grave goods. It must have been the grave of a woman, for there was a quantity of gold jewellery (rings, earrings and bead necklaces). Sadly, though, it seems that out of ignorance he gave everything he found to a gypsy as payment for tin-plating the coppers he used for cheese-making. Later the same man, again by chance, came upon a second grave close to the first. This probably belonged to some great warrior, because it contained a sword as well as several pottery vessels. When the shepherd attempted to remove the sword it disintegrated, and he also broke the pottery.

Figure 5.1 The Cave of the Cyclops, Yoúra. A rock-cut reservoir for water collection, with the 'bones of the Cyclops'.

Figure 5.2 Geometric vessel from the archaeological site at Palió Chorió.

Figure 5.3 An ancient quarry near Kastráki, Alónnisos. It is clear that massive blocks of stone have been removed and built into the enclosure of the fortress.

Let us hope that systematic investigation will bring to light further traces of the cultural inheritance left to us by the Dorians of ICOS. The Dorian establishment at Áyos Konstandínos where the graves were found was probably a farmstead, not a town. (There are many such small settlements throughout the inland parts of the island.) Their towns must be sought in the long-established sites at Kokkinókastro and in the vicinity of Palió Chorió. The weapons, jewellery and pottery must have been the products of local workshops, since there was little trade at that period. As we mentioned above, one element in the population, the Dolopians, were given to piracy. The same happened on the neighbouring islands, where the scattered population was still pre-Hellenic, deeply influenced by the cultures of various races. The chaos of this transitory period allowed these peoples to revive their former occupation of piracy, and to curtail cultural development. This may explain why today there are no signs of the dominant culture of this 'dark' period, in any of the smaller islands.

5.3 Greek Colonisation (8th–7th Centuries BC)

The 8th and 7th centuries BC were a time of chaos. The Dolopian pirates continued to infest the seas around the Northern Sporades as before. In this period there were pirates on Skíros and Skópelos and to a lesser extent on Alónnisos and the other Northern Sporades, controlling the channels between the islands. Throughout the rest of Greece feudal regimes were established, and the population increased, creating a land shortage. This gave rise to local disputes and social divisions, and impelled the Greeks into a second major period of colonisation, beginning in the 8th century. With this explosion of colonising activity the income of farmers increased, with large profits from the systematic cultivation of vines and olives. Manufacturing techniques also developed and the design of ships was improved. The need to find new land to farm became pressing and the men of this period founded colonies.

Our islands had the good fortune to be colonised, around 750 BC, by the energetic Chalcidians, from CHALCIS (modern Chalkídha) in Évvia.[10] The Chalcidians also established colonies at CYME (Latin CUMAE) in MAGNA GRAECA (southern Italy), and in Sithonía, the middle finger of the Chalkidhikí peninsula (OLYNTHUS and some thirty other towns there). The Chalcidians, a highly developed people, both culturally and economically, were attracted to the copper mines and forests of Chalkidhikí (which took its name from the colonists). Alónnisos and the safe harbours on the adjoining islands (Vasilikós on Peristéra, Planítis and Áyos Pétros on Kirá Panayá) formed an indispensable trading and naval bridge between CHALCIS and Chalkidhikí.

OLYNTHUS was the first colony to be founded, and after that the other colonies of this powerful Evvian people began to spring up one by one. As one ancient author puts it, 'the Chalcidians resettled all those places that had become desolate'.[11] Trading stations on the coast were established first, and then permanent towns. At the same time they settled in the Northern Sporades, where the same pattern of colonisation can be observed. Kokkinókastro was their most important trading port, followed by an undoubtedly subordinate town at the site of present-day Palió Chorió.

As metalworking techniques developed so also did farming methods. Merchant fleets transported the wine of Alónnisos to cities throughout the Mediterranean and brought back not only merchandise but also the discoveries and technical accomplishments of other peoples. These exchanges stimulated the creation of many new gainful occupations. Once the Chalcidians of Icos had solved their economic problems they began to turn to cultural matters. They imposed a plutocratic system. Craftsmen made great advances.

Pottery, new types of textiles, iron weapons and implements such as ploughshares, and the tools of various trades were transported to the Black Sea and sold along with the principal export, 'Ician wine'.[12] The local sailor-merchants would bring back grain, skins and other products.

Unfortunately, today we have no material evidence of this cultural and economic advancement that took place on Alónnisos, for the simple reason that the later inhabitants of the island found fine cities already established in key places and continued to use them. In the course of time, through repairs and rebuilding and large-scale reorganisation of the street plan, and natural disasters, the traces of the original cities have disappeared.

Nevertheless, the existence of such a significant culture can be deduced from the later Archaic and classical cultures of the island, which endured and thrived thanks to the ceaseless physical and mental labour of the Chalcidians. (It is not surprising that the inhabitants of the Italian peninsula in the 8th–6th centuries BC thought that Greece was inhabited only by Chalcidians.)

On the other islands around Alónnisos the Chalcidians did not establish settlements, but they undoubtedly used the islands as ports of call, and particularly Kirá Panayá, whose harbours were so important in the ancient world. These were the years when Planítis (Kirá Panayá's northern harbour) played such an important role as a naval trading station. It is likely that the Chalcidians built some kind of guardhouse there, probably in the position of the present castle.

The harbour did not only function as a refuge. Ships also anchored there to take on supplies of water and food. Water would have been as abundant then as it is today, and foodstuffs would also have been in good supply from the farming and stockbreeding in the fertile interior of the island. We hope that future generations will discover and record further information about this culture that preceded the Greek miracle that unfolded in these islands in the following centuries.

5.4 The Archaic Period (7th–6th Centuries BC)

Greek culture, first consolidated in the 'Dark Ages' (before the 8th century BC), developed to a very high level during the Archaic Period and evolved into the unrivalled civilisation of the classical age. In the transitional, Archaic Period, art and letters were no longer the privilege of the aristocracy, and intellectual and artistic developments involved much broader strata of society. Contacts with the long established and highly developed civilisations of the Orient and Egypt gave a new impetus to Greek art. In the Northern Sporades, as elsewhere, there was a general economic and cultural flowering.

Indeed, Alónnisos was in the front rank in this period, with rapid development in almost every field. Her wine was, as ever, in great demand. Her merchant and war fleets were enlarged. Her extensive pine forests enabled her to make great strides in the art of shipbuilding. Existing mining facilities were strengthened and improved. The city at Kokkinókastro evolved into a major northern Aegean trading post. An important factor in its later development was the Persian conquest of the Macedonian and Thracian littoral in 515 BC.

For a while, wine-producing towns such as MENDE (on the western finger of Chalkidhikí), MARONEA (on the Thracian coast) and THASOS (on the island known by the same name today), could not engage in trade with, or export their wine to, other Greek cities. From the castle on the hill by Palió Chorió, wine production in the interior was regulated, while the agricultural inhabitants were endlessly carrying their wine in skin bags to the warehouses by the shore.

The island's third guard post at Kastráki took on a more important role at this period. The greater part of the fortifications that remain there today is of Greek workmanship. On a small spur of the hill there is a wall 1.2 m high, 1.6 m wide and about 60 m long. Within this splendid wall can be made out a rectangular building 8 m x 6 m. At first sight, viewed from the western side of the island, it looks like a military outpost of Kokkinókastro, protecting the main town of the island and controlling the unprotected western shore. From the wealth of finds in its vicinity, however, it appears that the large building within the fortification was the residence of some important person, a governor, or perhaps of some religious functionary. It was there that a farmer found one of the coins struck in Alónnisos to serve its trading needs. That coins were minted at this period in ancient ICOS I have not found mentioned in any archaeological periodical.

My tentative personal opinion is that, in the first place, the volume of trade carried on here made it essential for the island to have its own coinage. Besides, neighbouring PEPARETHOS (i.e. Skópelos) had its own coinage at this period. ICOS, which was only a little behind PEPARETHOS economically would, logically, also have had its monetary autonomy.

Furthermore, from my careful searches in the catalogues of foreign coin collections (including the British Museum), I concluded that no other region had issued the coin found on Alónnisos, whose characteristics show the high level of expertise in metalworking of the local workshops.

Another reason why I consider the silver coin of ICOS to be from the Archaic Period is that it was found in the same spot as coins from the Cycladic islands of Sífnos and Tzía (also known as Kéa), which were struck at the end of the Archaic Period and bear witness to the wide extent of ICOS' contacts with the other trading centres of the time.

The bunch of grapes on one side of the coin[13] suggests the need of people of this period, on the one hand, to publicise their basic product and, on the other, to express their connection with the fruit that was almost sacred to them.

At the beginning of the 5th century BC the great geographer Scylax of CARYANDA may have visited Alónnisos. At any rate, the late-4th-century *Periplous* that bears his name and which may well be a compilation from earlier accounts of voyages, including possibly that of Scylax, refers to ICOS and the adjacent islands in

Figure 5.4 Ancient tomb of the Geometric Period at Áyos Konstandínos, Alónnisos, where there are also traces of occupation.

Figure 5.5 Ancient coins. *Courtesy of Kóstas and Angéla Mavríkis.*

in terms remarkably similar to those used by Strabo some three centuries later:[14]

> In the Aegean sea there are the following islands: opposite ERETRIA, SCYROS with a city, ICOS, which has two cities, PEPARETHOS which has three cities and a port, and SCIATHOS with two cities and a port. After these I returned to the mainland from which I had turned aside.[15]

To this same period must be ascribed the first systematic attempts at fortification on Kirá Panayá, the ancient HALONNESOS. The wall that stands majestically above its northern bay and commands the whole of the northern Aegean is considered to date, in the main, from the end of the Archaic Period. It is significant that whoever studies the layout of the fortifications will find a close similarity between the fortresses on HALONNESOS and ICOS. On both islands, in addition to the large fortresses, there are smaller guard posts: at Kastráki on Alónnisos (ICOS) and at Tzavétis on Kirá Panayá (HALONNESOS). It appears that the latter, like its counterpart at Kastráki (see above), functioned not only as a guard post for the undefended side of the islands, but also as the residence of some important person.

Notes

1. Hourmouziadis, Asimakopoulou-Atzaka & Makrís (1982), vol. 1, p. 368.
2. Scymnus, *Periegesis* 579–80.
3. Ovid, *Metamorphoses* 7.469–70. Translation from Miller (1977–84), vol. 1, p. 375.
4. Tholos tombs are beehive-shaped stone structures characteristic of Mycenaean culture. [Translator]
5. Quoted in Sampsón (1970).
6. See p. 40–5.
7. *Greek Anthology* 7.2. Translation from Paton (1916–18), vol. 2, pp. 3–5.
8. Quoted in Graindor (1906).
9. See pp. 50–1.
10. The links between Alónnisos and Évvia have remained close until today. At the beginning of the 20th century 70% of the population of Alónnisos had come here from Évvia (see Ch. 2).
11. Scymnus, *Periegesis* 586–7.
12. Grace (1961).
13. The coin from ICOS is very similar to coins from Chíos. For a later coin from ICOS, see p. 128.
14. See p. 45.
15. Scylax, *Periplous* 58–9. ERETRIA was on the southwest coast of Évvia, facing the mainland and thus not literally 'opposite' any of these islands, of which SCYROS is the closest to ERETRIA. From SCYROS the author moves in logical geographical progression through the other islands, following a northwesterly then westerly course back to the mainland. [Translator]

6

CLASSICAL, HELLENISTIC AND ROMAN PERIODS

6.1 Alónnisos in the Heyday of Athenian Power

IT WAS In the classical period that Greek culture reached its highest point. All the Greek regions experienced an economic and cultural flowering. Alónnisos, with a sound economic and cultural base, entered the classical period at the zenith of its development. Its wine, much sought after in the great markets, was the linchpin of its trade and brought great prosperity to the island.

There was the beginning of the systematic operation of large workshops for the production of amphorae and other earthenware vessels, the main one near the bay of Tsoukaliás on the west coast, and a smaller one at Vamvakiés on the east. All the amphorae had the word *Ikiōn* stamped on their handles. This stamp was a sign of the origin and guarantee of the authenticity of the exceptionally good local wine. Such stamped inscriptions were found in 1846 on an intact amphora by Papadhópoulos, and again in 1865 by Stephani.[1] After the Second World War, Chrístos Athanasíou found a broken handle with the same word on it.

Figure 6.1 A pot from the classical wreck at Peristéra (see Chapter 15).

It is significant that similar amphorae (of the Solocha type)[2] from Alónnisos have been found by archaeologists as far afield as Elizavetovskoe on the Black Sea and ALEXANDRIA in Egypt, as well as at PELLA in Macedonia and in the ancient Agora of ATHENS.[3] These important discoveries indicate the great demand in the classical period for the products of ICOS. Ician and foreign merchants and sailors brought to the island not only material wealth but also knowledge, new techniques, customs and manners. The island assimilated new cultural and economic elements. As long as the shadows of the Persian Wars did not touch the island, it continued to develop undisturbed. The Icians remained neutral, since the vast Persian armies constituted a deadly threat to the unprotected island.

Extraordinary artistic activity is one of the chief characteristics of the period. There are examples of fine metalwork, including jewellery, items for daily use, decorative objects, arrow heads and inscribed sling shots. One branch of this art was the minting of coins. A copper coin of the island shows Poseidon on one side and on the other a trident with two dolphins and the word *Ikiōn*. This coin is very similar to an example from HALICARNASSUS in Asia Minor, and it is not at all improbable that there is some connection between them. A drawing of this coin was published in 1883 in a numismatic catalogue by Imhoof-Blumer and the coin was republished some fifty years later by Rogers.[4]

Figure 6.2 Ancient coin struck in Alónnisos – obverse.
Courtesy of Kóstas and Angéla Mavríkis

Figure 6.3 Ancient coin struck in Alónnisos – reverse, with dolphins and the inscription IKIΩN
Courtesy of Kóstas and Angéla Mavríkis

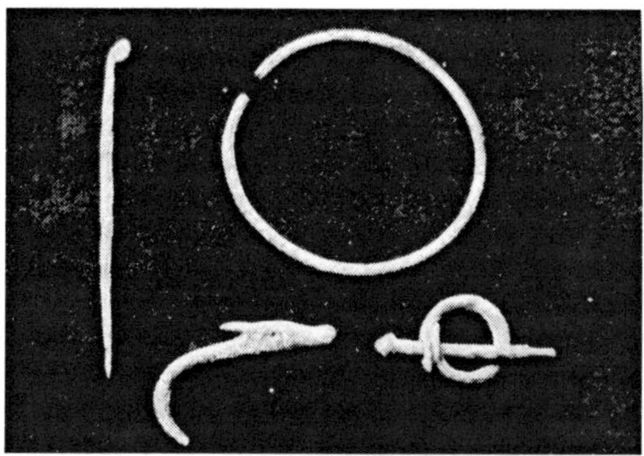

Figure 6.4 Various items of jewellery from classical Alónnisos. *Courtesy of Kóstas and Angéla Mavríkis.*

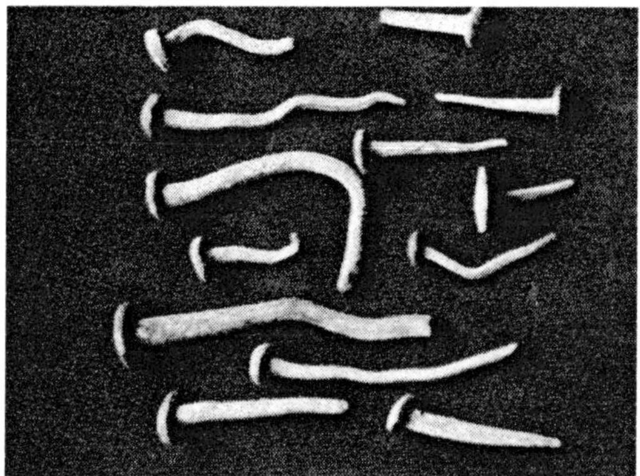

Figure 6.5 Nails for shipbuilding from the classical period. *Courtesy of Kóstas and Angéla Mavríkis.*

Figure 6.6 Rings of classical date from Kokkinókastro. *Courtesy of Kóstas and Angéla Mavríkis.*

The coin of Icos shows the age-old connection of the inhabitants of our island with the sea. Geographically remote, Alónnisos has been dependent, from antiquity to the recent past, chiefly on seafaring and fishing. For the people of Icos, Poseidon, the Olympian god of the sea, would have represented the maintenance of secure mercantile communications, the vital link with the mainland that facilitated the influx of technical and cultural innovation. In recognition of this the inhabitants of the island used their coins to express their devotion to him. Apart from the representation of the god on the coin there would surely have been, somewhere on the island and close to the sea, a temple in his honour.

The art of sculpture was cultivated by local craftsmen and the statues from local workshops are of a high quality. In many of the graves that were opened at various times by the inhabitants of the island, statuettes were found that bear witness to the level of artistic achievement. Unfortunately, once again the ignorance of the inhabitants about their ancient heritage has not left us many examples of the sculptor's art. Such examples of sculptures as the local people found they either gave to their children as dolls to play with, in which case they were eventually broken, or sold to various shrewd visitors who exploited the innocence of the country people to make a good bargain.

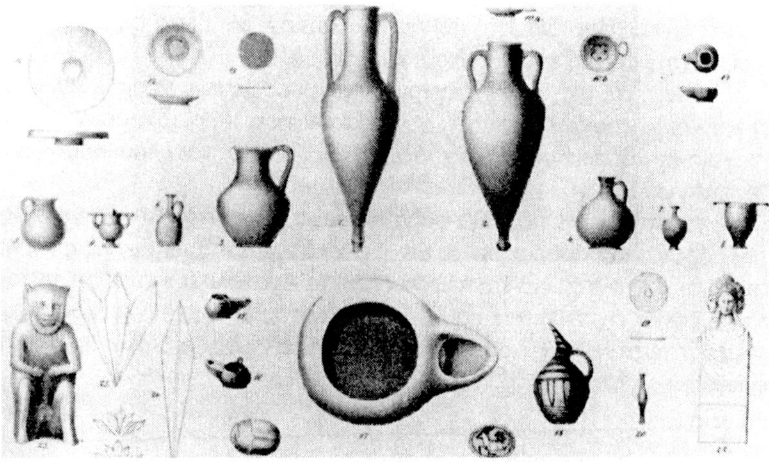

Figure 6.7 Grave goods from Kokkinókastro (from Fiedler, 1841).

According to the recollections of old people on the island, statues were found in the cemeteries near Palió Chorió, near the church of Profítis Ilías below the village, and at Kokkinókastro. Some of the statuettes were of metal, chiefly tin, but most were of local materials such as clay from the abundant red soil or the hard white stone (magnesite) which is found at many points on the island. Those of marble were carved from blocks brought from neighbouring Skántzoura. In referring to local materials we must remember the metallic deposits of Peristéra, where pre-war operations for the extraction of ore uncovered traces of ancient mines. The engineer in charge of these operations was impressed by the techniques of the ancient miners who had followed veins with great precision, whereas his own men were continually losing them. This knowledge must have been developed on Icos, where the population was descended from the ancient Chalcidians, who pioneered mining techniques.

Another characteristic of this period is the manner in which the dead were buried. Karl Fiedler, a 19th-century German investigator, excavated nine graves at Pitsoúria (the ridge above Kokkinókastro which also overlooks the bay of Chrisí Miliá). The excavation yielded surprising results. In all other ancient Greek tombs the grave goods were placed in the same chamber as the body. In Alónnisos they seem to have paid special attention to the comfort of the dead in spacious tombs, and constructed, in addition to the basic burial space, a second compartment, separated from the burial space by a stone partition, which functioned as a repository for goods.[5] Evidence to indicate the purpose of this unusual and distinctive burial practice has not come to light.

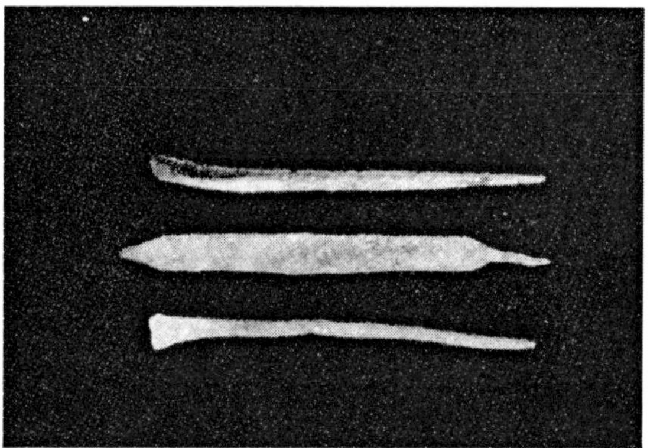

Figure 6.8 Medical instruments of the classical period from Alónnisos.
Courtesy of Kóstas and Angéla Mavríkis.

Classical cemeteries have been found in many other places on the island, and the very number of them suggests a large population, supported no doubt by the expansion of trade. With few exceptions, the graves were not particularly rich, though they have yielded many interesting artefacts. Scarabs and other examples of Egyptian art have been found in classical graves, providing evidence of trade with Egypt. Neither sarcophagi nor impressive funereal monuments are found on the island, owing to the shortage of suitable hard stone.

The vase painting of the period is delicate with its own specific motifs. It generally follows the Athenian style, depicting, on a black background, scenes of everyday life on Alónnisos.

There is no doubt that textile manufacture had developed throughout the island, in all the agricultural settlements as well as in the main towns at Kokkinókastro and on the site of the present Palió Chorió. We find loom weights scattered throughout the length and breadth of Alónnisos. The sheer quantity of these finds points to the development of a widespread textile industry, rather than mere domestic weaving. The raw materials would have come from local flocks, or could easily have been brought here by ship from other regions. But the second stage in production must have involved considerable development of specialised skills for the island's fabrics to be sought after. Near Ráches, a hill on the west side of the island about 4 km from Palió Chorió, large numbers of murex shells, from which the ancients extracted purple dye, have been found. Purple cloth was in great demand throughout the classical, Roman and Byzantine periods.

Figure 6.9 Loom weights. *Courtesy of Kóstas and Angéla Mavríkis.*

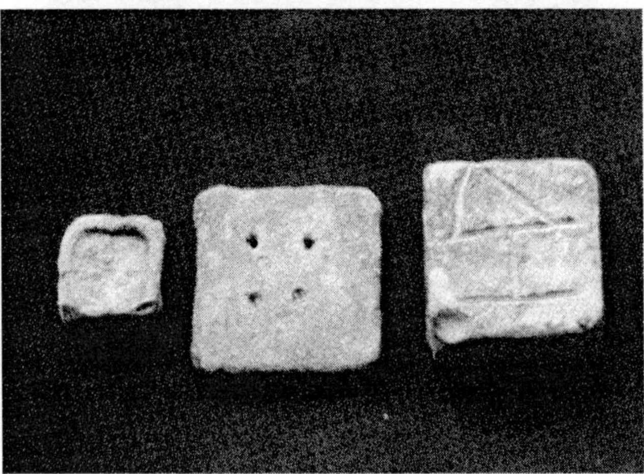

Figure 6.10 Weights for scales from Kokkinókastro.
Courtesy of Kóstas and Angéla Mavríkis.

Figure 6.11 Lead amphora seal of classical date from Kokkinókastro. *Courtesy of Kóstas and Angéla Mavríkis.*

Classical fortifications can be seen at various points on the island, and exhibit the characteristics of the period. In the fort at Kastráki (a small hill on the west side of the island above Megáli Ámmos) patches of classical work can be distinguished in the outer walls, as also in the forts at Kokkinókastro and Áyos Ioánnis. The repair, extension and improvement of these fortifications, which served the needs of the Delian League,[6] was made possible by the increased wealth of the island. On both Alónnisos and Kirá Panayá, in addition to the main fortresses there were smaller fortified lookout posts in prominent positions to control the unprotected shores. There are substantial classical walls at Koumarórachi in the northern part of the island overlooking the east coast, but these are of an agricultural nature, built by inhabitants of an agricultural settlement to separate their animals from their arable land so that they would not destroy the crops.

In the classical period ICOS had a democratic system of government, as is evident from the fact that it joined the Delian League in 476 BC. It appears that ICOS had an important place in this alliance, since it paid a tribute of 1,500 drachmas to ATHENS, while SCIATHOS paid only 1,000. All the members of the League were city states with democratic constitutions and well-developed mercantile and manufacturing sectors. The oligarchic states, on the other hand, had allied themselves (before the 6th century BC) with SPARTA, the second most powerful city state in the Greek world. In exchange for retaining their independence, these states supplied and supported SPARTA in her foreign affairs, including her wars.

It is much to be regretted that the work by Phanodemus known in Greek as *Ikiaka* ('Ician Affairs') has been lost. Phanodemus, writing possibly as early as the 4th century BC (and certainly no later than the mid 1st century), described in this book the history and constitution of ICOS. If we had this valuable evidence about our island today, many more pieces of the historical jigsaw puzzle could be fitted into place. We know of the existence of this historical work from the *Ethnicorum*, a geographical dictionary by Stephanus Byzantius (5th or 6th century AD), but sadly it cannot help us to further our researches.

The basic administrative bodies would have been at Kokkinókastro, the economic centre of the island, and the constitution of ICOS would have mimicked that of democratic ATHENS. The groups who exercised power in ICOS would have included craftsmen, merchants, sailors, fishermen and those who owned land and property. The institution of slavery would have chiefly benefited the richer merchants and landowners.

For the effective working of democracy, education was necessary and, above all, rhetorical skills. This presupposes the existence of teachers. The sophists were the new breed of philosophers who taught rhetoric and the exact sciences for a handsome fee. There is an archaeological find, the ring of an Ician sophist, evidence of the philosophical advancement of the island which would have followed as a natural consequence upon its economic success. The high standard of living is clearly evident, and the people of this period sought intellectual and cultural outlets. The philosophical movement was born at the right time to fulfil this need.

Figure 6.12 Finger ring of an Ician sophist.
Courtesy of Kóstas and Angéla Mavríkis.

Theatre developed on our island. as well as both the exact and the theoretical sciences. Unfortunately, though, no examples of writing from this local flowering of classical Hellenism have survived to our day; nor have any related monuments (ancient theatres or temples) been found here. It is natural that such writings of Icians as may have survived for a time would have aroused little interest in later periods, since the unrivalled culture of the classical period produced a plethora of more important works. And monuments are few, since most have suffered the ravages of time. Many were demolished by later inhabitants who used the stone in the construction of new buildings and terraces. The ancient wall at Palió Chorió is a case in point. The locals reduced it to its foundations to provide building material for their houses.

Throughout the classical period, the development of the island kept pace with the economic and cultural rise of ATHENS. In 476/5 BC, ICOS joined the Delian League, which had evolved after the defeat of the Persians in 477 BC through alliances between ATHENS and the Greek city states of Asia Minor and the Aegean islands, among them ICOS, drawn in part, no doubt, by the Athenian general Cimon's campaign to rid the Aegean of the pirates, whose activities caused such hardships to the inhabitants of those islands.

The sense of security that the protection of ATHENS offered would have been the decisive factor. From then on there were continual contacts between ICOS and ATHENS, and many Icians went to live in ATHENS and PIRAEUS. A grave stele was discovered in Pireaus (it is now in the National Archaeological Museum in Athens, see below, Figure 6.17 caption, p. 140) which bears the inscription 'Collon, son of Leucados, an Ician' (see Figure 6.17, p. 140). This Collon had evidently lived in PIRAEUS and was probably a merchant. This is perhaps the only extant inscription referring to Alónnisos and from it we learn the names of two of our remote ancestors. It has been published several times, beginning in the early 19th century.[7]

We have no information about the appointment of Athenian citizens to oversee their Ician allies. The authority that the Athenian garrisons exercised in nearby SCYROS would surely have extended to our remote island. Strabo tells us that SCIATHOS, PEPARETHOS, ICOS, HALONNESOS and SCYROS all had cities with the same name.[8] These cities would have adopted the lifestyle of their powerful ally, electing their officials democratically and having their own gods and festivals.

The Athenian drachma entered into the economy of the island. The silver drachma might be called the dollar of classical times, and advantageous exchanges could be made with it. In several places on the island large numbers of such coins have been found, providing evidence of intense economic activity. A farmer near Áyos Ioánnis, turning the soil prior to sowing, found forty silver drachmas, but being unaware of their value he gave them away. Often in the past when graves were discovered and opened – whether by chance, as when a mule slipped on the covering slab, or in the course of field clearance, or in search of corner stones for house building – silver coins depicting an owl (the symbol of Athena) were found. It was the custom of the ancients to place a coin in the mouth of the deceased so that he could pay Charon, the ferryman, to row them across the river Styx to Hades.

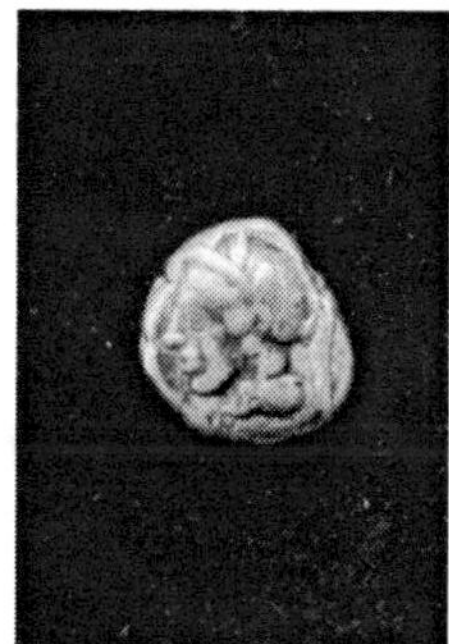

Figure 6.13 Athenian drachma found on Alónnisos.
Courtesy of Kóstas and Angéla Mavríkis.

6.2 Classical Remains on Alónnisos and the Other Islands

Remains from the classical period are scattered throughout all of the islands. At Koumarórachi on Alónnisos there was a settlement whose population evidently engaged in intense productive activity. The ground there is covered with pottery sherds and a counterweight from a press used for the production of wine or oil has been found. Near the church of the Dormition of the Virgin on the slopes of Vounó and at the oil press (both near Palió Chorió) there are sherds of the classical period and other signs of occupation. At Mourteró and Áyos Dhimítrios there are similar indications, but they have been obscured by later habitation.

Figure 6.14 Marble architectural members from Alónnisos. Both are from the classical period.

Figure 6.15 Counterweight from an oil or wine press. Áyos Pétros, Kirá Panayá. In the centre is carved a man's face.

Throughout the island we find traces of classical farmsteads, which would have been inhabited by autonomous family groups who exploited their land for crop growing and animal rearing. They might build anything from two to ten houses and auxiliary buildings (stores and stables), often with some rudimentary fortification, as protection from pirates or other enemies.

Sherds of every type of pottery of this period are found in various places on the other islands. Next in order after Alónnisos comes Kirá Panayá, which is rich in classical remains. Kirá Panayá was a fertile island with two large plateaus and two incomparable harbours, which were a potent force in attracting population. The fortress at Tzavétis was rebuilt at this time and the dressed stone blocks show a high standard of workmanship. The main fortress at Paliókastro overlooked the ancient town in the bay of Planítis. The inhabitants of the town would have been involved in farming, fishing and stockbreeding, and would have sold their products to the merchant ships that stopped there, or exchanged them for other goods.

The Athenians considered the strategic position of Kirá Panayá to be of great importance and maintained friendly relations, economic and cultural, with the island. We have no definite information on the number of inhabitants, but we estimate that about 500 people lived there. There is an ancient cemetery near the path to the monastery. The graves have been robbed and must have been opened a long time ago. In the interior of the island their are buildings of dry-stone construction, whose habitation began in the Neolithic Period and continued through the classical period and even extended into modern times. The island has still to be investigated as far as the classical remains are concerned, and it no doubt holds many secrets.

On Yoúra there is the cave of the Cyclops which the few ancient inhabitants of the island considered a sacred place. On Skántzoura, at Pirgákia, there are buildings that were used as dwellings or as strongholds, standing on a peak above the plateau of the island. In recent years they have been restored. On Psathoúra, after the catastrophe that submerged the ancient city, those things that gave the island its particular identity were lost. In this out of the way place, though, there would surely have been a fishing settlement. There is a surprising quantity of classical sherds on Grámeza. This small islet, with its fertile plain, held a well-protected settlement of considerable size. On the islets of Lechoúsa and Megálo Polemikó close to the sea, fragments of fine black-painted pottery have been found, probably from the graves of sailors.

6.3 The Conflict between ATHENS and SPARTA

After the initial advances in the early classical period, the destructive demon of the Greek race came into play. It is recognised that when the Greeks are united they are capable of the most extraordinary economic, cultural and military achievements, which seem to overstep the bounds of the possible. Again and again, though, they no sooner reach the peak of success than internal divisions appear and fratricidal wars break out. Cultural and economic regression follows and the mutual slaughter leaves deep wounds which are slow to heal. The city states were separated into two camps, one led by democratic ATHENS, the other under the leadership of oligarchic SPARTA.

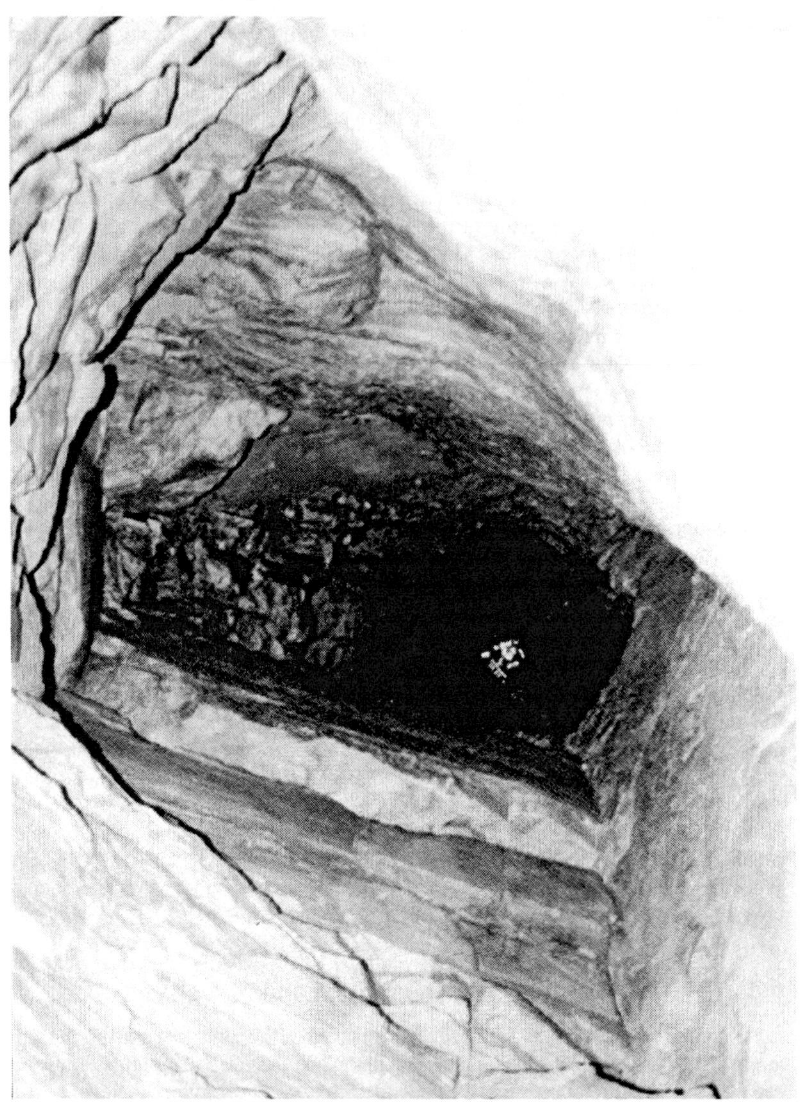

Figure 6.16 A well, cut through marble, on Skántzoura.

A disastrous civil war broke out in 431 BC and everything was laid waste. All resources were diverted into war for a period of twenty-seven years. ICOS and HALONNESOS provided forces for the war. In the end the alliance was defeated, ATHENS was humiliated and her allies subjugated to SPARTA. The Spartans came to our islands, abolished the democratic system and established an oligarchy. They imposed heavy taxes and oppressive laws and made life difficult for the inhabitants.

Fortunately the tyranny came to an end after the naval battle of CNIDUS (394 BC), in which the Athenian general Conon decisively defeated the Spartan fleet which for ten years had dominated the Aegean and controlled our islands. From 394 to 387 BC our islands enjoyed a spell of freedom and life began to run smoothly again. The two great powers, exhausted by the destructive conflict, were more concerned with survival than expansion. The civil war had led the Greeks into dreadful acts of cruelty and oppression. Worst of all, though, was that both sides made alliances with their common enemy, the Persians.

First the Athenians under Conon and then the Spartans under Antalcidas approached the Persians. Antalcidas concluded a shameful treaty, by which the Greek cities of Asia Minor and Cyprus were assigned to the Persians, in exchange for their support of the Spartan cause. The same agreement also guaranteed the autonomy of all other Greek city states, including the islands of the Northern Sporades. According to the terms dictated by the Persian king, Artaxerxes II,

> the other Greek cities, both small and great, should be left independent except for LEMNOS, IMBROS and SCYROS; and these should belong, as of old, to the Athenians.[9]

This guarantee, though, was little more than a formality, since in practice the Spartans, aided by the Persians, and on the pretext of maintaining order, came to the northern Aegean, and established oligarchic regimes in ICOS and HALONNESOS and other islands of the archipelago. Democratic principles had, however, been well established, and those who supported them, in alliance with Athenians living there, exploited popular resistance to the oppressive policies of the Spartans, and in 378 BC led the islands into the Second Athenian League. The citizens of ICOS and HALONNESOS, recalling their experience in the First Athenian (the Delian) League, demanded, in concert with other city states, a greater degree of autonomy and a more flexible organisation. This time there would be no reason for Athens to exact tribute and the autonomous states would avoid the former disasters.

The Athenians, however, did not honour their undertakings for long. In 358 BC they turned against their allies, demanding large amounts of tribute and appointing Athenian officials to govern them. Naturally, the allied cities reacted forcefully, and a war ensued which lasted for two years (357–355 BC). The Northern Sporades certainly did not side with ATHENS, but it is not certain that they joined in the revolt that checked the expansion of Athenian power. Another powerful state now appeared on the horizon.

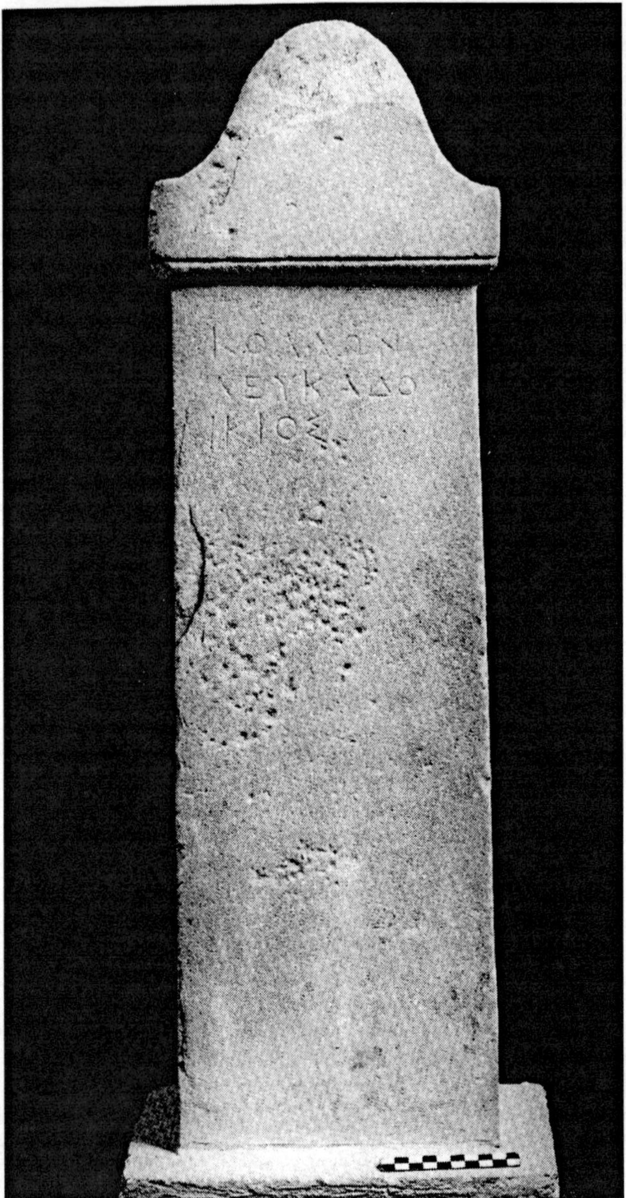

Figure 6.17 Names of ancient Alonnisiot citizens – grave stele of the Ician, Collon, son of Leucados, who lived in PIRAEUS (the port of Athens).

6.4 The Macedonian Conquest

Philip II, king of Macedon from 359 BC, found fertile soil in the conflicts of his time. The conjunction of the good work of his predecessors and Philip's exceptional personality brought the Macedonian state out of obscurity and transformed it into a dominant power. ICOS, HALONNESOS and the other Northern Sporades now became bases for the Athenian fleet in its confrontations with the Macedonians. The islands had fine harbours and abundant supplies and were generally well disposed towards the Athenians. As Demosthenes told the Athenians in about 350 BC, 'You have the advantage of winter bases for your troops in LEMNOS, THASOS, SCIATHOS, and the neighbouring islands, where there are to be found harbours, provisions, and everything that an army needs.'[10]

Philip of Macedon in his attempt to gain access to the Aegean seized AMPHIPOLIS and the coastal cities of PYDNA and POTIDAEA. ATHENS was unable to respond aggressively. Weakened by the wars she maintained a defensive policy and sent a part of her fleet to the Northern Sporades in order to check Philip's expansionist aims.

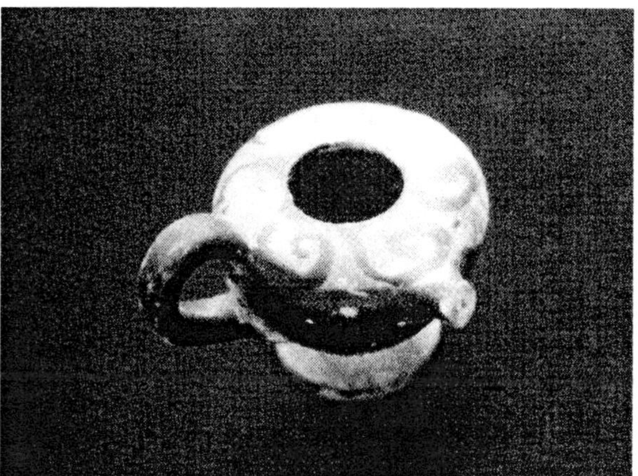

Figure 6.18 Oil lamp from a tomb at Kalóvolos.
Courtesy of Kóstas and Angéla Mavríkis.

Having dealt with the threat from his barbarian neighbours to the north, the Macedonian king had set his sights on the whole of the Greek lands. Step by step he added to his empire the PANGAEUS region and various territories in MAGNESIA and other parts of Greece. This visionary leader realised the importance of naval power and set about building his fleet. In order to advance swiftly into southern Greece he set up naval bases and in 354 BC he captured PAGASAE, the strategic harbour of the important city of PHERAE (which itself fell to Philip in 352). In 353 he made a surprise attack on the islands of the northern Aegean, which the Athenians had always considered to be their property. Philip's aggressive policy roused strong anti-Macedonian feeling in ATHENS, and the orator Demosthenes became Philip's most fanatical opponent.

The situation reached crisis point when, in 343 BC, a large Macedonians force invaded the island of Kirá Panayá, ancient HALONNESOS. They landed an army on the island, captured and killed or drove out the pirates who, seizing the opportunity offered by recent instability in the region, had taken over the island. Although the pirates had come as conquerors, they depended on the local population for their food supplies and other services, and were in close co-operation with them. They were well protected in the castle at Planítis, from where they could make surprise attacks on the boats they selected as their victims.

Three years previously the two rival powers had concluded a peace, which was specially favourable to the Macedonians, who had just captured OLYNTHUS. Influenced by this agreement, and as a gesture of good will, Philip offered to make a gift of HALONNESOS to the Athenians. The Athenians were outraged since they considered the island to be theirs. Consequently, Philip could not offer it to them as a gift, but must return it to them. Their reasoning may seem strange, but the Athenians wanted to preserve their prestige and pride, which they thought that their northern rival had impugned. Philip disagreed, with some justification, since he had taken the island from pirates, not from the Athenians. It therefore belonged to him, was part of his empire, and as such he could make a gift of it. For the Athenians there was an important legal distinction between 'giving' and 'giving back'. The intractable situation developed in the course of a year into a serious legal wrangle, and in 342 BC Demosthenes delivered his speech *On HALONNESOS*:

> Men of ATHENS, [...] Philip begins by saying that he offers you HALONNESOS as his own property, but that you have no right to demand it of him, because it was not yours when he took it, and is not yours now that he holds it. Moreover, when we ambassadors visited him, he used similar language, to the effect that he had captured the island from pirates and that therefore it belonged absolutely to him. It is not difficult to refute this claim on the ground of its unfairness. For all pirates seize places belonging to others and turn them into strongholds from which to harry their neighbours. But a man who should defeat and punish pirates would surely be unreasonable, if he said that the stolen property wrongfully held by them passed into his own possession. For, that plea once granted, if some pirates seize a strip of Attic territory, or a part of LEMNOS or IMBROS or SCYROS, and if someone dislodges these pirates, what is to prevent this place, where the pirates are established and which is really ours, from becoming the property of those who chastised them? Philip is quite aware that his claim is unjust, but, though he knows this as well as anyone, he thinks that you may be hoodwinked by the men who have engaged, and are now fulfilling their engagement, to direct Athenian policy in accordance with his own desires. Nor again does he fail to see that in either case, however you dub the transaction, the island will be yours, whether it is presented or restored to you. Then what does he gain by using the wrong term and making a present of it to you, instead of using the right term and restoring it? It is not that he wants to debit you with a benefaction received, for such a benefaction would be a farce; but that he wants all Greece to take notice that the

Athenians are content to receive maritime strongholds from the man of Macedon. And that is just what you, men of ATHENS, must not do.[11]

There is a view, which has had its supporters from antiquity to the present, that this is not a speech of Demosthenes. Those who hold this view allow that Demosthenes returned to this theme many times, indeed, more often than anyone else, and that his chief aim was to persuade the Athenian ***ekklēsia*** (citizens' assembly) not to accept the island as a gift but as something returned to them as of right. Unfortunately, however, they assert, it is not Demosthenes' words that have been preserved here, and the speech *On HALONNESOS* has been wrongly attributed to him, since it was actually delivered by Hegesippus. This view was supported by Libanius (AD 350), the great sophist from Antioch. On the other side, maintaining the genuineness of the Speech of Demosthenes, are ranged the elegiac poet and founder of the famous library of ALEXANDRIA, Callimachus, and Dionysius of HALICARNASSUS. They maintain that the speech clearly demonstrates the legal expertise of its author, Demosthenes, who had made a very extensive study of the law. However, the consensus now is that the speech was attributed to Demosthenes in error, and that it is in fact a speech of Hegesippus. In the ***ekklēsia*** many people addressed this burning issue, not only the anti-Macedonian orators, Demosthenes and Hegesippus, but also the pro-Macedonians, Aeschines and Demades. The interest of so many eminent men of the period in the island of HALONNESOS indicates the importance of our islands for the Athenians as much as for the Macedonians.

Let us review, in order, the events that led to the delivery of this speech, and let us see why the greatest orator of all time employed his rhetorical skills with such passion to reject the arguments of Philip II. The events that affected the island and so closely concerned the two rival powers were as follows. Having entered the Delian League, HALONNESOS remained faithful to the Athenian cause for over a century. In 355 BC the pirate Sostratus, from PEPARETHOS, attacked and seized the island and for twelve years used it as the base for his piracy. Though he enslaved the inhabitants of the island, he did not treat them too harshly, for fear they would complain to their former allies, the Athenians, about the repression. It appears that he adopted a policy of demanding 'harbour tax' from passing vessels, rather than simply destroying them.

In 343 BC the Macedonians drove out Sostratus and his pirates, took possession of the island and established a garrison there. In the same year Python Byzantius, a famous orator, was appointed ambassador for the Macedonians and sent to ATHENS, with a letter from Philip to assure the Athenians that their northern neighbours had no hostile intentions. The Athenians were somewhat wary and sent an embassy to Philip under the leadership of Hegesippus, in order to settle the terms of a treaty to their best advantage. Philip, however, decisively rejected the Athenian proposals, which were mainly concerned with AMPHIPOLIS. In the following year (342 BC) Philip again sent ambassadors to ATHENS, bearing another letter in which he tried to find a solution to the impasse of the previous year. There was, however, an undeclared military reason for these diplomatic efforts: the clever Macedonian general wanted to attack Thrace while diverting the Athenians' attention and delaying their response by diplomatic means. The speech *On HALONNESOS* was part of the debate in the ***ekklēsia*** which followed the receipt of Philip's letter.

After his expulsion from HALONNESOS, Sostratus returned to his birthplace, PEPARETHOS, with which he had maintained close friendly and commercial contacts. He persuaded his fellow islanders to take up plundering, and in 341 the Peparethians made a surprise attack, captured HALONNESOS and imprisoned the large Macedonian garrison. From Demosthenes' (or Hegesippus') statement that 'the Peparethians took the island', it appears that the Athenians had no connection with the expedition. Indeed, the attack was almost certainly instigated by the pirate Sostratus.

When Philip was informed of the hostile action of the Peparethians, he was furious and sent ambassadors to PEPARETHOS demanding the return of the Macedonian garrison and the island. The Peparethians refused and Philip, father of the most glorious victor in history, ordered Alcimon, admiral of his powerful fleet, to burn the whole of PEPARETHOS and to show no compassion. Alcimon sailed to PEPARETHOS, conquered it and punished the inhabitants as an example to others, pillaging the island from end to end. The Peparethians, surprised by the force of the attack, complained to ATHENS and their other allies that they had abandoned them. At this point Sostratus' career must have come to and end. If the Macedonians did not kill him in their vicious assault on PEPARETHOS, either the Peparethians or the Athenians would have punished him as the instigator of the disaster.

Figure 6.19 Ancient inscribed lead slingshots found on Alónnisos.
Courtesy of Kóstas and Angéla Mavríkis.

The Athenian leaders ordered that Demosthenes be tried on a charge of complicity, asserting that he had persuaded the Peparethians to undertake such an ill-advised attack on HALONNESOS in a time of peace with Macedonia. Half-heartedly the Athenians ordered their general, Ctesiphon, to undertake reprisals against Macedonian coastal cities, but fortunately no serious incidents ensued.

A letter of Philip to the Athenians written in AD 340 sums up the events of the previous years and gives us some indication of the spirit of the times:

> Philip to the Council and People of ATHENS, greeting.
>
> To the embassies that I have repeatedly dispatched to ensure the observance of our oaths and agreements you have paid no attention, so that I am forced to send you a statement of the matters in which I consider myself wronged. But you must not be surprised at the length of the letter, for I have many charges to prefer, and it is necessary to put them all clearly and frankly.

There follow several paragraphs on general themes, before we come to those that interest us most:

> The following affront should also not be passed over. Though formerly you confined yourselves to the charges I have mentioned, your arrogance is now such that, when the people of PEPARETHOS complained of the latest 'outrage,' you instructed your general to demand redress from me on their behalf. I actually punished them less rigorously than they deserved, for they seized HALONNESOS in time of peace and refused to restore either the fortress or the garrison in spite of my repeated remonstrances. But you, with full knowledge of the facts, ignored their offences against me, and only considered their punishment. Yet I robbed neither them nor you of the island, but only the pirate chief, Sostratus.
>
> Now, if you say that you handed it over to Sostratus, you admit that you employ pirates; if he captured it against your wishes, why this indignation against me for taking it and making the district safe for traders? In my regard for the interests of your city, I offered you the island, but your statesmen urged you to refuse it as a gift and demand it as an act of restitution, in order that, if I submit to their dictation, I may thereby confess that I have no right to the place, but if I do give it up, I may arouse the suspicions of your democracy.
>
> Conscious of this, I challenged you to submit your claims to arbitration, so that if the island was adjudged to be mine, I might give it to you; if yours, then I might restore it to your people. I repeatedly demanded a trial, but you paid me no attention, and the Peparethians occupied the island. What, then, was I to do? Was I not to punish those who had violated their oaths? Was I not to take vengeance for such a wanton outrage? For if the island belonged to the Peparethians, what right had the Athenians to demand it back? If it was yours, why are you not angry with the Peparethians for seizing the territory of others?[12]

Relations between Macedon and ATHENS continued to deteriorate, culminating in the battle of CHAERONIA in 338 BC, in which Alexander the Great, renowned for his military abilities, fought side by side with his father. The Athenians and their Theban allies were decisively defeated and submitted to the Macedonians, and all the islands of the Northern Sporades passed into Macedonian control. This battle is considered as a turning point, since it paved the way for Alexander's conquest of the world. At a pan-Hellenic conference in CORINTH, in 337 BC, in the aftermath of the battle of CHAERONIA, Philip II was proclaimed leader of the Greeks against the Barbarians. United under the leadership of the Macedonians, the Greeks now had the opportunity to punish the Persians and to unite the two major empires of the time. With the blessing of all the Greek cities Philip set about preparing for a campaign against Asia. But Philip was assassinated in the theatre at AEGAE in 336 BC, and the leadership was assumed by his charismatic son, Alexander, then aged twenty.

Endowed with exceptional political and military skills, Alexander confirmed his authority throughout Greece and embarked on the great campaign that took him as far as India. No one could stop or even check his forceful progress. The great victor, wanting to secure his rear, had established pro-Macedonian oligarchic regimes in the Greek city states, with Macedonian overseers and emissaries. From then until they regained their strategic importance some years after Alexander's death, our group of islands were a mere dot in the vast empire founded by the greatest general in the history of the human race.

6.5 The Hellenistic Period

After Alexander's untimely death in 323 BC, his empire was divided among his Macedonian generals. Egypt was ruled by Ptolemy, and Syria (roughly the area of modern Israel, Palestine, Syria, Iraq, Iran and Afghanistan) was ruled by Seleucus, while Macedonia and most of Greece, including our islands, came under the command of Antipater. Conflicts continued between these generals and their descendants in the Hellenistic kingdoms they founded, and our islands passed into the jurisdiction of the Ptolemaic kings of Egypt, who used them as forward bases for trading with the Macedonian heartland.

In general terms the Hellenistic period was a time of prosperity for ICOS and the surrounding islands. Although the conflicts between Alexander's successors continued, the winds of progress began to blow through the whole Greek world. The two great civilisations of the Greek west and the Persian east saw a period of prosperity and learning during which a great university was founded at ALEXANDRIA in Egypt, and the combination of the knowledge of Western Asia and India with that of the Greeks led to great achievements in science, philosophy and art.

The stability of this period enabled our island to resume the systematic cultivation of vines and to export its excellent wine to many new, rich markets. Trade was on the increase and once more reached the high levels of the Archaic and early classical periods. The workshops at Tsoukaliás stepped up production of amphorae, which had fallen off during the previous century. Wine was sent out to all the Greek maritime cities, and the ships returned laden with their goods.

At Kokkinókastro, and later at Palió Chorió, and in the area around these centres, the local population devoted themselves to a variety of specialist occupations. Wine production was only one of many productive crafts. Techniques of metalwork were perfected, and fine and delicate works of art were created.

The Hellenistic influence on local art is clearly evident. The makers of statuettes employed the new distinctive forms and created fine miniature sculptures from hard limestone, which is found in abundance on the island. Hellenistic tombs have been found in several places, including Kokkinókastro, and from the grave goods it appears that the inhabitants had a particular preference for Egyptian art work (scarabs, glass beads etc.). Trade was carried on using golden coins from all the kingdoms, but the copper 'ptolemies' found in many locations on the island were the most common. Much gold from this period has been found, but unfortunately details are not available.

The fortresses at Kokkinókastro and Palió Chorió, and the smaller outposts and Áyos Ioánnis and Kastráki continued to be used as defences against pirates and usurpers. There the Macedonians installed their representatives and governed in co-operation with the local pro-Macedonian faction. The Macedonians also controlled trade, but allowed some autonomy to those whom they favoured. In the countryside the farmsteads flourished as did the craft industries of weaving, metalworking, pottery and sculpture. The settlement at Kokkinókastro must have been the most important and the one most involved in commerce. The citadel at Palió Chorió controlled wine production and the other industries of the hinterland.

Figure 6.20 Limestone head from a statuette of Aphrodite, found where the Hotel Mediteraneo now stands. *Courtesy of Kóstas and Angéla Mavríkis.*

A new spirit of ambition in every sphere, originating in the vast new and rich kingdoms of Egypt and Syria, swept through Greece. The Hellenistic kings, descendants of Alexander's generals, inspired by Alexander, who was now regarded as a demigod, encouraged science and letters. As an island devoted to trade, ICOS had wide-ranging contacts and was exposed to all the new influences. The people of the island assimilated and developed new knowledge and skills.

The burning of the library at ALEXANDRIA may be considered the greatest disaster in the history of culture. It was the library of the Ptolemies who had ruled our island at one time. Among the books lost forever there would surely have been geographical and other texts referring to the Northern Sporades.

HALONNESOS (Kirá Panayá), which had formerly been the most important base in the northern Aegean, fell into disuse during Alexander's campaigns. Later, though, when his successors were struggling for power, it began once more to play an important role. Antiochus III of Syria, Attalus I of PERGAMUM (in Asia Minor) and Philip V of Macedon, in the course of the conflicts between them, all used the island as an anchorage, a refuge and a supply base. The inhabitants of HALONNESOS must have remained neutral during the invasions from the east. They would not, in any case, have been too well disposed towards the Macedonians, whose subjects they were, and would have tended to favour their opponents.

There is a view that the fortress on Kirá Panayá was destroyed by Philip V in desperation, to deprive his distant enemies of a forward base from which to attack his kingdom, his tactic being 'if you can't use it, destroy it'. After that Kirá Panayá disappears from the historical map until the Byzantine period. Without a fortress the island could no longer be protected from the successive waves of pirates who traversed the Aegean and it was abandoned.

In Hellenistic times there was a small settlement on Pipéri, in the natural amphitheatre that the locals call *Dhaskálou ta magazákia* ('the Teacher's cottages'). After the Second World War some fishermen from Alónnisos used to go to this spot to look for saddled bream. Feeding shoals of these fish can be spotted easily because of their luminescence. Watching from above the locals can estimate their numbers and then bombard them with dynamite. The fishermen had to cross a narrow and precipitous neck of land in order to reach a rocky platform, from which they could observe the fish. There among the remains of buildings several of the fishermen picked up Hellenistic coins. This settlement, which could only be approached from one direction, would have been easy to defend and would, at the same time, have served as an important vantage point from which to observe the movement of ships in the northern Aegean. The fertile plain occupying much of the rest of the island would have sustained a moderate population. In the other islands too there would surely have been small numbers of inhabitants involved in agricultural work.

Suddenly the region was threatened by Attalus I, king of PERGAMUM, who reigned from 241 to 197 BC. Having gained victories against the Seleucid kings of Syria, Attalus came to Greece in 211 and made an alliance with the Romans and Aetolians (from central Greece) in their war against Philip V of Macedon. Attalus joined forces with the Roman general Sulpicius, and in 207 attacked and laid waste PEPARETHOS, intending to use it as a base from which to launch attacks against Philip V of Macedon. Attalus and Sulpicius would certainly not have missed the opportunity of looting the islands around Skópelos, and particularly Alónnisos, since these were part of the Macedonian Empire.

In response, Philip sent a fleet to our islands which anchored in the channel between Alónnisos and Peristéra and from there launched attacks against the islands, and in particular PEPARETHOS (Skópelos), which he easily recaptured and garrisoned. Attalus withdrew his forces and returned to Asia Minor. Some years later, in 200 BC, not having the means to rule the islands, Philip preferred to lay them waste, destroying their cities, so that they could not be used as military bases or as supply stations by his enemies.[13]

Though the Northern Sporades were within the Macedonian domain for most of the Hellenistic period, they maintained a degree of autonomy. The inhabitants were opposed to the oligarchic system of the Macedonians and demonstrated their anti-Macedonian feelings. They were never the allies of the Macedonians but their vassals, and would probably have preferred conquerors from the east, such as Attalus, to their Macedonian oppressors. The Ptolemaic kings of Egypt, who also claimed the islands, were too far away to respond to the Macedonian occupation. It must have been in this period that the partial destruction of the city walls at Kokkinókastro took place and the decline of the area set in as people left.

6.6 The Roman Period

Once they had conquered all their immediate neighbours, the Romans turned their attention to the lands of the Greeks. The intervention of the Romans in Greek affairs initiated a major change. Once established, their rule brought peace and stability. We have already noted the Roman involvement in local wars against Macedon. In 199 BC a Roman fleet arrived in our islands, and the Romans proclaimed them free once more. In 196 BC the local people began to rebuild their fortifications, recently demolished by the Macedonians. Antiochus III of Syria, flouting the power of the Romans, who had recently defeated him, set out from his kingdom in 192 BC and, using our islands as a bridge, attacked the rich lands of Thessaly.

In the following year, defeated once more, Antiochus plundered the islands and returned to Syria. This was the last assault on our islands by any of the inheritors of Alexander's empire, and proved to be only a brief interlude in the Roman advance. From then on the Roman conquerors remained in our islands. After several recent devastations, ICOS and HALONNESOS no longer had the capacity to act as independent city states. Nevertheless, life as part of a Roman province was relatively easy, apart from the heavy taxes and the presence of pirates.

The prestige of the Romans was reinforced when, in the course of the Macedonian Wars, they defeated Philip V, in 197 BC, and his son, Perseus, in 168. Finally, in 145, the Romans under Mummius were victorious at CORINTH and took control of the whole of Greece.

In 88 BC Mithridates VI, king of Pontus, entered into a ferocious conflict with the Romans. Most of the northern Aegean islands were captured by his admirals Archelaus and Metrophanes. The latter conquered the Northern Sporades and used them as a base for piratical raids on the mainland shores, which were under Roman rule. For six years Metrophanes bled our islands dry with continual looting, transferring the spoils to storehouses on SCIATHOS. He was finally defeated in 82 BC by the Romans under the leadership of Sulla. The Pontic admiral was forced to abandon the islands, and returned to his homeland on the Black Sea with the remnants of his fleet.

Roman resources in the region were still not adequate to maintain the freedom of the seas, and Cilician pirates now began to take over the Aegean islands. From their base in Cilicia, in southern Asia Minor, they launched attacks in all directions, and with a fleet of about a thousand ships ravaged the entire Aegean. Many of them were active in the Northern Sporades because of the large quantity of shipping passing through the region.

Our unfortunate ancestors suffered terrible misfortunes under the scourge of the Cilician pirates, who treated them as their subjects and used the islands as bases from which to attack the rich regions nearby (Évvia, Thessaly, Chalkidhikí). The audacity of the pirates infuriated Rome; and Pompey, equipped with a large fleet, undertook, in 78 BC, to clear the seas. However, the pirates' operations were so broadly based that it took eleven years of battles on sea and land for the Romans to drive the Cilicians out of the Aegean.

Finally in 67 BC, at the conclusion of this famous pirate war, our islands were relieved of the deadly pirates, and life resumed its normal rhythm. The Romans, however, dazzled by the mass of material goods they had so easily acquired, began to quarrel over the spoils. The ensuing Roman civil wars lasted from 49 to 31 BC, and our ill-fated ancestors were to take the side of one or other party and then to bear the consequences

The second civil war (42 BC) was a conflict between Antony and Octavian. Antony had grown up in ATHENS, where he had received a Greek education. Consequently he was well disposed towards the city, and in the course of the war presented some of the Northern Sporades to ATHENS. According to Appian,

> to the Athenians when they came to ask him for TENOS he gave AEGINA and ICOS, CEOS, SCIATHOS and PEPARETHOS.[14]

By now, though, ATHENS had lost all its old lustre and was unable to breathe any new life into the islands. Instead she treated them as possessions and exacted heavy taxes. The unbearable tax burden which Rome and then ATHENS imposed, and which local governors arbitrarily increased for their own enrichment, reduced our island to a wretched state.

Much later, during the reign of the Emperor Hadrian (AD 117–38) the Peparethians captured the island. Philostratus mentions the man who controlled the island and alludes to the manner in which he exploited it:

> Furthermore, Hymnaeus of PEPARETHOS, who is on friendly terms with me, sent one of his sons here some four years ago to consult Protesilaus through me about a similar marvel. When Hymnaeus happened to dig up vines on the island of ICOS (he alone owned the island), the earth sounded somewhat hollow to those who were digging. When they opened it up, they found a twelve-cubit [over 4 m] corpse lying there with a serpent inhabiting its skull.[15]

We glimpse in this excerpt the decline of ICOS. The rich landowner from PEPARETHOS had seized and was exploiting the island, no doubt with the blessing of the Romans. He must have been well disposed towards them and been allowed to undertake the exploitation in return for certain payments, first to the local treasury and then to Rome. He systematised production and introduced new cultivation methods which have been maintained to the present day. Once it had become the private property of a landowner, ICOS entered on a long period of obscurity.

The city at Kokkinókastro was finally abandoned and its remaining inhabitants, who were mainly poor workmen, retreated to the citadel at Palió Chorió, where they stoically confronted their decline. Pirate attacks, which once more became more frequent, contributed to making the Aegean islands a backwater.

Hymnaeus the Peparethian, who visited the island from time to time, kept a luxurious court – which secret and unauthorised excavations have brought to light – on the small hill below Palió Chorió where the church of Áyos Taxiárchis now stands. Many coins of the Roman period were found there, which shows that trade was still carried on in this region. Unfortunately the remains have been covered up by house building, and for further information a new excavation will have to be undertaken.

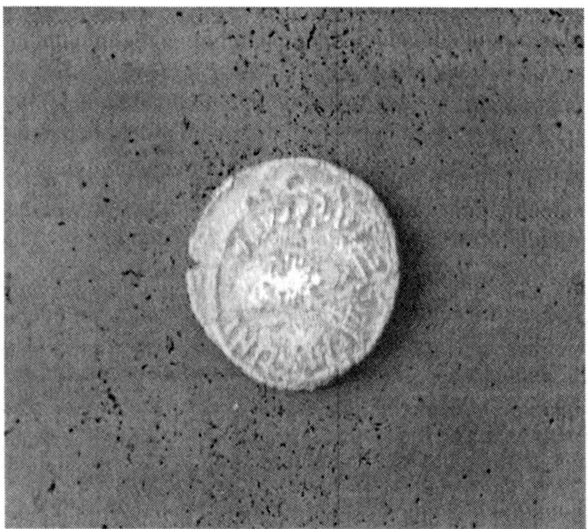

Figure 6.21 Roman coin found on Alónnisos. *Courtesy of Kóstas and Angéla Mavríkis.*

There are traces of a poor Roman farmstead at Koumarórachi and in the small well-watered valley nearby. Fear of pirates drove the population away from the shores and they sought out natural hollows and areas hidden among the hills. In the Roman period the fame of Peparethian wine spread. This wine was probably Ician wine, mixed with other wines to enhance the taste. In the same way, in the 20th century, merchants on Páros in the Cyclades took wine from Alónnisos, added their own for the aroma and exported it to France as top-quality Parian wine.

The definitive decline in the later Roman period left its marks everywhere. Throughout the island there are few remains of buildings from this period, indicative of low level of activity in these years. Alónnisos lost the elements of higher culture and became a purely agricultural island.

The Romans used Yoúra as a place of enforced exile.[16] It was the worst prison they could have found, since it is the most rugged and inhospitable island in the Archipelago. Those confined there lived in caves, chiefly in the one the locals call 'the cave of Márkos' (and more recently, in the interests of tourism, 'the cave of the Cyclops'). In this cave large numbers of lamps and other household vessels for everyday use have been found.

The once much quarrelled-over island of ancient HALONNESOS (Kirá Panayá) seems to have fallen completely out of favour. At Vasilikós on Peristéra, though, there is no shortage of traces of habitation in the Roman period, but chiefly of an agricultural nature. Similar but more extensive traces are found on the plateau of Stefáni in the southern part of the island. The island seems to have recommended itself only for agriculture.

The general cultural decline is clearly evident on all the other islands. There are scattered remains which indicate very poor living conditions and suggest that these islands were used only for the grazing of animals.

Figure 6.22 Oil lamps from the Cyclops Cave, Yoúra, 1964.
Courtesy of Thomas Vestrum.

Notes

1. *Inscriptiones Graecae*, vol. 12, part 8, No. 665.
2. Named after Solocha on the Black Sea where several amphorae of this type were found in 1912–13. [Translator]
3. Doulgéri-Intzessiloglou & Garlan (1990), pp. 371–3, 388.
4. Imhoof-Blumer (1883), p. 134; Rogers (1932).
5. See pp. 444–51.
6. The Delian League was an alliance of Aegean states, under the leadership of ATHENS, against the Persians. It was founded in 478 BC on the island of DELOS, where its treasury was housed until 454, when it was moved to ATHENS. [Translator]
7. See *Inscriptiones Graecae*, vol. 2, part 3, No. 3039, where details of earlier publications will be found.
8. See p. 45.
9. Xenophon, *Hellenica* 5.1.31. Translation from Brownson (1918), p. 403.
10. Demosthenes, *First Philippic* 32. Translation from Vince, Murray *et al.* (1926–49), vol. 1, p. 87.
11. Demosthenes, *On Halonnesos* 1–6. Translation from Vince, Murray *et al.*(1926-49), vol. 1, pp. 151–3.
12. *Philip's Letter* 1 and 12–15. Translation from Vince, Murray *et al.* (1926–49), vol. 1, pp. 335, 341–3.
13. Livy, 26.24, 27.29–30, 27.33, 28.3–7, 31.28; Polybius, 10.41–2.
14. Appian, *De bellis civilibus* 5.7. Translation from White (1912–13), vol. 4, p. 387.
15. Philostratus, *Heroicus* 8.9. Translation from Maclean and Aitken (n.d.), p. 210 (with spelling of proper names altered). The *Heroicus* is a dialogue about the cult of Protesilaus, a hero of the Trojan War. The speaker here is one of the characters in the dialogue. Hymnaeus would have come to consult the oracle in a cult centre devoted to Protesilaus. [Translator]
16. See Simópoulos (1970).

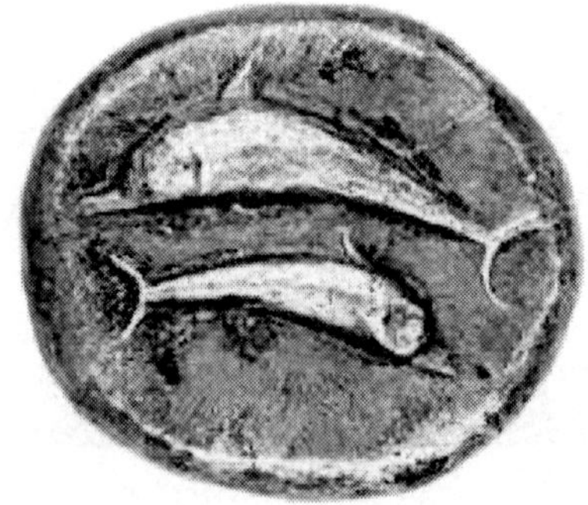

7

THE BYZANTINE EMPIRE

SUDDENLY in the midst of the Roman Empire, which little by little was beginning to weaken, a pioneering non-materialistic religion was born. Christianity began in obscurity, but with the sacred preaching of the apostles assumed great proportions. Poor men believed in the new religion which declared them the equals of their masters. From the small body of his followers, the divine words of Christ spread like lightning through the then known world.

7.1 The Coming of Christianity

The preaching of St Luke the Evangelist in THEBES (a city northwest of ATHENS) was a first step in the expansion of Christianity to our islands. By the 2nd century Christianity had already spread to Évvia, which maintained close links with the Northern Sporades. The people of Alónnisos were living at that time under an oppressive feudal regime controlled by the rich men of Skópelos.

The new teaching, which was brought to our island by sailors, touched the souls of our unfortunate ancestors. Christianity was the opportunity they had been waiting for to feel free and independent once more. Their feudal overlords saw the new ideas, which they considered madness, as a threat. They saw the converts as revolutionaries and opposed them by every means available. The Christians had to teach the divine words in secret, and in secret the faithful embraced the new religion.

Christianity was given a great boost by the first Byzantine emperor, Constantine I,[1] who adopted and established the religion, so that it became the property of all the downtrodden Greeks. From then on the poor and oppressed began to hope for salvation from their sufferings. After the proclamation of 313, the so-called Edict of Milan, promulgated at the instigation of Constantine and his mother, St Helena, to establish religious toleration, the hitherto powerful gods of Olympus were slowly forgotten. In our island Christianity was now supreme.

The religion, which had spread in secret, was now officially sanctioned. Some thirty or forty years after the proclamation of the first Christian emperor, the bishopric of Skópelos, which included Alónnisos and Kirá Panayá, was established with St Reginus as its first bishop. In the climate of general enthusiasm more and more people converted to Christianity. Forgetting their poverty, pirates and the problems of daily life, the islanders identified themselves with the new religion, which became synonymous with Hellenism throughout the Greek world.

Forty-eight years after the official establishment of Christianity, the Emperor Julian the Apostate tried to stamp it out. Julian, the champion of classical learning, dreamed of an empire in which the ancient culture would be revived. A basic precondition for the success of his enterprise was the abolition of the new religion and the return of the Twelve Gods of Olympus, and he unleashed a new persecution of Christians. In the Northern Sporades, and particularly in Skiáthos, Skópelos and Alónnisos, the local governor tortured many in order to make them deny their faith, and those who refused were put to death. This was the last attempt of the pagans to weaken and displace the Christian faith, but it failed, here as elsewhere, and from then until now our islands have remained entirely Christian, inhabited by a largely Greek population.

7.2 Island life in Byzantine Times

Throughout the Byzantine period our islands were a place of exile. Like any outlying part of the Byzantine Empire they had a governor whose job it was to control taxation and maintain order. The governor's residence was the large castle at Palió Chorió, which now became the administrative centre of Alónnisos, and which was restored in Byzantine times. For greater security the builders reduced the fortified area, abandoning the ancient walls that lie well outside the new enclosure. Farmsteads continued to exist, but, in fear of pirates, the people cultivated fields close to the security of the fortress.

The building work was carried out in a practical fashion, economising on both materials and labour by using the steep rocks on the east side as part of the fortification. Those houses of the village that were built on the very edge of the cliff were given small windows which could also act as embrasures. The fortress had a massive central gate (the key can still be seen in the municipal office in Patitíri) and a much smaller postern which could be opened and closed more easily. Outside there were secure hiding places for those who might not reach the castle in time in case of an assault. One such hiding place can be found in the gorge of Flórina. It is a natural underground chamber whose entrance is difficult to spot. The descent into this hideout was by ladder, and food and water were stored there in readiness for emergencies. The story is told that a mother who once sought refuge there had to strangle her child lest its crying betray her hiding place.

Alónnisos and the other smaller islands were too far from Constantinople for the imperial capital to exercise effective control. Their inhabitants could not rely on the protection of the Byzantine navy, but became easy prey for pirates or other invaders. Consequently, these unfortunate people had little chance to improve their lives, but were chiefly concerned with their security and survival. Nevertheless they triumphed over their disadvantages – the isolation, the difficulty of importing goods and other adversities – and left us splendid monuments of early Christian art. The virtuous islanders, who placed their hopes in the new religion, made extraordinary efforts. Large monastic centres grew up on Alónnisos at Áyos Dhimítrios and Áyos Pétros.

At Áyos Dhimítrios there was an important and flourishing monastic centre with a large church (a three-aisled early Christian basilica 37.4 m long and 17.3 m wide)[2] and a number of ancillary buildings (including baths and residential quarters) around it. Rather surprisingly the whole complex is situated close to the sea, and would thus have been exposed to attack. The location and general arrangement is similar to that of some later monasteries on Mount Athos. The site was probably chosen because the area is fertile and well watered. In modern times, the local inhabitants found large numbers of coins which were turned up by their pigs digging for roots. From the abundance of coins one gets some idea of the economic prosperity that existed (at least at times) in the Byzantine period.

Figure 7.1 Byzantine coin from the vicinity of Áyos Dhimítrios.
Courtesy of Kóstas and Angéla Mavríkis.

There was another important monastic centre not far down the coast at Áyos Pétros on Alónnisos.[3] The largish church (15 m x 9 m) in the bay of the same name (the next bay south of Stení Vála) and the various remains of buildings in this fertile area bear witness to the existence of an important settlement. In these two churches, which are situated fairly close together, can be seen architectural members such as columns and capitals of white marble which have been brought from elsewhere. These two sites together constitute the most important evidence of the Christian civilisation, which inaugurated a new era – an era in which through the power of Christianity our ancestors preserved unaltered their national identity and made progress in many areas. Besides, at this time there was intense commercial activity in this part of the island.

In the Middle and Late Byzantine periods the consolidation of Christianity was already a fact. Throughout the island, churches were built as an expression of the inhabitants' deep faith. Wherever there were concentrations of farms new churches were built. At Áyos Dhimítrios, only 100 metres from the already existing church, a second one of more moderate size was built. The ossuary was preserved until the Second World War, when it too was destroyed. The cemetery is in the area near Mourtítsa. In Byzantine times the whole surrounding area was exploited for agriculture. The ancient terraces, which are still visible today, indicate the extent of this exploitation.

Near Koumarórachi, where a fairly large population was concentrated, there are the remains of a small chapel. Most of its stones have been reused in the terracing and today the only surviving part is the sanctuary, where carved marble has been found.

In the area of Pangíria on Alónnisos, on the skirts of the hill known as Tourkóvigla, the visitor today encounters the remains of many Byzantine churches.

Near the village of Vótsi lies the church of Áyos Andhreas, and among its ruins can be seen sculpted columns and marble architectural members, including a fragment with the sign of the swastika. There were undoubtedly several Byzantine churches in Palió Chorió itself, but these were later demolished and new structures built on top of them.

Of all the buildings of this period the most significant architecturally is the monastery near Saránda Avrayés. Nowadays the ruins are covered by dense vegetation and access is difficult. The walls of the sanctuary have been preserved and are a work of art. The entire church, as is evident from the remains, was built of enormous blocks of stone, cut to fit together perfectly and to give from the outside the impression of a solid mass. Close to the sanctuary there are parts of carved marble columns and capitals of considerable size. Stones from the church walls were later reused in the terracing nearby. The church is built on a slope and must have been an impressive sight, dominating the area. Apart from being the monastic centre it must also have served as a church for the surrounding region which seems at that time to have been densely populated (Mourteró, Kalamákia, Vamvakiés). At Kalamákia, near the Byzantine kiln, a local farmer found some large engraved blocks of marble, which he showed to an archaeologist. It seems that there had been a second church in the area.

With the passage of time, links with Constantinople were strengthened and the island adopted certain Byzantine customs, including the building of family chapels within the properties of wealthier families. In the Middle Byzantine period there was a great expansion of monasticism, for political as well as religious reasons. Not only on Alónnisos but also on the other islands the number of monks increased dramatically. They built monasteries in prominent positions and embarked on the extensive exploitation of the potential of the uninhabited islands. In order to become self-sufficient they developed stock-rearing, and applied themselves with great determination to the cultivation of the land, laboriously transforming wasteland into productive fields. In a short time all the uninhabited islands were brought into use and great monasteries sprang up.

On Skántzoura, in the area now called Palaiomonástiro ('Old Monastery'), the first monastery of the island was built. It was close to the shore and controlled the harbour. From the monastery every vessel is visible, from no matter what direction they approach. The church was of fine workmanship, and around it the remains of other structures are visible, including the scattered cells in which the monks lived. The small size of the cells expressed the ideals of the spartan monastic life, and at the same time fulfilled functional objectives, being quick to build and easy to heat in winter. A wall a metre thick was constructed right across the island, dividing it into two parts. The western half was used for animals and the eastern, whose plain is more fertile, for seed crops and tree planting. The olive was cultivated, and many olive trees and vines were planted near the old monastery, around the edge of the plain and in various upland plateaus. Traces of this laborious agricultural endeavour, hidden now among the scrub and cedars, bear witness to the importance and size of the monastic community on Skántzoura, which was dedicated to the Annunciation of the Virgin.

At the same period, on the neighbouring island of Pipéri, there was another flourishing monastery also dedicated to the Virgin, in this case as *Zoodhóchos Piyí*

('Life-giving Spring'). Its foundation is the subject of a legend. A ship sailing in the northern Aegean ran into heavy seas. The crew, forty young disciples and their teacher, made a vow that if they were saved from nature's wild rage they would devote themselves to God. The storm carried them to Pipéri, to a place out of the wind where they were saved and found refuge. They remained on Pipéri and became monks, building a church and the famous *Saránda Keliá* ('Forty Cells'), whose layout the older people still remember today.

The church was built in a carefully chosen spot, close to the spring, which, as though by a miracle, gushes from the summit of the hill. Pipéri quickly became a notable monastic centre. The monks planted olives and vineyards and fruit trees and all the level plots were cleared and prepared for sowing with cereals. The countless terraces that they built are lost now among the pines, which spring up everywhere and silently cover every trace of human activity (there were 16,000 of them when some were felled for timber in 1965, and by now there must be even more). These terraces had a peculiarity in their construction: the monks had the foresight to leave a gap for drainage in times of heavy rain. Eventually an oil press was established. The millstones are still there today, testimony to former activity on the island over a long period A second, subsidiary monastery was built at the spot known as *Dhaskálou ta kalívia* ('the Teacher's huts'). The name alone puts us in the picture.

On Grámeza, on the eastern side, there is a church that seems rather large for this small island. It was certainly dedicated to the Virgin but to which of her festivals, or under which of her titles, we do not know. A few monks were established there and lived a self-sufficient life. The island appears barren and rocky, but on its summit there is a plateau which with great labour was cleared of stones and made productive. Water was provided by a spring in the surrounding crags which still exists today. Communications were non-existent, since the island had no harbour and all transport was extremely difficult because of the steep terrain. The church contained architectural elements in marble, but at the beginning of the 20th century many of these were carried up to the summit of the island to construct a house for the labourers attached to the monastery. A visit to this wild place is certainly worth the traveller's effort, in order to experience the real meaning of the solitary monastic life.

We do not know whether there were monks on Yoúra in the Byzantine period. The existing church is from a later period. According to tradition Yoúra was popular with Byzantine officials on account of its fine hunting (chiefly of wild goats).

On Psathoúra there are traces of Byzantine buildings on the property of the Phílippas family from Skópelos, who, according to the lighthouse keeper Yeóryos Agállou, found several Byzantine coins. There are also traces of a post-Byzantine church.

Of all the remote islands it is Kirá Panayá that stands out. In the Byzantine period it served as an important centre. There the largest of the monasteries was situated, commanding the bay of Áyos Pétros. From the monastery the monks could control the whole harbour. The church was large and of exceptional workmanship. Substantial quantities of carved marble indicate its grandeur. It must have accommodated a considerable number of monks, who would have been involved in stockbreeding and cultivation.

Figure 7.2 The old monastery of Áyos Pétros, Kirá Panayá.

The island provided the optimum conditions for livestock, with rich vegetation capable of feeding as many as 3,500 animals. It was also ideal for crops. The two large plateaus, amonting together to about 40 hectares, could produce large quantities of crops, chiefly cereals. (Many Byzantine irrigation systems survive to this day.) It was customary in monasteries to offer bread to visitors, and a great deal of wheat was required to provide for the needs of the monks themselves and of those to whom they offered hospitality.

The wheat was stored in barns in the middle of the plain of Áyos Pétros, where the walls of rectangular structure, constructed with lime mortar, still remain. They are overgrown, of course, with bushes which are of a rather unusual type. These long-lived bushes have enormous trunks and look more like huge trees. I discovered to my amazement that they are a species of rush, which over many years transforms itself into a tree. A little further on towards the seaward side there is a small ancillary church of similar date. Inside we found fragments of marble on which time had left its mark.

If one walks from the beach of Áyos Pétros towards the houses of the shepherds one comes across a strange relic. Next to the shepherds' allotment is a beautiful relief head on a dressed block of stone. Apart from the head, the shape of the stone is purely functional and it must have served as the keystone to the arch of some doorway or the counterweight of a press. This strange find was brought to light in the 1960s by two shepherds from Alónnisos who were employed by the monastery. They were living there all the year round and making cheese. They came across this huge stone while they were digging their allotment.

In all the islands there were 'servants', labourers attached to the monasteries who lived there either seasonally or all year round. Alone or with their families these men had sought refuge on the fertile but largely unpopulated islands where they worked for the monks. Apart from their food they received a certain proportion of the profits.

When Byzantium was at the height of its power the Aegean was secure from foreign incursions. With the gradual weakening of the empire came the first threats from the Muslims and the Latins. Almost all of our islands, their inhabitants driven to despair by the continual raids (chiefly by Saracens), were abandoned. If anything was left, it probably ended up in the holds of pirate ships.

7.3 The Sale of Kirá Panayá to the Monastery of the Great Lávra

The despair which took hold is evident in a document preserved in the monastery of the Great Lávra on Mount Athos. It records the sale of the island of Kirá Panayá, or Yimnopelayísion as it was then called, to St Athanásios the Athonite in the year 993. The two monks who sold the island had inherited it from Sávvas, the abbot of the monastery on the island, who had been a friend of Athanásios. Sávvas in turn had inherited it from the monk Séryos, the founder of the first monastery on the island.

As soon as he encountered the place, Séryos was inspired by its natural beauty and tranquillity and realised that it was the most suitable island for a monastic retreat. Immediately, in 973, he purchased the island from the imperial authorities to whom it had belonged until then. The sale price was 40 gold *nomísmata*,[4] but he also undertook to pay an annual tax of two *nomísmata*. After the death of Séryos, Sávvas took over the monastery, and while he was abbot, the authorities demanded a further 36 *nomísmata* for the ratification of the sale. The document of the first sale and that of the later ratification were seized with other items by Saracen pirates. A third document restating the terms of the original sale and its ratification, in which the monks requested a new document confirming their title to the island has, however, survived, as has the confirmation they received.[5]

After the death of the second abbot, Sávvas, and the pirate raid, the monks abandoned the monastery and dispersed. Two of the monks, named Kosmás and Loukás, sought refuge on Mount Athos and persuaded St Athanásios to buy it and to annex it to the monastic properties of the Great Lávra. Here is part of the text of the bill of sale of Kirá Panayá to St Athanásios the Athonite:[6]

> I Kosmás, a priest, and I Loukás, a monk, disciples of the late lamented monk Sávvas, abbot of Yimnopelayísion, have inscribed the Holy Crosses and signed this document with conviction and in accordance with our own views and wishes, without any compulsion, force, threat or coercion, but with due thought and consideration for Athanásios, monk and priest and abbot of the Imperial Lávra of Athos and his successors and all future occupants.
>
> After our abbot, the late lamented Sávvas, had gone to his eternal rest, I Kosmás, monk and priest and his successor, admitted three new monks,

> one of whom has died, while the other two, Makários and Lavréndios remain on the island. After the Saracens had come to Yimnopelayísion and remained twelve days on the island, during which time they captured many boats together with their crews [...] the *Topotirítis*[7] Paspalás, who had been commissioned by our Holy Emperor, took me from there and brought me to a military camp where we remained for four months.
>
> When I returned to the island, I found not a single monk nor any of the monastery's possessions. But even before this, we had been informed by those travellers who passed by the island in their ships, that the pirates had taken all our possessions, including the sheep and other animals [...]. All my fellow monks had left, and since the island was now desolate I too wanted to depart from there for ever.
>
> But I took counsel with Loukás, who thought that we should not leave the monastery completely empty and uncared-for, nor abandon the place that was dedicated to God for monks to dwell to become a dwelling place for worldly people, but that we should, rather, consider in what way the monastery might be re-established for the glory of God and the salvation of our Emperor and all Christians.
>
> To this end, then, we travelled to the Holy Mountain and came to the monk called Athanásios, who was the abbot of the Lávra, and falling at his feet we begged him to take care of the island and to re-establish the monastery, both as a friend (as he had been) of our late lamented abbot, the monk Sávvas, and as a friend of *Kir* Michális the *Protospathários*,[8] who had written again to Athanásios, the monk and Abbot of the Lávra, requesting him to take care of this monastery.

As Kosmás and Loukás go on to explain, this *Kir* Michális had been instrumental in obtaining the confirmation of the title to the island after the loss of the original documents. The current sale price of 70 gold *nomísmata* is mentioned, and the two monks declare, 'with God as chief witness' that the present document guarantees to Athanásios and his successors ownership of the island in perpetuity. The document concludes with a curse on any party who should go back on the terms of the agreement:

> may he be an outcast from the Christian faith and call down upon himself the curse of the 318 Holy Fathers.[9]

The scribe then adds his own name, stating that the document

> is written and signed by the hand of Efthímios the monk, in the presence of the witnesses whose names are appended, in the month of September in the year AD 993.

The witnesses who were present were Efraím, Kosmás, Theofílaktos, another Kosmás, Efstrátios, another Theofílaktos, and Yermanós. Each signature is preceded by the phrase 'Being present at this meeting, I have signed with my own hand.'

Notes

1. Constantine had been one of three co-emperors who shared between them the Roman world. Having defeated the other two, he became sole emperor and established a new capital in the ancient Greek colony of BYZANTIUM, which was renamed Constantinople (now Istanbul). The eastern part of the Roman Empire, where Greek rather than Latin was the lingua franca, came to be known as the Byzantine Empire. The Western Empire fell to the barbarians in the 5th century (it was reconquered, but only briefly, in the sixth), while the Eastern, Byzantine, Empire lasted for a further thousand years until Constantinople was taken by the Ottoman Turks in 1453. [Translator]
2. Lazarídhis (1966), p. 262.
3. Nikonános (1972), pp. 424–5.
4. In the 8th–11th centuries the gold *nómisma* (plural *nomísmata*) was the highest denomination coin used in the Byzantine Empire.
5. These documents are published in Lavriótis (n.d.).
6. Published in Lavriótis (n.d.).
7. A *topotirítis* was a deputy to a military or naval commander. [Translator]
8. *Protospathários* was a title conferred on various high-ranking officials in the Byzantine imperial hierarchy. *Kir* is an honorific roughly equivalent to 'my Lord'. [Translator]
9. 318 is the traditionally accepted number of bishops who participated in the Council of NICAEA (AD 325), the first of the Ecumenical Councils that defined Christian orthodoxy. [Translator]

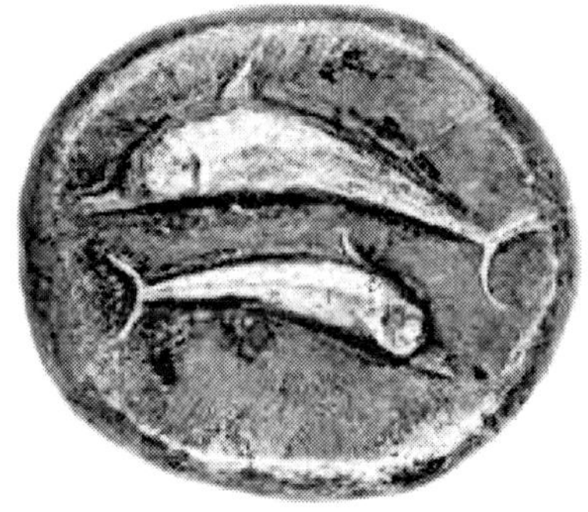

8

VENETIAN AND TURKISH RULE

DEEPLY INGRAINED in the minds of the older people on the island is the phrase, 'When the Pope of Rome destroyed the churches'. If we want to give historical substance to this expression we must go back to the Latin pirates, or more specifically to the Latin crusaders,[1] who in 1204 in the course of the Fourth Crusade captured and looted Constantinople.

8.1 First Venetian Occupation (1204–1276)

In Ayía Sofía they took a donkey into the sanctuary in order to load it up with the sacred relics.[2] This drunken horde of plunderers transported the goods they had looted from churches by way of our islands to the Latin cities, chief among these being Venice. During their passage through our islands they did not miss the opportunity for further plunder. Wherever they stopped they seized whatever they could find, having lost all Christian fear of God. They then began a systematic hunt for Orthodox priests, whom they turned out of their parishes or monasteries.

The Latin pirates treated the local population extremely harshly, particularly if they were Orthodox. The most merciless of all were the warrior monks who belonged to the order of the Knights of St John, who may have been responsible for the destruction of the monastery on Skántzoura and the monasteries of Áyos Dhimítrios and Áyos Pétros on Alónnisos. The sufferings lasted for more than fifty years until the City[3] was recaptured by the Byzantine emperor Michael VIII.

It was these westerners, supposedly our fellow Christians, who fatally weakened the Greek Byzantine state, and seized parts of it for themselves. At the time of the Fourth Crusade, various noble Venetian families appeared on the scene and came in time to dominate the Aegean. The Northern Sporades were soon annexed to the Venetian Republic. This powerful maritime empire was unable to exercise direct control of trade throughout the Mediterranean and sought instead some indirect method of controlling the seas, islands and seaboard cities, one that would not involve great expense to the Venetian state. To this end, Venice issued a decree that

> any Venetian of noble birth who so desires may with his own forces and at his own expense take possession of islands and seaboard cities in Greek lands anywhere within the bounds of the Venetian domains. Having taken possession of them he shall have the right of full authority and government of those regions. He shall also have the right to transfer his possessions to his descendants as though they were his personal property.

Marco I Sanudo and many other noble fortune hunters set out from Venice in eight galleys in the year 1207 and seized many islands in the Aegean, as well as territories on the mainland shores. The leader of the expedition distributed the captured lands among the nobles who had co-operated in the undertaking. Alónnisos was allotted to the Frankish barons Andrea and Geremia Ghizi.[4] Through alliances and intrigues they acquired further territories, including Skíros and the rest of the Northern Sporades, as well as Tínos and Míkonos in the Cyclades. Later they obtained part of Kéa, the whole of Sérifos, and extensive possessions in Negroponte (as the Italians called Évvia) as well as the region Acháïa in the Peloponnese and Chandhakás (modern Iráklio in Crete). They were aided in this by Domenico Michiel and Piero Giustiniani.

Our ancestors, then, were ruled by the Barons Ghizi, who repaired the Byzantine fortress at Palió Chorió and organised local defences. With the privileges they granted in the early years of their rule a new spirit of enterprise developed on our island. The impregnable fortress protected the inhabitants from Arab, Turkish and Latin pirates who regularly attacked our islands.

From within the fortress a secret underground passage was constructed, its entrance covered with stone slabs. The passage led out of the fortress and emerged in dense virgin forest on the east side of the hill. From there, under the cover of the trees, the people could reach their hideouts. The stone slabs over the entrance were carefully cut so that they fitted together perfectly. This passage existed until recently but was partly destroyed in the earthquake of 1965. According to tradition there were 74 houses built into the outer circuit of the Venetian fortress. The fortress was home to the Venetian governor and a small garrison to ensure the security of his domain. The governor's quarters were in the *Cazarna* (Venetian dialect for Italian *Caserma* meaning 'barracks'). Alónnisos was subordinated to Skópelos but maintained a degree of independence. The Venetians practised religious toleration. The first period of Venetian occupation was, however, characterised by rivalries, alliances with pirates and civil disputes.

By 1251, when Geremia Ghizi died, the Ghizi brothers had become, after the Sanudo family, the most powerful rulers in the Aegean. Geremia's children were all daughters and they did not have the right to inherit his share of the dukedom, which passed into the hands of his brother, Andrea. Andrea Ghizi died eight years later in 1259, and his son and heir Bartolomeo thus became the ruler of all the lands belonging to the Ghizi dynasty. At this date the governor of the Northern Sporades was Lorenzo Tiepolo, who had married Marquesia, the elder daughter of Geremia Ghizi. Together this couple governed discretely and wisely and were well loved by the impoverished inhabitants of the islands.

The quarrels in the Aegean sometimes verged on the absurd. A good example is the so-called 'dispute about the donkey'. A donkey belonging to Bartolomeo was stolen by pirates, who sold it to Guglielmo Sanudo in Síros. Sanudo was not prepared to return the donkey and Bartolomeo initiated a military campaign to retrieve it. Sanudo responded in kind and the bloodletting was only stopped by the forceful intervention of Venice's official representatives.

In 1259 the malicious Filippo Ghizi appeared on the scene and seized and looted the Northern Sporades. Filippo had married Geremia Ghizi's younger daughter, Isabella, and adopted his wife's family name. Lorenzo, aided by the local people, managed to reassert his authority over Filippo and restored the former peace and good order to the islands in 1261. For seven years there was continuing enmity between Filippo Ghizi and Lorenzo Tiepolo, which ended only when Tiepolo resigned his governorship and returned to Venice (where he was rewarded with a title), leaving the islands to the mercy of his bitter enemy. Filippo behaved very harshly towards the inhabitants who had nurtured such a special regard for his adversary, meting out death, arson and imprisonment, and making himself the scourge of the islands. He used our islands as bases from which to launch attacks on neighbouring islands, and entered into alliances with pirates of all kinds. Just when the Byzantine Empire was showing signs of recovery, piracy reached a new peak.

8.2 The Byzantine Reconquest (1276–1453)

In 1259 Michael VIII Palaeologus came to the throne of the Despotate of Níkea (ancient NICAEA). He was the most energetic of the rulers in those Byzantine lands that remained in Greek hands, and under him Níkea developed into a powerful empire. On 26 July 1261, his general, Stratigópoulos, retook the much desired city of Constantinople with relative ease. Michael Palaeologus was now established in the heart of the Byzantine Empire and made desperate attempts to restore its former glory.

In 1276 the admiral, Aléxios Filanthropinós with the Latin knight Licario, his second-in-command, liberated Évvia and the Northern Sporades from the Venetians and drove out all the Venetian soldiers. Licario managed to take prisoner Filippo Ghizi after attacking the castle of Skópelos during the summer months. During the siege those within the castle ran out of water and were obliged to surrender. Filippo was taken to Constantinople where he threw himself on the emperor's mercy. In exchange for granting his freedom Michael Palaeologus demanded that the islands belonging to the Ghizi family become part of the Byzantine Empire. Filippo agreed and handed over Alónnisos, Skiáthos, Sérifos, Amorgós and Kéa.[6]

Byzantine governors were installed in these islands, but they were not adequately supported by the official Byzantine fleet of Michael VIII, who was conducting campaigns in many sectors against his hated Frankish enemies. Not only did the emperor impose insupportable levels of taxation to cover the costs of his wars, but the pirates, with no effective check on their activities since the departure of the Venetians, once more terrorised the islanders.

A few specific acts of piracy have been recorded. In 1308, Catalan mercenaries, under the command of Frederico of Sicily and Ferdinando, returning from Asia Minor, where they had fought for the Byzantine emperor Andronicus II Palaeologus, plundered our islands, which happened to lie in their path. A few years later, in 1326, Turkish pirates raided all the islands of the Northern Sporades. And in 1403 a Turkish pirate by the name of Süleyman laid waste and pillaged our islands, and then overwintered here.

In general, the Palaeologan period was not a happy one for Alónnisos, and when the Byzantine Empire was finally destroyed by the Turks the people gladly accepted the protection of Venice.

8.3 The Return of the Venetians (1453–1475)

The exhausted city of Constantinople was besieged by the Ottoman Turks in 1453 and fell after a heroic defence on 29 May. The Turks established themselves in the city and steadily extended their domain. Chaos and insecurity reigned in our islands at that period. They were more than ever overrun by pirates who, now that the Byzantine fleet was destroyed, had nothing whatever to fear.

Life on the smaller islands became virtually impossible. The threat of Turkish expansion hung over the islanders, and their most pressing need was to find the protection of some Frankish duchy. They considered first the neighbouring house of Gattilusio in Lésvos, but turned instead to the Venetians, since their earlier period of rule in the islands had been fairly benign. Representatives from all the islands met together and formally handed over the islands to the Republic of Venice, with the proviso that the Venetians would guarantee them certain privileges.

The Venetian admiral Lorendano – one of the victors in the naval battle at Náfpaktos in the Gulf of Corinth (better known as the Battle of Lepanto) where in 1571 an Ottoman fleet was defeated by consortium of Christian fleets – considered the islands a most undesirable possession. The islands had been laid waste and their economies destroyed by the pirates.

The inhabitants of the islands, being clever diplomats, sent representatives to negotiate with the Genoese house of the Maonese who were lords of Chíos. They made no secret of their negotiations, intending that news of them should reach the ears of Lorendano. The Venetians were fanatical enemies of the Genoese dynasty on Chíos, and would do anything to prevent them extending their influence in the northern Aegean. By this stratagem the islanders avoided being occupied by the barbarous Turks and received the protection of Venice.

The powerful Venetian state sent two representatives with the title of *Rettore* ('Rector'). One rector was responsible for the islands of Skiáthos, Skópelos and Alónnisos, the other for Skíros. The inhabitants were allowed a certain degree of independence and retained their own autonomous bishopric. Venetian authority was exercised by the commander of the Venetian garrison and his subordinates. There would presumably have been groups of local elders who would have made the everyday decisions about administrative, religious and economic matters. Judicial authority lay with the rectors, who were accountable only to the governor of Negroponte (Évvia) at Chalkídha.

The rector responsible for Alónnisos was based in Skópelos and oversaw matters from there, with occasional visits to the fortress at Palió Chorió (the Alonnisiots were very poor in those days and life even in the fortresses of the island was very frugal). The first rector of Skópelos was Paolo Bonzi.[7] Altogether there were 22 rectors who governed our three islands (Skiáthos, Skópelos and Alónnisos) during the second Venetian period.

Among them was a certain Niccolò Giorgio (1474–75), the last of the Latin governors before the first Turkish occupation. From him, perhaps, are descended the family whose name has been Hellenised as Tzórtzis and who are still living on Alónnisos. If not descended from him, they must have adopted this name in the Venetian period.

Figure 8.1 Fishermen at Patitíri, 1968. *Courtesy of Athanásios Páppos.*

8.4 First Turkish Occupation (1475–1486)

The Turkish fleet began to operate on several fronts in the Aegean, with the aim of gaining control of the profitable trade in this sector of the Mediterranean. The Turko-Venetian war in the Northern Sporades raged for several years, but by 1475 the Venetians were in retreat, and abandoned the islands to the mercy of the Turks. The islands came into contact for the first time with their future Turkish masters. The Turks considered them to be infidels who had co-operated with their enemies and treated them in a harsh and inhuman fashion. The first Turkish occupation was short-lived, however. The Turks had probably never intended to establish themselves permanently on the islands, which would have required maintaining a garrison with all the attendant expenses. They remained for a few years and then abandoned the islands which became once more a part of the Venetian sphere of influence.

8.5 Venetian Rule (1486–1538)

In order to gain the support of our ancestors in the war against the Turks for the control of the Aegean, the Venetians now treated them with greater respect and accorded them many new privileges. Once again the main agricultural activity would have been the cultivation of vines, improved by new methods derived from the wine-loving Venetians.

In general terms the periods of Venetian rule were relatively good times for the three islands of Alónnisos, Skópelos and Skiáthos. They enjoyed a certain degree of security in the midst of the general turmoil in the Aegean. Venetian rule certainly left its mark on our own island of Alónnisos. The Venetians had close contacts with the local population, and memories of this period remained strong, as is evident in many local idioms and personal names.

Even today many women on Alónnisos have the Christian name Sinióra (from the Italian *signora*), and there are other women's names of French or Italian origin still current on the island, such as Muresó and Sirainó, while our general vocabulary has been enriched by many words of Italian origin, particularly those relating to the winds and weather. There are many place-names, too, which bear witness to the passage of the hot-blooded Venetians: Marpoúnda, Zarboúnda, Tzórtzi Yalós, Stení Vála, Mourteró, Flórina, Spartínes. There was also a definite influence on the local architecture, and many houses built in the Venetian style can still be seen in Palió Chorió.

Throughout the later periods of Venetian rule, the smaller islands must have been completely empty and abandoned. Because of the numerous and increasingly ruthless pirates who sheltered in their harbours, all normal life and activity ground to a halt. The monasteries on the remote islands had long been abandoned to the ravages of time. Many questions relating to Venetian rule in the Northern Sporades remain unanswered. Perhaps future researches in the archives of Venice will help us to find more about trade, social and professional relations, shipping and other matters. All this information is no doubt there, but would require careful and laborious searching through an enormous number of files.

8.6 Turkish Rule (1538–1830)

By the 16th century the Ottoman Empire was well established. The Sultans had realised that in order to achieve and maintain a position of supremacy they would have to construct a powerful navy. They succeeded by making an alliance with the Barbary pirates, fellow Muslims from North Africa. Chief among them was the notorious Barbarossa, known to the Turks as Hayrettin Paşa who, in 1520, was appointed first admiral of the Ottoman navy. The cunning Sultan, Süleyman I (known in the West as 'the Magnificent') thought that by appointing the pirate his admiral he could acquire the most powerful fleet in the world, and at the same time rid himself of a thorn in the flesh of the Ottoman Empire. Apart from his piratical activities, Barbarossa was a fanatical enemy of all Christians, and his activities struck fear and terror into the hearts of the people of the Aegean islands. As first admiral (in Turkish Kapudan Paşa), Barbarossa continued to tyrannise the Aegean islands and seaboards, but now on behalf of the Sultan. He achieved great successes and was soon the most notorious man in the Mediterranean.

Figure 8.2 The bay of Tzórtzi Yalós. *Courtesy of Thomas Vestrum.*

The red-bearded admiral, with the authority of the Sublime Porte,[8] set out from Istanbul with pomp and ceremony at the head of a huge fleet. He had 70 warships and 50 auxiliary vessels, carrying 250,000 troops in addition to their crews. Nothing could withstand this armada. In 1538 the fleet arrived in the Northern Sporades, which along with many other Aegean islands were still in the hands of the Venetians. Barbarossa seized and devastated most of Skópelos, taking many prisoners. He then turned his attention to Alónnisos, razed all its fortifications to the ground, and took the Venetian administrators prisoner, before moving on to the Cyclades. After the passage of this merciless 'Redbeard', Alónnisos was completely depopulated. Those who were not killed were taken as slaves to the shipyards of Istanbul or the slave markets of the east; and the few who evaded capture hid for a while in caves and later escaped to voluntary exile in neighbouring Évvia or Thessaly.

The arrival of Barbarossa was the worst disaster that our island suffered in the whole of its long history. Everything came to a standstill and the island remained uninhabited for many years. The total devastation of Alónnisos left it entirely defenceless against pirates, and this affected its future development. Fear of the triple domination of Latins, pirates and Turks reduced the exiled inhabitants to despair. Most of those who had fled preferred to remain far from danger. The few who later dared to return were condemned to a life of extreme poverty, which was the only way of not attracting the attention of pirates greedy for spoil. Foreign travellers who visited the island some years after Barbarossa's raid found the seventy-odd houses of Palió Chorió still in a ruinous condition. There was a further setback in 1570 when Kemal Reis, Barbarossa's successor as Kapudan Paşa (and known in that capacity as Kiliç Aslan or Kiliç Ali Paşa) attacked Alónnisos, destroying whatever had been restored.

After that, it seems that the island remained deserted for several decades. It was not really in the interests of the Ottoman Empire for Alónnisos and other islands in the Sporades to remain uninhabited and unworked, and early in the 17th century the Sultan granted our islands a special privileged status in order to give a stimulus to their repopulation. Under the terms of the Sultan's ferman (edict), the islands were now subject to the Kapudan Paşa. They retained the right to religious toleration, and paid tithes but not capitation. They had autonomous local government, with the right to elect their own elders. There was a Turkish governor, who, together with a Turkish military officer, saw that order was maintained and gave judgement in civil cases. Any outstanding legal differences were referred to the governor of all the Northern Sporades, the Kapudan Paşa, once a year. The Turkish governor was stationed in the old Venetian *Cazarna* ('barracks') and from there governed the very few (about 300) inhabitants of Alónnisos.

The Turkish occupation is a fairly obscure period, and much of what is known about comes from the folk tradition, passed on to us by the very oldest inhabitants of the island. The following story was told to the folklorist Athanásios Páppos by an old lady, Angelikí Malamaténiou, known as *i Chondrína* (the 'Fat One'), who was born in 1880.

> According to the tradition, during the period of Turkish rule, all the Alonnisiots were shut up inside the castle [at Palió Chorió]. There, where the offices of the *Kinótita* were before they were demolished, lived the Turkish governor with his Arab servant. It was next to the gate of the castle and anyone wanting to go out through the gate had to pass by the house of the Turkish governor. Anyone who was particularly clever or energetic was in danger of being killed or expelled by the Agha.[9] In order to protect a particularly clever and energetic boy from the Agha, his uncle took him on his travels. They travelled for three years, at the end of the three years they

> dropped anchor at Patitíri. The young man couldn't wait to go and see his family in the village as soon as possible. There was a wedding that day in Kopriá.[10] There was wine, and having been away for so long the young man took the opportunity to get well and truly drunk. The moment came when it was his turn to dance with the bride. The Agha was watching the dancing from his window. When he saw what a dashing figure the young man cut, he sent his Arab servant to bring him to his office.
>
> 'Hey, you,' said the Arab, grabbing him by his breeches, 'the Agha wants to see you.'
>
> 'Alright,' said the young man, 'I'll just finish my turn with the bride and then I'll come.'
>
> 'Now!' said the Arab, giving a sharp tug at his breeches.
>
> Excited as the young man was by the wine and the dancing, he pushed the Arab very forcefully, and the Arab fell flat on his back. The wedding celebrations came to a halt, and the Arab ran back to the Agha's house to fetch his gun.
>
> 'Run for it!' they told the young man.
>
> So he was running in front and the Arab was running after him with his gun. Below the threshing floors there was a wood and the young man went in there to hide.
>
> The Arab kept watch on the rock by the threshing floors. He spotted the young man's red fez and shot him. He cut off his head and brought it to the Agha as though it were a cannonball. The villagers immediately informed the uncle, the captain, the strapping sailor, who was still down at Patitíri. In a furious rage the captain killed the Agha and dragged the Arab off to the walnut tree that used to stand by the well. There the captain strung him up by his feet and beat him until he gave up the ghost.
>
> The people of Alónnisos were then without a governor until the news of the Agha's death got out. In retaliation the Turks came to Liadhrómia [Alónnisos] and killed all the old sailor's relatives. Even his second cousins didn't escape the Turkish knife. They killed about twenty people.[11]

Here is another tradition from the Turkish period, as related by Konstandínos Chrístou, who heard it from Miltiádhis Chrístou:[12]

> In Alónnisos today there are three large villages: Patitíri, so called because they used to bring the grapes there and extract the must in the *patitíria*[13] by the shore; Vótsi, which takes its name from the hero of 1913, Níkos Vótsis;[14] and Rousoúm. During the period of Turkish rule there was a Turkish landowner, who, thanks to his rank, had managed to acquire a large estate in the vicinity of Rousoúm. In those days the place had another name.
>
> This landowner was called Orsum. He was on friendly terms with the Turkish governor and oppressed the poor inhabitants who worked on his property for a crust of bread. An Alonnisiot pirate felt sorry for his fellow islanders and killed Orsum and his whole family too so that his unworthy seed should not continue. From then on the bay has been called Rsoúm (or Rousoúm, because it's easier to say). The pirate took up residence in the landowner's house.

An alternative explanation of the name Rousoúm is that it was here that the *rusuum* (an Arabic term for 'taxes' used by the Turks) had to be paid to the tax agents of the Sublime Porte.

The bay of Tourkonéri ('Turk-Water'), on the west side of Alónnisos, was so called because it was there that the Turkish ships took on supplies of water. Another place is known as *tou Toúrkou to mníma* ('the Turk's grave') because some officer of the Turkish navy was buried there. According to tradition this grave was the favourite spot for searching for hidden treasure.

Figure 8.3 Patitíri from above, 1964. *Courtesy of Athanásios Páppos.*

Throughout the Ottoman period, the fleet of the Kapudan Paşa overwintered in the Northern Sporades, but the admirals preferred the harbours of Skópelos and Skiáthos to those of Kirá Panayá or Vasilikós on Peristéra, because of the adjacent towns that could furnish supplies and offered opportunities for social life and entertainment. This is one of the reasons why shipbuilding and trade developed on these two larger islands. Skópelos took the lead, and Alonnisiots used to go there to find work and to obtain goods from the Skopelites who travelled widely. A characteristic example of this is the costume known as the *Mórka*. This costume had the garishness of court costumes of the European Renaissance. Skopelite sailors brought it from European ports to our islands. This style of dress delighted the female population, who began to wear it, and it gradually became established. From Skópelos it spread to Alónnisos, and thus we have the unusual situation of two Aegean islands with identical traditional costume.

It was during the Turkish period that a distinctive form of folk culture developed throughout Greece. In cultural matters, Alónnisos, a poor and remote island, was little touched by later influences, and its songs, proverbs and folk tales, and customs associated with weddings and saints days, preserve a pure and unalloyed folk tradition, unique of its kind.

Figure 8.4 A traditional wedding in Palió Chorió.

Another characteristic of this period was the strength of religion among the inhabitants of Alónnisos and the lesser Northern Sporades. After the fall of Constantinople to the Turks in 1453, the Greeks began to strive for a national identity and to rally around the Orthodox religion. The groundwork in the Northern Sporades had already been done with the granting of the right to an episcopal seat by the Venetians.[15] The policy of religious toleration was continued by the Sultan Mehmet II, known in Turkish as Fatih ('the Conqueror'). Between the resettlement of the island after the depredations of Barbarossa and Kemal Reis and its liberation in the early 19th century, many churches were built. The people who returned to the island needed the facilities to fulfil their religious obligations. Churches were built first within the castle at Palió Chorió and later, from time to time, others were built in the surrounding countryside.[16]

Notes

1. 'Latin' (in Greek *latinikós*) is a way of characterising, from a Greek perspective, western Europeans of the medieval or early modern period. [Translator]
2. The 'Great Church' of Ayía Sofia was the principal church of the Byzantine capital, Constantinople, and the focal point of Orthodox Christianity. [Translator]
3. Today, as in Byzantine times, Greeks often refer to Constantinople simply as 'the City'.
4. 'Frankish' and 'Franks' (*frangikós* and *Frángi* in Greek), like 'Latin' and 'Latins', refer to western Europeans in general. [Translator]
5. Athanasíou (1964).
6. Nasoúlis (1950).
7. For this and other details in the above account see Ikonómos (1883), pp. 27–9.
8. The name of the entrance gate to the palace of the Grand Vizier in Istanbul, 'Sublime Porte' came to refer to the government of the Ottoman Empire. [Translator]
9. 'Agha' (*Agás* in Greek, Ağa in Turkish) was a widely used title in the Ottoman Empire, applied to various civil and military officials. Here it denotes the 'Turkish governor' of Alónnisos just referred to in the previous sentences. [Translator]
10. Kopriá is the village square in Palió Chorió. [Translator]
11. This story was published in the November 1974 issue of the journal *Vórii Sporádhes*.
12. For information about Miltiádhis Chrístou see pp. 201, 205–8
13. *Patitíria* are large tanks in which the grapes were trodden.
14. See pp. 211–12.
15. See p. 168.
16. For details of the surviving churches, see pp. 329–34.

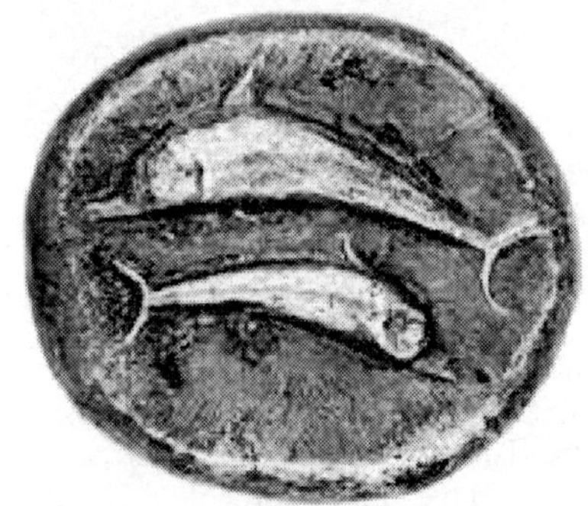

9

GREEK INDEPENDENCE: REVOLUTION AND PIRACY IN THE NINETEENTH CENTURY

Figure 9.1 Boats at Patitíri, 1958. *Courtesy of Ioánna Tzórtzi.*

OUR REGION, as we have said before, has always been ideal for pirates. An important crossroads throughout Greek history, it could hardly have been ignored by profiteers and fortune hunters, and from remote antiquity to the present piracy has flourished almost continuously. Dolopian, Phoenician, Cilician, Frankish, Thessalian and Macedonian pirates, among others, have, at various periods, operated in these parts; and their presence made sea voyages far more perilous than they would otherwise have been. The victims of piracy, and the ships looted by pirates are innumerable, and there have even been examples in the 20th century. There are only a few pirates from ancient times whose names we know, and some of these have been mentioned in earlier chapters. From recent centuries, though, many are known to us, either from books or from the folklore and folk history of the island, which the old people still recall.

The history of piracy in the Northern Sporades begins with the Dolopians, who established themselves very quickly, often with the help of local inhabitants. The Minoans were the first to clear the Aegean of the scourge of piracy, but after the collapse of Minoan civilisation the pirates came back in even greater force. Many maritime city states, inspired by the idea of quick profit, devoted themselves to piracy. Cimon of ATHENS came towards the end of the Archaic Period and restored order to the sea routes, but Athenian control was short lived.

Throughout the classical and Hellenistic periods the level of piracy steadily increased, reaching a peak in the Roman period. Through superhuman efforts the power of Rome defeated the pirates, the fear and terror of the seas. But anarchy returned to the northern Aegean during the Byzantine period, despite the efforts of the emperors to maintain control. In the medieval period piracy flourished as never before, with crusaders (who often had the blessing of the great Catholic powers), Arabs, and fellow Greeks all operating as pirates in our waters. With the foundation of the Greek state, the first President, Kapodhístrias, initiated a campaign to stamp out piracy in the Aegean. There were still isolated cases of piracy right up to the Second World War,[1] but after Greek Independence the fear of piracy was no longer widespread.

Pirate attacks in our region have been of two principal kinds. The first was invasion by large pirate fleets which took possession of our islands, looted them and used them as refuges and bases for their operations. Sometimes these were the fleets of independent pirates, sometimes they belonged to some ruler who plundered the islands on the pretext of military necessity. The second kind was the surprise attack on unsuspecting ships by pirate gangs using small boats, propelled by oars or sail. For the first category there is no shortage of written evidence, but for the second we must often turn to folk tales to supplement what little hard evidence we have.

Before we survey what is known about pirates operating in and around Alónnisos and the smaller islands in the 19th century, let us look first at a local folk song, still sung by some of the old people of Alónnisos. The text of this carnival song was given to me by the folklorist, Athanásios Páppos who has studied the folk culture of the island.[2] The song gives us a glimpse of the torments that our impoverished ancestors suffered at the hands of pirates.

Out of the East in a golden ship, out of the East we came
And on the ship twelve pashas sat. How beautifully they sang!
And on the ship twelve wretched slaves, twelve slaves there, bound in chains.
And one of the slaves let out a groan, and all the ship stood still.
The captain heard the poor slave's groan and from the stern he cried,
'Which is the man who groaned so loud and all the ship stood still?
If he's a member of the crew, then my house shall be his.
And if he's one of my galley slaves, I swear I'll set him free.'
The slave spoke out, 'Twas I that groaned and all the ship stood still.'
'Are you hungry, Slave? Are you thirsty? Have you no clothes to wear?'
'Not hungry, Sir, nor thirsty, Sir, and I have clothes to wear.

But I suddenly thought of hearth and home and the plight of my poor wife.
I was but three days a bridegroom and now twelve years a slave,
Twelve years seen none but foreign lands, none but barbarian shores,
For nine years eaten bitter fruit, and never a glimpse of freedom.'
A fine swift horse they found for him, a whip placed in his hand.
'Godspeed, then, Slave,' the captain said, 'your freedom's well deserved.'
No sooner had he said goodbye than he'd gone forty miles.
By the time the captain's words were done, he'd made it eighty-five.
And as he raced along the road, and as he flew along,
An old man in a field he spied and he was tending sheep.
'God bless you and good day, old man.' 'And God bless you, my boy.'
'Long life to you, but tell me now to whom this field belongs.'
'To darkness 'n' desolation, boy, to my poor son Yannákis,
That was but three days a bridegroom, and now twelve years a slave.
And his poor wife this very day must wed another man.'
'Long life to you, but tell me quick, can I get there in time?'
'If your horse be swift enough, my boy, you'll reach the house in time.'
And as he raced along the road, and as he flew along,
An old dame by the stream he spied and she was washing clothes.
'God bless you and good day, old dame.' 'And God bless you, my boy.'
'Long life to you, but tell me now to whom these clothes belong.'
'To darkness 'n' desolation, boy, to my poor son Yannákis,
That was but three days a bridegroom, and now twelve years a slave.
And his poor wife this very day must wed another man.'
'Long life to you, but tell me quick, can I get there in time?'
'If your horse be swift enough, my boy, you'll reach the house in time.'
He whips his horse, he spurs it on, he bursts into the house.
'Make way, my friends. Stand back, you guests. The bride must treat us all.'
And with the first drink that she pours she holds him with her eyes.
She pours the first, she pours one more, all fix their eyes on him.
And when she knows for sure it's him, she stops and cries aloud,
'Ladies, go home. And all you guests, go back now to your houses.
My husband has returned to me, my darling has come back.'
They fall into each other's arms, expire like burnt-out candles.

Some of the pirates active in the early 19th century also played a role in the revolutionary movements that led eventually to the establishment of the independent Greek state, which was internationally recognised in 1830. Because of the great distance from the centres of the revolutionary movements, and because of its small population, Alónnisos did not generally play an active part in the important events that liberated Greece from slavery;[3] though its few sailors and their ships no doubt served the national cause.

The only man from the island positively known to have fought against the Turks during the Revolution of 1821 was a certain Captain Mengés. After the struggle he returned to the island as a cleric. In the register of male citizens of the *Dhímos* of Alónnisos he is listed as Dhimítrios Papavasilíou, and this name also appears in a document of 1829. Since that time all the descendants of Papavasilíou have been addressed as Mikés (possibly the forename of Captain Mengés before he assumed a new name as a cleric).

Figure 9.2 Patitíri, 1958. *Courtesy of Athanásios Páppos.*

From the middle of the 18th century various revolutionary movements sprang up in Thessaly, Macedonia, Évvia, Chalkidhikí, to name only the areas closest to the Northern Sporades. But the size of the Turkish army, the lack of support from abroad and the hasty and disorganised nature of their actions condemned these movements to failure.

9.1 Revolutionary Buccaneers before the War of Independence[4]

In 1806 Nikótsaras raised the flag of freedom and, using our islands as a base and refuge, launched attacks against areas under Turkish rule. In the spring of that year he came to Alónnisos to enlist volunteers for his fleet. Many of those he recruited were revolutionary soldiers who had fled to the islands to escape the reprisals of the ruthless governor of Epirus, Ali Paşa. On 10 July 1807 Nikótsaras returned and anchored in the strait between Alónnisos and Peristéra, where he captured a ship belonging to Angelís Limiótis, as a contemporary witness, Ioánnis Inglésis, reported in a letter to the people of Skópelos.

In 1807 Yánnis Stathás founded his Free Greek Fleet which was based in the Northern Sporades. Stathás gathered together a fleet of some seventy ships with which he made devastating raids on Turkish-held lands. They were pursued by the furious Turks but managed to escape and return to their refuge in the Sporades. So great was the devastation caused by their raids, that they were seen as posing a threat to the stability of the Ottoman Empire. The Sultan was obliged to command Ali Paşa to grant an amnesty to stem the tide of dangerous refugees escaping to the islands from mainland Greece.

In 1808 Papavlachávas took up the reins. Though his movement had some success on land, it was at sea that he really distinguished himself. From Kassándhra (the western finger of Chalkidhikí) he transferred his sphere of operations to the Northern Sporades. Based on Skópelos, with the help of the islanders he built a fleet of fast warships. He inflicted incalculable damage on the Turks, but the Sultan later thought it prudent to grant him an amnesty.

After the deaths of Stathás and Papavlachávas, the revolutionary struggle was taken up by other pirates, notable among them Yeóryos Zorbás, Vássos, Dhoumbiótis, Tsélios and the Lázos brothers. They were fearsome men who inflicted great damage on the Turks. With their small fleet they would spread out and strike various areas that were under the Turkish yoke. After an attack they would return to the Northern Sporades and remain there for a while.

According to tradition, Nikólaos Tsélios, began his piratical career on Peristéra, where he commanded a gang of buccaneers. Their usual tactic was to make surprise attacks on ships using the much frequented passage to the east of Peristéra. Near the cape which is now named after him, he would hide in a bay with his fast 12-oared boat. When the lookout gave the signal that there was easy prey approaching, the pirates would emerge from their hideout and row hard until they overtook some slow-moving sailing boat.[5]

Tsélios first appears on the stage of history in 1815, when he engaged in a battle at Márkesi on Skíros with the forces of the local Turkish naval commander. In their rage after the battle, the Turks unjustly accused the Skirians of harbouring pirates and hanged two of the village elders. In 1816 Tsélios increased the size of his band by joining forces with Liólios, another famous pirate of the period, and together they raided Skíros.

The vicious attack was successful and very profitable. They looted and destroyed more than thirty houses; several young women were raped or taken prisoner. Some of the women were later returned in exchange for ransom. As a consequence of this catastrophe many of the Skirians were unable to pay their heavy Turkish taxes and were obliged to leave the island, fleeing to Psará, Chíos or Smyrna, not only to escape the local Turkish authorities, but also in fear of a second attack by the pirate fleet.

9.2 Pirates Hunted by the Turkish Navy

The islanders' initial enthusiasm for the rebels gave way to resentment in the face of their insatiable demands for food and war materials, and they became unwilling to help them further. A state of enmity set in between the arrogant sea captains and the ordinary people of the islands, and battles ensued. Even in Alónnisos there were several skirmishes, though generally the people of the island, who were few in number, adopted a servile attitude towards the numerous and demanding pirate gangs. On Skíros, after the raids of Tsélios and Liólios, the locals came to loathe and detest the pirates. They even went as far as to co-operate with the Turkish admiral, Topal Paşa whose forceful intervention put an end, for the time being, to the pirates' activities among the smaller islands, forestalling total devastation. It was in the aftermath of these events that our islands were first called the Dhemonónisi ("Devil's Islands"). The Turks called the islands Şeytan Adaları (which means the same), and the pirate flotillas they called tayfalar (in Greek, *taïfádhes,* 'troops' or 'troopships').

Márkos was one of the pirates hunted down by the Turks, who had put a price on his head. Pursued by a large Turkish caravel Márkos and his crew had sought refuge on Yoúra, an island whose numerous caves could easily shelter 500 people or more. The caravel had anchored on the east side of Yoúra to take on water. Márkos, thinking that even if they came after him the Turks would never be able to find him on this wild island, fired on them from a cliff directly above the ship and killed several of their men. The startled Turks put out to sea, but when they spotted Márkos' band scrambling up the mountainside and saw how few of them there were, they felt humiliated, and determined to terrify this shameless 'infidel'.[6]

They dropped anchor at Megáli Vála, a deep bay at the south end of Yoúra, and landed a large party of soldiers, who made their way to the monastery. Either because they were threatened by the Turks, or because they did not have good relations with Márkos and his pirates, the eleven monks living there at the time, betrayed the pirates' hideout to the officer in charge. One of the monks led the way to Márkos' cave, the same cave that today, for the benefit of tourists, is called 'the Cyclops' Cave'. (This cave is currently being excavated and many important finds have come to light.)[7]

The pirate on guard saw them coming and informed his captain. But the Turks were now quite close; it was too late for the pirates to escape. They were trapped within range of the Turks' flintlocks, and a battle ensued. The Turks greatly outnumbered the pirates and drove them back inside the cave, where they kept them pinned down for several days. Eventually, driven by hunger, Márkos and the other survivors, tried to break out. They were exhausted and in an impossible position, and did not manage to get past the enemy. They dispatched a number of Turks, but in the end they all fell.

The game warden, K. Kiriazís, told me that not so long ago there were large quantities of lead among the stones at the entrance to the cave – concrete evidence of the battle that took place there. In the 1960s, though, some Alonnisiot fisherman took away all the lead and melted it down to make weights for fishing nets.

After the battle, the Turks buried the dead, thanked the monks and departed. But this was not the end of the story, for one of Márkos' men had managed to remain concealed in the cave. When the danger had passed, he made his way to the monastery at night and killed all the monks as revenge for their betrayal. For almost 150 years the skeletons of the monks lay undisturbed in a cave near the monastery until they were destroyed by cows belonging to the game warden. There is an alternative story to explain skeletons in the cave. Because of its great height the island of Yoúra is often struck by lightning. On that particular day, so the story goes, it was raining and ten of the eleven monks were in the church for the usual

Figure 9.3 Boatyard, Patitíri, 1961. *Courtesy of Nikólaos Agállou.*

services. They had sent the eleventh, the youngest monk, to fetch water from the boat and to see that everything was alright. Returning to the monastery, the young monk was surprised by the total silence. When he entered the church he found all the other monks dead, struck down by a bolt of lightning. Since he couldn't open the stone tombs single-handed, he dragged the bodies to the nearest cave, about 200 m west of the church.

The first tradition seems the better explanation of the ten skeletons, though the second is not improbable, since even in recent decades the game wardens who lived on Yoúra would dash out of their houses at the first sign of lightning to seek refuge in the caves.

9.3 The War of Independence (1821–28)

After the outbreak of the War of Independence in 1821 (referred to in Greek as 'the Revolution'), and the initial failure of the revolutionary movement in most of mainland Greece, many of those who had taken part fled to the Northern Sporades. The total number of refugees in Skópelos and Skiáthos at this period reached about 70,000; and the present population of Alónnisos is largely descended from revolutionary refugees from Thessaly, Macedonia and Évvia.

To begin with the islanders welcomed these bedraggled revolutionaries, but they became so numerous that the islands could not feed them. Hunger and destitution pushed many of them into piracy, and serious problems developed between the pirates and the other islanders. Many of the military leaders of the revolution became ferocious pirates, using force of arms to sequester local boats, sinking the boats they did not need, and engaging in looting and killing.

The most famous of the revolutionaries from Thrace and Macedonia who took to piracy were Karatásos and Yátsos, while the most bloodthirsty of all of them was Captain Stirianós. The local population suffered a great deal at the hands of these cruel leaders.

Besides, the presence of the revolutionaries put the islands at risk of Turkish reprisals, and this was a further cause of resentment towards the revolutionary pirates. The arrival of Turkish troops could mean the wholesale slaughter of the population, as indeed happened on the island of Psará, near the coast of Asia Minor. Consequently, the islanders lived in constant fear of the Turkish fleet, as the following stories illustrate.

There was, at this time, an old woman who went every Saturday evening to the church of the Análipsis (Ascension) which overlooks the sea at the northern end of Alónnisos,[8] to light a candle.

One Saturday, in the summer of 1824, when she had lit her candle, she felt tired and fell asleep by the church. While she was sleeping a woman dressed in black appeared and woke her, saying, 'Get up', but the old woman was so tired that she just fell asleep again. The same woman appeared again and prodded her, this time saying, 'Get up! the Turks are coming.'

The old woman opened her eyes and saw frigates approaching. Running as best she could she reached the village about an hour before dawn.

When the sun rose the frigates could be seen heading for the port below the village. The people hid all their valuable possessions and anything made of copper and went to the Church of Áyos Nikólaos[9] to pray. Suddenly the wind picked up and the frigates set off eastwards. It was this fleet that shortly afterwards burned the island of Psará from end to end.

On another occasion a frigate appeared at Vrisítsa, north of the village. The villagers went to hide near the church of the Panayía,[10] where there was virgin oak forest. (In times of famine, the villagers made bread from acorns.) A little boy called Yórgos was crying from hunger. When the villagers saw the Turks approaching the cemetery nearby, the boy's father killed his child to prevent his cries giving away their position. The villagers spent the night outside among the trees and returned to their houses only when the frigates had left.

Figure 9.4 Boat belonging to Agóstrofos in trouble after a southerly gale, Patitíri, 1965.

Near Yérakas there was a small hamlet of herdsmen's houses. For fear of pirates it had been built inland, where it couldn't be seen from the sea. The Turks got to hear of it, though, and the fleet made a surprise attack. They took the animals and anything they found of value. The old people they killed, and the others they took to sell as slaves. Before they left they set fire to the houses, and this locality has ever since been known as *Stachtomágaza* ('Ash-houses').

9.4 The Greek State's Campaign against Piracy

The successful outcome of the Revolution led to the creation of a nation state of Greece, which included the Northern Sporades but not the adjacent mainland regions of Thessaly and Macedonia. Continuing piracy was one of the most pressing problems confronting the new state. The government received petitions from the elders of Skiáthos, Skópelos, Skíros and Iliodhrómia (Alónnisos), asking that measures be taken against the pirates, and Kapodhístrias, the Greek President (*Kivernítis*), entrusted Admiral Andhréas Miaoúlis with the task of stamping out piracy in the Northern Sporades.

Miaoúlis set out on 18 February 1828 with the frigate, *Ellás*, the gunboat, *Filéllines*, and an armed fishing boat. With his great daring and his prestige as one of the great leaders of the War of Independence, the famous admiral succeeded, through a combination of force and diplomacy, in carrying out his mission. A total of 79 pirate ships surrendered to Miaoúlis. He set fire to 41, sent 29 to Póros to add to the Greek fleet, and took six with him. In the previous year (1827) pirates in the region had attacked and looted 80 ships. Now many of them were taken to military camps in mainland Greece. The idea was to turn them into regular soldiers, and save the islands from their destructive activities. The Greek authorities understood that it was only poverty and hunger that had driven many of them to piracy.

Figure 9.5 Building development at Patitíri, 1965.

Many of the pirate captains and crews from the Northern Sporades were rounded up and taken to a military base at Elefsína, near Athens. But some, including Mítros Liakópoulos, Yeóryos Zorbás, Stávros Vasilíou, Karatásos and Dhoumbiótis, remained on the islands and continued to enrich themselves through piracy. Their great success encouraged many of those who were in the camp at Elefsína to make their escape and return to their islands to resume their piratical activities. The government ships would take them away, but they kept breaking out and coming back. Those pirates who had remained on the islands all along at first offered the justification that their families would not be safe anywhere else. Later they changed their tune and said that the Turks of Tríkeri were planning to attack the islands and their families would certainly be in danger if they were not there to protect them.

The activities of the pirates affected not only the people of the Northern Sporades but also those on nearby mainland coasts, both Greek and Turkish, and even the monks of Mount Athos. When the local pirate leaders combined forces with those who had escaped from Elefsína, they were once more a formidable force, and no ships could travel safely in our waters. The most terrible of all these pirates was Mítros Liakópoulos. A petition from the elders of Skópelos to Anastásios Lóndos, the *epítropos* (chairman) of the governing committee for the Northern Sporades, gives an account of acts of piracy committed in Skántzoura at this time:

> We consider it our duty to inform you that Panayótis Poúpas, a Skiathite, who is here now, having just arrived from the port of Skíros, which he left yesterday, saw, with his own eyes, soldiers, about forty in number, making their escape from the camp in a *trechandíri*[11] and proceeding towards Linariá.[12] As soon as they arrived there they spotted a *skambavía* coming from Kími [in Évvia] and attacked and captured it. The *skambavía* was loaded with flour and sheep's butter belonging to Krizótos' son.
>
> Yesterday evening they tied the aforesaid *trechandíri* to the *skambavía* which they had captured at Skíros and went to Skántzoura where they captured another boat, a *sakolévi* loaded with barley. The leaders of these men, Liákos Kartaválas among them, are the vilest and most wicked of mariners, and they also approached the ship of the aforesaid Panayótis, intent on plundering that too, and would have succeeded if Mr Michális, the brother of Apostaláras, had not been present, for he recognised them and spoke to them and prevented them from plundering it.
>
> They told him that they intended to go to Kirá Panayá and, if they could get there, to take away their families who had been living on the island. Michális told them that their families and many others had already fled from there. We have taken the necessary measures, as far as we are able, that is to say, we have set the necessary guards on all the beaches of our island, and tonight we are all standing by and keeping watch. As regards these matters please advise us as soon as possible what is to be done.
>
> We remain, your obedient servants, in Skópelos, 16 June 1828, T.S. Aléxandhros Dhapóndes, Konstandís Englézou, Konstandínos Trimakoúlis.

This is some indication of the anarchy that reigned in the Northern Sporades in that year. Kapodhístrias was obliged to intensify his efforts to root out the cancer of piracy. This time he appointed Aléxandhros Mavrokordhátos and Captain Andónis Kriezís to assist Admiral Miaoúlis in the renewed campaign. Other prominent officers involved included Kanáris and Papanikolís. Government order No. 24, issued on 23 January 1829, instructed Miaoúlis

> to depart with all speed for the islands of Skópelos, Skiáthos, Skíros and Iliodhrómia [Alónnisos] and to take such measures as your wisdom and experience shall dictate. To this end you have the authority to issue proclamations to the local people, and orders to the local elders and soldiery, in order, by those means, to control and direct affairs in such a manner as to put an end once and for all to the sufferings of the inhabitants, restore order in internal affairs, and remove every pretext for, and means of

> contributing to, criminal acts and piracy, many of which are attributable to the local soldiery.

This brilliant admiral would achieve two objectives in this campaign. The second objective, after stamping out piracy, was to strengthen the official Greek navy through the sequestration of the pirates' ships.

One of Miaoúlis principal targets was Nikólaos Tsélios whose piratical activities have already been referred to. A cutter from Miaoúlis' fleet cornered Tsélios inside the harbour of Planítis on Kirá Panayá. The harbour has only a single narrow entrance, and there was no way out for Tsélios. The devilish pirate suddenly hit on the solution. He and his crew went ashore in a small auxiliary boat. There he commanded his puzzled men to get the boat on their shoulders as fast as they could and head off towards the interior of the island. Carrying the boat they quickly made their way overland to Vromopigádha, on the west coast of the island, thus escaping certain arrest. From Vromopigádha, rowing hard, they made the passage to Alónnisos, leaving the astounded sailors in the cutter to follow them as best they could. The Greek authorities never apprehended Tsélios and both he and his partner, Liólios, died in Istanbul.

Verónis was a pirate who had had good relations with the people of Alónnisos over a long period. When the wind was in the south he would tie up at Yália (a bay on the west coast, just north of Palió Chorió), but in other weathers he anchored on the east coast at Rousoúm, by the large flat rocks on the northern headland of the bay, which has since been known as Cape Verónis.

For the poor people of Alónnisos, Verónis was a kind of Robin Hood. He shared out the foodstuffs he had looted and provided dowries for many of their daughters. He was best man at weddings and a godfather at baptisms and generally developed friendly relations with the islanders. The village elders even gave him fields, in the area now known as Choúni Veróni. (Verónis' Vale) near Patitíri. It is said that, when the newly founded Greek state was clearing the area of pirates, a certain Dhrosákis informed the authorities about the connections between the Alonnisiots and the pirate.

Verónis then sent an ultimatum to the inhabitants of Palió Chorió: either they handed Dhrosákis over to him or he would burn down the entire village (which then consisted of 32 houses). The people of the island were divided into two parties: those who wanted to deliver the traitor to the pirate, and those who were against it. The latter won out, and the entire population was obliged to move temporarily to neighbouring Skópelos, for fear that Verónis would carry out his threat. The pirate came upon an old woman at Agállou Láka,[13] and asked her why there was no one working in the fields. She explained to him the ins and outs of the situation, and Verónis sent two of his men to the deserted village to burn half the houses, the ones whose owners supported Dhrosákis.

Later Verónis was granted an official amnesty by the Greek state. He returned to Alónnisos and got married. He took on the responsibility of protecting the island. The other pirates were all afraid of him, and attacked Alónnisos only when Verónis himself was away. Unfortunately he had only daughters and his name died out. He had married into the Alexíou family.

Figure 9.6 Constructing the harbour, Patitíri, 1971 (a).

Figure 9.7 Constructing the harbour, Patitíri, 1971 (b).

Captain Makrís and his gang were based on Pipéri and attacked merchant vessels passing both east and west of the island.. There were five members of the gang, and they would take up lookout posts at high points along the ridge of the island. Each was within sight of the next man or men in the chain, and when one of them spotted some ship within the area of their operations, he would inform the others by signs and they would all run as fast as they could to Sikiá to launch their boat. In those days the monastery's shipyard was at Sikiá, near the north end of the island, on the west coast, and it was paved with stone slabs. (It was destroyed in 1944 by a storm of unprecedented violence.) From the shipyard, the pirates would row hard and attack the ship with muskets. They would loot it, usually killing the crew, unless they were locals, in which case they would demand ransom for their release.

The pirates had made their homes in caves on the island and had developed good relations with the local monks. On the monks' side the good relations were partly motivated by fear, but they also benefited from the pirates' presence, since the pirates regularly gave them a share of the spoils, things that were of no use to the pirates, or superfluous to their needs, including food, fabrics, candles, books and household utensils.

Figure 9.8 Patitíri, 1971. *Courtesy of Athanásios Páppos.*

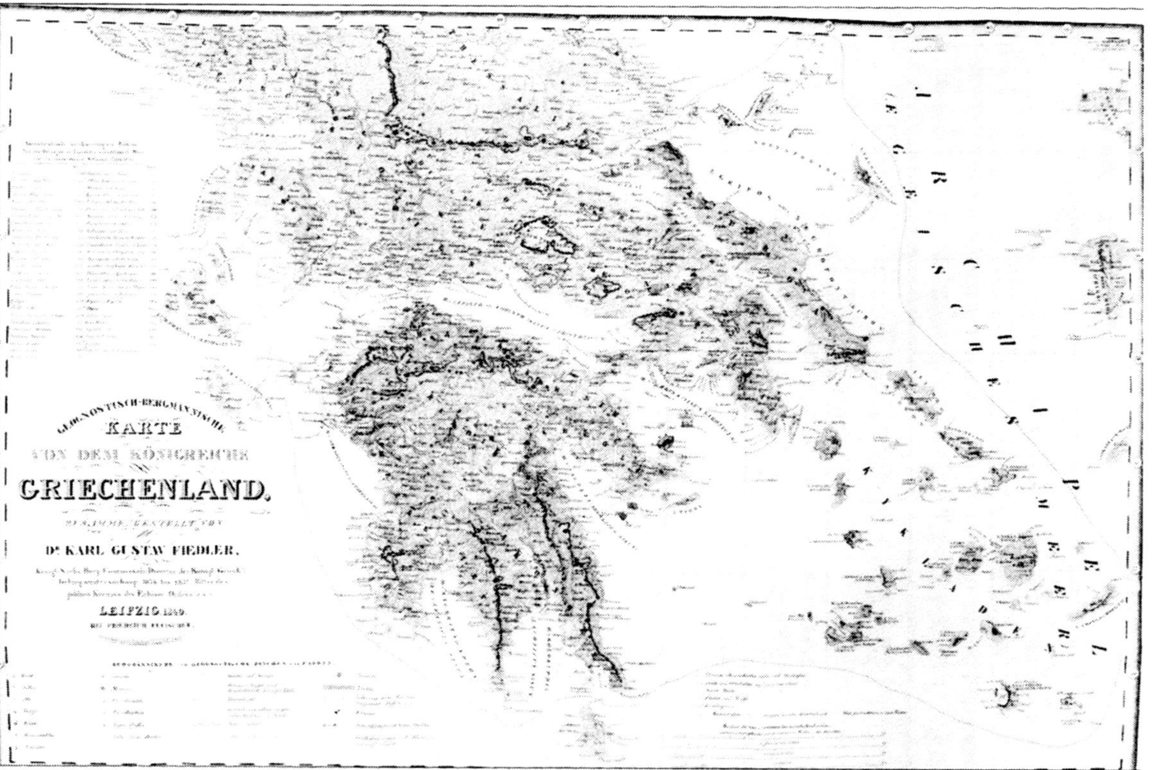

Map 10 The original boundaries of the Greek State as they were from 1830 to 1863. During this period piracy gradually declined. *Source*: *Kóstas and Angéla Mavríkis' collection of old maps.*

The other members of Captain Makrís' gang were Líkas, Stamoúlis, Mítros and Pólikas. Their activities were known to the Greek government, and when Miaoúlis sent Kanáris to Alónnisos and the smaller islands to flush out the pirates, Kanáris undertook to confront members of the gang on Pipéri. The story goes that he first captured their boat and thus prevented their escape. He then landed two parties of soldiers, one on either side of the island and took the pirates by surprise. Líkas and Mítros were killed in the struggle. The pirates, however, killed two of the government soldiers.

Stamoúlis gave himself up but the officers, enraged by the death of their comrades, hanged him from a pine tree in the place since known ironically as *tou Stamoúli i Vígla* (Stamoúlis' Lookout). The other two, the leader Makrís and his right-hand man, Pólikas, were pursued and eventually surrounded on a hilltop. What happened next gave rise to a story of the hidden treasure that did the rounds in Alónnisos. Makrís handed Pólikas his gun to hold off the pursuers, giving Makrís time to run and hide several leather bags full of spoils in some hole or crevice and run back to their vantage point. In the ensuing battle, Makrís was soon shot dead; Pólikas gave up without offering any further resistance and was led away for trial.

There is, however, another version of the arrest of the pirates. According to this story, one of the pirates was sick and the others left him behind while they went to Áyos Efstrátios. If there was any danger, he was to light three fires in the night. The sick pirate was found by field guards and gave away the signal. The field guards promptly lit the three fires. The next morning the pirates arrived at Pipéri to see what was going on. The field guards took their boat and surrounded them in their mountain retreat. The rest of the story is the same. From that day to this, the story of the hidden treasure has continued to gain ground, and Makrís' treasure is still discussed on Alónnisos today.

Manólas was a ruthless pirate based on the small island on the west side of Alónnisos which has since been named after him. On this island there are sea caves where he concealed his boat. Manólas and his band lived permanently on the island and slept in the caves. Their base was a strategic point, from which they could watch both the western side of the island and the channel between Alónnisos and Skópelos. They would observe all the movements of ships and calculate when to attack. In their fast rowing boat they made surprise attacks on heavy sailing ships. They also attacked unsuspecting boats which anchored overnight in the nearby harbour of Agállou Láka, or further south at Vrisítsa. It is probable that Manólas' pirate band was exterminated by the government troops. Manólas himself is said to have died of wounds on his island.[14]

Stéfanos was a pirate based on Peristéra, which, though less mountainous than Yoúra or Pipéri, is difficult to land on and riddled with caves. Stéfanos had his hideout on the rugged hill of Stefáni, since named after him. His skull still lies today next to a prominent rock called *i patsá tou Stefáni* ('Stéfanos' Footprint'). There is a mark on the rock shaped like a footprint. It is said that one day when Stéfanos stepped onto this rock he was immediately shot down by government officials. Another story which has been passed from mouth to mouth, but has some historical basis, concerns the hunting down and capture of three pirates who lived on, and operated from, Alónnisos, where the local population had suffered much at their hands. After the village elders had lodged a complaint against them, a cutter of the Greek customs authorities came to the island.

The pirates were hiding out at Leptós Yalós, on the eastern side of the island. There they ordered the shepherd who had given them hospitality to kill a kid and roast it for them. As they were eating, the captain read the shoulder-blade[15] and became frightened. He ordered his men to set off for Yérakas (at the north end of Alónnisos) and to steal a boat there so that they could escape to some other island. A detachment from the cutter set off in pursuit and, led by the shepherd from Leptós Yalós, they soon picked up their tracks. Later though they lost them, and might not have found them again if the customs officers had not spotted a garter which one of the pirates had lost. When they reached the harbour at Yérakas, the officers saw a boat already disappearing into the distance. On the boat were the three pirates and a man from the small settlement nearby whom they had taken hostage. The frightened relatives of the hostage had gathered that the pirates were heading for Pipéri.

The commander of the detachment sent a shepherd on foot to the village to tell the crew of the cutter to pick them up at Yérakas. The cutter arrived in the evening and by dawn the next day they were at Pipéri. The pirates saw them come ashore to pursue them, and set off at a run for the other side of the island to make their escape by boat from the monastic shipyard. But the chief customs officer who knew he was dealing with cunning rogues, had had the foresight to send another, smaller detachment to guard the boat. The pirates made an attempt to launch the boat but in their haste and fear they knocked it off its supports. In the end they gave themselves up and the customs officers promised them an amnesty. However, when they got the pirates to Skópelos, they killed them.

The English traveller and archaeologist, Allan Wace, visited Skiáthos in 1905 and gathered information about the history of the island. He gives an illuminating account of the problems posed by pirates from Alónnisos for the people of Skiáthos:

> The new town [Skiáthos] has existed only since the foundation of the Greek kingdom. Before that the people lived in Kástro, which is now a deserted fortress on a rocky headland at the northernmost point of the island. The tip of the headland, on which the castle stands, has been cut off by human agency, and the channel formed is spanned by a bridge, which has now fallen into disrepair. [...] Facing inland, a strong gate protected the bridge, and the little artificial island itself was surrounded by a wall. The inhabitants withdrew into this almost inaccessible nest out of fear of the pirates who had their hideouts on the deserted islands around Alónnisos, and especially those between that island and Peristéra. That is why those lonely reefs were called the Devil's Islands. The pirates became such a nuisance that the Greek government was obliged to send Kanáris himself to root them out. It is said that on one occasion the pirates even managed to seize the castle, attacking from the north where the rock slopes down towards the sea.[16]

Two other pirates, Andriótis and Kóros, who were both active on Alónnisos are worthy of mention. Andriótis controlled the main approach to the channel between Alónnisos and Skópelos. He kept his boat hidden in the cave that now bears his name and he lived above it.

Figure 9.9 Patitíri, 1972. *Courtesy of Athanásios Páppos.*

On the seaward side of the hill known as Vounó, north of Palió Chorió, there are a number of small concealed openings which lead into large underground chambers. These the pirates had adapted to their needs, so that they could live there and maintain a constant watch on passing ships. Their tactics were the same as those of other pirates, overtaking large ships in their fast rowing boat. They brought the spoils back to their caves and exchanged them with other pirate crews or with receivers of stolen goods who had connections on Skópelos.

Kóros used to beach his boat on the islet that now bears his name in the bay of Glifá. He lived in a cave above the bay in the spot known as Tsoukaná Choúni (Tsoukanás' Vale) and from there controlled the narrow sheltered harbour of Stení Vála, immediately to the south. Kóros probably attacked the larger boats that tied up in the harbour for the night. The crews, exhausted after a long day's sailing, would not realise in time that they were being attacked and would be slaughtered or find themselves prisoners of the cunning pirates. The story goes that Kóros hid his treasure on the island now known as Kóros, and, sure enough, at the beginning of the 20th century, a local man found a pot full of coins there.

9.5 Piracy in the Kingdom of Greece

As a result of the concerted efforts of Kapodhístrias and his admiral Miaoúlis, there was a period of respite from piracy. But after the assassination of Kapodhístrias (in which, incidentally, the son of the pirate, Tsélios, played a part), anarchy ensued as three factions fought ferociously for power, bringing the country to the brink of civil war.

Personal interests undermined the order that Kapodhístrias had brought to Greece; the public treasury was emptied; and the Northern Sporades were overwhelmed once more by pirates. In 1832 the people of Iliodhrómia (Alónnisos) complained repeatedly to the *éparchos* (governor) of the Northern Sporades that the situation on the island had become insupportable, in consequence of the barbaric behaviour of the pirates.

Under the terms of the London Protocol of 1830 Greece was to become a monarchy. Eventually, in 1832, a young Bavarian prince named Otto from the House of Wittelsbach was chosen, with the approval of Britain, France and Russia, to become the first King of the Hellenes. Otto did not arrive in Greece until 1833 and for the first two years of his reign, until he came of age, power was in the hands of a Regent.

Under the new regime, fresh measures were undertaken for the suppression of piracy. After a further decade of concerted action the newly constituted kingdom achieved its objective. Nevertheless, isolated acts of piracy and pillaging continued for many years, particularly in remote regions like the outer Northern Sporades which then lay only just inside Greek territorial waters. The most northerly frontier between Greece and the Ottoman Empire was 14 nautical miles north of Psathoúra, and our islands continued to serve as a refuge for pirates who raided the shores of Turkish Macedonia. When King Otto visited Pipéri in 1841, the fear of pirates was still very much a fact of life, as the following story illustrates.

Figure 9.10 Drawing up a caïque, Patitíri, 1973. *Courtesy of Fótis Tzortzátos.*

At that time, old Físos lived on Pipéri. He was an Alonnisiot shepherd, from the Agállou family, who kept flock of goats on Yoúra. His strength and appearance were such that the pirates feared and respected him, though they were generally on good terms with him. Físos welcomed them to his house and gave them food, while they supplied him with tobacco and gunpowder. It was mainly in the winter that the pirates used Pipéri as their refuge.

A Greek from Asia Minor had entrusted his son, Líppas, to Físos' care. The boy had arrived with his gun, a silver musket and 120 gold pounds. On Pipéri the monks, shepherds and pirates all lived together amicably and everything was fine for a while. But one of the pirates, Karavélis, couldn't rest easy with the thought of the 120 pounds so close at hand. One day around noon, encountering the boy on the shore, he attacked and robbed him. Físos, or Patliás (meaning 'thicket') as he was also called on account of the dense mat of hair on his chest, realised that something was afoot. He asked Karavélis, 'Where's the boy?' but Karavélis could only mumble in reply. Físos tied him to a tree (which has since been uprooted) and went to find Líppas. He found the boy dead and returned to Karavélis in a fury. He made the three men gathered round him draw lots to see which one would execute Karavélis. The lot fell on V. Tzórtzis, but he was a good friend of Karavélis and refused to kill him. So Físos took his gun and shot Karavélis through the heart.

Later Físos was arrested and tried in the court at Chalkídha in Évvia. His sentence was light, though, and he was soon out of gaol. In prison he got to know some pirates who revealed to him where they had hidden their money, with the idea that Físos should bring them half of it when they were released from prison. Físos went to the spot they had described to him on the tiny island of Pappoús between Yoúra and Kirá Panayá. He found the money, took out half of it, but left it rather inadequately hidden, while he made a trip to Psathoúra, intending to pick it up on his way back. In the meantime, though, a Skopelite called Marlítsis who happened to land on Pappoús found the money. He took it and later used it to acquire a large property on Skópelos. Físos was ashamed to go back to Chalkídha and admit that the money had been stolen from under his nose. The pirates would never have believed him.

The rest of the money remained, and still remains, buried. This is one of the many local tales of hidden treasure. It is natural that wherever pirates have operated the existence of treasure hoards will be suspected. Today, though, the idea has taken such a hold on the popular imagination that many stories on this theme have been invented.

9.6 An Act of Piracy in the Early 1900s

In the early years of the 20th century, the Agállou family were living on Yoúra as shepherds, and they had good relations with pirates. Some pirates agreed to capture a boatload of sheep from Macedonia and to bring them to Yoúra for the Agállou family. In those days Macedonia was still Turkish, and the sheep belonged to Turkish landowners. The pirates duly stole the sheep and brought them to the island. The Agállou family promised to pay the pirates when they sold the lambs in the spring.

Figure 9.11 Patitíri, 1977. *Courtesy of Fótis Tzortzátos.*

At Easter the pirate captain went back to Yoúra to collect his debt. But he found only the Kiriazís family living there, and they knew nothing about the deal. They told them that the Agállou family had cleared off and gone to live in Peristéra. The pirate went to Peristéra and found them at Vasilikós. They were waiting for him. They had no money and no intention of paying, and now proceeded with the plot they had hatched.

Figure 9.12 Patitíri, 1981. *Courtesy of Kóstas and Karen Kaloyánnis.*

One of the Agállou men told the pirate to go round in his boat to Peristéri bay on the south coast of the island, taking one of the family with him; meanwhile he would go over the hill, collect the money on the way, and meet them on the beach. This Agállou ran and took up a position on Cape Mávros on the west side of the bay. When the boat came by, he fired at the pirate and killed him.

Some time later the relatives of the murdered man went to Yoúra in search of him. They threatened to kill the Kiriazís family, thinking it was for them that their relative had stolen the sheep. A certain Kiriazís was woken in the night by a noise outside his house, and in his terror he thought he could see someone there. To save himself he fired, but the suspicious shadow turned out to be one of his goats. The dead pirate's family with the help of the authorities eventually apprehended the Agállou who had shot him, and Agállou spent many years in gaol.

Notes

1. See p. 272.
2. Páppos published the song in the journal *Vórii Sporádhes* ('Northern Sporades') in November 1974. On Páppos himself, see p. 319.
3. Greeks commonly refer to the period of Turkish rule as *i Sklavía*, 'the [period of] Slavery'. [Translator]
4. Apart from the folk traditions of Alónnisos, the main sources for this and subsequent sections of the chapter are Kefalliniádhis (1984), Konstandinídhis (1988), Nasoúlis (1950), Theocháris (n.d.) and Dhapóndes (1994).
5. The same hideout was used again in the Second World War (see pp. 245–6).
6. *Giaoúris* in Greek, from the Turkish word gâvur, a derogatory term for non-Muslims.
7. For the archaeological significance of this cave, see pp. 102–4.
8. See pp. 339–41.
9. See pp. 330–1.
10. This church of the Panayía was probably the monastery of the *Kímisis tis Theotókou* (Dormition of the Virign) on the slopes of Vounó. [Translator]
11. The *trechandíri*, as well as the *skambavía* and *sakolévi* which are also referred to in this petition, are all varieties of small sailing ships. [Translator]
12. Linariá is a port on the west side of Skíros. [Translator]
13. A *láka* is an area of low-lying ground within a forest which has been cleared of trees and rocks and used for growing crops. There are many such fields on Alónnisos, known by the names of the families who owned them. In this case, though, Agállou Láka is also the name of a bay on the west side of the island. [Translator]
14. See pp. 63–4.
15. Reading the shoulder-blade is like reading tea-leaves or coffee grounds. Taking the shoulder-blade of an animal which has been cooked and eaten, the future is read from the shape of the bone and shape and position of any marks on it. [Translator]
16. Wace (1906), pp. 129–30.

10

LOCAL WAR HEROES, 1903–1922

AGAIN and again patriots from these islands answered their country's call. They gave of their best, fighting nobly, and did not dishonour their arms. In every phase of recent history we shall see the participation of our fellow islanders. They did not simply take part in the wars, but showed incomparable courage on all the critical fronts, and wrote their own history with their bodies. In honour of these modern heroes, of whom we should be proud, the following pages are written.

Unfortunately, by the time I was writing this book, most of them were already dead, and we could have no direct contact with them, but their relatives have helped enthusiastically with the project. I have added what little information I was able to glean from the archives of the Directorate of History of the Army General Staff,[1] and provided brief descriptions of the personalities of the combatants.

10.1 Local Heroes of the Macedonian Struggle (1903–1909)

The first combatants were those who took part in the Macedonian Struggle. At the beginning of the 20th century Alónnisos and the surrounding islands, with only about 600 inhabitants between them, constituted one of the most sparsely populated regions of Greece. By then, our islands had already been free from foreign rule for seventy years. The people had developed a national consciousness and were ready to help their small homeland of Greece extend its borders and become a significant European nation. Lying close to Macedonia, which was still under Turkish rule, these islands were of great strategic importance. The inhabitants of Alónnisos and of the lesser Northern Sporades were familiar with the Macedonia littoral through their trading activities, and were thus able to contribute to the military ventures of the partisan struggle in Macedonia (1903–09).

Miltiádhis Chrístou and Konstandínos Malamaténios from Alónnisos, and Theódhoros Athanasíou from Peristéra all responded voluntarily to the call of oppressed Macedonia. Greek it was and Greek it must remain. They left their families behind and risked their lives daily in the mountains and coastal plains of the neighbouring land, together with their fellow Greek combatants from Macedonia itself and from all parts of Greece. It is due to their initiative and self-sacrifice that the present borders of our country include the bloodstained earth of the descendants of Alexander the Great.

Athanasíou and Chrístou came back, honoured and proud, while Malamaténios sacrificed his life, fulfilling his ultimate duty to the nation.

10.1.1 Theódhoros Likoúrgou Athanasíou

Figure 10.1 Participant in the Macedonian Struggle, Theódhoros Athanasíou.

The Athanasíou family came to Alónnisos from Kerasiá in Évvia. Their ancestors were armed bandits who had risen up against the Turkish conquerors. When reinforcements from the Sultan arrived, the revolutionaries sought refuge in our islands. One of the Athanasíou warriors put down roots and established a permanent home here. Since then the Athanasíou family has become one of the largest and most successful families on our island. Likoúrgos Athanasíou moved to Peristéra and set himself up there, becoming engaged in stock rearing. His son, Theódhoros, a man of physical and mental vigour, grew up in that barren place, but left the island to become a soldier. While he was serving in the army, Macedonia, was suffering the incursions of Bulgarian *comitadjis*. These were members of parastate organisations that had the support of the Bulgarian authorities. Beneath the noses of the Turks, the *comitadjis* terrorised the Patriarchist Greeks, in their attempt to Bulgarise this ancient Greek region.[2] The *comitadjis* tortured, killed and used the most terrible methods to eliminate Greek culture.

It was during this campaign of terror that an event took place which led our patriot from Alónnisos to become a willing participant in the Macedonian Struggle. An entire school with all its Greek pupils was burned down by the cowardly Bulgarians. This so incensed Theódhoros that he determined to go to Macedonia and fight for his Greek compatriots. At this point the Greek Macedonia Committee in Athens had only just been inaugurated. Many officers 'on leave' and 'deserters' from the ranks, with the tacit approval of the Greek state, made their way to Macedonia to protect the Greeks from the inhuman conduct of the *comitadjis*. Among the first Greek partisans to set foot on Macedonian soil in 1903 (in fact, the fourth, according to military records) was Theódhoros Athanasíou. Theódhoros had been endowed by nature with many graces. He had good eyesight, a vigorous, well-trained body and, more importantly, a steady hand. This last gift, as we shall see, won him the title of best Balkan marksman. Theódhoros immediately put himself under the command of Pávlos Melás, and the two men were united in the silent friendship of comrades-in-arms. Now began the great struggle that was to last six years, and throughout that time the Greek partisans defended, and ultimately saved, Macedonia from the Bulgarian incursions. From the accounts of events provided by Theódhoros' descendants, I add the following particulars.

In the difficult conditions of guerrilla warfare, partisans had to fight the *comitadjis*, protect themselves from the Turks, make propaganda and avoid the local pro-Bulgarian informers. It is recognised now that Macedonia remained Greek thanks to the military acumen and the undivided patriotism of these Greek partisans. Theódhoros himself recalled that they had attacked the *comitadjis* many times. With a cape and a gun he would go around from village to village and encourage the Greeks, punishing criminals and traitors. And with only this cape he slept in the mountains in the bitter cold of the *vardháris* (a violent wind of southern Macedonia). The snow could be as much as a metre deep; and when it snowed the combatants would sit around a fire, waiting for the snow to stop and then freeze over, so that they could walk on it again. Theódhoros had the role of tracker and sniper. With his sharp eyesight he always went ahead of the others and enabled them to avoid traps or undesirable confrontations. His fame as a marksman even reached the Bulgarians, who promptly put a price on his head. On one occasion, from a distance of a kilometre, he managed to pick off a member of a group of *comitadjis* who were fleeing from a village that they had just looted and burned. As Theódhoros himself told his relations, the Macedonian partisans took no care for their own lives. In fierce battles and engagements, they fought with the confidence that they would always be the victors. Theódhoros himself always aimed to shoot his opponent in exactly the same spot on the body; and this for two reasons: first to ensure death was instantaneous; and secondly to leave his 'signature' on the victim. (Here it should be noted that the Mannlicher rifles of the Greeks were inferior to the Mausers used by the Bulgarians.)

Laying bets as to who would prove the best marksman was one of the very few forms of amusement these men had during the six-year struggle. Only rarely did they risk going down into the villages for other entertainment, for fear that they would be betrayed, as indeed they sometimes were. On one such occasion, when they found themselves surrounded in a village, they made holes in the brickwork of the houses and managed to creep out under the noses of the far more numerous Bulgarians. Both Pávlos Melás and, later, Thodhorís' immediate commander, Kóstas Garéfis, had such confidence in his personality and patriotism that they appointed him paymaster. In this capacity, Theódhoros handled all the money (in the form of Turkish pounds) which was used to pay those who killed enemies with a price on their heads, as well as for more routine matters such as buying provisions and paying informers.

Athanasíou also passed through a dreadful swamp, where, moving about in strange boats, both sides had to contend with appalling conditions. There he learned to smoke, to help to pass the long hours of immobility. Theódhoros was a comrade of Dhías, the famous messenger of the Macedonian Struggle. And Melás, valuing his character, used him for secret missions. Captain Garéfis, the leader of Theódhoros' band, intended, once the struggle in Macedonia was over, to unite their children in marriage. Garéfis was from Miliés in Pílio and wanted for a son-in-law a man like his first officer.

One day the band attacked the *comitadji* leaders, Loukás and Karatásos,[3] in a shack where they were sleeping. The Greeks had agreed on the password *lemóni* ('lemon'). Anyone emerging from the shack without giving the password was to be shot as a *comitadji* by the Greeks who stayed outside to cover the shack. Garéfis came out of the hut so pleased with his success that he forgot to give the password. As a result, he was shot and killed by his own men.[4] His band, which consisted of 17 men, was now dispersed to other sectors, and Theódhoros Athanasíou joined the band of Captain Zígras. Theódhoros had been with Garéfis for three years (1903–06) and was shattered by the death of his comrade and leader. The activities of Zígras and his band in central Macedonia were heroic and impressive. In their propaganda they used psychological tactics. Towards the end of the campaign a Macedonian village whose inhabitants were Bulgarians refused to go over to the Greek side. Then the Greek partisans, Athanasíou among them, rounded up all the village elders and began to argue with them. The elders maintained their stance until the Greek captain lit a match and warned them that they would have to decide before the match went out, otherwise he would burn them all. The bluff worked and one by one the Bulgarians changed their tune.

After the Macedonian Struggle, Athanasíou returned to his island, but was called up again by the prime minister Venizélos, to serve in the Balkan Wars of 1912–13. He was among the first Greeks to set foot in Thessalonica, when the Turks surrendered the city in November 1912. Later he was decorated for his part in the battle of Kilkís-Lachanás (June 1913).[5] The Bulgarian riflemen had no trouble picking off the Greek officers whose gold braid shone in the sun. Before the order came from the commander-in-chief not to wear gold braid, their only protection was provided by the Greek marksmen. Athanasíou was the most skilful of these, and he managed to kill the Bulgarians' best marksman from a distance of more than a thousand metres. This man was concealed on the opposite hillside, which was held by the Bulgarians, with only his head showing, on the lookout for Greek officers, who, however, did not dare to emerge from their trenches. Athanasíou pinpointed the marksman and for hours kept him covered. He would have to kill him with the first shot, otherwise the Bulgarian would take cover. Eventually, with absolute composure, he fired; and the enemy stayed where he was.

When King Constantine I requested to meet Athanasíou, he failed to recognise him, since Athanasíou was not wearing any insignia, and he spoke to him brusquely. Later the misunderstanding was cleared up and the king not only apologised to Athanasíou, but also congratulated him.[6] Later, in a contest of military skills between the Balkan armies, Athanasíou won first prize. The Queen of Greece was so excited by the contest and the victory of this man from Alónnisos that she presented him with her own gun, a Mannlicher bearing the royal insignia. This hero's weapon was respected even by the Germans who occupied the island in the 1940s. They not only did not take it, but saluted the hero in military fashion.[7] Later the gun was taken by the *Ierolochítes* who showed a complete lack of respect for the old campaigner. The *Ierolochítes* were members of the *Ierós Lóchos* ('Sacred Company'), an elite corps recruited and trained by the British in Egypt during the Second World War, in preparation for the liberation of Greece. They were picked for their royalist and anti-Communist views, and would have had little sympathy with members of the largely left-wing Greek Resistance with whom Theódhoros was involved.[8]

The exploits of Athanasíou continued in Peristéra. During the 1930s, at Paliofánaro, at the northern tip of Peristéra, he found a shipwrecked man, wrapped in a tarpaulin and on the point of death. Athanasíou carried him on his back all the way to his house, a distance of nine kilometres. There he gave him first aid and managed to save his life. In 1940 Athanasíou welcomed and gave refuge to many allied servicemen on the run from the Germans, as well as members of the Greek Resistance, including the partisan leaders, Koumoundhoúros (who was also a British Intelligence agent), Channás, and Artémis. Theódhoros and his tough wife Elisávet were tortured many times but they never gave away the identities or the activities of their companions. Many allies and local people owe their lives to this heroic couple from Vasilikós.

10.1.2 Miltiádhis Konstandínou Chrístou

Figure 10.2 Participant in the Macedonian Struggle, Miltiádhis Chrístou.

At the very beginning of the Macedonian Struggle, Miltiádhis Chrístou abandoned his family in order to offer his valuable services to the Greek cause. He left behind two infant daughters and a wife, and joined the band led by Theocháris Zarkádhas. His field of action was Eastern Macedonia, where the Greek partisans, who were few in number, were making superhuman efforts to control their sector. Each of their divisions had some speciality, for it required intelligent deployment of limited resources to confront naval as well as land-based forces. Miltiádhis' division handled the supplies for all the partisans in Macedonia, partclarly in the Yannitsá area (west of Thessalonica), but also wherever else there were shortges. They had to transport volunteers and munitions, avoiding informers as well as Turkish and Bulgarian forces. They had to move continually under the noses of the enemy and to co-ordinate their liaisons with absolute precision. Their service was the umbilical cord that linked the Greek partisans in the hinterland with Mother Greece. Provisions were brought across the border by train, though this was a risky business. From there the partisan captains of Eastern Macedonia assumed responsibility.

Figure 10.3 Captain Miltiádhis Chrístou.

Captain Miltiádhis had taken part in many missions. His sword, which his son recently showed me, was thoroughly battle-scarred. Miltiádhis was a friend of Pávlos Melás, who gave him a Mannlicher rifle. He also had very good relations with the irregular officers, Yaklís and Mitroúsis, who later stayed in his house on Alónnisos when matters got out of hand in Chalkidhikí. Captain Miltiádhis had no sense of danger and his reckless and heroic deeds showed him to be both an energetic combatant and a capable sailor. Later on, he smuggled out many allied servicemen – reportedly 1,186 in all – under the noses of the German and Italian occupying forces. For this he was specially honoured by the British Commander-in-Chief in the Middle East, Field-Marshall Alexander, who came to Alónnisos in a destroyer to decorate Miltiádhis Chrístou and his son Kóstas.[9]

Captain Miltiádhis was endowed with great strength, and had proved himself to be the best mountaineer on the island – the cliffs which he climbed with ease would tax the abilities of an experienced alpinist. Some of his exploits were extraordinary. One day he went to Skópelos to sell blackfish. On the shore at Skópelos twelve gendarmes were cursing and beating some locals, who were too frightened to defend themselves. Miltiádhis ran into the crowd and began to strike at the gendarmes, who fled in terror. Then, being drunk, the gendarmes quarrelled with their commander and beat him. After that they went out on to the balcony of the gendarmerie and began shooting at random. The village streets of Skópelos quickly emptied. Miltiádhis was so infuriated at this mindless behaviour that he marched up to the gendarmerie, knocked them down one by one and took their guns. Having collected twelve revolvers, he returned to Alónnisos where he calmly sold them. In 1916–1917, during the blockade by foreign powers, Miltiádhis was the only Alonnisiot who managed to get past the warships and bring supplies of food to the island. On one such trip he was apprehended by a British vessel. The captain summoned him to the bridge to explain himself. Miltiádhis pulled out a concealed pistol and made as if to arrest the captain, who, being duly amused, congratulated Miltiádhis and gave him a meal. Then the Alonnisiot departed leaving the British crew speechless.

During this same period a mine came ashore at Pánormos, on the west coast of Skópelos. Miltiádhis had opened it and was extracting the explosive, when a military vessel arrived to defuse the mine. Miltiádhis opened fire on the crew, who beat a hasty retreat. At the naval base the sailors reported the incident and Miltiádhis was summoned to Vólos for trial. In the court he conducted his own defence and, when asked why he had tampered with the mine, replied that he had done it for the safety of shipping. The judge was furious at this obvious lie, but Miltiádhis stuck to his story. Then he took the detonators out of his pocket and threw them down on the bench, declaring that he had *not* taken them for fishing, and if they wanted them, let them keep them. The judge replied, 'You take them and go.' The accused was declared innocent and the chamber was emptied at once.

On several occasions Miltiádhis rescued certain notorious thieves, Yangoúlas, Tzamítros and Babánis, transporting them from Chalkidhikí to Évvia. On the way he would entertain them in his house in Palió Chorió, where they pretended to be merchants. But they quarrelled incessantly among themselves and Miltiádhis had a job to keep the peace. In his old age Miltiádhis lost his sight, but even that did not put a stop to his exploits. Blind though he was, he still opened mines, with the help of his son, to extract the explosive for fishing. He died a respected elder, who, with his stories and his advice on many subjects, had been an asset to his fellow islanders.

10.1.3 Konstandínos Yeoryíou Malamaténios

Kóstas Malamaténios was an Alonnisiot who enlisted in the Macedonian guerrilla band of Captain Yaklís. Yaklís' band was responsible for a number of acts of piracy in the early 1900s in Macedonia. His men would land at night near coastal villages and steal from the Turks. Later they turned their hands to transporting volunteers and armaments for the Macedonian Struggle. When things got difficult they would seek refuge on Psathoúra. Since this was Greek territory the Turks could not pursue them there. The Greek partisans in Macedonia were hard men who often fell out among themselves. In one such dispute Malamaténios got into a fight and received a knife wound in the leg. He was left to recuperate in a Turkish area in the care of a friendly Greek couple, but before his wound had fully healed he went to rejoin Yaklís. Soon after, the band was betrayed and they found themselves pursued by a large force of Turks. In their flight, Malamaténios fell behind because of his wounded leg. Mitroúsis Gongolákis, a leading member of the band, who was from near Sérres and spoke Bulgarian, killed Malamaténios so that he could not be captured and tortured by the Turks. Gongolákis was afraid that under torture Malamaténios might betray the identity of his comrades, or their hideouts, or other information of value to the enemy. Later Gongolákis killed himself in preference to being captured. The Turks had surrounded him and two of his men in a church. There was a shoot out in which several Turks and one of Gongolákis' men were killed. With only one bullet left, Gongolákis called out that he was ready to surrender. With his last bullet, he shot the Turkish officer as he entered the church, and then fell on his sword. His remaining comrade gave himself up and was subjected to frightful torture.

10.2 Alonnisiot Heroes of the Balkan Wars (1912–1913)

In 1912–13 Greece went to war against Turkey under the leadership of the renowned politician, Eleftherios Venizélos. The Greek Royal Navy secured our islands for the Greek state, one after another. Among the many Alonnisiots fighting in the Greek navy was the stoker, Dhimítrios Gioulís, who served on the battleship *Avérof*. Admiral Koundouriótis could always tell from the speed of the ship whether or not Gioulís was on duty. Victories following one upon the other extended our borders progressively northwards through Macedonia. Later the Greek army proved stronger than the Turkish defence of Bizáni and captured Yánnina.[10] After the Greco-Turkish war of 1912–13, war was declared between Greece and Bulgaria in July 1913. After the bloody victory at Kilkís, to the north of Thessalonica, our army advanced and captured Eastern Macedonia and Western Thrace. All these acquisitions involved heavy losses. In almost all of these bloody battles the brave men of Alónnisos helped to realise our vision of a Greater Greece. The part played in the Balkan Wars by Theódhoros Athanasíou, who survived, has already been mentioned. The following seven Alonnisiots lost their lives, fulfilling their duty to the homeland, and are installed in the pantheon of heroes, a source of pride for succeeding generations. (Some of the details are taken from the archives of the Army's Directorate of History.)

Figure 10.4 Alonnisiot sailor in the Balkan Wars, 1913.
Courtesy of N. Anagnóstou.

10.2.1 Charálambos Chrístou Mourísis

Charálambos Mourísis took part in the siege of Yánnina as a regular soldier. Yánnina was protected by the impregnable fortress of Bizáni. The Greeks made a series of tactical assaults, but for a long time it was impossible to break the Turkish defence. The Greek army finally took Bizáni and entered the city, where our soldiers received a tumultuous welcome from the local population. Mourísis was wounded in the assaults during the first year and was transferred, seriously injured, to the military hospital at Pátras, where he died on 19 October 1913. Other men from Alónnisos fought with him. In Epirus the winter of 1912–13 was one of the coldest ever recorded, and when the soldiers returned to Alónnisos they produced the following song, which Kiriákos Efstathíou, still remembered at the age of 95:

> We do not fear Bizáni's guns
> Nor yet the mountains high,
> But only this bitter cold.

10.2.2 Panayótis Yeoryíou Tsoukanás

The battle of Kilkís-Lachanás in June 1913, was of great significance in establishing the frontiers of present-day Greece. The order was that Kilkís must be taken by the Greek army at whatever cost. There were 18 Greek regiments ranged against 20 Bulgarian. The Bulgarians, however, had fortified their positions and dug trenches. On the basis of common logic the capture of Kilkís was an impossibility. But morale was high and the Greeks did not count the bullets which fell around them like rain and they advanced unchecked. Among them was the Alonnisiot, Panayótis Tsoukanás, who from the first day of the battle flung his body fearlessly in front of the enemy fire. In the end he gave his life, at the very moment that Kilkís was overwhelmed by the Greek army. The Greek losses were heavy: 2,701 dead and wounded was the final reckoning for the three days of what was one of the noblest battles of the Balkan Wars.

10.2.3 Konstandínos Chrístou Nikoláou

Konstandínos Nikoláou and his comrades heroically defied Bulgarian bullets, in the hard-fought battles around Kilkís. After the Greek soldiers drove out the Bulgarians, who retreated in disorder. Meanwhile, isolated divisions of the Bulgarian army continued to make counter attacks. On 18 July 1913 an unofficial Greco-Bulgarian ceasefire was agreed. Nevertheless, irregular groups of soldiers carried on the fight, and Konstandínos Nikoláou was killed on 21 July, three days after the ceasefire in the Kilkís sector.

10.2.4 Konstandínos Agállou Agállou

Konstandínos Agállou served as a marine in the Greek army. He was wounded – it is not known where or in what circumstances – and died in the military hospital at Dedeagatch (now Alexandhroúpolis) in Thrace, in July 1913.

10.2.5 Konstandínos Dhimitríou Vláikos

Konstandínos Vláikos took part in the battles of Kilkís-Lachanás and followed the Greek army throughout its winter campaigns. In their trenches and underground dugouts the soldiers lived in inhuman conditions, sleeping in the mud and rain, and being in constant fear of enemy shells. Vláikos' constitution could not withstand the rigours of the winter, and in the spring he was transferred to the military hospital at Thessalonica with a serious form of tuberculosis, from which he died on 11 March 1913.

10.2.6 Stamátios Ioánnou Agállou

Stamátios Agállou served in the Greek Royal Navy. There was an occasion when he and hundreds of other sailors were about to disembark from a transport ship. The ship entered a naval base and drew alongside the quay. In their excitement the sailors all rushed to one side and the ship rolled over. Agállou was struck on the head and drowned.

Figure 10.5 Members of the Vláikos family, Pipéri, 1934. *Courtesy of P. Vláikos.*

10.2.7 Nikólaos S. Xidhéas

Nikólaos Xidhéas also served in the Greek Royal Navy and suffered a similar fate to that of Stamátios Agállou. He was wounded and drowned in a collision.

10.2.8 Nikólaos Ioánnou Vótsis and the Naming of Vótsi

Having referred to such a heroic period for the Greek nation, we must relate how one of the bays of Alónnisos took its name from a certain glorious hero of the naval struggle.

1912 was a difficult year for Greece. Following a peace accord in the Black Sea, the Turkish fleet was withdrawn from the naval blockade of the Bulgarian ports, and was concentrated in the Dardanelles, ready to move out into the Aegean, in the hope of achieving a victory that would halt the decline of the Ottoman Empire. Towards the end of the year, the tension was defused by the great naval battle off Cape Helles at the entrance to the Dardanelles (15–16 December 1912), at which the Turkish fleet was outmanoeuvred by the Greek warships and retreated into the straits. Two months earlier, an act of unusual daring had raised the morale of the Greeks. Lieutenant Nikólaos Ioánnou Vótsis in the Greek Torpedo Boat No. 11 blew up the Turkish battleship *Fetih Bülent* in the harbour of Thessalonica at 11.30 p.m. on 30 October 1912. After this exploit Vótsis went to the village of Vromerí near Kateríni in southern Macedonia. There he and his companions rested and then sailed to Oreí in Évvia where the Greek fleet was based. From there they set out, via Chalkídha, for Piraeus to replace the three torpedoes that had destroyed the *Fetih Bülent*. Bad weather, however, forced them to anchor in a small natural harbour on Alónnisos. They were given hospitality by the people of the island, who, when they afterwards learned of their honoured guest's great triumph, renamed the bay that had sheltered him from the weather *Kólpo tou Vótsi* ('Gulf of Vótsis'), now usually known simply as Vótsi.

Figure 10.6 Vasilikós, Peristéra, 1957. *Courtesy of M. and D. Papavasilíou.*

10.3 Heroes of the Asia Minor Campaign (1919–1922)

It would have been inconceivable for Alonnisiots not to have been represented in the much debated campaign in Asia Minor.[11] All those who took part are dead now, but they were able to communicate their rich experiences to their children. It is unfortunate that, while they were still alive, there was no researcher to gather from the men themselves a precise account of the events that unfolded on the heroic but troubled front in Asia Minor.

There were many factors contributing to the disorderly retreat and the uprooting of the Greek population of Asia Minor, among them the National Schism (the internal political division in Greece between the Monarchists and the Venizelists), which affected even the exhausted army, the soldiers' long absence from their homeland in their struggle on behalf of their fellow Greeks, and the inertia of the last months of the campaign in 1922. All of these had a negative impact on the morale of the army and led to the shameful defeat of September 1922.

Investigating the part played by Alonnisiots I felt indignation and anger, not with the Turks, but with the Greeks themselves, who 'turned and tore out their own eyes', in the words with which Venizélos characterised this black page of Greek history, in a speech delivered on Mount Athos in 1930. In order of the importance of their contributions to their country, we refer to the following Alonnisiot heroes of the Asia Minor Campaign.

10.3.1 Colonel Konstandínos Dhioyénous Theodhórou

Konstandínos Theodhórou was born in Skópelos on 6 October 1868, and he himself always thought of Skópelos as his home. He had, however, some distant relatives on Alónnisos, and it is for this reason that Alonnisiots consider him to be one of their heroes. His name is inscribed on war memorials in both Skópelos and Alónnisos. After his death, his son, who reached the rank of admiral, wanted his remains to be transferred to his own homeland of Skópelos. Let us first consider his career as it appears in his file in the Army's Directorate of History.

Konstandínos Theodhórou enlisted in the Greek army in 1884 and took part in the Greco-Turkish War of 1897, in charge of a platoon. After 11 July 1901 he is referred to as a second lieutenant. By 1912 he was serving as a lieutenant and was decorated for his acts of valour. In the following year in the hard-won battles of the Balkan Wars he was promoted to captain. Many officers had been lost in the wars of 1912–13 and the army needed to replace them. Those who had a record of heroism or greater charisma rose more rapidly in the hierarchy. In September 1915 Theodhórou was made a major, and two years later a lieutenant colonel.

On the Asia Minor Front in 1919–21 he was in charge of operations at the Sakarya river where he again distinguished himself by his heroism. During this campaign he reached the rank of colonel (October 1919), and was appointed commander of the garrison at Bursa. The one black mark in his career is his exploitation of his position for personal gain. From Alonnisiots and Skopelites who served at the Asia Minor Front we learn that Colonel Theodhórou obtained 'gifts' from Turks through blackmail and amassed thousands of Turkish pounds.

From 11 January to 10 March 1922 he was commander of the Sixth Infantry Regiment. Because of the notorious factionalism within the army he was not informed of the order to retreat. Neighbouring commanders saw Turkish planes dropping leaflets, which warned the Greek soldiers not to harm Turkish villages and threatening to burn them alive if they did. From this they understood that the front had collapsed. The signal for retreat was communicated from one regiment to another in chain fashion, but the officers decided not to inform Colonel Theodhórou for two reasons: first, because he was of a different political persuasion; and, secondly, because they knew that, if he was kept in ignorance of the general retreat, he would, as an honourable officer, continue to fight and thus hold up the Turkish advance until they themselves had reached a safe distance.

Theodhórou indeed fought heroically, but finally surrendered to the Turkish army. However, the people of Bursa, who bore him a grudge, tortured him in a terrible manner. First they forced him to eat excrement, threatening to kill his men if he refused, and then they strung him up in an olive tree and proceeded to gouge out his eyes and cut off his feet, leaving him to die slowly from loss of blood. He was officially regarded as missing in action, and the Greek state awarded him a posthumous promotion to the rank of lieutenant general.

10.3.2 Níkos Malamaténios

Níkos Malamaténios is an unjustly neglected hero of Alónnisos. The aged Mítsos Kiriazís, who was a conscript in 1919, tells Malamaténios' story as follows:

> My brother-in-law served in the Greek army for many years. He deserted, but in the end he went back. Desertion was a natural phenomenon in the army at that time, when many men had been serving continuously for more than eight years. We had a regular correspondence. He used to send me letters from Thrace, where he was stationed with his regiment. In the last letter I received he told me he was going to be transferred to Asia Minor. Then nothing more. Apóstolos Kaloyánnis met him at the front, at Afyon Karahisar, and according to him Malamaténios was killed during the retreat by boiling water which the Turkish villagers threw down from their windows.

In my researches in the Army's Directorate of History, I did not find the name of Níkos Malamaténios among the missing or dead of 1922.

10.3.3 Ioánnis Yeoryíou Tzórtzis

The story of Ioánnis Tzórtzis is told by his son, G. Tzórtzis:

> My father served for a total of twelve years as a soldier. He enlisted in 1912 and was discharged in 1924. He took part in many battles on different fronts in Asia Minor. With the skill and dexterity of an accomplished musician he made a *laoúto*[12] from a wild pear tree, and organised a band of musicians to entertain the troops. Towards the end of the campaign he had been transferred to the Afyon Karahisar sector, and during the disorderly Greek retreat he ran day and night for eighteen days to reach Smyrna.[13] He was with his captain who had a horse. They didn't go through the Turkish villages, because the people had been armed and were firing at them from their houses. They had to stop by the road to rest or sleep. Another Greek soldier, afraid of the ferocity of the Turkish irregulars, stole their horse while they were sleeping. Now they had no choice but to run. But the captain couldn't keep up the gruelling pace. Exhausted, he called his adjutant to him, gave him the address of his brothers, said goodbye to him, and stoically awaited a violent death at the hands of the barbarous Turks. Eventually my father made it to Smyrna. From there he was shipped to Chíos with the rest of the army, and continued to serve for another two years.

I personally remember Uncle Yannákis (a diminutive of Ioánnis), from the times when I first went to Kirá Panayá on fishing trips. I was twelve then, and he, a little old man, would be keeping an eye on the water melons and vegetables in his garden to protect them from the fishermen. Thirsty for company, he would tell his stories; but at the time they seemed to me like fairy tales.

Figure 10.7 Ioánnis Tzórtzis in Asia Minor, 1921.

Figure 10.8 Ioánnis Tzórtzis in Asia Minor, 1922.

Figure 10.9 Ioánnis Tzórtzis playing the santouri at the monastery on Kirá Panayá, 1963. *Courtesy of G. Tzórtzis.*

Figure 10.10 G. Tzórtzis playing the *laoúto* to visiting fishermen on Kirá Panayá.

10.3.4 Panayótis Kónstas

The following account is from my conversation with Níkos Kónstas, the son of Panayótis.

> My father fought for nine years in all. He was three years in Asia Minor. He fought in several battles and his division defended Afyon Karahisar. I was shocked by his accounts of the bestiality of the Turks. During the retreat he had seen Turkish prisoners with worry beads made from the nipples of Greek and Armenian women. They had raped them and then cut the nipples from their breasts. They vied with each other to see who had the longest string of worry beads. My father walked for many days without resting. In the end he got to Smyrna.
>
> There the sailors from the French and British ships were like animals. They cut off the hands of the miserable refugees with axes when they tried to save themselves by climbing aboard, and then they laughed at them. Is that how the civilised nations of Britain and France behave? After many hardships my father managed to make his way back to Greece. He had a lot of adventures on the way and it was a long time before he reached Alónnisos. Comrades of his who got back to the island before him thought that he was dead. His relatives wept and mourned. They sang his praises and built a memorial. Then he appeared, like a ghost. But he spent only a few days leave on the island at that time. He served another two years in the

army, until the situation was stabilised in 1924 with the revolutionary movement of Plastíras.[14] Then he came back to the island and took up farm work.

10.3.5 Apóstolos Kaloyánnis

This account was given by his son, G. Kaloyánnis.

> My father served as a soldier for eight years on the Asia Minor Front. He was in the medical corps and he helped to save the lives of many soldiers. One of them was a man from Glóssa [on Skópelos]. When, many years later, this man from Glóssa learned that my father had come out alive from the inferno of Ionia,[15] he came to Alónnisos to thank him personally. My father's worst experience came at the end of the war. He was among the last to reach the shore and the Turks were breathing down his neck. The Greek warships couldn't take any more on board. There was an argument and they took only the officers. His situation was tragic.
>
> He had just seen his comrade from Alónnisos killed by boiling water which the Turks threw from the windows.[16] Fortunately, at the last possible moment, a naval officer from Alónnisos spotted him and took him on board. Those who were left behind were slaughtered like sheep. This officer was called Xidhéas. He was executed by the Germans in 1944.[17] My father was deeply indebted to Xidhéas and promised that, if he had a son, Xidhéas would baptise him. That's how Xidhéas came to be my godfather. After he returned to the island, my father rarely spoke about the war. As a nurse he was able to help many islanders, using the experience he had gained on the battlefield.

10.3.6 Sotíris Dhrosákis

Sotíris Dhrosákis, with the rank of sergeant, distinguished himself on the Asia Minor Front. There, throughout the whole of the campaign, he was constantly among the heroic soldiers in the front line. In 1946 he came back to Alónnisos to represent the whole village in the anti-forestry case, but was murdered by right-wing paramilitaries.[18]

10.3.7 Ioánnis Tzórtzis

Ioánnis Tzórtzis fought for many years in the Greek army as a gunner. He was with Colonel Nikólaos Plastíras in the Ukraine campaign of 1917, but particularly distinguished himself later in Asia Minor. In recognition of his military proficiency he was given the rank of sergeant. He was in the front line throughout the whole campaign, and was involved in many clashes with the Turks on the Afyon Karahisar front. When Mustafa Kemal attacked, Tzórtzis' division was smashed and each man looked to his own safety. For about twenty days the Greek soldiers ran day and night to avoid being killed. On the road they agreed among themselves to rest standing up, leaning on their rifles, so as not to be overcome by sleep. But they were so debilitated that they slumped to the ground and fell asleep against their will. They awoke in the afternoon of the following day and began to run again. The Turkish irregulars were gaining on them and there was still some distance to cover. They met a Greek colonel on a white horse. They saluted him and asked him where they should go and what they should do. He told them that the army was being reorganised in the town of Kula, and that they should go there. They made a diversion and cautiously approached Kula. A preliminary reconnaissance revealed that the Turks were in control of the town. Tzórtzis and his companions waited until nightfall, and then escaped under the noses of the Turks, making a wide circuit. In great fear they passed through the lines of Turkish soldiers who were hunting for Greek forces, and reached Smyrna. From there they managed to get a passage to one of the Greek islands.

10.3.8 Nikólaos Efstathíou

This is Nikólaos Efstathíou's story as related by his son, Ilías:

> My father served in the Greek army on and off for eight years. He had terrible experiences of war, particularly during the retreat when the front at Afyon Karahisar collapsed. Pursued by the Turks, the Greeks ran to save their lives. My father had a pony which he rode and led by stages so as not to overtire it. He had already been eight days on the run (the retreat was chaotic and the pursuit merciless), when he suddenly came upon an exhausted soldier whom he recognised as a fellow Alonnisiot.
>
> He stopped and gave the man something to eat and drink. With what little he had left, half an army loaf and a small canteen of water, he revived his compatriot, and they set off again together. When night came they agreed to rest for just one hour and then to carry on. My father looped the horse's bridle round his hand and, exhausted, fell asleep. But his devious compatriot stole the horse and left him to sleep until morning. He was woken by the sound of gunfire and cannon.
>
> Terrified, he followed the road he was on, which, thanks to his good luck, brought him to the railway line. He was suffering from hunger and thirst. He drank water from the depressions left by horses' hooves. He continued to follow the railway tracks until he heard a train approaching. It was crammed absolutely solid with Greek soldiers and civilians and there wasn't room for a single extra person. My father saved himself by an act of desperation. He grabbed hold of some rail on the outside of a carriage and held on with what strength remained to him, balanced on one foot, all the way to Smyrna.
>
> From Smyrna he got to Thessalonica, and from there he made his way on foot to Vólos. He was owed money by an acquaintance of his in Xerochóri [a village in Évvia]. A frightful image kept returning to his mind. Next to the trenches a large shell had exploded, right where the horses were kept, creating a great pile of bodies, guts and blood. The horses' lifeless heads were still dangling from their bridles. This horrific image haunted my father for the rest of his life.
>
> When he got back to Alónnisos he ran into the soldier who had left him helpless and without his horse. His explanation was that fear had driven him to this devious act. It was such a relief for our mother when father returned to the house. Life had been very hard for her without him.

There were other men from Alónnisos who took part in the Asia Minor campaign. Unfortunately their close relations are all dead now, and it is difficult to find out the precise details of their contribution to their country. Research, however, is continuing.

10.3.9 Men who Served in the Greek Royal Navy

During the operations in Asia Minor, apart from the soldiers at the front, there were many Alonnisiots who served as sailors or marines, such as K. Efstathíou, Dh. Kiriazís, V. Dhimákis, Stamátis Kaloyánnis and S. Frantzéskos.

Kaloyánnis and Frantzéskos married girls from Smyrna. Kaloyánnis had been stationed in Buca just outside Smyrna. During the retreat he went to a friend's house to see if they were alright, but found only the terrified daughter of the family. The rest of the family had abandoned the house and fled, and in the panic the girl had got left behind. Kaloyánnis took her under his protection. When a ship refused to take her on board, he knocked down a Turkish boatman, took his boat and managed to get them both aboard another transport vessel.

Later they married and after living for some years in Athens set up house on Alónnisos. One day a passing cargo vessel from Néa Fókea (on the Kassándhra peninsula of Chalkidhikí), loaded with grain for Skópelos, stopped at Patitíri. Kaloyánnis enquired about some of elderly relatives of his wife's who lived at Néa Fókea.

The sailor he spoke to told him that not only were those relatives still there, but that the whole family from Buca had returned after many years, all except for a girl who had been lost there. Thus, completely by chance, and after so many years, a reunion was brought about. Kaloyánnis and his wife got aboard the cargo vessel and went to Néa Fókea. There, working in the fields, they found the girl's parents, who could not believe their eyes when their long-lost daughter suddenly reappeared. Such reunions were, unfortunately, very rare, particularly where girls were involved.

Refugees from Asia Minor did not come to settle in Alónnisos because there was little scope for land requisition on our island, mainly because there was very little cultivable ground on the island and what existed was already under cultivation. Skiáthos was another matter: the Greek population of Çeşme was resettled there, and became involved in trawl-fishing.

10.3.10 Dh. M. Vláikos

Vláikos did not serve in Asia Minor, but in the concurrent campaign against the Bulgarians on Greece's northern frontier, where he died in 1920. His camp was bombarded by an enemy plane and Vláikos ran to take cover. By an unlucky chance a bomb landed close to his chosen hiding place and he was killed. His companions, who had not reacted so quickly, remained in the camp and suffered no harm. Vláikos was in fact the only member of his regiment who met his death in this unfortunate incident. The official telegram announcing his death came like a canon shot to our small island, which was plunged into grief. Today the old people of Alónnisos remember Vláikos as one of the finest young men the island ever produced.

Notes

1. *Yenikó Epitelío Stratoú, Dhiéfthinsi Istorías.*
2. In 1870, eight years before Bulgaria became an autonomous principality under Ottoman suzerainty – it did not declare full independence until 1908 – the Orthodox Bulgarians, with the encouragement and sanction of the Ottoman Sultan, had established their own ecclesiastical authority, the Bulgarian Exarchate, and were no longer under the jurisdiction of the Greek Patriarch in Istanbul. The struggle between Greeks and Bulgarians for the affiliation of the people of Macedonia was often couched in terms of allegiance to the Exarchate or Patriarchate, though ethnic and linguistic identity were the underlying issues. The *comitadjis* were the agents of the Bulgarian Macedonian Committees (hence their name) whose aim was to impose Bulgarian language and culture, and gain the allegiance of the population of Macedonia with a view to its eventual annexation to Bulgaria. For a detailed account of the Macedonian Struggle in English, see Dakin (1966). [Translator]
3. The names Loukás and Karatásos are transliterated from the Greek, but it is not clear whether these are Greek names (there were certainly some ethnic Greeks fighting on the Bulgarian side) or Hellenised versions of Bulgarian names.
4. This seems likely to be the truth about Garéfis' death, rather than the received view that he 'was shot and killed by one of Loukás's men who had escaped during the battle' (Dakin, 1966, p. 235, n. 77). [Translator]
5. At the heart of the Balkan Wars was the disposition of Macedonia, in the context of nationalist aspirations in the Balkans. In the First Balkan War, which erupted in 1912, the three Balkan powers of Greece, Bulgaria and Serbia cooperated militarily against the Turks, but they could not agree on the vital question of how to distribute the territory surrendered by the Ottoman Empire. By the Treaty of London (1913), the Turks ceded all their European possessions to the Balkan allies, with the exception of Eastern Thrace (still part of Turkey today) and Albania, which became independent. However, the Treaty of London did not determine the division of territory among the allies, and Greece and Serbia divided Macedonian territory between themselves in a bilateral agreement, prompting Bulgaria to attack both. In this Second Balkan War, Greece and Serbia won victories that ensured major territorial gains at the Treaty of Bucharest in August 1913. The following account of the shooting of the Bulgarian marksman belongs to this latter campaign. See also pp. 204–8. [Translator]
6. As Crown Prince and then King, Constantine had been Commander-in-Chief of the Greek forces in the Balkan Wars. His father, King George I, whose reign began in 1863, was assassinated in Thessalonica in March 1913. [Translator]
7. See p. 255.
8. The *Ierós Lóchos* was part of the British strategy characterised by Níkos Th. Kaloyánnis as creating a 'praetorian guard' (see p. 279, in Nikos Th. Kaloyannis' contribution to the chapter on the Second World War). The original 'Sacred Company' was a group of 300 elite soldiers in THEBES in the 4th century BC. The name was also adopted by a band of volunteers in the Greek War of Independence. [Translator]
9. Konstandínos (Kóstas) Chrístou's own account appears on pp. 266–7.
10. Bizáni is the name of a range of hills guarding the southern and northeastern approaches to Yánnina (also known as Ioánnina) in Epirus. The hills were heavily fortified with numerous Turkish artillery emplacements. [Translator]
11. With British encouragement, a Greek expeditionary force entered Asia Minor in 1919, anticipating that, in the carve-up of the Ottoman Empire then being negotiated, those areas of western Turkey with a large Greek population would be annexed to the Greek state. Both the Greeks and the British underestimated the growing strength of the Turkish Nationalist Army of Mustafa Kemal (later to be known as Attatürk). The Greek forces were extended on two broad a front; the British would not provide military support; and by the end of 1921 it was clear that the defeat of the demoralised Greek army was inevitable. [Translator]

12. The *laoúto* is a traditional Greek folk instrument, a type of lute. See the illustration on p. 217. [Translator]

13. Smyrna (Zmírni in Greek, İzmir in Turkish) is a major port on the west coast of Turkey. [Translator]

14 It appears that the narrator, Níkos Kónstas, has condensed events here. The revolution led by Colonel Nikólaos Plastíras took place in 1922 and led to the abdication, for the second time, of King Constantine I (1913–17, 1921–22), and his replacement by his son, George II. In 1923 King George was forced to leave the country (he returned in 1935), and in 1924 Greece was declared a Republic. This last event is, presumably, the stabilisation of the situation to which the narrator refers. [Translator]

15. 'Ionia' is the ancient Greek name for the Aegean seaboard of Asia Minor and the adjacent islands. Not to be confused with the Ionian Sea and the Ionian Islands (which include Corfu, Ithaca and Zákinthos) on the western side of the Greek mainland. [Translator]

16. The comrade was Níkos Malamaténios (see p. 214). [Translator]

17. This is Thanásis Xidhéas, whose photograph appears on p.235. An eye-witness account of the execution of Xidhéas and several others will be found on pp. 233–8. [Translator]

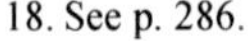

18. See p. 286.

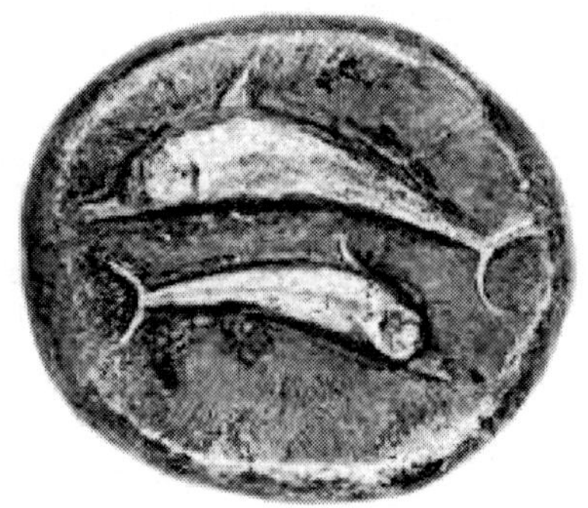

11
THE SECOND WORLD WAR

Figure 11.1 Court hearing held in Palió Chorió, 1936.
Courtesy of Michális and Evanthía Vláikos.

AFTER the resolution of the Asia Minor situation and the return of the soldiers to their homes, Alónnisos like the rest of Greece, entered a period of recovery. In spite of the political instability and economic problems, life on Alónnisos resumed its regular rhythm.

11.1 The Interwar Period

People were busy with resin tapping, timber felling and charcoal production, and the cultivation of the land, especially the vineyards. The population increased and there were many immigrants. The export trade in the most plentiful products (resin, wine, charcoal) made it necessary for some Alonnisiots to become involved in shipping. They bought cargo vessels and went into business. Wine was brought down by mule from the widely scattered presses in wineskins and deposited in cisterns in the harbour. From there, again using skin bags it was transferred to barrels in the holds of the ships.

At that period many olive presses were constructed and produced oil of high quality. It was this oil that saved the population in the catastrophic world war that followed. The process of production of olive oil was as follows: donkeys walking in a circle turned two great stones that ground the olives. Then they were put into goatskin 'envelopes' and pressed in a wooden press. Hot water was used to separate the pure oil, while what was left usually ended up in the sea. The oil was transported, again in skin bags, to huge earthenware jars which were stored in small warehouses.

Figure 11.2 Agricultural work on Alónissos.

Figure 11.3 Agricultural work at Alónia.

Many people were involved in stock breeding, not only on Alónnisos, but also on those of the surrounding islands which had been purchased by the *kinótita* of Alónnisos. The remaining islands belonged at this period to the monastery of the Great Lávra on Mount Athos, which exploited them, taking 25% of the agricultural produce.

In the 1920s the then President of the *kinótita* needed the wooden boxes that held the local archives. In order to free them for use he burned their precious contents, thus destroying a great treasure house of knowledge.

Figure 11.4 Wedding celebrations in Palió Chorió, 1932. *Courtesy of P. Vláikos.*

11.1.1 Mining on Peristéra

In the 1930s a private individual leased the mineral rights on Peristéra and began to extract iron and chrome. He opened a total of five galleries in different places. At first he found iron ore in viable quantities, but later the veins ran out. The galleries were opened by blasting with dynamite.

The rock was so hard that wooden props were not necessary. The ore was brought by mules to the beach and taken off in wooden vessels. The company ceased operating before the war. Today the galleries offer an excellent opportunity for visitors who are interested in the pre-war period. They are sound and safe, and with a torch one can walk to the end. The length varies from 20 to 90 metres.

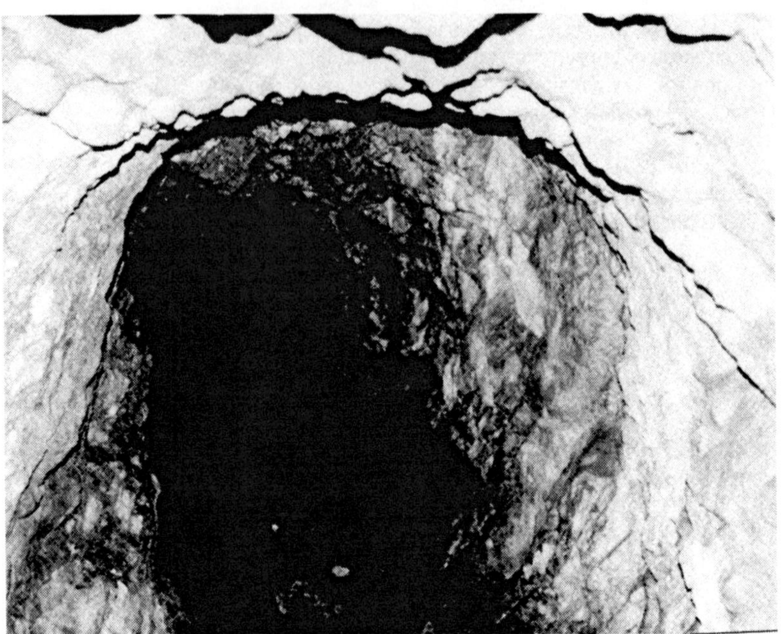

Figure 11.5 One of the five galleries for iron and chromium mining on Peristéra, 1930–1940.

11.1.2 Industries on Alónnisos

A list in the municipal office of Alónnisos shows that at this period the following types of industries were operating within its jurisdiction: olive mills, flour mills, wool carding establishments, lime-kilns, and tile factories. There were six olive mills, all hand-operated. The names of their proprietors and the dates of their foundation are listed in Table 11.1.

Table 11.1 Oil mills on Alónnisos in the 1930s.

Proprietor	*Founded*
Vasílios Tsoukanás	?
Yeóryos Karakatsánis	1920
Evángelos G. Anagnóstou	1924
Panayótis Apostólou Vláikos	1925
Aristídhis Athanasíou	1928
Ioánnis G. Strouflíotis	1932

There were three flour mills. One was owned by Ioánnis K. Kaloyánnis and had been operating since 1900. Another, owned by the Alexíou brothers, no longer exists. Níkos Athanasíou fixed up two 18th-century mills in the bay of Yália, below Palió Chorió. The windmill was not very successful, but the water mill did well and continued to operate until 1950. The windmill has recently been restored to working order, and the site of water mill has become a water storage and pumping facility, though the original mill building is in ruins.

11.2 The War on Alónnisos

Figure 11.6 Soldiers from Alónnisos in Albania, 1940.

As soon as war with Italy was declared in October 1940, all the young men of Alónnisos and the smaller and now uninhabited islands, which at that time were still full of life, were called up to serve their country. With other men from all parts of Greece they fought energetically against the insolent Italian invader. Patriots from Alónnisos were in the front line throughout the campaign. Most of them were herdsmen or muleteers inured to life in the mountains. On the Albanian front they distinguished themselves, fighting heroically. Although outnumbered, the Greeks halted the advance of the better equipped and thoroughly modernised Italian army, and then drove the Italians back in disorder. Italy was humiliated on the international stage. This was the first glimmer of hope for the nations involved in the war, the first indication that the Axis Powers could be defeated.

On 6 April 1941 the German army entered Greece from Yugoslavia. Again, Alonnisiots were among those who placed their bodies in the path of the iron-clad barbarian. The Greeks and the Serbs were the only peoples who were not afraid of Hitler's all-powerful army. In the end the Greek front collapsed under the impulse of this lightning attack, and the Swastika was raised all over Greece. But the Greeks had performed their miracle, delaying by two months the German invasion of Russia.

Soldiers from Alónnisos, barefoot and bedraggled, but full of pride, took the road home. They covered the whole distance on foot from the Albanian Front, or from the last line of defence against the Germans, as far as Vólos. They found food in the villages they passed through, a dry crust or a bit of cheese, so that they could continue their journey. They handed in their weapons at collection points designated by the army.

After about four weeks of tramping they reached Vólos. From there, in cargo boats, trawlers and dragnet boats or whatever other means they could find, they returned to their island. The island rejoiced to see its soldiers again. Men and women wept with joy and relief. Gradually the soldiers began to readjust to island life once more. Their first concern was to rid themselves of the troublesome lice. The women boiled their clothes in great cauldrons and skimmed off the insects with twigs.

Figure 11.7 Members of the Alónnissos militia and Youth Movement under Metaxás, Palió Chorió, 1938. *Courtesy of N. Anagnóstou.*

As the front collapsed and the Greek and allied forces retreated southwards, many Australian, British, New Zealand and Cypriot soldiers, who had come to strengthen the Greek defences, were trapped behind enemy lines. As the Germans, Italians and Bulgarians extended their control to all parts of Greece, the position of these soldiers became very difficult. The Alonnisiots who had not yet recovered from the trials of the difficult campaign, swung into action once again. Organised now in EAM, the National Liberation Front,[1] they took responsibility for the safe evacuation of their allies.

They even welcomed them to their own houses and kept them there, at great risk to their own lives, until the organisation's caïque came to take them to the Middle East. The local cell of EAM included the brave Kaliarína and her husband on Skiáthos; Ioánnis Channás, Yeóryos Karádhis and K. Agállou on Skópelos; Yeóryos Alexíou, Evángelos Yeoryíou Anagnóstou, Mítsos Dhrosákis, and Panayótis Vláikos on Alónnisos; Kóstas Chrístou on Kirá Panayá; Theódhoros Athanasíou and Kóstas Malamaténios on Peristéra; Chrístos Malamaténios on Yoúra; and Evángelos Andoníou Anagnóstou on Pipéri.

They transported the allied soldiers from coastal villages in Pílio and brought them to assembly points in the Northern Sporades, from where they were taken in groups by caïque to the Middle East. Among such assembly points were Cape Verónis on Alónnisos, the 'Cave of the English' on Lechoúsa, the Cave of Máka on Peristéra, and the Liadhromítiko cave on Yoúra. Along with the allied soldiers went those members of the Greek army who wanted to reach Greek military headquarters in Egypt in order to continue the struggle. Cretan soldiers were also trapped. These men all escaped under the noses of their Italian pursuers. After the German invasion, the Italians, with their shameful defeat in the Píndhos mountains fresh in their memories, behaved very harshly towards the local inhabitants. In the first years of the Occupation the Italians were in control of our islands.

With Vólos as the centre of their operations and guard posts on Skiáthos and Skópelos, the Italians controlled the Northern Sporades. Drifters and big commercial vessels were armed and used as pursuit boats. With these they made surprise attacks on Alónnisos and the surrounding islands. Their aim was to break the network that was arranging the escape of allied soldiers, and to wear down the morale of the inhabitants.

In the end they achieved very little. Later, when the Italians left, the control and surveillance of our region passed to the Germans. By then, however, almost all the allied soldiers had been transferred to the Middle East. After consultation with the central committee of EAM, certain leftists had organised ELAS and ELAN, the Greek Popular Liberation Army and Navy respectively.[2] There was a third organisation whose remit was to observe and record the movements of the Germans. In practice, a man from Glóssa on Skópelos by the name of Paplomatás and another man from Tríkeri, who went round the islands in his caïque, gathered information and passed it on to the partisan leadership in Pílio.

Towards the end of the war, the Germans, with the help of local informers, tried to eliminate EAM. One act intended to demonstrate their power was the execution of the heroes of Alónnisos. With their headquarters in Skiáthos and guard posts in Skópelos and Kirá Panayá, the Germans controlled all the ships in the northern Aegean. The ruthless German governor of the Northern Sporades, Mileoúnis as the locals called him because he demanded *million*s to release the ships, maintained order until the penultimate year of the war. After he was captured by the partisans the Germans lost control.[3] The bombardment of their convoy in the open sea near Psathoúra and the sinking of one of the German ships exposed their weakness.

11.2.1 The Testimony of Kóstas Tsoukanás

The most important events of this period have been described by eye witnesses, among them Alónnisos' first doctor, Kóstas Tsoukanás, whose account follows.

> In January 1941 I was sent to the Military Hospital at Aidhipsós in northern Évvia as assistant surgeon. There we treated soldiers wounded in the war who were mainly suffering from frostbite. Following the collapse of the Albanian Front – brought about not by the Italians (for we had defeated them) but by the invasion of the German forces – around 20–25 April (at Easter), just after we had been bombed, a German unit arrived and we handed the hospital over to them.
>
> We put on our civilian clothes and I returned to my home in Alónnisos, where I offered my services as a doctor to my fellow villagers. 1941 passed without health problems among the population of the island, but in 1942 there was a great famine and a shortage of medicines, and we even had two deaths from starvation. There were no occupation forces on Alónnisos, though there were Italians on Skiáthos and then Germans on Skópelos, so we didn't feel the full force of the Occupation, except for certain dreadful events to which I refer below.
>
> At that time, EAM was being organised on Alónnisos as well as another organisation for the evacuation of British and Greek soldiers to the Middle East. The then president of the *Kinótita*, Y. Alexíou, played an important role in the latter (often risking his life), as did Vangélis [Yeoryíou] Anagnóstou with his small motor boat. Throughout the occupation, he transported Britons and Greeks from the Northern Sporades, Pílio and Évvia to the shores of Asia Minor. The first serious incident happened as follows.
>
> It was February 1942. One bitterly cold winter day Vangélis Andoníou Anagnóstou came to my house in Vótsi (a small settlement on Alónnisos). He told me that on his way from Stení Vála (a natural harbour on Alónnisos) he had run into soldiers – Italian soldiers – who were going towards the village [Palió Chorió]. With a few phrases of broken Greek they had asked him to tell them whose caïque was taking British soldiers to the Middle East. He certainly knew the man in question, but he got away from them and came to tell me what had happened. It was a little after midday. I put on my waterproofs and ran through the wind and rain to inform the president, whose house was about 800 metres from mine. We found him in the warm, seated round a lighted stove with some other men, drinking wine. As soon as they heard what was afoot they vanished, fleeing, as it later emerged, to Malamaténios' hut in the mountains. The island policeman found them (how exactly I don't know) and a struggle ensued. The president was wounded but escaped along with his companions. At midnight an Alonnisiot knocked on my door and asked for medicines and bandages for the wounded man. No sooner had he left than two Italian soldiers arrived and demanded to know where I had hidden the wounded man. When I told them I knew nothing, they left. A bit later, towards dawn, the Italian detachment returned with their chief officer. This time they brought along, with their hands tied, Malamaténios and his wife, Mítsos Dhrosákis, the wife of the president, and various others whose names I

> don't remember. They began to torture them and beat them with sticks to make them say where the others who hadn't been arrested were, and who else was in the organisation. After the beating they brought them outside and left them kneeling in the sleet. Then they brought them inside again. The officer (this torturer was a big man called Antonio) gave the order, 'Avanti' ('Let's go'), that is, 'Let's get on with the beating.' As for me, my heart was trembling, lest they returned to the question of who had tipped off the men and enabled them to escape. In the end, after this rough treatment, they were all set free but they were in an indescribably awful state. The president we later learned died from loss of blood on the voyage to the Middle East.

It is worth giving some further details about Yeóryos Alexíou, who had been president of Alónnisos since the time of the Metaxás government.[4] Alexíou, a fervent patriot, joined the Resistance network, and by his own efforts saved many allies and Greeks. In his house, situated in an isolated spot at Cape Verónis (on the north side of the bay of Rousoúm), he could hide and feed allied servicemen on the run. Someone from Skópelos betrayed him and he fled to Malamaténios' house on Vounó, the hill to the north of the village. The deputy president of the island, Strouflіótis, led the policeman, Gourlós, to Alexíou's hiding place. There was a fight in which Gourlós stabbed Alexíou twice with his service bayonet.

Figure 11.8 Members of the Alónnissos militia and Youth Movement under Metaxás, Alónnisos, 1939. *Courtesy of Nikólaos Anagnóstou.*

Thinking that he had killed him, Gourlós went off to inform the Italians. Alexíou, however, came round and was helped to a cave not far from his own house. There he was given first aid and the bleeding stopped. The news went round the village and old Likoúrgos decided, at great risk to himself, to take Alexíou to Lechoúsa. There was a cave there that served as an assembly point for Greek and allied servicemen. He took him there to wait for the next caïque going to the Middle East. The inhabitants of Vasilikós on Peristéra undertook to feed him, bringing him bread, cheese and water. When Kóstas Athanasíou went, after about a month, to collect Alexíou from the cave on Lechoúsa, he found him in good spirits – he was even cracking jokes. But when he was moved the wounds opened again and he began to bleed. On the voyage to Turkey there were no first aid facilities and he died shortly after arrival in Smyrna, where he was buried in the grounds of the Greek Consulate.

Figure 11.9 Members of Metaxás' Youth Movement in Palió Chorió, 1938. *Courtesy of Ólga Tsoukaná.*

We return now to Dr Tsoukanás' account:

> The second important event was as follows. One morning a convoy of eight SS ships approached Alónnisos and German soldiers came ashore. The people recognised them from a distance and by the time they arrived in the village they had locked their houses and disappeared into the forest. My wife, who was a dentist, my young son and my mother remained in the house. It happened that I myself had gone off to Skópelos on some business or other before the SS ships arrived.
>
> Finding the houses locked up, they began to break down the doors with their rifle butts in their search for the villagers. They made holes in the wine barrels and oil jars. The commanding officer came to my house and found my wife. She invited him in and offered him *loukoumádhes*[5] which she had just made and something to drink, which he declined. He asked her why the houses were locked and where the inhabitants were. Her answer was that everyone had gone out to work in the fields as they did every day. He was convinced and ordered his men to stop breaking down the doors and to abandon the search.
>
> They set off towards the interior of the island. Soon a soldier brought my cousin, Apostólis Vláikos, to the officer, and presented the officer with a note which Vláikos had thrown away as soon as he saw the soldier, since it was from his brother-in-law, Vangélis [Yeoryíou] Anagnóstou, who, as we've seen, arranged the evacuation of Britons and Greeks to the Middle East. The soldier who arrested him suspected something and had therefore brought the note to his commanding officer. The officer gave it to my wife so that she could read it and tell him what it said. My wife coolly told him that it was from his brother telling him to go to Skópelos. He believed her and let Vláikos go free.
>
> The third incident was when an Italian detachment came to the village on Alónnisos and ordered us to find and arrest a certain captain in ELAN, Vangélis Paplomatás from Skópelos, who was in hiding here, threatening reprisals if we failed to find him. We all dashed out, the whole village, into the surrounding countryside, on to the slopes of Kalóvoulo, to make it look as though we were searching. 'Vangélis! Vangélis!' we shouted. But Vangélis managed to get away to safety, swimming through rough sea to the island of Áyos Yeóryos, and from there to Skópelos, using an old door as a raft.
>
> The fourth and most serious event took place on the Feast of the Dormition of the Virgin, 15 August 1944. The church in the village cemetery is dedicated to the Dormition, and every year the whole island gathers there on 15 August. All the people of the village, as well as those of us who lived at Vótsi, were getting ready to go to the festival, when we heard that nearby on the beach at Spartínes a caïque had put ashore a group of Greek partisans. But then Apóstolos Vláikos, who was nicknamed *Dháskalos* ('Teacher'), arrived at my house and told us that they were not partisans but Germans, whom he had seen two days before on the neighbouring island of Kirá Panayá. We didn't know what to believe, and some of us set off for the village church while the others stayed at home. Almost the whole village went to the church for the festival of the Virgin.

Figures 11.10–11.17 Alexíou and the eight others on these pages were all shot by the Germans in 1944 (as described on pp. 233 and 236–8). ***This page***: *top left*: Alexíou; *top right*: Phloroús; *bottom left*: Zmirnéas; *bottom right*: Agállos Anagnóstou. ***Opposite***: *top left*: Yeóryos Mourísis; *top right*: Thanásis Xidhéas: *bottom left*: Kiriazís; *bottom right*: Dhrosákis. Note: there is no photo of the ninth victim, Agállos Agállou.

When the service was over, the village bells were rung and a town crier went round calling all the men to assemble in the village square without the women and children, and saying that any man who didn't come and was found outside the square would be shot on sight.

The men were gathered in the square, myself among them. The Germans had set up machine guns around the square and were covering us from all sides. Suddenly a villager by the name of Panayótis Mikés was spotted near the village well from an observation post and shot and wounded. Then the interpreter asked those assembled in the square whether there was a doctor among us. 'Yes,' they replied in chorus and I was called out and told to go and see to the injured man. He had been shot through the thigh, but the bone was not broken and there was no haemorrhaging. I bound up the wound and returned to the square where everyone was assembled. There I was confronted by the following spectacle. Eleven men had been roped together one beside the other. Most of them were EAM cadres. My father was among them. They had their backs to the crowd.

I was very worried. I approached the German interpreter and asked him what was going on. He replied coldly that these men were going to be executed because they were partisans. I begged and pleaded with him. I told him that we didn't have any partisans here and that no one from our village had gone to the mountains to join the partisans and fight the Germans.

'You must believe me, and if you doubt it make enquiries now, straightaway. That old man tied up there – he's my father – is he a partisan too? He had a big caïque but he gave it to the German authorities.'

He immediately understood and told me not to worry. He went over to the leader of the detachment and began to talk to him. The latter shouted angrily, but he ordered them to release my father, who went away. Since there was nothing I could do for group as a whole, I tried to save my cousin, Apostólis Vláikos.

I went up to the interpreter again and said, 'Surely it wouldn't be right to kill this man when he works for Germany? He collects the resin that the island produces, under his own care and supervision, and sends it to the factory in Chalkídha.'

'In his case it is impossible,' he told me, 'because he's been sending signals to the organisation that evacuates the British soldiers.'

I pleaded with him then, saying that Vláikos was my relative and that he had no connection with those people. The interpreter gave me some hope that he would try. He went back to the officer, who got furiously angry and would not listen. At this point Apostólis turned to speak to the officer, but the officer, with his pistol in his hand, ordered him not to speak and to turn round again immediately. The interpreter, however, said to him 'Speak, speak.'

He began to say that he worked for the Germans, collecting resin, but at that point the interpreter untied him. Before he could get away and take cover the order to fire was given and the nine remaining men fell dead to the ground, and if any then showed any sign of movement he was given the *coup de grâce*. Only one of the nine individuals, Thanásis Xidhéas, had managed to get free. He had jumped from a considerable height, from the spot where he'd been tied up with the others,[6] but he had received a bullet in the chest.

> When I went up later I found him dead just ten metres away. We had all watched this macabre spectacle, terrified. Finally they ordered us to stay put until they had gone away and were out of sight. They took with them Apostólis Vláikos, carrying him on a cartridge case, but when they reached the shore they let him go. When they had gone far enough not to see us, we got up and approached the bodies and checked that they were all dead. Their relatives took them up and mourned them, and then buried them. I was sorry to learn that while we were all gathered in the square, the Germans had thrown some incendiary bombs and burned down the house of my uncle, Panayótis Tsoukanás, a member of EAM, who had not come to the square, but made a run for it. They were going to burn down the house of my cousin, Apostólis Vláikos, as well, but his wife was three-months pregnant, and, respecting this, they refrained from setting fire to the house. After these events, all the people, frightened, grief-stricken and despairing, abandoned the village and sought refuge in the forest.
>
> What interests me is how the members of EAM could have made such a mistake as to think it was a group of Greek partisans approaching; and how the Germans were able to make their raid when the partisans were all here, and how they were able to pick out the EAM organisers and other activists whom they arrested. Thanásis Xidhéas, who was executed, had met the Germans on the road when he was on his way to the church, and had told them 'Germany has finally collapsed.' Yeóryos Mourísis had boasted that he'd sunk one of their ships. Since they'd found Zmirnéas first on Skópelos and then on Alónnisos, they had decided that he was a go-between for the partisans. Agállos Anagnóstou was killed despite his youth, because they'd learned of his brother's involvement in the transport of British servicemen to the Middle East. The others were all members of the local EAM group.

In fact the man who betrayed most of these members of the Resistance and sent them to their deaths was a certain Fótis Psarós.

Dr Tsoukanás' account gives us a general picture of how events unfolded in Alónnisos. I shall now try to give a more detailed description of some of these events, beginning with those terrible hours the inhabitants lived through after the executions.

As soon as the Germans had gone, all the men disappeared into the surrounding hills for fear that they might return. The heavy work of gathering up and burying the bodies was left to the women, who stayed behind in the village. In the midst of the unbearable pain of the unexpected and cruel loss of loved ones (husbands, fathers, sons), the women took the dead heroes home to their houses. They carried them in blankets, for many of them were disfigured by bullets and couldn't be picked up for the blood. They took them to their houses to lie there overnight. But those villagers who were in league with the Germans came out into the square and started saying that the Germans would come back that night and those who had the dead in their houses would be punished. The bereaved and grief-stricken women, fearing reprisals, had to carry their dead to the church of Áyos Yeóryos in Kástro (the upper part of the village within the old fortifications).

Nothing happened during the night, and in the morning they took the bodies out of the church, which was now covered in blood, and carried them to the cemetery. They opened the tombs themselves, but in the afternoon they found the priest who'd been in hiding, and he read the funeral service for all the dead together, though they were buried individually.

Another significant event of the period was the reorganisation of the *eparchíes* by the government in 1942, probably to make things easier for the Germans. Until 1942 we belonged both ecclesiastically and administratively to the *eparchía* of Évvia. Since 1942 we have been part of the *eparchía* of Skópelos, although ecclesiastically we are still part of the Bishopric of Chalkídha in Évvia.

11.2.2 The Testimony of Evángelos Anagnóstou

Let us now look at an extract from the published *Journal* of Evángelos Yeoryíou Anagnóstou,[7] who describes himself as 'owner and captain of the Motor Boat *Eléni*, Registration: Vólos 1099'. Anagnóstou gives his own views of some of the foregoing events.

> On the day the Italians and Germans first set foot on Greek soil, and the Greek patriots began a life of suffering, my own life also took a dramatic turn because I became involved in sheltering and evacuating British soldiers and officers.
>
> My first trip with my boat, the *Eléni*, was to Zagorá in Pílio to buy potatoes. I went with a merchant from Skópelos called Yeóryos N. Lemonís. Before we made the trip to Zagorá we went first to Vólos, where we had an agreement with a man from Paleá Mitzéla [a village on the east side of the bay of Vólos] by the name of Yeóryos Samsarélos.
>
> We would go there and he would give us potatoes. But when we got to Mitzéla he said to us, 'I'll give you the potatoes' – actually we were going to buy them from him – 'but you must do me a favour in return. I'm hiding two Englishmen in my shop and I want you to take them to your islands, to Skópelos or Alónnisos, because if the Germans find them here they'll burn my place down. To save these men we've got to get them out of Greece, to Turkey if there's some way to get them there.' I made up my mind and I said to him, 'When it's dark, we'll take them to Skópelos and then we'll have to see what happens after that.'
>
> We loaded the caïque with potatoes and we got the two Englishmen on board and set off in the dark from Paleá Mitzéla. When we got to Cape Gouroúni – it was barely light, the sun had just begun to rise – we saw a caïque flying a German flag. We didn't know what to do. We thought of hiding the Englishmen in the hold with the potatoes. So we got to work double quick, dug a hollow in the potatoes, shoved the men in there and covered them up with potatoes.
>
> Then we waited in agony to see what would happen. The other boat had Germans in for sure, but they just kept going towards Thessalonica and didn't pay us any attention. We were just a small boat and they didn't suspect anything. Things were just beginning then and they didn't bother much about the caïques. The Germans hailed us from their caïque. At that point I said, 'God help us,' but they didn't inspect us and we went on our way and got to Skópelos.

Figure 11.18 Two boats of the kind used to smuggle stranded Allied soldiers, Vótsi, 1945. *Courtesy of Michális and Evanthía Vláikos.*

We got the Englishmen out into a cave at Áyos Konstandínos [on the west coast of Alónnisos] where there's a little island. I went round to Skópelos town and unloaded the potatoes. Then I went back to where I'd left the men and picked them up and took them to Alónnisos [i.e. Palió Chorió] and met up with Ioánnis Dh. Channás, who was going to arrange their transport, and he said to me, 'We'll take them to Skíros and find Captain Michális' – Pandelís Eyenítis – 'and he'll take them to Turkey in his caïque.' We set out during the night, and made it to Skíros by morning. We found Captain Michális' boat and they set off for Turkey, while we took our boat back to Alónnisos.

A bit later on I went to Vólos with my boat, and on the way back I stopped off for the evening at Skiáthos. The customs officer at Skiáthos was an old friend of mine and when he met me he asked me where I was going. 'I've come from Vólos and I'm on my way to Alónnisos.' The customs officer was called Evángelos Chrisofákis, and he said to me, 'I'll tell you a secret, and I hope I won't regret it, and you'll keep it secret so no one finds out it was me that told you. There are Englishmen here. We've hidden them in a house. Sirainó Kaliári has got them in her house, and if you can take them I'll bring them tonight when everything's quiet and no one will see them, and you can take them aboard and go, and do what you can to look after them and find some way for them to escape.' Fuel was in short supply at the time, and I told him, 'I've got no petrol for the engine. If you could find me a bit of petrol.' So he found a couple of cans of petrol on another boat and gave them to me, and about midnight he brought the Englishmen and I set off for Alónnisos. By morning I was at Cape Verónis as the place is called. Yeóryos I. Alexíou has a house there and he took them in. I'd arranged with Ioánnis Channás to hide them in Alexíou's house, since it was by itself and on a headland where you could land a caïque to make a getaway. It was this that eventually lead to Alexíou's death, as I shall describe below.

A few days later Sirainó Kaliári came over from Skiáthos in the trawler her husband keeps for fishing, bringing eight Englishmen with her. In the meantime an officer had been here. He'd come from the Middle East to get together certain Greeks to take them to Turkey. He'd had discussions with Ioánnis Channás and they'd asked me to get them away to Turkey. I'd agreed, since he said to me, 'For every man you take in your caïque you'll be paid six English pounds.' I decided to take them aboard at Cape Platsoúkkas [just north of Vótsi], the eight that Kaliarína had brought, the four Englishmen I'd brought myself from Skiáthos, together with some Greeks and the officer who'd been sent here, whose name I learned – he was called Yánnis Karabótsos – twenty men in all.

I took a sailor from Kaliáris' trawler, an old man from Çeşme, to help me with the boat. His name was Theódhoros Kaplánis and we set off late in the afternoon, about five or six o'clock one day in July 1941. We sailed past Skíros and the next day reached Psará [a small island, west of the north end of Chíos]. At first light we stopped at Andípsara [west of Psará] and got them all out on to this island, and told them to hide all day in the caves by the sea, and in the evening we would come and get them and set off again. With Uncle Theódhoros I took the boat to another little island off Andípsara and moored it behind a large rock where it was more or less out of sight of the opposite shore. There we spent the whole day, worrying whether we'd manage to make the crossing to Turkey.

Before we set off from where I'd left them all, this officer called Yánnis took me aside from the others and said to me, 'Captain, we're going to get rid of two of our company here on the island, now that we've found out who they are. They're not suitable for transfer to the Middle East.'

I didn't know which men he was talking about and I said, 'It's a great sin to do such a thing, because I shall be a guilty party too.' And I begged him not to do this deed, because one of the men who had come in my boat was a fellow villager, Nikólaos Th. Kaloyánnis, and I was afraid that he was talking about him, because they hadn't wanted us to bring him along with us from the village. It suddenly came to me that he meant he was going to kill them, and my suspicion was correct.

Later after we had set off and got near to Turkey, he came and sat next to me at the tiller, and said to me, 'Those who are sitting together talking next to the mast are big communist cadres. Mítsos Dhrosákis hid them in his house on Alónnisos. It appears they were known to him.'

The men were from Vólos. Anyway, the officer didn't do what he'd thought of doing, perhaps because he'd listened to me. When I came back from the little island where I'd hidden the boat, I took them all on board. Not one of the company was missing, and we set off from Andípsara in daylight, before it began to get dark, because a trawler from Psará came by, with its nets out for whitebait, and they told us there were no Germans on Psará. They only came occasionally when they were looking for someone, but today it was clear.

'You've nothing to fear till your past Psará,' they said, 'but from there on you're in God's hands.' They asked me if I'd got any bread to give them. 'It's months since we saw bread at home.'

I gave them some bread which we still had left in the boat and one of them wished me a thousand blessings. The trawler went with us as far as the harbour of Psará. It was still light when we passed Psará and went on towards Turkey. About two or three in the morning after we had passed Kardhámila in Chíos and were approaching the channel between Chíos and Agnoúses [also known as Inoúses] we encountered a German patrol boat with two or three collaborators on board.

We recognised them easily. It passed right next to us. It had its sail up and was going with a following wind towards Chíos. And we had our sail up too. They hailed us and asked where we were going, and we said we were going to Chíos town.

'Come alongside, come downwind,' they told us. We replied that our engine wasn't working properly and that we'd have to tack first to come downwind.

When we'd seen the boat from a distance one of the British had said to me, 'I've got four Mills hand grenades. We'll use them if comes to it. As long you can get close to the other boat, so I can throw them easily, we'll have a hundred per cent chance of success.'

But luckily we escaped. It seems they didn't suspect anything and we went on our way. In two or three hours we reached Turkish waters. By then it was getting light. We passed through the channel between Agnoúses and Turkey, and then through the group of islands the Turks call Günya. We went on and arrived at Çeşme about midday. Then the Turkish authorities arrived with the Greeks from the Consulate in Smyrna who were assigned this work. They took the British soldiers but the eight Greeks had to remain on the boat. They wouldn't let them go ashore, except for the officer, Yánnis, who had Turkish papers on him. That night they stayed inside the boat. They wouldn't even let them outside to sleep. But they said they would bring us food on the boat, and they left a Turkish guard to make sure no one got out. The next day they told us to leave, but there was a strong wind blowing. Another caïque that was there – it was from Chíos and belonged to the Greek Consulate – set out.

On board was the brother of the vice-consul, Nikólaos Dhiamandáras, who came from Chíos. But he came back and said, 'The wind's too strong. This boat can't sail.' So we stayed there until some time after midday. I don't know how we sorted things out, but then they took the Greeks ashore. We stayed about two days in Çeşme and Mr Dhiamandáras paid me only for the twelve British servicemen, six pounds each, and he gave me it in Greek money. For the Greeks he paid nothing, but he gave me two barrels of petrol, which was good, since you couldn't get any at the time. We took some food which they had given us and on the fourth day we set sail from Turkey and returned to Greece.

We left Çeşme at about seven or eight in the morning and reached a point on the Turkish mainland opposite Agnoúses. We waited there until it got dark before proceeding. When we reached open sea near Psará the wind was very strong. We went to Andípsara once more to wait for it to die down. It was a north-northeaster and we couldn't have made any headway. We stayed at Andípsara until it got light and the wind dropped. The wind was blowing from the southeast now, so we set sail, and the next day arrived at Alónnisos.

I sent Uncle Theódhoros home to Skiáthos in a caïque and paid him as I had agreed, even though he'd said he wanted nothing, except to see once more the land of his birth. His family came from Çeşme, but he had left as a refugee. Now our journey, in which we had suffered much from rough seas and the fear that the Germans would arrest us, was finally over.

After that I made many trips before winter set in, sometimes to Chalkidhikí to get supplies of grain, sometimes to Lésvos for oil. Around February 1942 the Italians came to our village because someone – I didn't know who – had given away the secret that British soldiers were being evacuated from our island. They had the names of those they wanted, and they and came and arrested them. They began by taking a few people, the wife of Yeóryos I. Alexíou, her father and some others – and beating them till they were half crazy, hoping they would talk. They took them to the secluded house of Vasílios Tsoukanás, and there they beat them.

The next day they came to the village and asked the deputy president, Konstandínos Strouflıótis, and the policeman, whose surname was Gourlós, to hand over the customs officer, who was called Mandoúvalos, and Yeóryos I. Alexíou, and Koumoundhoúros, who was from Vólos, but they had been told that the Italians were looking for them and had fled their houses and gone to Vounó, the hillside facing the village, to the cabin of Spíros Y. Malamaténios where they could keep an eye on what was going on. Then the policeman and the vice-president set out to arrest them, for the policeman knew where they were. They had an understanding with the customs officer that if they were wanted they would warn them so they could escape but, instead of warning them, he went to arrest them. When they saw the policeman and the vice-president approaching they thought they were also coming to hide. But they were coming as enemies. They arrested the customs officer who thought it was a joke, but Alexíou refused to give himself up. So the policeman set on him with his knife and stabbed him twice in the shoulder and he fell down dead. They took the customs guard and left. They went and handed him over and reported that they had killed the other man, which was what they thought.

Alexíou came round, though, and Spíros Y. Malamaténios helped him to get away and then some others took charge of him and took him over to the island of Peristéra. But his wounds wouldn't stop bleeding. In the meantime the Italians, who had no confidence in the policeman, went and arrested Spíros Malamaténios along with his wife, and Dhimítrios Dhrosákis, Panayótis Chrístou and some others and took them to Vólos. They'd been looking for several other men too, myself included, but they didn't find them in the village. At the time I was at Kirá Panayá with my caïque.

Figure 11.19 The house of Spíros Malamaténios at Vounó, where Yeóryos Alexíou was in hiding.

> I heard what had happened and went down in another, smaller boat to find out more, because I'd been told that the Italians were also looking for me and that when they'd gone to my house everyone was crying, thinking they would arrest me too. The Italians had gone now but we didn't know when they would be back to make more arrests, and I decided to go to Turkey so as not to fall into their hands. Yeóryos Alexíou who was on Peristéra, together with Ioánnis Channás, Yeóryos Karádhis and K. Koumoundhoúros from Vólos, all escaped with Captain Michális who had come over from Turkey, but the unfortunate Alexíou never made it to Smyrna. He died as soon as they arrived and was buried in the Greek Consulate. But when I decided to leave I had no one to take with me, yet how could I sail the boat alone? So I took Nikólaos Y. Floroús, nicknamed Kafiréas. The Italians were after him too. He came alone without his family even knowing he had gone.
>
> As for me, I left a wife and three children to the mercy of God, whatever might happen. My oldest child, a boy, Níkos, was eight, the next, a girl, Eléni was five and the younger girl, Sinodhí, was about one and a half, and I abandoned them and fled to the Middle East. I went first to Kirá Panayá with Nikólaos Floroús to get my caïque and then we set off about 15 or 16 March 1942. After about twenty-four hours' sailing from Kirá Panayá we reached Kaloní in Lésvos, where we stayed three or four days because of the weather, and then we set off again one night for Turkey. We got to Çeşme about 30 March and stayed ten to fifteen days. The Greek and British authorities there asked us to undertake missions to Greece, but we told them, 'We came here to save our skins, and we came because of you, and we shan't go back. Send us anywhere else to work but not to Greece. We've abandoned our families to save British servicemen, and now you owe us something.'

From this journal of Evángelos Anagnóstou we get an impression of the situation during the first years of the war. Anagnóstou was a refugee in the Middle East for three years. During that entire period his family had no news of him at all.

While we are dealing with the first years of the war, we must also mention Yeóryos Serendás, a Russian agent, who had been exiled to our island by the Metaxás government. He spoke seven languages and was a civil engineer. In 1942 when Germany declared war on Russia he was evacuated by Níkos Kaloyánnis so that he would not be killed by the Germans. They had met when Serendás was in the Middle East directing a major construction project for the Euphrates dam.

11.2.3 Tzoúmas and Paplomatás

When the Italians left and the Germans arrived, our island was thrown into confusion by the capture of Tzoúmas and Paplomatás.

A caïque belonging to the Resistance was on its way to Kirá Panayá with four men on board. In the open sea off Ladhádhiko in southern Peristéra the ignition burner for the diesel engine broke down. Using the oars they got the boat into the concealed inlet once used as a hideout by the pirate Tsélios. One of the men went off to Skiáthos to get it fixed.

Figure 11.20 Angelikí from the Anagnóstou family on her wedding day, 1946.

Two of the three men remaining on the boat, Tzoúmas and Paplomatás, who both came from Peristéra, thought it best to get away and hide, in case their position was discovered. They went off to find Theódhoros and Kostís Athanasíou, who took them in. The third crew member was called Artémis and he spoke fluent English, having spent several years in America.

He refused to abandon the boat and stayed to guard it. Suddenly from where he was sitting he saw a mast rounding Cape Tsélios, and he just managed to hide among the nearby rocks in time. It was a German patrol boat, which, seeing the hidden caïque fired a shot.

After firing a further volley of warning shots they made an inspection, and assuming the boat had been abandoned they towed it to Skópelos. From there they sent out a search party to find the partisans who had abandoned the boat. Artémis, meanwhile, set off on foot to Vasilikós to warn the others. Tzoúmas and Paplomatás escaped from Vasilikós. But Artémis, who seemed to be a marked man, hid in the Cave of Máka, waiting for Captain Michális' boat to take him away.

The hunt for the three men began. The leader of the expedition was an Alonnisiot collaborator named Stamátis who had at first been a good patriot, and had taken part in the evacuation of British servicemen. He was even among those listed as members of the Resistance by the Italians.

For some unknown reason he had sided with the Germans and become their representative on the island. Along with two other collaborators he was appointed by the Germans to apprehend the two fugitives. He went to Peristéra and Alónnisos and ordered that none of the small boats should leave harbour. Then he learned from his colleagues that the men they were after were somewhere in the vicinity of Patitíri. Tzoúmas and Paplomatás had in fact split up in order to have more flexibility. Tzoúmas had gone to a hut to get water to drink. The woman who lived there (she was called Ánna) said to him, 'Wait here while I go and get it.' But she betrayed him to his pursuers.

Tzoúmas was inside the house. He heard a noise and came out and saw that they were almost upon him. He began to run and they started to shoot at him. Stamátis, the collaborator, was amazed that they didn't hit him, and afterwards told the German administration that Tzoúmas must have been wearing a piece of the True Cross. Near the hut there was a cliff, a sheer drop of about 15 metres. Tzoúmas was a man of great physical courage and prowess (his house was full of medals for his heroic acts in the Albanian Front), and he decided to jump off the cliff rather than be captured. He fell about 15 metres on to rocky ground but wasn't seriously hurt. At the point where he landed he later built a shrine which is still there today.

His pursuers came down by the footpath and found him dazed. One of the young men in the party was going to knife, him but his father who was also among the collaborators, stopped him. They took Tzoúmas, half conscious, to Skópelos and from there he was sent to Thessalonica together with Konstandínos Chrístou.

On this trip the Germans had brought with them the captain-owner of the fishing boat they had just commandeered, but he was of no further use to them and so they killed him and dumped his body in the sea.

Figure 11.21 Tzoúmas at the blessing of the shrine marking the spot on the cliff from which he leapt to escape his pursuers.

Tzoúmas was incarcerated in the prison camp at Karabournoú, on the south side of the bay of Thessalonica, but Paplomatás had managed to escape from the ship and made his way to Cape Kókkino (where the lighthouse stands in the bay of Mikrós Mourtiás). There K. Garifállou Agállou received him and took him in his boat to Sáres, the headland on the east side of Skópelos harbour. To avoid reprisals Agállou gave out that Paplomatás had set off swimming and then got across in a boat he'd found.

As for Tzoúmas, one night when the weather was bad and there was no moon, he got under the barbed wire of the camp and plunged into the cold waters of the Thermaic Gulf. He got away and made contact with the Resistance in Macedonia who arranged for him to escape to Turkey.

Figure 11.22 Sailor Andhréas Papavasilíou, 1940.

Towards the end of the war, in Asia Minor where he was serving in the armed forces, Tzoúmas ran into Stamátis, the man who had tracked him down. The Alonnisiot collaborator froze as soon as he saw Tzoúmas. Tzoúmas forgave him, however, and told him to work for the good of the country from now on. But Paplomatás, who was more revengeful, did not let him off when his turn came.

Towards the end of the war, when the Germans were withdrawing and the Resistance was gaining the upper hand, Stamátis had made a trip in his boat, taking along his son and his brother, Kostís. They were transporting oranges and tangerines from Chíos to Chalkidhikí. But the Resistance had been tipped off and Paplomatás and others were waiting for them.

Stamátis saw them first and hid among the fruit. The partisans asked the other two if they knew where their captain was. Naturally the son would not betray his father, nor the other man his brother. They said, 'If you tell us where he is we won't harm you. Otherwise, if we find him, we shall kill you too.' Then they searched the boat and found Stamátis. They seized them all and took them into the hills. There before the father's eyes they killed the son who was innocent. Stamátis himself insisted that the boy had done nothing.

'Kill me,' he said, 'since I'm guilty, but let him go free.' But they had just laughed at him, and then they killed his brother too. The brother's death was undeserved and he left behind a large family. They tortured Stamátis himself for several hours and finally they hanged him from a plane tree.

11.2.4 A Plane Crash at Marpoúnda

Another event that stuck in the memory of the inhabitants of our island was the crash of a German plane near Marpoúnda. M. Kaloyánnis tells the story:

> An aeroplane appeared from the direction of Skántzoura flying low and heading for the village. The pilot was trying to make a forced landing, probably because of some serious mechanical problem. His intention must have been to splash down in the sea. But he didn't make it and a few metres before the sea he crashed into the tops of some pine trees, opposite the little island. The plane suffered considerable damage but it didn't blow up. Three of the crew escaped, seriously wounded, while the fourth was killed when a pine branch went through his neck.
>
> The Alonnisiots treated the wounded men, and the police went off to inform the German guard post on Skópelos. The Germans came with a patrol boat and took away the wounded and gathered together the wreckage of the plane, and some of them went after two locals who were trying to make off with various items.
>
> They were firing at them, but they managed to escape, though only just. The German authorities thanked the locals for the care they had taken of the dead pilot. They had laid him in a coffin which they decorated as they would have done for one of their own people. The Germans demonstrated their 'gratitude' in Kopriá in 1944 with the execution of the 11 Greek patriots.

11.3 The War on Kirá Panayá

The Axis Powers immediately recognised the vital strategic importance of Kirá Panayá. In the northern harbour they established a guard post manned by 25–30 soldiers. Their sector of operations was the northern group of islands, and three patrol boats were permanently stationed at Kirá Panayá. As soon as they were established there they took it into their heads to take prisoner the son of the old soldier Vláikos who lived at Áyos Pétros. He was forced to bring a goat every day and bread for his captors. The old people say that the Germans had a huge cauldron which was continually boiling into which they would put the whole goat, just as it was. From Kirá Panayá they would go out on frequent patrols and make surprise appearances in the surrounding islands.

11.3.1 An Event at the Monastery on Kirá Panayá

Figure 11.23 At the monastery on Kirá Panayá, 1964. *Courtesy of Thomas Vestrum.*

The Germans decided that the monastery on Kirá Panayá was another place that needed to be garrisoned. They sent five or six soldiers from the guard post which had already been established on the small island of Pétra in Planítis bay, and from then on there was a permanent monastery guard at the Athonite establishment.

One day a fishing caïque large enough to carry a gun of considerable diameter anchored at Yoúra, and took on board the Alonnisiot Chrístos Malamaténios. The crew of this allied boat was made up of British servicemen and members of Greek Resistance. Their aim was to annihilate, or at least scare off, the German guards at the monastery of Kirá Panayá, so that they would be less likely to spot the allied submarine which was engaged in secret missions off the east coast of the island.

Under sail, so as to make no noise, they landed in an inlet close to the monastery, but not within its bay. From there they climbed up under cover of darkness and approached the stone wall around the monastery courtyard. Near the entrance a German was keeping watch. It was cold and he was wearing the Nazi soldier's full-length cape.

In the dark the Greeks mistook him for a monk and in a whisper, they called to him in Greek to tell them how things stood. He was surprised but reacted promptly, throwing a hand grenade and running for cover. He dashed inside the outer courtyard, closed the gate behind him and raised the alarm. He went up to the cells and reported to the officer in charge and the battle began.

The Germans were firing from the windows at the wall where the allies were hiding. They returned the fire but it was pointless. The position was well defended and neither side could get anywhere since they were completely hidden from each other. Finally the attackers withdrew before the defenders could be reinforced from the guard post at Planítis, which was about an hour away.

Figure 11.24 Balcony at the monastery, Kirá Panayá, 1964. *Courtesy of Thomas Vestrum.*

As they retreated they deliberately left behind a British Thomson revolver and some English cigarettes, so as not to provoke reprisals against the local people. Under fire the boat with its engine full ahead got away from the shore. They headed out to sea in the direction of Grámeza and then stopped and began to bombard the monastery but without scoring a hit. Fearing a renewed attack, however, the Germans abandoned the monastery and rejoined the main guard post at Planítis.

Figure 11.25 Monastery, Kirá Panayá, 1969. *Courtesy of Fótis Tzortzátos.*

11.3.2 Vasílis Kónstas Remembers

The following account was provided by Vasílis Kónstas.

> When the war in Albania ended we tramped for twenty days before we reached Vólos. For the rest of the war I stayed on Kirá Panayá. I lived in the monastic buildings and had my own goats, from which the monks used to take a share. However, in the confusion of war and with food being so scarce we didn't give them any.
>
> But the Germans on our island consumed 200 of our goats and three cows. Old Vláikos used to kill and skin the goats and take them to them every day. They used to shoot the cows in the field and gut them on the spot. Then they would carry the animal tied to a big beam with three men in front and three behind and hang it from a large olive tree, where they would proceed to cut off slices and cook them. At Áyos Pétros there were four more Germans with their own patrol boat and I used to bring them water every day. The Rumanians [in the German army] would continually ask me if I'd seen enemy ships and I would just tell them that what they saw, I saw.

11.3.3 The Sinking of Three Torpedo Boats at Planítis

The following account was provided by Dhimítrios Malamaténios.

> Towards the end of the war we were fishing at Kirá Panayá, at Planítis to be precise. The German army had almost completely withdrawn and three British torpedo boats had arrived at Planítis. They tied them to the rocks with their sterns towards the sea and sent a lookout to the highest point of the island. We were across the bay from them and could see them clearly. Suddenly we heard an aeroplane
>
> The crew did not prepare to defend themselves since, although Planítis is a closed harbour, there are no cliffs to provide protection from attack. The British hastily abandoned the boats and hid in the bushes. Seeing this we did the same. Among the crew were two Greek officers who did not hide but grabbed machine guns to repel the attack. The aeroplane was British, but seeing the men take cover and grabbing machine guns they assumed they were Germans. The plane began to make dives and to attack from both sides. The bullets were whistling and ripped through the bodies of the two Greek gunners.
>
> The British plane made repeated dives until all three boats were sunk. When it was over the crew came out of the bushes and set about salvaging whatever was floating. A group of two or three dropped the bodies of the Greek officers into the sea with irons tied to their feet according to naval custom, so that they would sink. The rest got busy mending the holes the aeroplane had made in the boats with lead and copper plates. Having done that they began to bale out the water. Since the boats were tied up close to the shore they were resting on the bottom but were only half-submerged. Eventually they got them afloat again, got the engines going and made off.

11.4 The War on Other Islands

11.4.1 Peristéra: The Testimony of Konstandínos Athanasíou

The following account was provided by Konstandínos Athanasíou, the son of Theódhoros Likoúrgou Athanasíou whose story has already been told.[8]

> As soon as the Albanian Front collapsed, we came back to our homes at Vasilikós on Peristéra and continued the struggle there. The place where I lived was lonely and sheltered, so the organisation for the evacuation of allied soldiers recruited me and my father. Our job was to shelter and feed (with what little we had) allies and Greeks who were on the run.
>
> They had to get to Çeşme in Turkey and from there to the Middle East. In the winter we hid them in the caves of Mákaris and in summer around our house. Our other job was to supply petrol to the caïque that would come and take them off. At that time the transport was in the hands of a Mr Yeóryis from Vatiká [in Évvia]. To begin with the petrol tank was next to my house, but after frequent visits from enemy search parties I buried it in the ground.

Figure 11.26 Vasilikós, Peristéra, 1964. *Courtesy of Linda.*

The whole process ran smoothly until our work was betrayed by someone from Skópelos by the name of Prokópis. This man, angry that the Alonnisiot, Karayánnis, hadn't taken him along with the British soldiers from the island of Áyos Yeóryos, revealed the whole evacuation plan to the Italians. It was winter, and raining, when about fifteen Italians, aboard a caïque they had commandeered, belonging to a man known as Chácholos ['Bumpkin'] from Skópelos, anchored at Vasilikós. My wife spotted some men leaping out of a caïque and informed us. My younger brother Likoúrgos was ordered by my father to take some detonators which we used for fishing and hide them. As he came out of the house he got frightened and began to run. The Italians started firing at him but they missed.

Later I learned that the Italians who came had shot at Uncle K. Agállou. He had tricked them, falling down and playing dead. A few metres below there was a cow belonging to Malámis, and they slaughtered it and cooked it in a hut by the sea. At the same time they came and arrested me and asked me about the British soldiers. I played dumb and in order to escape I told them there might be a caïque at Peristéri, a bay on the south coast of Peristéra. We went there and looked down from above, but we saw nothing, since the caïque was a figment of my imagination. We went back and the commanding officer ordered four soldiers to beat me unmercifully. They carried out the order and were continually asking me where the British were hiding. Fortunately a caïque had come by the day before, bound for Psará, and taken them. Otherwise they would all have been killed. Fearing for his own skin, some neighbour of mine reported to the officer that I knew about the British, and they set to again with a will and beat me some more. Finally, crippled and exhausted from the beating, I was seized by two unarmed Italian soldiers who were supposed to escort me to my house.

> Afraid that they would kill me, I gathered all my strength, got away from them and went to Vounó. After that I was living 'in the trees' for the rest of the war.
>
> Italian search parties used to come regularly, about once a fortnight, to the harbour of Vasilikós. I, however, was always safe in the caves with my father, and usually sound asleep.
>
> By the time the Italians handed over to the Germans, the evacuation of allied servicemen had been more or less completed. The new overseers continued to come with search parties about twice a month, and the following two events were connected with their visits:
>
> (1) The famous Alphons, a man of wavering allegiances, but with strong Greek sympathies, visited my father, in his role as a German officer. 'My dear old Thodhorís, where is your gun?' he asked. 'Behind the door,' my father replied.
>
> Alphons took it down, and asked him if he had bullets or if he'd like them to give him some. My father replied, untruthfully, that he neither had nor wanted any. Alphons saluted him in military fashion and left. Thus the Germans respected the old warrior's weapon, but after the war the *Ierolochítes* came and insolently took away his gun.[9]
>
> (2) One day when my sister Angelikí was minding the goats she saw a British submarine which had surfaced on the far side of Peristéra. In all innocence she mentioned it to an Alonnisiot boat owner named Matzitákias, but he reported it to the German guard post on Kirá Panayá. The Germans sent a patrol boat and a detachment of soldiers came and took us so that we could show them the spot.
>
> Naturally by then there was nothing to be seen. One of the soldiers, a Rumanian, observing the Parkéta reef, insisted that it was a submarine. I disagreed and he got angry and was going to shoot me. I was saved by an officer, who looked through his binoculars and was assured by him that it really was a reef.
>
> After this they came regularly, but they did no bother us. After the bombing of the convoy during the German withdrawal, the beach at Livadhákia[10] was littered with the bodies of drowned Germans. Such things had happened before during the war, and from a fellow islander living on the plateau at Vouní I heard of a tragicomic event.
>
> Some boy had gone down to the beach and found a Nazi cap and uniform. He was very pleased with himself and put them on and set off towards his village. The people in the village lived in constant fear of attack and spread the word that a German soldier was approaching. Everyone hid. Later when they discovered their mistake the boy got a good telling off.

The Alphons mentioned in Konstandínos Athanasíou's account was one of the strangest people who passed through our islands. Before the war he came to Tríkeri (also known as Paleó Tríkeri), a tiny island in the large bay south of Vólos, and began to work on the caïques, mainly trawl-fishing.

He was a well-educated man who had sought refuge in Greece, and his way of life was like that of a monk. He preferred to share the hard life of simple sailors, but had to give this up when his hand was badly injured. During the 1930s he fished for many years with Agállou from Alónnisos. According to the old people, he recorded everything he could discover about the islands and knew every nook and cranny. Shortly before the war he went to Germany where he wrote a book about the fishermen of the Aegean.

During the war he turned up again as a German officer. But he loved the islanders and in the course of the war he saved the lives of many of them. With his detailed knowledge of the region, he used to go around in patrol boats briefing his conquering fellow countrymen about the islands. After the war he returned to the island of Tríkeri, where he converted the living quarters in the monastery of the Panayía into a hotel, and married a local Greek woman. With his education and his eccentric character he became well known in his motherland and many people came from Germany to visit him. In the end he was struck down by an incurable disease and retired to a cave where he peacefully yielded up his spirit.

11.4.2 Yoúra: The Testimony of Eléni Floroús

It was early August 1944, when four German soldiers and a junior officer came to the tranquil island of Yoúra. One of them was a Rumanian. He wore a German uniform with peasant boots. Their purpose was to take all the men from the island to the guard post at Planítis on Kirá Panayá. At that time there were about fifty people living on Yoúra, all herdsmen. They were there because of the big olive crops on Alónnisos. You had to keep the goats away from the olive groves, which was no easy matter. Since it was summer everyone was up in the hills where the shepherds had spring and summer quarters. There the simple herdsmen used the caves or made tin shacks where they lived and made cheese. The Germans landed in the big bay and proceeded to round everyone up in Perivoláki, on the west coast of Yoúra. My grandmother, Eléni Floroús was there and remembers the events:

> Suddenly six armed Germans appeared in front of us. I was alone and very frightened. The two boys who were there with me, Kostís Tzórtzis and Tássos Kaloyánnis, had run off in fright and I had no chance to warn the rest of the inhabitants. These wild beasts – that's what they were – began a search. They knocked down the piles of clothes, overturned the baskets, tipped the cheeses off the shelves and broke them open in case we'd hidden hand grenades inside them.
>
> Then, pointing to the milk, they asked me if I'd brought it from Tragórema for the British soldiers. I played the innocent and said I knew nothing about them. Then a Rumanian who spoke quite good Greek asked me if I had thread to sew his button on. He wanted to find out if the British had given us reels of sewing thread. I calmly unravelled some thread from my sock and gave it to him. He was furious and said he wanted a reel. I told him I had none and the search began again.
>
> At that very moment Uncle Mítsos Athanasíou's boat came into view, on the way from Valsámia to Chalkidhikí. For amusement the Germans began to fire at him from a great distance and the old man was obliged to turn back towards the land for safety. I saw my chance, and grabbing a jar of English jam and stuffing it down my dress I ran off as though I was chasing a hen and hid it under a large stone that fear gave me the strength to lift up. When they'd finished smashing the place up, they seized me and pushing me in front of them went off to arrest the others. My husband had

just had time to hide his gun in a bright green holly bush and had gone only a few steps before he ran into us and turned white. The Germans pushed him along the road striking him and the other men they rounded up. In the other huts there were English goods, soap and cigarettes, but as luck would have it they didn't find them.

They took the men in the patrol boat to Planítis where they beat them unmercifully. The torturer was a short German who beat them with a special stick, its branches trimmed but left as sharp points. He wanted information about a British submarine which had surfaced in the area. He didn't manage to break them, though, and eventually let them go.

But they hadn't gone far when a certain Matzitákias told the Germans that Floroús, my husband, was the brother of the fugitive, N. Floroús, and a new round of beating and torture began. In the end they took him with them to find his brother on Alónnisos. He said he would find him at Isómata, but there he made a run for it and made it to Áyos Pétros on Alónnisos. When it was dark he took his uncle's boat and rowed all night arriving at Yoúra exhausted. It was a superhuman effort, when you think that even a small motor boat takes three and a half hours. I was weeping all the time because I thought he was dead.

All the other men from Yoúra returned straightaway the next day, but my husband only came home after five days. With me helping they got him into a cave until his swollen and bleeding legs got better. From then on he was on the run and constantly in hiding. We didn't see the Germans again, except in passing patrol boats. Later during their withdrawal the bodies of many drowned Nazis were washed up on the shores of our wild island. The impoverished locals stripped them and took their clothes, their boots, and, if they were officers, their revolvers. Because of its many sea caves the caïques that transported the allies to the Middle East could find refuge on Yoúra.

On many occasions local caïques deposited hunted allied soldiers in these caves, until the partisans came by to take them to Turkey. I once went on a boat like that. There were English soldiers and Greeks and the captain was Vangélis [Yeoryíou] Anagnóstou. He was delighted to see us. He asked us about his family and for news of the war and gave us cigarettes and chocolate. They had been hiding in a cave and had put up a tarpaulin so they couldn't be seen from the sea.

11.4.3 Pipéri

During the war the Anagnóstou family were living on Pipéri. Evángelos Andoníou Anagnóstou was a member of the intelligence group set up by the Resistance. From time to time they would ask him about the movements of German patrol boats. He was armed with a Mannlicher rifle belonging to his cousin Agállou who was later executed. As soon as someone told the Germans where he was and what he was doing, they came to arrest him. But he saw them coming and hid. They terrorised his younger brothers whom they found alone in the sheepfold.

Then they stole their cheeses and left. Later they sent someone from Alónnisos to instruct Anagnóstou to hand over his gun to the German guard post at Skópelos. He went, and was saved thanks to the persuasive intervention of 'Von Kóstas', a Skopelite interpreter. After that, as he himself relates, there were no further German visits to the island. Some Greek patriots were in hiding on the island for a while and they regularly came to him for bread. Their hiding place was so remote that it was never found out. E. A. Anagnóstou himself writes as follows:

> What I particularly remember is how they used to hide the allied caïques en the way to the Middle East. They were all without masts and they had sandbags around the hold. They came close inshore where the water was deep. They hung lots of tyres from the side that was against the rocks and camouflaged the boats with tarpaulins. When they'd covered the boat completely, they climbed up the surrounding heights and watched for the enemy. That's what they did in the daytime and sailed on at night so as not to be seen. They would go aboard, role up the tarpaulins and start the engine with the exhaust in the water to cut down the noise. They would always paint local names on the boat (Skópelos or Alónnisos) before they set off and were lost in the dark. These precautions were necessary because of the numerous German boats that patrolled the area and the numerous warplanes carrying out reconnaissance from the air.

11.4.4 Psathoúra

During the war the Agállou family lived on the remote island of Psathoúra. Yeóryos Agállou helped his father, the lighthouse keeper, from 1941 to 1945. His father was appointed to the post by the Greek puppet government that was in the service of the Germans. The light in the lighthouse had to be kept switched off unless the order to light it was given. According to Yeóryos Agállou's own account there were two significant events on the island in this period. The first was an aeroplane crash and the second the sinking of a German ship, mentioned above. Both incidents are described in Chapter 15, below.[11]

Many 'local' caïques used to anchor offshore or close to the beach, and if challenged they could always say that they were on their way to Chalkidhikí for wheat or other goods. On one occasion, Agállou observed the Greek submarine *Papanikolís* surface several times before disappearing into the deep water off Psathoúra, but he could not get near it. With the help of allied ships it had managed to sink a convoy, from which bodies and various objects washed up on the beaches of several islands, including Psathoúra. Many such convoys passed by during the German withdrawal. A corvette or an anti-torpedo boat would escort transports, tugs pulling barges, petrol tankers and wooden sailing ships. The convoys were all on their way to Thessalonica.

In 1943 the first scientific expedition came to what is now the Marine Park of the Northern Sporades. In the early summer a group of scientists, headed by the Dean of a German university, a certain Dr Beck, came to Psathoúra. Their guide was the famous officer Alphons. The scientific mission toured all the islands of the Northern Sporades. On Psathoúra and the neighbouring islands they collected samples of plants, small animals, snakes, insects and sea creatures. Their 'scientific' research in the sea was carried out as follows: they would throw dynamite into the sea to kill the fish and then photograph them and study them when they came to the surface. They also took sponges from the sea and various living organisms which they kept in glass jars.

Figure 11.27 Pipéri, 1951. *Courtesy of N. Anagnóstou.*

Figure 11.28 Wives of the lighthouse keepers, Psathoúra, 1953.

Figure 11.29 The inhabitants of Psathoúra in front of the lighthouse, 1953.

Figure 11.30 Fetching water, Psathoúra, 1953.

11.4.5 A Bombing Incident on Pappoús

Some Skopelites had taken their boat to the small island of Pappoús, and were fishing there when a German plane happened to come by. The sailors were afraid and got out on to the rocks to hide. The pilot saw them running and, assuming the boat belonged to the Resistance, started to bomb it. The boat sank, but an old woman with a small rowing boat rescued the men, and took them to the nearby island of Grámeza where they hid among the cliffs. Later she took them across to the monastery on Kirá Panayá.

11.4.6 Skántzoura

On Skántzoura nothing of great significance happened during the war. There was an old monk living on the island, and the family of Yóryis Kiriazís, who didn't got involved in the Resistance, although they were good patriots. Many times Italian and German patrols stopped at the island. But they were only using it as a refuge for the night. Since it was near Évvia, the island was used at first as an assembly point for allies before they were sent on to the Middle East. Many Greeks, mainly from the surrounding regions, found refuge on Skántzoura. Among them were eight Greek patriots from Ayía Ánna in Évvia who were being pursued by the Germans. In desperation they came to the island in a small boat. From there an Alonnisiot took them to the Middle East. They left their boat and their nets with the monk, so that they could collect them after the war. After the bombardment of the German convoys, all sorts of useful things were washed up on Skántzoura.

11.5 Alonnisiots in the Prison Camps

All the patriotic actions described above were a problem for the invaders, and from the start local informers were recruited to co-operate with the Italians and Germans. At first it was the Italians, who, with the help of such informers, were able to arrest a large number of those patriots who had been helping allied soldiers to escape. Some were deported to prison camps, including three men arrested on Alónnisos. The first two were the boatmen Panayótis Chrístou and Mítsos Dhrosákis. The third was a brave activist, the customs officer, Mandoúvalos, who did not survive the barbarous conditions of imprisonment. Later, during the German occupation of our islands, Konstandínos Chrístou was captured by fellow islanders and handed over to the Germans. The stories of these four men follow.

11.5.1 Konstandínos Chrístou

Konstandínos Chrístou, the son of the Miltiádhis Chrístou who took part in the Macedonian Struggle,[12] was born in 1921. He learned his patriotism from his father – the ideal of freedom and the hard struggle that is necessary to attain it. At a young age he got involved in the national Resistance, and he was one of the first men on our island to organise transport for allied soldiers, including New Zealanders, Australians and Cypriots, who were trapped behind the lines and waiting anxiously to get across to Turkey.

Figure 11.31 The hero of the national resistance, K. Chrístou, when he came to lay a wreath and to recall the difficult years.

Together with his father, who owned a caïque, Konstandínos Chrístou evacuated 150 British servicemen from Katiyóryi, a village in Pílio at the beginning of May 1941. They sailed for five days braving the dangers of German patrols. In the same month they came back to Elliniká in northern Évvia and picked up 15 allies and three Greeks, and then three more at Alónnisos, and took them to the coast of Asia Minor, opposite Chíos. On another mission in June they evacuated 23 allies from the same village, Elliniká, and transported them to Skíros, where Y. Efstathíou and the Alonnisiot Panayótis Vláikos took over and transported them to Turkey.

That same year Chrístou was arrested at Almirós near Vólos by the Italians guarding the airfield and charged with illegal trafficking in arms. By good fortune he had not managed to get any material and nothing was found on his boat. He was led off to the Avérof prison, but after a month he was released for lack of evidence. His clothes in tatters and without food he made his way to Pílio There he was obliged to steal a boat when he ran into two armed Italians who wanted to question him. He caught them off guard and left them unconscious. Taking their guns, he seized the boat and tried to make his escape. He meant to get back to his island but it was an old boat and he found himself alternately rowing and bailing without rest. In the end it sank just south of Skiáthos, near the small island of Tsoungría. By chance a fisherman was passing and took him to Loutráki, the harbour below Glóssa, on Skópelos. From there he walked to Skópelos town. In the harbour there he met a fellow Alonnisiot who asked for his shoes in return for taking him back to the island. Disgusted at the behaviour of his fellow islander, he none the less gave them to him and, when they arrived, walked up to the village barefoot.

In 1943 his name was put forward for the post of onshore lookout for the Fourth Squadron of allied ships in the Middle East. Eager to serve his country, he took up the post and went off to Kirá Panayá. There he joined the Resistance, recorded the movements of the Germans and Italians and passed information to allied vessels so they could avoid traps and German patrol boats. This was done by lighting signal fires at Anixiatiká, the highest point on the island. His activities became known to local collaborators, who, on the instructions of the German military authorities on Skópelos, made a plan to capture him. Chrístou was well armed and the collaborators were afraid of a direct confrontation. Cunningly they arranged for a fellow Alonnisiot, whom Chrístou thought of as a good friend, to get him drunk. Then a band of Alonnisiots and Skopelites would come from Skópelos to apprehend him.

When the two men had drunk a whole bottle of *tsípouro* (the local grappa), the others arrived and tried to get him to their caïque. On the way he managed to get away from them, but being very dizzy from the drink he fell down. They tied him to the mast and, proud of their success, took him to Patitíri, where the leader of the German collaborators on Alónnisos took charge and brought him to the authorities on Skópelos. On the way they taunted him, saying, 'You're going to die, you scum.' But he replied, 'Then I shall die for my country, as a patriot, not as a traitor.'

Mileoúnis,[13] the governor of the Northern Sporades, who was based in Skiáthos, had come to Skópelos to carry out the interrogation in person. Holding his revolver against his temple, Mileoúnis threatened to kill Chrístou if he did not talk. Mileoúnis was ignorant of the code of loyalty observed by the Resistance and the allies. Chrístou refused to speak and in a rage Mileoúnis immediately signed a warrant for his transfer to the notorious concentration camps in Germany. He was taken directly to Thessalonica with another prisoner, Tzoúmas.[14] Chrístou's father was a tragic figure who went to Vólos hoping to buy his son's release, but Konstandínos was already in the P. Melás concentration camp in Thessalonica, and his father lost all trace of him.

In the camp in Thessalonica, when they had gathered the required number of prisoners to make up a transport (650), they sent them off for Germany. They were jammed in, 70 or 80 people to a railway wagon, with no space to sleep. They could only sit pressed tight against each other. Their only provisions came from the Red Cross in Thessalonica. In Yugoslavia, Serbian partisans were added to the train and it continued on to Germany. In Hungary they made a stop at a railway station and groups of people came up and asked who they were. '*Banditen*' the Germans replied, and the crowd started shouting insults and throwing stones at them. The men on the train called out. 'We're partisans, not thieves.' But in vain – the Hungarian people and their soldiers gave the prisoners the first taste of the psychological warfare that was to follow.

Disheartened the prisoners gave up their attempt to influence the fanatical crowd, whose leader was a Hungarian army officer. Without justification the Hungarians shouted abuse and spat at the prisoners, threw stones at them and banged on the outside of the train (but it may have all been show, to please the authorities). Then Konstandínos Chrístou stood up on the pile of Red Cross blankets to reach the window. The other prisoners handed him the latrine bucket and when the train moved off he poured it over the Hungarian officer. Then the whole station began to laugh it him and he didn't know where to put himself since he was covered in excrement.

In Germany the Greeks were put in the same camp as the Serbian partisans. Their remaining Red Cross provisions and their blankets were immediately confiscated. They were each given a green trench coat left over from the First World War with the letters 'KG' on the shoulder (*Kriegsgefangene*, 'Prisoner of War'). Around their necks they hung metal identity tags. Chrístou's tag had the number 1144.41. Later he went around many of the German camps as part of a labour brigade. Chrístou remembers the names of the camps where he was held like a nightmare litany: Essen, Düsseldorf, Nordholz, Mempel, the Rheine airbase, Bechtheim, Valonne,[15] and also, according to the Red Cross, Celle, Hannover, Wutzetz, and Friesack.

There they lived in wretched conditions. They slept on the concrete floors of wooden huts, pressed close together to keep warm. In the morning they would find that some had died from suffocation. Their rations were meagre. Each morning they got coffee and a slice of black bread with margarine and a little jam. They ate again in the evening, when they returned from work, but only thin cabbage soup. On Sundays they added some dark bran to the soup which made a kind of porridge.

Konstandínos Chrístou continues the story:

> When we went out into the villages to work we searched among the refuse for potato peelings or any other scraps. The German women pitied us and when they threw their rubbish out they wrapped bread and butter in paper for us to find, even though they were strictly forbidden to give us anything.

Our main task was to clear the roads after the bombing raids, to salvage the German civilians' possessions from the ruins and to dig defences, though we did many other things as well. On St Basil's Eve [31 December] we decided in our committee to go on hunger strike. Our idea was that since we were certainly going to die it was better to die from a bullet than starvation. That evening we didn't go to get our food.

The guards came and would have beaten us all night long, but luckily there was an air raid that night and we were spared their batons. Our hunger strike succeeded, since from then on they gave us double rations in the morning and the bran porridge twice a week. Out of 650 men only 35 survived. I remember vividly when we were working at the Rheine airbase there was a tremendous allied bombardment. The pandemonium went on all night. The earth shook from the bombs and the sky was lit up by the flares and the anti-aircraft tracers. Our hut was blown into the air and we suddenly found ourselves out in the open. Terrified, we ran and jumped into a ditch where we stayed till morning when the bombing stopped. Such were our living conditions.

When the Russians came, the Germans retreated, taking us with them in a column four abreast, for two or three kilometres into the interior of the country. Starving as we were, we pulled up nettles from the road and ate their tips. If we left the column even for a second they would shoot us. From time to time we came upon dead horses. With the little penknives that we had, each cut of what he could without leaving the column. Finally they brought us to a halt in a wood outside a village. They told us we could rest in the wood. Meanwhile the Russian army was approaching from the east, the Americans from the west. We heard artillery and small arms fire. In the morning we awoke to find our guards had abandoned us.

They had gone to a nearby village and donned civilian clothes to escape the fury of the allies. When we understood that we were free, we danced for joy. There were many pig farms in those parts and we fell on the pigs and ate them raw. Many of our company died there from eating so voraciously after days without food. Fortunately the British came and took charge of us and put a stop to this. They looked after us, since we were nothing but bones. We walked like living skeletons. We were comparatively lucky, being liberated fourteen days before the end of the war. Otherwise we would all have been dead. The British gave us appropriate food and drink and in about four months we were restored to health.

One day, when I was better, just before we left for Greece, I was taking a walk in the village and I saw some roses in a garden. I went in to cut one, and out came a German who started to shout at me. I couldn't restrain myself and unleashed all my pent up feelings against him and beat him unconscious.

In the station where we assembled I met P. Chrístou and Y. Kaliáris. I went to Greece by train and then to my island. My family were indescribably happy though they thought they were seeing a ghost. They had thought me dead and had put out *kólliva* for me.[16] When we were in Germany we were not allowed to communicate with our relatives. I had been a prisoner of war in Germany from September 1943 until the end of the war. Since then I've lived in Palió Chorió and been involved in various occupations, but mainly sailing and music (I played the *klaríno*).[17]

> After the war an anti-torpedo boat came to Patitíri, bringing Alexander himself, the commander of the British forces in the Mediterranean. They called out my name and that of my father through a loudspeaker, and an islander came up from Patitíri to tell us. When we went aboard the warship they began to play the Greek national anthem. They decorated us and presented us with citations and entertained us. Unfortunately I don't have these citations any more, because when the British exiled Makários to the Seychelles, hanged Dhimítrios and Karolís, burned down Afxéndios and committed so many other atrocious crimes in Cyprus, I felt soiled by their barbarous medals. As an act of patriotism, in 1956 I sent these tokens of distinction to the *Nomarchía*[18] for them to return to England.

11.5.2 Panayótis Chrístou

Panayótis Chrístou was an Alonnisiot who with his caïque helped to evacuate many allied servicemen. He was a member of the Northern Sporades network which was established for harbouring and evacuating allied servicemen stranded in Greece. He was betrayed by local informers including some of his own relatives and arrested by the Italians in 1941. He was taken to the Kassavetía prison in Vólos and sentenced to several years in gaol. After four or five months he was transferred to Italy. He remained there for about twelve months and the conditions there were very good, but then he was transferred to a prison camp in Germany.

Germany at that time needed a labour force for its war industry. Along with him went Y. Kaliáris from Skiáthos, who with his wife, the legendary Kaliarína, saved hundreds of allies. Another was Mandoúvalos who had also been arrested in Alónnisos. Until the end of the war they worked at Dachau. For a year Panayótis Chrístou was in the mines, in wretched conditions. Fortunately for him he specialised in very fine artistic work and enjoyed better treatment. His job was to paint bombs and do the lettering on them. In the factory where he worked someone urinated on one of the bombs and was summarily hanged and his body left there all day as an example. Every day Panayótis saw companions die, but as if by a miracle he survived to the end of the war despite the inhuman conditions of this camp, which was notorious for its barbarity. When he came back to the island he brought with him two cakes of soap made from the fat of prisoners and many photographs. When he died, his wife, under emotional strain, threw them all away.

At the end of the war he was saved by the Americans and, after four months of rest and recuperation, returned home. When they liberated prisoners in Germany, the allies recorded all their names, and Panayótis Chrístou was informed that in another division there was a certain K. Chrístou. He was delighted, thinking it was his brother. A meeting with the other Alonnisiot prisoner was quickly arranged. It was not his brother, but his first cousin Konstandínos Chrístou (whose story has already been related) and they spent four months together waiting to be sent back to Greece.

Panayótis Chrístou's wife had been left with two children and had to endure alone the hardships and hunger of the war. For five years she had no news of her husband, and when she heard he was on his way home she was overjoyed. As long as they were in Germany they were not allowed to send letters and no one here knew anything about their men. The Red Cross were forbidden to enter the camps. Panayótis was able to send a letter only after he had arrived in Greece.

11.5.3 Mandoúvalos, the Customs Guard

Mandoúvalos was not an Alonnisiot but deserves a mention since he was active on our island. As a true patriot with a strong character, he was an active member of the organisation for the evacuation of allied servicemen. He had a strong bond of friendship with Y. Alexíou and together with others they rescued and shielded British, Australian, New Zealand and Cypriot service men.

Unfortunately someone informed against him and he was captured by the Italians. When he tried to escape he was injured in a gully and transferred to the Kassavetía prison in Vólos. When he recovered, he was transferred to Italy, and after a year there was taken to Dachau, and worked in the Bavarian mines. Shortly before the liberation he fell seriously ill, and being unproductive he ended up in the camp ovens where they made the human soap.

Many years later, Mandoúvalos' father, who cut a sorry figure, met Panayótis Chrístou and asked him about his son. Panayótis told him the sad tale of how his son had met his unnatural end only a few days before the war ended.

11.5.4 Dhimítrios Dhrosákis

Dhimítrios (also known as Mitroúsis or Mítsos) Dhrosákis was the son of an Alonnisiot schoolteacher. His father had educated him, intending him to be a doctor. But Mítsos was interested in commerce and went off to Brazil. There he went into business supplying ships, and prospered. But he contracted a serious illness, which was exacerbated by the damp climate of Brazil, and he was obliged to return to Alónnisos, where he opened a cafe in Patitíri. He bought a large boat and in addition to running the cafe transported various goods. But, as a Greek citizen, when the war came, he went to the Front.

When the Front collapsed he came back to the island and took an energetic part in the protection and evacuation of allies. With his caïque he picked them up from the embarkation points and took them across to Peristéra. Many of them he fed with his own food and hid in his own house. Local informers denounced him to the Italians and he was led off to the Kassavetía prison in Vólos. There he was given a heavy sentence and after four months was transferred by ship to Italy, along with Panayótis Chrístou. He remained in Italy for about a year.

When the Germans needed personnel for their war industries, they took all the prisoners from the Italian gaols, transported them by train to Bavaria. In Yugoslavia Mitroúsis' train was attacked by Serbian partisans, who easily annihilated the German guards and set the prisoners free. Mitroúsis quickly learned Serbian and joined the partisans in the mountains where he remained until the end of the war. There he developed a personal friendship with Field-Marshal Tito, who was at that time a partisan. Mitroúsis gave Tito a handful of Greek soil as a talisman. Later the British Intelligence Service came to Greece and made him their post-war representative on Alónnisos.

Figure 11.32 Merchant vessel on the way from Áyos Yeóryos to Vólos.
Courtesy of María Dhióma.

11.6 Hunger and Trade during the War Period

Famine first set in during 1942, when two people died of hunger in Palió Chorió. After that everyone began to plant crops all over the island from end to end. It was this that forced many herdsman to move to the other islands with their small flocks. Each family's meagre harvest was so valuable to them that the crops had to be protected from animals. In addition everyone threw themselves into olive growing, because as long as you have olive oil you won't 'swell' with hunger, as they say.

It was fortunate that in those years fish were abundant. Sometimes the sardines just jumped out on to the rocks and the locals gathered them up. For meat there were sea-birds, 'old women' as they are called, which people caught by climbing up the cliffs with torches. The birds would fly towards the light and crash into the rocks behind. They got so used to the meat of these birds that after the war they became a favourite appetiser. The wild goats on Yoúra were decimated by relentless hunting, and the survivors became so cunning that you might hunt for weeks without killing a single one. There were surpluses of two island products, wine and oil, but pulses and grains were in very short supply. In the spring there was plenty of cheese and other animal products.

Of necessity, to ensure survival, a new kind of trade developed. To begin with everyone paid in money and transactions were simple. Eventually money became useless and trade was conducted by exchanging goods. Alonnisiots with rowing boats or small sailing craft, took whatever surplus products they had to other places in the region to exchange for foodstuffs. Usually they took wine, oil and soap to the grain-producing areas in Chalkidhikí and the Loudhía valley near Thessalonica. There they could exchange one *oká* of wine for eight *okádhes* of grain, or one *oká* of soap for six *okádhes* of grain.[19] They also went to Pílio to exchange island products for potatoes. If the wheat and barley they brought back was more than they needed to sustain their families, they would sell the extra. Some who had large caïques exploited the situation, operating a black market, and for five *okádhes* of grain they might acquire a good field.

Some of the poorer people tried to cross the open sea in small boats to save their families from hunger. Uncle Níkos Papadhákis used to tell me his stories from the war. He took what little wine and oil he could spare and struck out in a small boat to exchange it. He took a goat with him and foliage for its fodder. The goat's milk was all the food and drink he had throughout his voyage. Several times he almost drowned or was nearly caught by German patrol boats.

One night, on his way from Lésvos to Chalkidhikí he stopped at Áyos Efstrátios to rest, and seven men who had been exiled on that island got into his boat. The exiles there were in a desperate situation owing to the barbarity of their Greek guards. Even the German governor of Lésvos, when he saw their wretched condition, ordered their gaolers to give them more food and to treat them better. Nothing would persuade those seven men to get out of Uncle Níkos' boat, and they begged him to take them away from the hell of Áyos Efstrátios. He took pity on them, and, evading the watchful eyes of enemy patrols, took them across to Chalkidhikí. They rowed like crazy all night as though they were going for the record and by morning reached the mainland. Later the boat was impounded by the Germans, but Uncle Níkos found it again after the war in Lésvos.

Many Alonnisiots rowed all the way to Évvia to sell salt and buy pulses, grain and potatoes. And there were others who used to fish with improvised tackle. They made fishing lines from horse hair and hooks from bits of wire. But these makeshift devices were effective because, luckily, the fish were so plentiful. From chick-peas and lentils they made a kind of paste called *fáva*. It had been the staple food of their ancestors for the past 300 years. Boiled wild greens with lashings of oil also had a special place on the menu during the Occupation. Sweets and sugar were replaced by grape syrup and such honey as the island produced. There was also trade in seals which were killed while they were sleeping for their skin and their blubber.

Their tough skin was much in demand for shoes, and in the absence of kerosene for lamps, seal blubber was burned to give light. Later car tyres were used to make shoes, but these were very expensive – two days' labour for a piece of tyre big enough for a pair of shoes. Throughout the war there were many black marketeers who got rich exploiting the situation, profiting from the power of hunger.

In 1944–45, with the war coming to an end, the island found its natural rhythm once more, with everyone working together to ensure a regular supply of food.

Figure 11.33 Typical Alonnisiot lateen-rigged wooden sailing boat, 1946.
Courtesy of Ioánnis Frantzéskos.

Figure 11.34 The art of traditional cheese-pie making is handed down from generation to generation. During the Occupation the women of Alónnisos made pies of all kinds (octopus, meat, cheese, courgette) to satisfy their large families.

Figure 11.35 Making Alónnisos-style cheese pies, Yoúra,.

11.7 Acts of Piracy during the War

In April 1942 a ship had stopped at Límnos to take on *tsípouro* (grappa), brandy and wine and was anchored at some harbour on the east side of the island. The sea was calm. In the harbour a local man invited the crew to join in the celebrations for the baptism of his son. They accepted the invitation and drank and danced all night, and when the wind got up they ignored it. But their unmanned boat was dragged by the wind; its anchors didn't hold and it was blown out to sea. It eventually ended up close to the rocks just below the monastery on Kirá Panayá. In the monastery there were some Alonnisiots and the monks Veniamín and Athanásios, who went down and stole the cargo from the boat. To avoid attracting suspicion they then sank the boat with hand grenades.

It was also in 1942 that a cargo boat from Límnos, having delivered a cargo of oil, soap and wine (belonging to the black-marketeers of Alónnisos) to Kassándhra in Chalkidhikí, was returning laden with barley, wheat, lentils, beans, grapes and almonds. The crew of four anchored in Peristéri bay on Peristéra, intending to proceed from there directly to their island. The people of Peristéra had received advance warning and with the co-operation of a partisan boat – the customs officer of Skiáthos was among the partisans – they attacked the boat of the black-marketeers and took the cargo. A small part was sent to Pílio for the partisans engaged in the struggle there, and the rest was divided between Alonnisiots, Skiathites and the crew of the partisan boat.

With the same boat the partisans also captured two other boats at Peristéri, one loaded with flour from Vólos, and one unladen boat whose captain worked for the Germans. They unloaded a third of the cargo at Peristéri and then took the boat round to Klíma on the east coast of the island, where they unloaded another third on the headland of the bay. Four days later the boats were transferred to the Middle East for the needs of the Fourth Allied Division. The rest of the cargo the partisans hid in their own houses or the houses of neighbours they could trust, or stored it in caves and old mines. In those days grain was like gold. For a 'gas-crate' of grain you could buy a whole field,[20] while a whole day's labour was valued at a handful of beans. In the end the captain went off to the Middle East, but after the war he resumed his trading runs.

As we have seen it was hunger that drove men to piracy in 1942. According to Gandhi, hunger is the worst form of violence and leads men to crime. If one recalls that at that time two people died of malnutrition in Alónnisos, one realises how hazardous life was in those years.

The very last act of piracy in these islands took place in March 1944 on the island of Pipéri, and was undertaken for purely patriotic and philanthropic reasons. The man responsible was a relative of mine, Evángelos (or Vangélis) Yeoryíou Anagnóstou, and I am extremely proud of him. At the height of the famine in 1944 he saved almost the entire island of Foúrni in the Dodecanese, and also enabled many of the inhabitants of nearby Ikaría to survive.

Captain Vangélis' crew consisted of two Greek sailors, an American gunner and two officers of American origin as passengers. On the way they met the caïque that had captured Mileoúnis, the harsh German governor of the Northern Sporades. In order to avoid a German attack they travelled with this caïque to Kouloúri in Pílio, and together with the two American officers they delivered the hostage to the partisans at nearby Venetó, and then made off as fast as they could for Pipéri with the aim of returning to Turkey. Evángelos Anagnóstou (Captain Vangélis himself) told the story in his *Journal*:

> We took our caïque and set off and in the morning we arrived at the island of Pipéri in the Northern Sporades. We found a small caïque anchored there, carrying five or six thousand *okádhes* of wheat destined for Lésvos and Chíos. The captain, as he told us himself, was from Aretós near Thessalonica, and his name was Sotíris. There were also two merchants who had wheat for the black market.
>
> Since the captain had told us they were black marketeers, when it got dark I said to them, 'Get your boat ready and come near ours and fix a rope so that we can tow you to Lésvos', so they wouldn't suspect we were going to take them to Turkey. Tom the American got into their boat with his automatic on his shoulder just in case they tried to cut the cable during the night and get away from us. In the morning we passed by Sígri on the west side of Lésvos and two or three hours later we were near Babakale on the Turkish coast and were now quite safe from German patrol boats. We kept in Turkish waters, crossed the Gulf of Edremit, passed the Moslonísia[21] and reached our base. There they began to unload caïque full of wheat into smaller caïques which took it to Ikaría and Foúrni to be distributed to the people there.

11.8 Accidents with Mines

In Alónnisos as many people were killed by mines during or after the war as were killed in other ways in the course of the war. A total of 11 individuals fell victim to an undeclared war. The treacherous mines were German, laid by the occupying forces in straits and harbours. In our area they were laid at Cape Kókkino (on the west side of Mikrós Mourtiás bay), and in various channels and coves. Many others laid in neighbouring regions such as Pílio and Chalkidhikí broke loose and drifted about, and were eventually washed up on the shores of Alónnisos and the surrounding islands. Many floating mines were located by local people. Throughout the first postwar decade minesweepers of the Greek Navy were continually neutralising mines following information provided by local officials.

Figure 11.36 Mines. Alónnisos' nightmare.

Three terrible events shocked the population of the island. In the aftermath of the war, and particularly during the Civil War (1946–49), the situation was desperate. The inhabitants were trying to restore the island and provide themselves with the necessities of life. Fishing gear was unobtainable and many made a living from mines. They used the explosives for fishing and then sold, bartered or salted the fish which were so easily caught by this method. (Because of the war the sea had not been fished commercially for many years and the fish stocks had grown enormously.) They would tow the mines to a place where it would be easy to deal with them. With only very basic tools they would remove the covers and take out the vitreous fuses. Once they'd got the fuses out, they'd remove the 200–300 kilos of hardened explosive. This they pulverised to ensure it would ignite, and put it into tin cans of various sizes, and inserted the detonators. They would watch from a boat or the rocks till they saw the glint of fish in the water and then throw their homemade bombs into the sea. A number of accidents resulted from these practices, as described below.

11.8.1 Seven People Killed by a Mine, Mourtiás, November 1944

In the autumn of 1944 some Alonnisiots found one of the larger types of mines at Cape Kókkino. It had come loose from its moorings and was floating. Using two boats they towed it close to the shore, where they attempted to open it with the limited expertise they had and only simple tools. It contained 300 kilos of dynamite in a solid matrix. The external cauldron-like body had protruding spring-loaded rods which were connected by wires to a central detonator. When a ship bumped into such a mine, one or more of the rods would be depressed, triggering the explosion.

Seven people were involved in this attempt, including Thanásis Likoúrgou Athanasíou, his eight-year-old son Kostákis and his elder son Vangélis who was 21. It is very strange that a child was involved in such a dangerous undertaking. The others were a man from Skíros and three Alonnisiots, Ioánnis Paraskevás and two other men who were both called Yórgos Floroús. The whole operation was observed from a safe distance by two other people, one of whom was the wife of one of the unfortunates; the other a shepherd who had left his goats at Kalóvoulo and come down to get his share of the spoils.

These eye witnesses suddenly saw smoke, and when it cleared there was nothing left but the lower parts of the boats below the waterline. In the village windows were shattered and the explosion was heard on Peristéra. Fragments of flesh, hair and clothes were scattered all over the hillside. According to the accounts of the witnesses, although they had kept the mine floating so the detonator rods wouldn't strike the rocks, one of the men had accidentally taken hold of one of the rods and set off the explosion.

11.8.2 A Mine Spreads Death, Manólas, December 1944

On the west coast of Alónnisos, which faces the mainland, mines were continually drifting ashore and getting stuck among the rocks. As Kóstas Kaloyánnis relates,

> One day when I was a boy, I saw from our hut in the hills something shining down by the shore. My father sent me to see what kind of a gift the gods had sent us. When I got near, I saw an iron object with a kind of door that was hanging open. I reached inside and began to cut the cables by hitting them with stones.
>
> Then, also with stones, I broke and pulled out three fuses. Then my mother came along and she was as ignorant as I was and together we tried to remove various bits and pieces by banging them with stones. When we

got home and my father saw our finds, he recognised them and practically fainted. Afterwards he exchanged the fuses for cigarettes.

The fishermen, Kóstas Agállou and Thanásis, who had just married a local girl, were not so lucky. They found a mine in the open sea off the rocky island of Manólas. The sea was dead calm and I could even hear their voices. They went nearer and gave thanks to God when they saw it was a mine. Suddenly a small caïque with two other Alonnisiot fishermen on board appeared. The two who had got the mine said they were going to take it close inshore to open it, and told the others to go round the other side of Manólas to take cover.

The other two were annoyed that they couldn't stay there to fish, but they went round the other side of the island and far enough out to sea to be safe. Kóstas and Thanásis towed the mine to a sea cave on the island where they could diffuse it without being seen. They didn't get the chance to do the job, because there was a big explosion and black smoke and dust poured out of the cave.

The other fishermen approached with caution to see what had happened. They waited for the smoke to clear, calling out in case anyone was still alive. When the dust settled they went inside but saw nothing but blood and little bits of flesh stuck to the sides of the cave. They went to inform the customs officer and the rest of the inhabitants, who had all heard the explosion but didn't know what had happened. Many boats went to the scene of the tragedy but there was almost nothing to retrieve. This event took place on the St Basil's Eve [31 December].

11.8.3 A Mine Kills Three at Kokkaliás on Peristéra, May 1948

An eye-witness account by Ioánnis Konstandínou Agállou:

> An Alonnisiot was ferrying the lighthouse keepers from Psathoúra to Patitíri. They happened to come across a mine in the sea off Áyos Dhimítrios and when they got to the harbour[22] they informed the customs officer. He in turn mentioned it to a group of fishermen who decided to go and open it. The group consisted of Konstandínos Athanasíou, whose boat they went in, with Nikólaos Vláikos and Y. Tzórtzis. They approached the mine, which was bobbing up and down on the water. At first they hesitated. The sea was calm. In the boatyards they spotted another fisherman painting his boat. They went to fetch him and it was K. Kaloyánnis. Together they tied up the mine and towed it with a 100-metre rope. They took it to Kokkaliás[23] on Peristéra. Athanasíou and Vláikos got scared and went five bays further on to take cover. From there they heard the deafening explosion. They went back certain of what they would find and were shaking when they confronted the horrific outcome. They informed the customs officer, and many local people, relatives and the curious, set off for the site of the explosion. They found nothing intact but the men's legs which had been in the water.[24] The other parts of their bodies were spread all round the bay. They brought the legs back to Patitíri and there are many who remember that frightful sight.

11.9 Addendum for the English Edition

by Níkos Th. Kaloyánnis

[Níkos Th. Kaloyánnis, who lives on Alónnisos, sent the author a detailed critique of the Greek edition of this book. He was particularly concerned about the book's political perspective on events of the Second World War and the immediate postwar period. The author invited Mr Kaloyánnis to write his own account of the events in which he was involved, for inclusion in the English edition. Mr Kaloyánnis agreed, but asked that what he wrote be translated in full and exactly as he had written it. The translator has complied with this request, even though this involves the repetition of part of an extract from the book by Evángelos Anagnóstou quoted earlier in this chapter (p. 241).]

I am going to write about a very small part of my life during the period of the Second World War. On 8 November 1941 the island's policemen summoned me to the police department. I went and stood in front of his desk, and asked him why he had sent for me. He answered with feeling, 'I sent for you to tell you that the Italians have learned about your activities in connection with the assistance you have given, along with your compatriots, to British soldiers, to enable them to get to Turkey; and I have received the order to arrest you and hand you over to them.'

He was referring to members of the British Expeditionary Force who had taken part in military campaigns against the Germans and Italians, and who, for various reasons, had not been able to retreat with the main body of the expeditionary force. The Greeks provided them with every assistance and protection and moved them forward from place to place until they reached Turkey, and thus avoided internment.

When the police officer informed me of the order he had received from the Italian occupation forces, I asked him, 'And what do *you* think should happen now? – first as a Greek, and then as a policeman.'

'But, look, you know, I have a family, I have children, there's nothing else I can do.'

'I, too, Officer, have a family and a child, but first and foremost I am a Greek and I will not allow you to hand me over to the Italian occupation forces.' I had decided to raise the stakes, ready to respond to whatever he might do.

Three days later, on 11 November 1941, the caïque belonging to Evángelos Y. Anagnóstou came the island with 16 Greek officers. Among them were Captain Yánnis Karabótsos and an Australian officer, as well as five Greek civilians: three from Vólos and two from Skiáthos. There were 24 of us in all. The capacity of the caïque was about ten persons – I mean, the capacity of the hold. We left the same day, in the afternoon. We passed by Skíros and continued on to Andípsara, an uninhabited island opposite Psará. For security reasons we travelled at night. There, on that uninhabited island, the first drama was played out.

Captain Yánnis Karabótsos, an agent of the Intelligence Service – the British were recruiting large numbers of agents at that time – had been sent from Cairo – now for the second time – to Greece, in order to enlist Greek officers who were dedicated loyalists and supporters of the fascist Metaxás regime. Karabótsos, carrying out the orders of his superiors, said to the captain and owner of the caïque, Evángelos Y. Anagnóstou – and here I transcribe the dialogue from page 99 of the book *Imerolóyon* (*Journal*), written by Evángelos Y. Anagnóstou and published in Athens by Papazísis in 1978:

> 'Captain, we're going to get rid of two of our company here on this island, now that we've found out who they are. They're not suitable for transfer to the Middle East.'
>
> 'It's a great sin to do such a thing, because I shall be a guilty party too.' And I begged him not to do this deed, because one of the men who had come in my boat was a fellow villager, Nikólaos Th. Kaloyánnis [the other man in question was Yeóryos Yourgoúlas, one of the three from Vólos],[25] and I was afraid that he was talking about him, because they hadn't wanted us to bring him along with us from the village. It suddenly came to me that he meant he was going to kill them, and my suspicion was correct.

The next day, at about nine o'clock in the morning we reached Çeşme. There we were 'welcomed' by the notorious Dhiamandáras, the Greek vice-consul who fleeced the Greeks who arrived there.

The Turks, in the course of the Second World War, played a double game. They were with the allies, and at the same time they were with the Germans. For each of the men the Turks received and sent on to the Middle East, the British paid five gold pounds, but the Turks sent large numbers of them back to Greece, many of whom fell into the hands of the Germans. Others they killed or despatched to work-camps in Germany. A proportion of the Greeks, at the suggestion of the British, passed as Greek Cypriots, and this was the case with us.

In the afternoon of the third day we had spent waiting in the hold of the caïque, the British ambassador came to see us and instructed us to tell the Turks, when they asked us, that we were Cypriots. Eventually the necessary formalities were completed, with both parties maintaining the subterfuge. After a stay of eight days in Çeşme we set of towards our destination. They took us to Smyrna, where we stayed two days. We went on by train to Aleppo in Syria, our final destination being Palestine. Kefar Yona, near Netanya in Palestine (now in Israel), was the headquarters of the composite First Greek Brigade.

Others who had come from Alónnisos to the Middle East were:

1. Yánnis P. Vláikos, who had been serving in the Navy. When the front collapsed, the battleship *Avérof* managed to reach Alexandria. Among the crew of the *Avérof* was Yánnis Vláikos. We met one another many times in Alexandria.

2. Níkos Y. Floroús, whom Evángelos Y. Anagnóstou took as crew on his caïque when he went to Turkey. From there, in the same caïque, they went to Cyprus and afterwards they crossed to Egypt. We met twice in al-Qasasin in Egypt.

3. Kóstas I. Alexíou who had been living in Athens. How he got to Egypt I do not know. Him I also met twice in al-Qasasin in Egypt.

And so our military life began. The First Greek Brigade was stationed in Syria and administratively subordinate to the Eighth Army. The commander of the Brigade was Pavsanías Katsótas. The commander of the Eight Army was General (later Field Marshall) Montgomery. In August 1942 the First Brigade was transferred and stationed outside Alexandria, in the rear of the El Alamein Front. Later it was sent up to the front line, in the southern sector of the front. On 26 October 1942 came the assault, the German defences gave way and began to retreat. Head of the German forces was Rommel, the Desert Fox, as they called him.

In January 1943 the First Brigade was transferred and stationed at Tripoli in Syria.[26] During the course of 1942 the Second Greek Brigade had also been set up. In late February and early March 1943 events of a political nature erupted in both Brigades.

The progressive democratic forces had rallied and had founded the ASO, the *Andifasistikí Stratiotikí Orgánosi* [Antifascist Military Organisation], in keeping with the antifascist spirit of the Second World War. The democratic forces, under the leadership of the ASO, demonstrated against the attempts of the British and their Greek subordinates to create a praetorian guard with the purpose, as soon as the war ended, of imposing on the Greek people the king who was their instrument.

After the events of March, there were arrests in both Brigades, and I was among the first to be arrested. With the 450 (approx.) antifascists whom they took from the two Brigades they formed the Eighth Battalion of Guards which they despatched to Tripoli in Libya, North Africa.

The antifascist struggle for the democratisation of the army continued. In April 1944 came the second wave of events. Our great 'friends' and 'allies', the British, reacted strongly against the demands of the armed forces, removing their masks and putting their cards on the table. They disbanded all three armed forces, army, navy and airforce, and put the ranks and many officers behind barbed wire. They then established the Mountain Brigade with a strength of about 2,500 officers and men: they had created the praetorian guard as had been their intention from the beginning.

The next stage was the despicable 'Lebanon Agreement' of 1944. This agreement paved the way for the brutal armed intervention of the British in December 1944. In the *Dhekemvrianá* [Events of December] the British took the place of the German occupation forces, and created even worse conditions of enslavement for the Greek people, with the equally despicable Agreements of Caserta (in Italy) and Várkiza (near Athens).[27]

These agreements were disastrous for the Greek people, since they gave birth to and nourished the parastate armed groups of the Soúrlidhes[28] and many others throughout Greece, and, worse still, brought into greater prominence the 'Security Battalions', the Chítes, Andón Tsaoús and others.[29] The orchestrated and controlled activities of the parastate organisations led to the Civil War. In 1947, during the course of the Civil War, the British passed the baton to the new American occupation forces, who have continued to exert their authority over us to this day.

Alónnisos, 4 September 1999
Níkos Th. Kaloyánnis

Notes

1. The Greek initials stand for *Ethnikón Apeleftherotikón Métopon*. EAM came to be dominated by the Greek Communist Party.
2. *Ellinikós Laikós Apeleftherotikós Stratós* and *Ellinikón Laikón Apeleftherotikón Naftikón* in Greek.
3. See p.273.
4. General Ioánnis Metaxás, a soldier turned politician, and dictator with fascist inclinations who ruled Greece from 1936 to 1941. See also p. 321, n. 4.
5. Traditional Greek sweets made from dough fried in oil, usually served with honey or rose syrup and cinnamon. [Translator]
6. The square in Palió Chorió extends to the edge of a small cliff. [Translator]
7. Anagnóstou (1978).
8. See pp. 202–5.
9. This was the gun given to Theódhoros Athanasíou by Queen Frederica (see p. 204).
10. Livadhákia is a bay on the east side of Peristéra, opposite the island of Lechoúsa. [Translator]
11. See pp. 380–5.
12. See pp. 205–8.
13. See p. 229.
14. See pp. 244–9.
15. Most of these names appear in the original in Greek transliteration and some of the identifications are uncertain. Some, such as Mempel, may be the names of factories rather than labour or prisoner-of-war camps.
16. *Kólliva* is a mixture of boiled wheat, dried fruit, sprinkled with flour and icing sugar, which is laid out in church during memorial services and distributed to those present or sent to absent relatives. [Translator]
17. The *klaríno* is a traditional Greek instrument similar to the clarinet. [Translator]
18. The offices of the Nomós (administrative region) of Magnisía in Vólos. [Translator]
19. 1 *oká* = 1.28 kg; *okádhes* is the plural. [Translator]
20. In those days, fuel oil was usually transported in standard wooden crates, two cans to a crate. The crates were reused for various purposes and the 'gas-crate' (*gazondeneké*) was commonly used as a measure of volume. [Information supplied by the author]
21. 'Moslonísia' is evidently the Greek name for the group of Turkish islands (Alibey Adası, Maden Adası, Karaada, etc.) on the south side of the entrance to the Gulf of Edremit. The name is probably related to Müsellim Boğazı (Müsellim Strait), the channel between the north coast of Lesvos and the Turkish mainland, through which they would have sailed after passing Babakale.
22. This presumably refers to the harbour at Patitíri. [Translator]
23. A bay on the south coast of Peristéra. [Translator]
24. The implication is that the men had been standing in the sea at the time of the explosion, and that the water shielded their legs from the full force of the blast. [Translator]
25. The information in square brackets is inserted by Mr Níkos Th. Kaloyánnis. [Translator]
26. In what is now Lebanon, but at that time Lebanon was still part of the French Mandate of Syria, though administered separately. [Translator]
27. The Caserta Agreement of September 1944 put all resistance forces in Greece under British command; the Agreement concluded in February 1945 at Varkíza near Athens followed the battles in the streets of Athens between British forces and EAM in December and January, and under the terms of this agreement EAM was required to disarm. [Translator]
28. The Soúrlidhes were named after their leader, Grigórios Soúrlas. [Translator]
29. These are all right-wing paramilitary organisations. The Chítes were members of an organisation known by the Greek letter *chi* (written 'X') under the leadership of Yeóryos Grívas (better known as leader of the anti-British EOKA movement in Cyprus in the 1950s).

Andón Tsaoús (also known as Andónios Fosterídhis) was the leader of a similar, smaller organisation. [Translator]

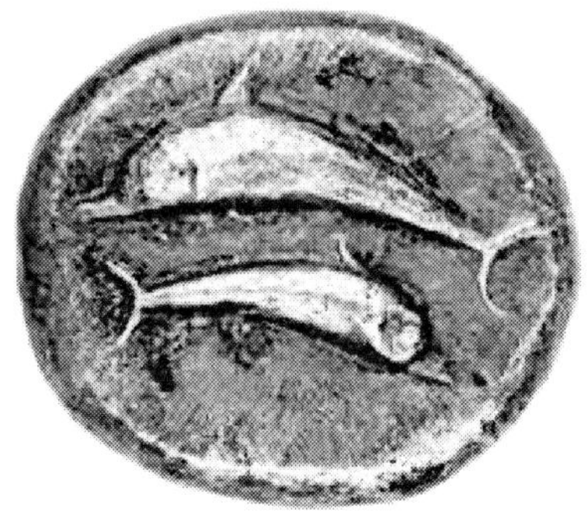

12

SINCE 1945

Figure 12.1 Merchant caïque approaching, Alónnissos, 1946. *Courtesy of Valándis Vláikos.*

At the end of the war the Germans abandoned our islands. The allies took over, guided there through Pílio by the Greek Resistance. The islands were free again. The prisoners of war returned after an absence of many years. So too the four local men who had sought refuge in the Middle East. Alonnisiots sought out and reclaimed the boats that had been requisitioned by the Germans. The island breathed a sigh of relief and concentrated on its own affairs.

12.1 Postwar Divisions

Those Alonnisiots who had sought refuge on the remote islands were ordered to be repatriated along with their animals. In a document from the archives of the *Ethnofulakí* (the National Guard, since disbanded) we read:

> Skópelos, 29 May 1945. To the President of the *Kinótita* of Alónnisos: please see to the removal from Kirá Panayía of the following inhabitants of Alónnisos who are pasturing their animals there without authority: (1) Konstandínos Kónstas (5 oxen, 12 sheep); (2) Nikólaos An. Anagnóstou (6

oxen); (3) Charíklia Dhrosáki (3 cows); and (4) Marigó Yamodhéna (1 mare).

For over four years there had been no regular army in Greece. All the men who, in the ordinary course of events, would have been called up during those years to do their national service (the 'classes' of 1941–45) were called up now. Soon, almost all the young men were enlisted in the national army. Peace was not to last long, and they soon found themselves involved in the tragic Civil War or 1946–49.

Liberation, at the end of September 1944, was followed by the crisis of December, the defeat of EAM and the Várkiza agreement, which paved the way for the triumph of the Right. The police force was re-manned with men recruited from the Security Battalions, or EDES (the National Republican Greek League)[1] and embarked on a witch hunt. On Alónnisos the horror of the executions at Kopriá (15 August 1944) was still fresh in people's memories.[2] Nevertheless, the majority of the Alonnisiots who had joined EAM during the Occupation ceased being active members and became the mere passive observers of the events that now unfolded. For the most of 1945 life resumed its pre-war rhythm, and that autumn the whole village joined in celebrations as in the old days, because the wine and grain were plentiful. Everything was going well until November 1945 when the police arrived on the island along with the prefect, Leonídhas, and the field guard, Kónstas.[3] Prior to their arrival, the right-wing elements, being few in number, hadn't dared to bother anyone, but once the police arrived they moved into action. Led by the forestry officer Níkos, from Ftelió (on the mainland, south of Vólos) they formed the Royal National Union of Youth. The first incident occurred at Patitíri when Yóryis Tzórtzis attacked the toughest member of the Youth Movement and in the scuffle took his pistol from him. When the police officer heard of this he asked old Yánnis, Yóryis' father, to return the revolver, since it was police property. After four days Yóryis handed it over to the policeman.

During the first half of 1946 the right-wing inhabitants of the island got themselves better organised, with the help of the anticommunist state machinery. One evening the forestry officer, the policeman and Father Lagós, the village priest, met together in a house, and the policeman told the others, 'Once the army takes over the government in order to stop the communists, you will be able to get the better of them.' Sitting in the office of the *Kinótita*, they wrote down the names of 32 people they considered dangerous. The list included Stilianós Frantzéskos, who was a friend of Níkos the forestry officer. Níkos went to the president of the *Kinótita* and asked him to delete Frantzéskos' name. In any case, with 32 names, the list was too long. In the end the number of those to be killed was reduced to 12. After this meeting the three like-minded men concluded that the democrats were in the majority on the island and that they would have to bring in 'forces', that is to say the *Kalambalíkidhes*. During this period of civil unrest many paramilitary and parastate organisations sprang up in our country. Far-right parastate organisations led by Spíros Kalambalíkis and Grigórios Soúrlas were active. Members of Kalambalíkis' gangs were called *Kalambalíkidhes*. They had their own patrol boats and hunted down men of left-wing views.

In March 1946, Mitroúsis, the representative of the British Intelligence Service, summoned some of those marked for extermination and warned them, 'Make sure you don't give them a pretext, or they'll start to step up the reign of terror around the villages.' And a certain Athanasíou, a builder who was working on Matzitákias' house, next door to the police station, overheard a police officer saying, 'They'll be dressed as field guards when they come.' But the men who had been condemned didn't take any precautions and on 1 July, the eve of the local festival of the Áyi Anáryiri, several of them were apprehended.

Around midnight the *Kalambalíkidhes* came to Palió Chorió. They went into the police station and began shouting at the policeman because he had not arrested the dissidents. The plan they now hatched was that while the night-long celebrations for the festival of the Áyi Anáryiri were still in progress, with everyone dancing under the olive trees, the local rightists would provoke a fight with the democrats. The police would then step in, arrest those they found there and hand them over to the *Kalambalíkidhes*. But Eléni, the wife of Yánnis Garifálou, overheard them plotting and went to inform those who were in danger. As a result the rightists found none of the people they were after at the festival, and went off to look for them in their houses.

They arrested the Dhrosákis brothers, Kóstas I. and Chrístos I., and Yánnis P. Vláikos along with Kostákis Vláikos. It was three in the morning. They were being guarded by a man from Skiáthos, but Yánnis Vláikos managed to push him into a ditch and the prisoners made a run for it. The *Kalambalíkidhes* chased Vláikos and four of them fired at him with automatics, but he was lucky and escaped. Having lost track of both Yánnis and Kostákis Vláikos, the rightists went to Káto Choráfi (between Patitíri and Palió Chorió), where they raped the wife of I. Vláikos. They also went twice to the house of N. Kaloyánnis, but he was expecting them. The first time he hid in the loft, the second time in a space under the floorboards which was scarcely big enough for a child.

Meanwhile, the two Dhrosákis brothers, Kóstas and Chrístos, who had not escaped with the other prisoners, had been taken off by boat from Patitíri, together with Níkos A. Athanasíou, who had been denounced by one of his neighbours, and Sotíris Dhrosákis, whose story is related below. Two Alonnisiots had come along on the caïque with the *Kalambalíkidhes* (one of them was Fótis Psarós). These men beat up Níkos Athanasíou and broke his arm, in an attempt to force him to tell them where the guns were kept. He told them that old Thodhorís on Peristéra had hidden guns during the Occupation.[4] So they went to Peristéra where they found Thodhorís in his hut with his family and old Miltiádhis. The *Kalambalíkidhes* barged in expecting the old men to be frightened. But they for their part calmly went on eating and asked the intruders what they wanted. Then the leader, Spíros Kalambalíkis himself, asked them where the guns were. Coldly and angrily Thodhorís told them that he had escaped a thousand dangers and he wasn't scared of them. 'In those days we fought to create Greece, and now you are destroying her.' As Thodhorís was speaking Miltiádhis, who was practically blind, seized the knife they had been using to cut the bread. 'Put the knife down, old man. Don't try to be funny,' said one of the men from Skiáthos. But Miltiádhis bravely replied, 'You want me to prune the bushes rather than you? You should have my eyes, then you'd see.'

Thodhorís now told them, 'You're right, I used to keep guns here, but I've handed them all in now. Come and look if you want.' They followed old Thodhorís up to a cave, leaving Níkos Athanasíou down below with his broken arm.

Thodhorís indicated by signs that he should make a run for it, but Níkos was frozen by fear. Thodhorís revealed to them that he had hidden Koumoundhoúros from Vólos there, when he was waiting to be taken to the Middle East. Kalambalíkis' behaviour immediately changed. He became friendly and said, 'Then I'll take him greetings from you.' Koumoundhoúros was now the head of the Intelligence Service for the whole of Thessaly. When they went back to the hut they told Athanasíou, 'Now we know you were lying.' In desperation he ran towards the cliff, fell, struck a rock and ended up in the sea. The *Kalambalíkidhes* finished him off. The first shot missed, but the second struck him in the chest and he went under. Later Dh. Malamaténios and a certain Kaloyánnis retrieved his body. They could see the dead man upright in the water as though he was walking. They got a large hook onto him and hauled him to the surface. They brought him to the village, where a proper funeral was held.

Sotíris Dhrosákis was another victim of the night's work. A retired teacher who had worked in many parts of Greece, and who, as a young man had fought in the Asia Minor Campaign, he was devoted to Alónnisos. He has been described as a political organiser and even as an communist leader, but it should be noted that, while he was inclined towards extreme left-wing ideology, he was not a fanatic. Dhrosákis had been appointed President of the Agricultural Association (*Agrotikós Sineterismós*) and was lobbying to get sulphur for the vineyards. He had also been elected representative of the forest owners' organisation, *Sinidhioktisía Dhasón* ('Joint Ownership of Forests'), and in that capacity Dhrosákis returned to Alónnisos in 1946 to prevent the wholesale destruction of the forests of Yeladhiás, at the north end of the island, which were threatened by Meladhiótis' logging operations. As a result of his efforts he was marked down by the *Kalambalíkidhes*. On the eve of the Áyi Anáryiri, Dhrosákis had been in Skópelos. When he got back to Alónnisos and heard that the *Kalambalíkidhes* were around, he went to hide on Yóryis Tsoukanás' caïque. But someone betrayed him, and the *Kalambalíkidhes* seized him and took him aboard their caïque, along with Athanasíou and the other two Dhrosákis men.

After their visit to Peristéra, they went on to Agnóndas on Skópelos, where they beat Sotíris Dhrosákis to death. At first he was beaten with canes, but when the canes broke the beating was resumed with pine branches. Wherever he'd been struck he was bleeding under his clothes. Dhrosákis taunted his captors, telling them that if they were men they would kill him with a bullet. But they replied that they wanted his soul not his body. They went on beating him until he died, by which time all his bones had been broken and he had been reduced to a shapeless mass. Although not directly responsible, the two Alonnisiots whose boat had brought him to Agnóndas were accomplices in his murder. After they had killed Sotíris, they beat up Kóstas and Chrístos Dhrosákis, who would also have died if Father Yóryis from Glóssa hadn't got them to the hospital in Vólos. Eighteen of the murderers who came to our island were from Skiáthos, the other three from Pílio.

12.2 The Civil War, 1946–49

While other countries were busy rebuilding after the destruction of the Second World War, Greece fell victim to a harrowing Civil War which had incalculable economic and social consequences. The events described above give some idea of the situation that precipitated the war. Hatred and fanaticism were intense. The Greek state, with the assistance of the British, and later the Americans, was determined to wipe out the communists. In the ensuing Civil War, many Alonnisiots fought in the regular army, and three of them lost their lives in circumstances which are described below. The leftists had to leave the island and move to other regions, chiefly Athens. In 1947 the Americans took command of our region, and from 1947 to 1949 Alónnisos was used as a place of exile for dissidents. 350 of them arrived here and rented houses up in Palió Chorió. The state gave them a pitifully small allowance. They included doctors and teachers and other professional people. The locals had good relations with them, but they were cautious, since there were informers keeping tabs on everyone. The scourge of emigration afflicted out island in the Civil War period. Many Alonnisiots went to the USA, Canada or Australia, but most of them later returned. Below are the stories of those who died fighting in the Civil War.

12.2.1 Yeóryos Konstandínou Kastánis

The soldier, Yeóryos Kastánis, was recalled to the national army and served on Mount Parnassus above Thíva (ancient THEBES). Parnassus was one of the best defended communist strongholds and many battles were fought there in the course of this catastrophic fratricidal war. The news of Kastánis' death was brought to Alónnisos by other soldiers, who gave the following account. One night in 1948, Kastánis' 12-man squad were in a forward position close to the enemy and sleeping after an exhausting march across the rough terrain of the historic mountain. Guards had been posted but they failed to spot the experienced partisans who took them by surprise and killed them. The camp was now at their mercy and they killed seven with a sub-machine gun while they were sleeping, and then quickly disappeared into the darkness. Kastánis was among those shot. The next day the squad failed to answer radio calls. Other soldiers came to their sector and found all their comrades cut to pieces by the bullets. Kastánis was buried in the bloodstained soil of Parnassus by his fellow islander, N. Kiriazís.

12.2.2 Konstandínos Nikoláou Efstathíou

Konstandínos Efstathíou was called up to join a regiment involved in the liquidation of communists in Northern Greece. In letters sent to his family, he gave terrifying descriptions of the many battles he took part in. The war of the 'brother-eaters', as Kazantzákis so appropriately called it, was merciless. Efstathíou was in the front line where battles were fought out hand to hand among the rocks of Ammoúdha, a mountain in central Greece. At one point his squad was within calling distance of the partisans, who kept them covered from higher up. The soldiers were protected by a steep outcrop, but dare not come out for fear of the marksmen who were patiently waiting. Efstathíou's squad had the misfortune to be led by an unworthy junior officer, who at one point ordered Efstathíou and another soldier to go to the mules which were tethered some way off. They refused, saying that it would be suicide to go out in the open. This officer called them cowards, and, threatening them with his revolver, forced them to carry out his order. Thus the two men fell victims of the enemy's trap. Later, in order to drive the partisans off Ammoúdha, the national army sprayed this impregnable mountain with petrol and set fire to it.

12.2.3 Dhimítrios Vouyouklís

Dhimítrios Vouyouklís was also conscripted to fight against the communist bands. Born in 1922, he was in the 'class' of 1943. He had completed his national service, returned to the island and become engaged, when was called up again, to a different regiment. He fought alongside Ioánnis Kaloyánnis, who related the following events.

On 8 October 1948 a group of partisans raided a village near Boukavíki in the region of Kastoriá (a town in northwestern Macedonia). A reconnaissance plane located the partisans on a mountain. They were roasting stolen sheep in petrol drums and having quite a party. The plane reported their position to the ground troops, and the next day the soldiers moved forward to make a surprise attack on the partisans. When they had spotted the aeroplane the partisans had deliberately ignored it and carried on enjoying themselves, but as soon as it had gone they went off to set an ambush. Vouyouklís' group fell right into the trap. Vouyouklís was killed in the exchange of fire, while Kaloyánnis, who was covering the rear, got cut off from the rest of them. It was a long time before he found his way back to the camp, where it was assumed he had been killed. In fact, the army had already sent a consolatory telegram to Alónnisos, and Kaloyánnis' friends and relations were mourning his loss. Two days later the mistake was corrected, but the news of Vouyouklís' death arrived.

12.2.4 Makrónisos

The prison island of Makrónisos, in use during and after the Civil War, is a black mark on our recent history, a place where many dissidents suffered and died. A number of Alonnisiots spent time there and were subjected to appalling treatment. Some of them were held there for as long as five years. Those who signed a 'declaration of repentance', rejecting communism and denouncing their comrades, were allowed to leave. Life there was hell. There were sadistic torturers who used the worst and most barbarous methods imaginable. Among the torturers, were, regrettably, two Alonnisiots. They were among the worst and had beaten, tortured and killed many prisoners. The method they followed was to beat prisoners almost to death, until they begged to be finished off with a bullet. They would even do this to fellow islanders.

Many years afterwards, one of the torturers, who was then a shepherd on Skántzoura, was badly injured. He was brought down to the shore and taken to Alónnisos by a man from Tríkeri. This Trikeriot had been a prisoner on Makrónisos, but after so many years he did not recognise his torturer. When he learned his name, he cursed himself for having carried the man on his back – the back which the injured man had scarred and ruined with his whip.

12.3 Postwar Recovery: the 1950s and Early 1960s

When the Civil War ended, Alónnisos mourned victims on both sides. The leftists who had been exiled to Alónnisos departed, and the local people got on with the peaceful business of life. Most were involved in wine production and other agricultural work. There were still no fishermen. Things were difficult. There was no wage labour available and people were obliged to go abroad or move to other parts of Greece.

Figure 12.2 A pupil setting out by fishing caïque for the secondary school in Skópelos, Alónnisos 1949. *Courtesy of Michalís and Evanthía Vláikos.*

Most of those who left went to live in Athens, which was then in the throes of major reconstruction. Greek shipping made great advances and played a significant role in international economic recovery. Going to sea was one solution to financial hardship which many men on the island embraced, since the wages were reasonable. At the same time stock breeding really took off and all the remote areas of Alónnisos were brought into use, as well as many of the sparsely populated islands.

On Yoúra, for the first time, the state appointed game wardens to protect the rare breed of wild goats. Their meat was considered a luxury and many poachers made trips to that remote island. On Psathoúra there were the lighthouse keepers and their families. They planted crops on the fertile island, and each family had a few animals. Kirá Panayá and Skántzoura, fertile islands with good grazing, attracted many *koligádhes* (tenant farmers) who worked with the monks. Relatively large numbers of people moved to these islands in the 1950s. The cutting down of the holly oak forest gave another boost to the local economy. Y. Malamaténios from Alónnisos lived on Pipéri with his family for sixteen years. They kept animals there and shared them with the owner of the island. Lively festivals were a common feature of life on all the islands in the 1950s and the inhabitants made merry despite their poverty. They were keen on the traditional songs of island life, and the long elaborate love songs known as *amanédhes* Their build makes them good dancers and distinguishes them from the people of other islands. Because of the war the seas had not been fished for several years. The first fishermen to start fishing again after the war brought in enormous catches. Some men working from Steni Vála once caught 3,000 kilos of sea-bream in a day!

Figure 12.3 Merchant boat at sea off Cape Patitíri, 1956. *Courtesy of Athanásios Páppos.*

12.3.1 Korean War: Ioánnis Karakatsánis

In 1953 a Greek division went to take part in the terrible war between North and South Korea. After North Korea's surprise invasion of 1952, which nearly drove the South Koreans and their American allies into the sea, a United Nations force was put together to which fifteen other countries, including Greece, contributed. North Korea was communist, and the capitalist countries helped South Korea to contain the communists within their existing borders. Among the men in the Greek division was Ioánnis Karakatsánis from Alónnisos. As he himself recalls, they embarked on a large transport ship and sailed for Seoul, the capital and principal port of South Korea, arriving in January 1953. From Seoul they advanced to the frontier where they spent eight months guarding a bridge. In July of the same year they returned to Greece, without calling at Japan. On the ship with them there were about 500 coffins destined for various countries.

Figure 12.4 Bringing goods from Vólos to Alónnisos, 1956.
Courtesy of Michális and Evanthía Vláikos.

12.3.2 Compulsory Public Service

An interesting aspect of life on Alónnisos in the 1950s is evident from a document issued by the *Kinótita* of Alónnisos dated 26 November 1950. It concerns the institution of universal public service. This new measure required every man on the island over the age of 18 to do three days' work for the *Kinótita* every year. If anyone didn't want to work, he had the alternative of paying the *Kinótita* the amount required to employ someone else for three days. The same edict also commandeered the services of every pack animal on the island for one day each year.

12.3.3 Agricultural Production

Another public document, dated 18 February 1951, gives us an idea of the large quantity of wine produced. The original document was destroyed, but not before it had been copied out by a later President of the island, A. Páppos. It includes the names of 277 individuals and records the numbers of barrels of wine on which each of them was taxed in the financial year 1950–51.

Figure 12.5 Man in Alónnisos, 1952. Courtesy of Marína and Panayótis Diniakós.

Figure 12.6 Relatives of the Warden, Yoúra, 1964. *Courtesy of Thomas Vestrum.*

The number of barrels per person varies from three to 60, and the total quantity of wine recorded is 3,962 barrels. It was taxed at a rate of 1,000 drachmas per barrel, and a barrel contained 50 *okádhes* (64 kilos).[5] Though informative, the document will not be entirely accurate, since it is a tax list. The wine producers would tend to hide a part of their production to avoid being taxed on it, and the actual annual production would be considerably more than the 4,000 barrels recorded. Wine was the island's most important source of income. Grape varieties cultivated included *limnió*, *rodhítis*, *koutoúres* (both white and red), *filéri* and *vradhianá*. The excellent taste of the wine was due to the pale soil, the altitude, the plentiful sunshine and the generally good climate of our island.

Another tax list, this time for the financial year 1951–52, shows the number of goats owned by each of 52 individuals.[6] The largest number recorded for any one person is 220 and the total is 3,439. On 26 March 1952, the committee of the *Kinótita* fixed the annual tax rates for animals grazed on common land. Small animals (pigs, sheep, goats) would be taxed at 4 drachmas per head, larger animals (oxen, horses, mules, donkeys) at 7 drachmas per head. (Today the special breed of oxen perfectly suited to conditions on our islands have gone.)

A survey made in 1960 records 60 wells and 36 springs. By 1964 the annual production of olives reached 165,000 kilos. Tables 12.1 and 12.2 show the number of animals on the island in 1961, and the quantities of animal products produced in the period 1960–63.

Figure 12.7 Women sorting dried plums, Alónnisos, 1954.
Courtesy of Kóstas and Máchi Efstathíou.

Table 12.1 Livestock on Alónnisos (1966).

Livestock	*Number*
Horses	35
Mules	98
Donkeys	131
Cattle	70
Goats	6,373
Poultry	1,600
Beehives	376

Table 12.2 Animal products from Alónnisos (1960–63).

Animal products	*(kg)*
Milk	88,825
Meat	21,205
Cheese	47,000
Honey	2,250
Goatskins	100
Wool	250

Source: Moutsópoulos (1982).

12.4 Further Setbacks

Figure 12.8 School celebration, Alónnisos, 1963. *Courtesy of Kóstas and Máchi Efstathíou.*

Figure 12.9 After the earthquake, Alónnisos, 1965. *Courtesy of Ioánnis Chíras.*

12.4.1 The 1965 Earthquake

9 March 1965 was a calm winter day like many others. A light rain was falling; and later turned to sleet. The inhabitants of our island and other islands in the region had returned to their houses, seen to their animals, and were huddled round their stoves enjoying the warmth. Farmers, most of them, they were tired from the day's labours. Families had finished eating and were sitting around and talking. (There was no television on the island then and people made their own entertainment.) Suddenly and without warning, at 10 p.m. a seismic tremor, measuring 6.4 on the Richter scale brought chaos. Walls cracked, roofs fell in, crockery on the shelves was shattered, women screamed, the animals went wild, whinnying and bleating in strange fashion.

Confronted by this primal and insidious enemy, the people ran for their lives. The rain and darkness added to their terror. They got away from the houses as fast as they could, the men helping the old people and the children, and made for the nearby forest for safety. Palió Chorió, Vótsi and Patitíri were emptied within minutes. The pinewoods at Káto Chorắfi and Spartínes were filled with people. Huddled together, soaked to the skin and in shock they waited for dawn. As the sun rose the full extent of the disaster was evident. The elders gathered the people together to find out who was missing. Two elderly women were the only victims of this new menace. It was fortunate there were not more. The two women lived in a small shack and had been crushed when the roof fell in. Relatives found them the next day and pulled their bodies from the wreckage.

The navy had been promptly informed and arrived the following day. The sailors began to distribute tents, dried food, medical supplies, clothes and blankets. The local people adapted to life under canvas, realising they were much safer in tents, since the aftershocks continued for more than a month. During that time people only made the rather risky visits to their houses to get household utensils and various other necessities. Eventually a group of army engineers came to the island. They demolished those houses that were beyond repair and cleared the rubble. Many islanders lived in tents for over a year waiting for their homes to be rebuilt. They accepted the situation stoically, and after they had got over the initial shock began to enjoy themselves. Many remember life in the tents as a time of constant conviviality.

The government took the next step, first making loans available to the earthquake victims and then building the so-called *Néo Ikismó* ('New Settlement'). This consisted of rectangular concrete structures more like hen huts than houses, which bore no relation to the island environment. It was nine years before the construction work was completed and the houses handed over to the local people.

One unfortunate result of the earthquake was that the archives of the *Kinótita* were destroyed for the second time.[7] They had been kept in a cupboard built into a wall. This was damaged and many documents got wet and were rendered completely useless. A positive outcome of the earthquake, however, was that a number of the soldiers who came to help with reconstruction met local girls, married them and settled here permanently. They were a welcome addition to the community and the special skills they had learned in the army a great help to the island.

Figure 12.10 After the earthquake: Alónnisos, 1965. *Courtesy of E. and D. Dhiómas.*

Figure 12.11 After the earthquake: a girl in traditional costume, Alónnisos, 1965. *Courtesy of Ólga Tsoukaná.*

Figure 12.12 After the earthquake a family in Patitíri, 1965. *Courtesy of María Dhióma.*

Figure 12.13 After the earthquake: living in tents, Alónnissos, 1965.

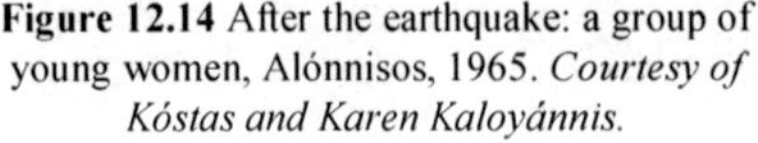

Figure 12.14 After the earthquake: a group of young women, Alónnisos, 1965. *Courtesy of Kóstas and Karen Kaloyánnis.*

Figure 12.15 After the earthquake: the first temporary shelters, Alónnisos, 1965. *Courtesy of María Dhióma.*

Figure 12.16 After the earthquake: people continue to enjoy themselves, Alónnisos, 1965.

Figure 12.17 After the earthquake: the Alexíou family in front of their tent.

Figure 12.18 After the earthquake: the police station in a tent, Alónnissos, 1965.

Figure 12.19 After the earthquake: visit of Queen Frederica, Alónnissos, 1965.

Figure 12.20 After the earthquake: Alónnisos 1965. *Courtesy of Ólga Tsoukaná.*

Figure 12.21 After the earthquake: Alónnissos, 1965. *Courtesy of Valándis Vláikos.*

Figure 12.22 After the earthquake: Palió Chorió, 1965.
Courtesy of Kóstas and Máchi Efstathíou.

Figure 12.23 After the earthquake: assessing the damage, Palió Chorió, 1965.
Courtesy of Michális and Evanthía Vláikos.

Figure 12.24 After the earthquake: view of Palió Chorió from above, 1965.

Figure 12.25 The feast day of Ayía Paraskeví, in the square at Vótsi.
Courtesy of Ólga Tsoukaná.

Figure 12.26 Many politicians came to the islands after the earthquake. They promised much but did little.

12.4.2 Destruction of the Vines

The basic income of the island was still derived from wine production. But suddenly there was bad news. On both Skiáthos and Skópelos phylloxera had destroyed the vineyards. On Alónnisos strict measures had to be adopted to prevent the infection being introduced with agricultural produce. However, some very stupid person brought in garlic and planted it beside a vineyard, and another brought manure from Chalkidhikí. In no time at all, the vines on Alónnisos had all withered. After the earthquake, this second great natural disaster struck Alónnisos.

12.5 Recent Decades

12.5.1 The Growth of Tourism and the Decline of Agriculture

In the early 1970s the islanders decamped from the old village to the earthquake-proof settlement by the shore. Houses were allocated by lottery to those who were eligible, and with each house went a plot of land. The worst thing was that when they moved into the New Settlement, the islanders abandoned the old village (Palió Chorió). In 1978 the school in Palió Chorió closed down, and other services ceased to operate. Everyone was confined within the limits of Patitíri, and the old village was deserted. Later on, most of the houses there were sold to foreigners.

The 1970s were characterised by the development of tourism. The people now established in Patitíri turned to the construction of buildings to serve tourists. There had been a certain amount of tourism before the earthquake, but now it really took off, growing steadily after 1970. The rate of emigration began to fall and many people came back to the island. Some agricultural production continued, but wine production never recovered. Table 12.3 gives statistics for agricultural and animal products in 1977. Today, twenty years later, agricultural production is minimal, and the only real interest is in olive growing and the production of oil. Meat, skins and other animal products are also in decline, though they are still important.

Table 12.3 Agricultural production on Alónnisos, 1977.

Crops	*(kg)*		*Animal products*	*(kg)*
Tomatoes	90,000		Milk	125,700
Clover	85,000		Meat	38,820
Grapes	60,000		Cheese	17,000
Barley	35,000		Honey	8,750
Green beans	15,000		Goatskins	1,050
Marrows	9,500		Mizíthra (soft cheese)	1,000
Onions	2,000		Wool	170
Artichokes	2,000			

Source: Moutsópoulos (1982).

12.5.2 An Alonnisiot Caught Up in the Cyprus Invasion

One highly significant event in the 1970s was the infamous Turkish invasion of Cyprus, the island of Aphrodite. N. Kónstas, a merchant seamen from Alónnisos, was caught up in the invasion. Kónstas tells his own story:

> Shortly before the Cyprus tragedy we were in Mersin. Mersin is a Turkish naval base.[8] We had brought a cargo of sugar which we were unloading in the civilian harbour. The military vessels were under steam and large numbers of soldiers were coming and going on the docks, clearly preparing for something. Later we learned it was Attila No. 1.[9] Our captain had a video recorder and he was filming the whole affair from the bridge, intending to hand the video over to the Greek Army General Staff. It was our bad luck that he was spotted from the harbour and a party came immediately to get the camera. The captain hid it and denied everything.
>
> For forty-two days we were kept prisoner in the harbour and repeatedly interrogated. They tried to intimidate us, saying that they would throw us into a snake pit, or employ various similar tortures, if we didn't confess.

Figure 12.27 The first group of French tourists, Alónnisos, 1969.
Courtesy of Fótis Tzortzátos.

> At times we heard artillery and gunfire, but we didn't know what was going on. Soon they were bringing back the bodies of Turkish soldiers killed in the landings. Two *postália* [large steel-hulled cargo vessels] tied up astern of us full of dead and wounded. They had been mown down by the Greek Cyprus Force and the Cypriots. The invasion would never had succeeded if the Americans had not treacherously intervened to broker an armistice, giving the Turks time to establish themselves on the Great Island.[10] As soon as they saw the numbers of their dead, the Turks went mad. The enraged crowd got into the boat next to ours and killed a Cypriot sailor. We ran to call the captain to find out what was going to happen. The radio had been sealed and we were isolated. There was a chance that the harbour would be bombed by our own side if the Turks didn't kill us. We asked the captain for the video camera and he gave it to us. To make sure it couldn't be found we burned it in the stove. As the crowd watched the ships with the dead in them they became more and more enraged. The harbour authorities had to put up railings 1.5 m higher than the ones already there, to prevent reprisals.
>
> Greek ships in other Turkish harbours were brought to Mersin. They assembled 80 of them there altogether with the aim of averting a Greek bombing raid. The situation was chaotic. The Turkish soldiers were getting more and more angry, and continued to interrogate us about the video recorder. Eventually, when things quietened down, the ships began to leave one by one, but they kept us there. In the end an officer came aboard with a party of soldiers, issued us with the route we must follow, checked the radio and went ashore. Bewildered, we untied the ship and headed out of the harbour. Two Turkish destroyers were waiting for us.
>
> They sailed along with us, one on the right, the other on the left. We were terrified. Their plan was to sink us. The captain ordered us to break open the radio and send out and SOS. Everything depended on it; it was our only hope of salvation. We sent out the SOS. Luckily for us it was picked up by a Russian torpedo boat. It came alongside but the Turkish ships stayed where they were. The Russian captain called for reinforcements and two destroyers came from the American Seventh Fleet. Relieved, we explained to them what was happening and eventually the Turkish ships withdrew. The American destroyers continued to escort us until we entered international waters.

At the time of the Cyprus crisis there was a rumour on our island that the Alonnisiot, P. Kaloyánnis, had been killed when his boat was bombed by the Turks. His boat did sink at the time of the events in Cyprus and it sank close to the Great Island, but it wasn't bombed. The probable cause was the shifting of his cargo of marble tiles in the No. 2 hold.

12.5.3 Communications and Services

It was through the initiative of Queen Frederica, following her visit to the island in the aftermath of the earthquake, that in 1965 a proper post office was established on Alónnisos for the first time. Before that, the inhabitants of Alónnisos were dependent on the post office on Skópelos.

Shortly after the 1965 earthquakes, the automobile first came to Alónnisos. There were no roads other than those that the army had made. The main route used by cars was the road linking Patitíri with Palió Chorió. There were two cars at first, and for a very long time they were the only two. Nevertheless, on one occasion, they managed to have a collision!

It was in 1969 that electricity first became available on the island. For several years it was generated locally. Later the public electricity company laid an undersea cable from Pílio to Alónnisos. The telephone had come to Alónnisos in the early 1960s.

In the immediate postwar period the only regular transport between the islands had been a wooden sailing boat, called the *Katerína.* This was later replaced by the *Paschális*, and eventually the car ferries began to call. In April 1985 the 'Flying Dolphins' (hydrofoils) of Yeóryos Livanós' Ceres company were first seen in Alónnisos.

The new itinerary had been the dream of the inhabitants of the Northern Sporades since 1972. The 'Flying Dolphin' put an end to the isolation of Alónnisos, drastically reducing travel time to the mainland. People no longer felt so insecure in cases of medical emergencies. Livanós' concern for the islands was reflected by the personnel of the company. The service is now operated by Minoan Lines who bought up the Ceres company.

12.5.4 Tássos Kaloyánnis' Gifts to His Birthplace

Tássos Kaloyánnis, the son of a poor shepherd family, left Alónnisos and went to America in pursuit of the great dream. Through courage and determination he succeeded. He set up his own construction company and soon prospered. In 1989 the new school buildings (*Yimnásio* and *Líkio*)[11] were completed at a cost of 150 million drachmas donated by Tássos Kaloyánnis as an expression of his love for the island. Kaloyánnis also funded the public gymnasium and the drilling of boreholes to augment the water supply.

12.5.5 Shipbuilding on Alónnisos

The traditional skills of shipbuilding survive on the island of Alónnisos even among the younger generation. Wooden fishing boats and wooden craft of other kinds are still in operation today. Indeed, many of them are in daily use. This fleet of wooden boats has had to be built and has to be maintained. Five individuals have adopted shipbuilding as their principal occupation. Níkos Kiriazís, Y. Alexíou and Kóstas Kaloyánnis are the old ships carpenters. Kaloyánnis set up a family business and has passed on the trade secrets to his two young grandsons, who are in their early twenties.

During the recent decades of peace, apart from the large caïques they have constructed many small boats, chiefly for fishing. The construction of even the smallest boat requires the same skills and is no less demanding and complex than the construction of a large one. Shipyards are a characteristic feature of the island. Several of them are still functioning today and using traditional manual methods. They are used mainly for dry-docking *trechandíria* (light, fast sailing boats) for inspection and maintenance. The method is as follows. A wooden platform, known as a *váza*, is submerged in the sea and the boat positioned over it. The platform is pulled on to a wooden slipway by means of a large capstan, which requires 4–6 people to turn it. A rope attached to the *váza* is gradually wound round the capstan, and the *váza* moves up the slipway like a wagon on railway lines, with the boat resting securely on top of it.

Figure 12.28 The traditional shipyard, abandoned.

12.6 Prospects for the Future

The islands of Alónnisos, Peristéra, Skántzoura, Kirá Panayá, Yoúra, Psathoúra and other smaller islands constitute a most interesting archipelago with very good prospects for the future. These prospects are founded on the islands' many resources and advantages, of which the principal ones are: the Marine Park (provided it is properly understood and suitably managed); the wealth and variety of the marine and terrestrial archaeology; the natural environment with its spectacular diversity of flora and fauna. These are discussed here in turn. Among the island's resources we should also include the Homeopathic Academy, which is discussed in the next chapter.

12.6.1 The National Marine Park of Alónnisos and the Northern Sporades

The Marine Park is a clearly defined protected area which includes Alónnisos and the other islands to the north and east and the sea around them. The Park was set up to conserve the rare flora and fauna, to prevent interference in or exploitation of the environment, and to preserve the cultural heritage intact. It was created at an opportune time and has been a saving intervention, ensuring that our islands can remain unchanged and unexploited in the difficult times through which we are passing.

Figure 12.29 The author with a seal of the species *Monachus monachus*.

Figure 12.30 The first release of seals back into the sea, Skántzoura.
Courtesy of Kóstas and Máchi Efstathíou.

The Marine Park is the best gift that our generation could pass on to those that follow. The creation of the Park was the fruit of separate efforts on the part of organisations and individuals who began to be conscious of the need for such an initiative around 1970. The first results of their lobbying were seen in 1986.

Two years later, in 1988, the *Nomarchía* of Magnisía published the pioneering official decision to protect the area where the Mediterranean seals live and breed, with the agreement of the interested ministries (Agriculture, Environment and Shipping). Government support and recognition grew and in 1992 the region was officially declared a National Park. From the time the idea was first conceived to the foundation of the Park there was a systematic abuse of the funds provided by the European Community. The only people who did not benefit were the inhabitants of Alónnisos, where the fishermen in particular were directly and adversely affected by the prohibitions of the law.

In the last few years there has been a concerted campaign by all the local interested parties for the appointment of a government agency to oversee the Marine Park and the management of the money allocated to it. The prohibitions that were hastily imposed were completely at variance with the wishes of the local people, and provoked the discontent and indignation on Alónnisos. Gradually, however, a compromise solution was hammered out (not, to be sure, without some behind-the-scenes political wheeling and dealing), a solution that will serve the needs of both the ecosystem and the people who live within it.

The Marine Park provides a biological breathing space among all the contamination that the Aegean area receives from unregulated human activities. The future progress of our entire region is bound up with it. Progress must above all respect the ecosystem, and it must always be based on the proper use of natural resources and not the relentless and ill-considered exploitation for short-term profit.

12.6.2 Archaeological Wealth

Much of this book is devoted to the description of the marine and terrestrial archaeology of the region. Some years ago, the then Minister of Culture, Mikroútsikos, announced the future creation of a Marine Archaeological Park, and we hope that this will become a reality in the near future.

The aims of the Archaeological Park will be, primarily, to catalogue and investigate the antiquities of the islands; and secondarily to enable travellers to visit them. Investigations will take place where the government officials judge it to be appropriate, and where they can implement measures for the security and protection of monuments or wrecks. For the present, the first step in this inspired theme is the creation of a centre for the conservation of the objects that are brought up from the seabed, and this is to be housed in the old gendarmerie building in Palió Chorió. The rich archaeological resources, if they are managed in a proper scientific manner, will contribute a great deal to our islands.

First and foremost, this small dot on the map, Alónnisos, will become known to the whole world, and we will confirm once again that the Aegean has always been an inseparable part of the Greek world from antiquity to the present.

12.6.3 The Natural Environment

When God adorned the world, his gift to Alónnisos and the surrounding islands was their stunning beauty. Moving from island to island one meets both the wildness and the serene beauty of nature in a harmonious whole. Whether you walk about the islands or dive in the sea around them, you meet extraordinary colours and motion, majestic sunsets, and panoramic views of astounding beauty. It is the wildness and peace of all these places that seizes your imagination and compels your love. The longer you stay, the more you will feel the pull of a strange attraction. Gradually you will discover that this feeling emanates from the harmony of the landscape. It is what the ancient Greeks called 'cure of the soul' to observe the alternation of wildness and calm.

When you go from high and rugged Yoúra (its peak 515 m above sea level) to level and low-lying Psathoúra (a mere 14 m), you have made the passage from black to white. And yet, between the two islands there is complete harmony. This supreme harmony makes me feel very small when I try with my humble learning to describe it. Even here, though, human agency has extended its destructive work. Man found a divine gift, but, failing to respect its value, through ill-considered interventions (and chiefly in recent years), he has disturbed the equilibrium, with the arbitrary construction work at Patitíri, the illegal dumping of refuse, uncontrolled fishing, pollution from merchant shipping, and the deliberate burning of forests. It is the common duty of every inhabitant and visitor to see that these islands remain as they are: wild, secluded and far from the ecologically and culturally destructive trends of recent years.

12.7 Concluding the Historical Survey

Throughout the march of history we have seen man on these islands slowly coming to terms with nature and using it for his own benefit. He developed specialised fishing skills, learned to produce exceptionally good wine, and built monasteries, taking advantage of the natural peace of the islands. The perfect equilibrium between man and nature persists even in our own days. When I was trying to find signs of buildings or other ancient remains on the more remote islands, I received help from local people who live or used to live there, and I observed this perfect adaptation.

On rocky and precipitous Yoúra, for example, getting about on foot is difficult and strenuous. When I asked for directions, I was often told, 'It's just down there', and this 'just down there' would turn out to involve an hour's walk. But for those who spend their lives in these untrodden places, walking is no effort. On Kirá Panayá a vast area rich in nutritious bulbs has been divided into squares in the minds of the local people. Fearing for the survival of this species, they never pull up all the bulbs in any one area and are prepared to walk some distance to make up the required quantity. On Skántzoura marines from a special operations group, the OYK,[12] caused extensive damage and the local people were as angry as if a part of themselves had been destroyed. On Peristéra, Palaeolithic man made his home in natural rock shelters, and modern man still uses rock faces for one or more natural walls of his stone-built houses. On Alónnisos the old people cannot understand why the young leave the fields uncultivated and appear to have no interest in them. For the old the earth is an indivisible part of themselves. It is not easy for visitors or even indigenous people to understand these things. Nevertheless, I have been impressed by the bond between man and the earth. This harmony that I have encountered goes beyond the limits of the human and approaches the divine.

Notes

1. The Greek initials stand for *Ethnikós Dhimokratikós Ellinikós Sindhesmós*. EDES was the principal non-communist force in the Greek Resistance. Even during the Second World War there had been armed conflict between EAM and EDES. [Translator]
2. See pp. 233–8.
3. 'Field guard' translates *chorofilakás*, i.e. a member of the old rural gendarmerie instituted in the early days of Greek independence, and now integrated into the regular police force (*astinomía*). Elsewhere in this book field guards are sometimes referred to as 'gendarmes'.
4. 'Old Thodhorís' is Theódhoros Likoúrgou Athanasíou, whose long career was described on pp. 202–5.
5. The officially recorded production amounts to more than 50,000 litres, the equivalent of over 70,000 standard 70 cl bottles. [Translator]
6. In the original Greek edition several pages are devoted to reproducing the two tax lists in full. While these documents are of great interest to Alonnisiots and others who know the island and islanders well, it was felt that for the English edition it would be sufficient to summarise the information contained in them. [Translator]
7. For the earlier destruction of the public records, see p. 225.
8. Mersin is on the southern coast of Turkey, due north of the eastern tip of Cyprus. [Translator]
9. 'Attila No. 1' was the Turks' code name for the first phase of the Turkish invasion of Cyprus, 20–22 July 1974.
10. 'Great Island' translates the name Megalónnisos, by which Greeks often refer to Cyprus.
11. *Yimnásio* and *Líkio* are two types of schools representing the two stages of Greek secondary education.
12. The Greek initials stand for *Omádha Ipovríchion Katastrofón*, literally, 'Submarine Disaster Group'.

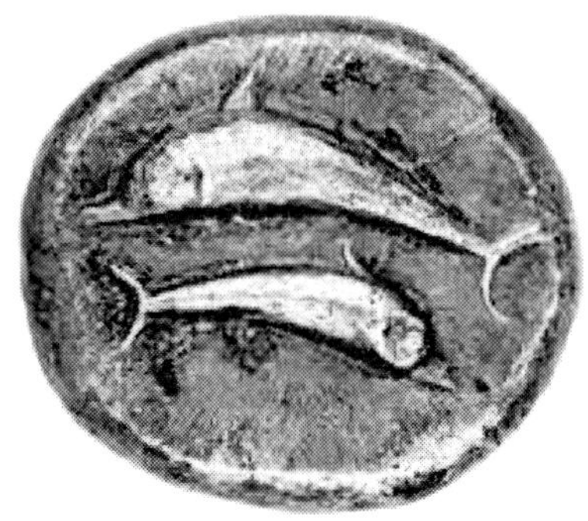

Figure 12.31 The clean waters of Alónnisos. *Courtesy of Thomas Vestrum.*

13

CULTURAL AND INTELLECTUAL LIFE : FOUR BIOGRAPHICAL SKETCHES

THERE WAS great poverty on Alónnisos in the early part of the 20th century, and the farming families of the island barely managed to subdue the earth and obtain the necessities of life. Intellectual pursuits had little place in our poor island and men of letters did not live here.

13.1 Vasílios Papavasilíou: Teacher, Priest and Artist

One exception was Vasílios Stamatíou Papavasilíou, or Papavasílis as he was known to his fellow islanders. Though born to a poor family, in 1875, he was able, through their sacrifices, to study in Lárisa, where he graduated with highest honours and became a primary school teacher. His first appointment was to the primary school at Glóssa on Skópelos. There he married, and his wife, who was very religious, encouraged him to become a priest.

He was ordained by Bishop Grigórios of Chalkídha in Évvia, and appointed village priest at Glóssa. As both teacher and priest, Papavasílis had much to offer to this small village on Skópelos. He raised the cultural level of his position and became a respected member of the community. Papavasílis and his wife had four children. Unfortunately, through diseases that were still incurable at that time, he lost his wife and one of his two daughters. He was left a widower with two young sons and a daughter. Devastated by the sudden loss of loved ones, he was unable to cope with his family duties, and took on a woman called Marigó to help him. She was a good woman; she supported him and the children flourished. As time passed, rumours began to circulate. The people of Glóssa made contemptuous references to their 'immoral priest' and came to hate him, despite all he had done for them. His son, Stamátis, left for Athens, where he became an animal trainer. His other son graduated with honours and was appointed primary school teacher on Skiáthos. There he was suddenly taken ill. He was transferred to a hospital in Athens, where he died. He was buried in Athens.

Papavasílis himself left Glóssa when he was appointed teacher in his native place, Alónnisos. On Alónnisos he did not act as a priest, only as a teacher. Through his teaching – of as many as 250 pupils at a time – our primary school (built in the late 19th century with a gift from Singrós)[1] came to be recognised as the best in Magnisía and received an award from the inspectorate of primary education. As a teacher he was austere and strict, but he was a charismatic communicator. He was also an athlete, and he trained his pupils according to the ancient maxim 'a healthy mind in a healthy body'. The athletic contests that he organised in our primary school were pioneering, even by today's standards. He himself had repeatedly won prizes in the Pan-Thessalian Games for discus, javelin and high jump. As well as being a teacher he was also an accomplished classical violinist.

Figure 13.1 Father Vasílios Papavasilíou, artist, priest, teacher and musician.

Ill fate dogged his footsteps, however. His daughter Nína died from meningitis in Vólos, and later he lost his elder son Stamátis. Shattered by his family tragedy, he turned to painting. His soul penetrated a world that few are able to enter. His paintings are of a rare quality, though the earlier ones are rather pessimistic. Several works by Papavasílis are now in America, including *The Dance of Zálongo*,[2] and some later paintings on themes from ancient Greek mythology, such as *The Chariot of the Sun* and *The Nine Muses*. He was also concerned with Biblical themes and painted a series of icons; and there is a self-portrait, which he made by looking at himself in the mirror.

Papavasílis was very fond of women and music. He had a large collection of gramophone records, including both classical music and traditional Greek love songs. Once, on a visit to Vólos, he encountered a street musician playing the violin. Papavasílis was enraptured and followed the man. At that time the clergy were forbidden to go near such spectacles. He was approached by a policeman who ordered him to move away, since he was a priest. Papavasílis got angry and made as if to strike the policeman, who fled in fear.

He performed many services for his island, and to the end he was a much loved and respected member of the community of Alónnisos. He died in 1941 from pulmonary oedema. The priest Grigórios reverently transferred his bones to the cemetery of the church of Ayía Paraskeví, where the icon screen is adorned with icons painted by Papavasílis himself, among them a St Nicholas, a St Panteleimon and an Annunciation.

13.2 Chrístos Athanasíou

Chrístos Yeoryíou Athanasíou, the youngest of the four children of Yóryis Athanasíou and his wife Marigó (from the Vláikos family), was born in Alónnisos on 4 July 1912. At that time, the father, Yóryis Athanasíou, acted as the island's doctor, practising every form of natural medicine, at a time when rural Greece was totally neglected by the Greek state. He was a deeply religious man and a *ieropsáltis* (cantor),[3] as well as a fine carpenter and a farmer. He had an excellent memory and a wide knowledge of history and ancient Greek literature, which he tried to share with his fellow islanders.

Chrístos Athanasíou, the son of this doctor-cum-carpenter-and-farmer, received his first education in Alónnisos from Papavasílis (see above), the priest, teacher, painter and musician. Later he continued his studies in Skópelos where he completed the first and second grades of the *Yimnásio* (the first stage of secondary school), and then in Kími, in Évvia, where he completed the third and fourth grades. At the famous *Yimnásio* at Kími he was considered a genius by his fellow pupils.

According to K. Konstandinídhis, who was one of his classmates, Chrístos Athanasíou could recall and recite from memory both the *Iliad* and the *Odyssey*. He tried to get into the Navel Cadet School, but was unsuccessful. In those days there were few places and they were mainly reserved for the sons of officers. It was at this point that his father died of a heart attack at the age of 49. Chrístos transferred to the *Yimnásio* at Vólos, joining the sixth grade, and passed his final exams there in 1931.

After this, though, disenchanted with the political situation in Greece, and lacking funds, he abandoned all attempts at further study and returned to live in Alónnisos. At the age of 21, he married Angelikí Alexíou and was appointed secretary for the *Kinótita* of Alónnisos. His first initiative was to press the committee to allocate money for the purchase of a radio and the formation of a basic library consisting of the marvellous volumes produced by the Eleftheroudhákis publishing house.

Thus it was Chrístos Athanasíou, who, in 1934 or 1935, brought the first radio to Alónnisos and set up two loudspeakers in the corners of the square in Palió Chorió, enabling this remote island to keep abreast with what was going on in the world, and to hear a little music. The arrival of the radio was a landmark in the cultural development of Alónnisos. The library, though, was ignored by the Alonnisiots, who couldn't afford for their children to study and develop intellectual interests, and Athanasíou himself was almost its only user. Whenever he was free from his secretarial work for the *Kinótita*, he immersed himself in the rich world of knowledge, seeking to open windows of light in the dark skies of the interwar period in Greece.

Then came the dictatorship of 4 August 1935,[4] and five years later the invasion of Greece by the fascist Axis powers.[5] Chrístos Athanasíou, as the head and chief breadwinner of a family was not called up as a combatant, but was enlisted in the Civil Defence on Alónnisos. The *Kinótita* office where Athanasíou worked also served as the local branch of what was then known as the TTT or 'the three Ts', that is to say, Posts (*Tachidhromía*) Telegraphs and Telephones. The dark days of the fascist occupation were extremely difficult for Athanasíou, as indeed they were for all Greeks. He did not align himself with any party or faction, though he despised the institution of monarchy which he regarded as demeaning to the Greek people. He was one of the many eye witnesses to the execution of nine resistance members in the old square of Palió Chorió on 15 August 1944 by a firing squad consisting of one German, several Rumanians serving with the Germans, and some Greek collaborators. Liberation found Athanasíou, like all of his fellow islanders, in a state of extreme poverty. Combining his carpentry skills (learned from his father) with what he had learned from the study of technical books, Chrístos Athanasíou became a shipwright. He built six sailing boats of thoroughly scientific design, with many complex and difficult elements in their construction, and some of them are still sailing the Aegean today.

After the war Chrístos Athanasíou was reappointed secretary to the *Kinótita* and resumed responsibility for the TTT. He had a son in 1946, whom he named Yóryis after his father. At the same time, in the immediate postwar period, he became involved in the practice of medicine, not empirically like his father, but after studying medical reference books. He used modern drugs and implements for the relief of pain and the healing of his fellow islanders. Alónnisos suffered as much after as before and during the war from the total neglect of the state, which now, instead of assisting its citizens, was chasing 'red chimeras'. Private doctors visited Alónnisos from time to time, chiefly to make money, and several times they denounced Athanasíou to the police for practising medicine without a doctor's diploma. Despite such problems, Athanasíou never refused his services to his suffering neighbours, since at that time there was no other doctor on the island.

In the postwar period he embarked on a thorough study of Homer, linguistics and the history of the Greek language. In 1956 the committee of the *Kinótita* of Alónnisos decided to dismiss him from his position as secretary. Thus almost twenty-five years of service in local government came to nothing. (In those days local government employees had no security, were not eligible for compensation, and received no pension.)

After that he shut himself up in his house and devoted himself entirely to his reading, and in particular to researching the history of Alónnisos. In fact, he wrote a history of Alónnisos and the surrounding islands. Many Greek intellectuals, such as N. Moutsópoulos (a professor in the Polytechnic of Thessalonica), Lipourlís (professor of philosophy in Thessalonica), the poet Klítas Kírou, and Yeóryos Vithoúlkas (see below), came to Alónnisos to visit Athanasíou and were impressed by the scope of his erudition. In his later years he was an avid reader of modern literature, both Greek and foreign, as well as ancient authors. In 1987 he had an operation to remove a cataract, but because of some complication he did not recover his full sight. He became disheartened, since he could no longer see to read, and died on 18 March 1988, leaving his writings on the subject of linguistics and the history of language.

Chrístos Athanasíou educated his son at home. Yórgos never went to *dhimotikó*, *yimnásio* or *líkio*. Through his father's instruction alone he passed the entrance exams for the School of Medicine in the University of Thessalonica, where he distinguished himself. When he graduated, he was appointed doctor on Alónnisos. There he did his best to help his fellow islanders, who all had great faith in him. He was active in cultural affairs and intensely interested in the intellectual advancement of the island.

13.3 Athanásios Páppos

After graduating in French Philosophy in the University of Athens, Athanásios Páppos returned to Alónnisos and listened patiently to all the old people of the island, collecting folk tales, proverbs, songs and information about traditional customs. His work saved from oblivion an important folk culture, in which long-standing local traditions, heavily influenced by ancient Greek mythology, blend with other elements brought to the island by the families who have moved here from other parts of Greece. The isolation of our island helped to preserve this cultural amalgam which survived into the 1970s, but has since been affected by the growth of tourism. When the Junta fell in 1974, Athanásios Páppos was elected President of Alónnisos. As President he promoted the culture of the island among local people and foreigners alike.

13.4 Yeóryos Vithoúlkas and the Homeopathic Academy

Yeóryos Vithoúlkas, one of the most famous innovators in homeopathy, was born in 1932. In the early 1960s he studied homeopathy in South Africa and then in India. His restless nature led him to embark on a new campaign to promote homeopathy. Through research, observation and publication, he raised the intellectual profile of homeopathy and established his reputation as a leading scientist. With acclaimed lectures in at international conferences and an impressive list of publications, he rose to the highest levels in the world of homeopathy. His books are widely read and have been translated into 14 languages, including Chinese.

In 1970 he founded the Athenian School of Homeopathic Medicine, and in 1975 the Centre for Homeopathic Medicine. He has also distinguished himself in the American scientific world. He was honoured by an international conference in Washington in 1974. Since 1978 he has taught in San Francisco, and in Suez. In the late 1970s he embarked on his sixteen-volume work on homeopathic pharmacology. Not content with his extensive bibliography and arduous continuing research, he created a new model which challenges the way in which we have previously understood the workings of the human organism and its behaviour in sickness and in health. This work has found many adherents; it has been widely accepted and has impressed the international scientific community, who recommended Yeóryos Vithoúlkas for the Alternative Nobel prize.[6] The Swedish committee awarded him the prize in 1996, making Alonnisiots very proud since we consider Vithoúlkas to be one of us.

Figure 13.2 Easter celebrations, Patitiri, 1975, not long after the fall of the Junta – a Junta placard is on its side behind the fire. *Courtesy of Valándis Vláikos.*

In 1995 Vithoúlkas founded the International Academy for Classical Homeopathy on Alónnisos. The Academy is housed in a stone-built building with all the modern audio-visual systems necessary for teaching and holding conferences. There are also ancillary buildings and a library of books related to the aims and functions of the Academy. Internationally recognised centres such as the Medical Academy of Moscow, and the medical schools of Bonn and Berlin co-operate with the Academy on Alónnisos. Based on the principles of its founder, it is an influential centre for education and research, which may contribute as much to Alónnisos as to the advancement of the science of homeopathy. Yeóryos Vithoúlkas' devotion to science is matched by his love of Alónnisos, prompting him to leave the place where he had lived hitherto and come to our island. He built a house here and has remained with us ever since, only leaving the island to fulfil his increasingly frequent scientific obligations throughout the world.

Notes

1. See p. 359.
2. Zálongo is a village in Epirus. The 'Dance' refers to the mass suicide in 1803 of a group of women from Zálongo, who, according to the tradition, danced their way off a cliff to avoid being captured by Ottoman troops. [Translator]
3. More than just a chorister, the *ieropsáltis* (or simply *psáltis*) has an essential role in the performance of many Orthodox services. [Translator]
4. On 4 August 1935 the prime minister, General Ioánnis Metaxás, with the king's consent, suspended parts of the constitution, dissolved parliament and assumed dictatorial powers, which he retained until his death in January 1941. [Translator]
5. The Italians invaded in October 1928 but were driven back into Albania. The Germans invaded Greece from Yugoslavia in April 1941. [Translator]
6. The Right Livelihood Award, established in 1980, by the Swedish-German author, Jakob von Uexkull, 'to honour and support those offering practical and exemplary answers to crucial problems facing the world today', has become known as the Alternative Nobel Prize. Awards are presented annually in the Swedish Parliament on the day before the Nobel awards. [Translator]

Figure 13.3 French tourists waiting beneath the austere phoenix symbol of the Junta.

Figure 13.4 The Homeopathic Academy of Alónnisos. *Courtesy of Anthony Hirst.*

Figure 13.5 Wedding celebrations in Palió Chorió, 1948 (a).
Courtesy of Michális and Evanthía Vláikos.

Figure 13.6 Wedding celebrations in Palió Chorió, 1948 (b).
Courtesy of Michális and Evanthía Vláikos.

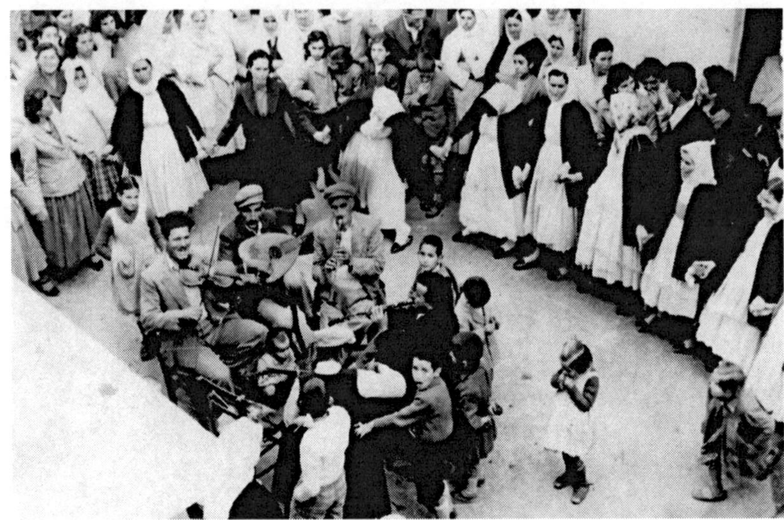

Figure 13.7 Wedding celebrations in Palió Chorió, 1956.
Courtesy of Nikólaos M. Anagnóstou.

Figure 13.8 Dancing at the School, Palió Chorió, 1960.
Courtesy of Marína and Panayótis Diniakós.

Figure 13.9 School outing, Palío Chorió, 1961. *Courtesy of Marína and Panayótis Diniakós.*

Figure 13.10 School outing, Palío Chorió, 1962.
Courtesy of Marína and Panayótis Diniakós.

Figure 13.11 A social gathering, Patitíri, 1972.
Courtesy of Father Grigórios Tsamáris.

Figure 13.12 Easter celebrations, Patitíri, 1967.

Figure 13.13 National Day celebrations (25 March), Patitíri, 1967. *Courtesy of Michális and Evanthía Vláikos.*

Figure 13.14 Father Tsamáris, Patitíri, 1969. *Courtesy of Father Grigórios Tsamáris.*

14

CHURCHES AND OTHER BUILDINGS

IMMEDIATELY after the catastrophic earthquake of 1965, P. Lazarídhis came and examined all the post-Byzantine monuments of Alónnisos, in his capacity of *éforos* (director) of the regional archaeological service. He recorded the extent of the damage in each church, together with details of their iconostases and icons. He also organised a programme of church repair and maintenance. His survey began in Palió Chorió where there is the largest concentration of churches.

14.1 The Churches of Alónnisos: Within the Old Village

14.1.1 Naós tou Christoú (Church of Christ)

Figure 14.1 Church of Christ in Palió Chorío, 1960. *Courtesy of Athanásios Páppos.*

Near the square in the old village (Palió Chorió) is the church of the Nativity of Christ, usually referred to simply as 'the Church of Christ'. The church is a strange shape and its architecture of an unusual style. It is a single-aisled basilica[1] with a dome, but influenced by Western models. Built in the 17th century, it bears witness to the island's Venetian connection. (Venetian influence is evident in the architecture of houses as well as churches.) At the time of the earthquake some cracks appeared, but they are not too worrying. At the entrance there is a narthex[2] with a women's gallery above. Inside there is a carved wooden iconostasis,[3] a beautiful example of local woodcarving which was brought here from the church of Áyos Nikólaos when it was demolished. The roof, with its dome, is covered with slates from Pílio. In 1965 three icons of the mid 17th century were recorded (a King of Kings and Great High Priest,[4] a John the Baptist and a St Nicholas). There are 22 others, of which 15 are from the 18th and 19th centuries. The Church of Christ is the largest in Kástro (the part of Palió Chorió within the old walls).

14.1.2 Áyos Athanásios (St Athanasius)

This church, also within the bounds of Kástro, is another single-aisled basilica, 8.65 m long and 5.78 m wide. The roof is a wooden construction covered with stone slates. The apse within the sanctuary, like that in the Church of Christ, is of the Armenian type. This suggests that this church was built at roughly the same time, in the 17th or 18th century. The iconostasis is recent and appears to be a replacement. Over the entrance there is an arch of the Arab type. One 18th-century icon, a St John, was recorded.

14.1.3 Áyos Yeóryos (St George)

This is located on a high point in the centre of Kástro. It is single-aisled, 6.85 x 4.2 m, with a barrel-vault roof. Again, the roof is covered with stone slates. It hardly suffered at all during the earthquake, but some plaster fell off revealing the murals behind. The iconostasis is old (17th century). The recorded icons are of the 18th century (a Virgin, a Christ and a St John), but there are older ones of the 17th or early 18th century (a St George, and an Annunciation with two saints above and four bishops below).

14.1.4 Áyos Dhimítrios (St Demetrius)

Áyos Dhimítrios was within the village, but it did not withstand the earthquakes of 1965. It was cruciform in plan, 6.8 x 4.45 m, with a semicircular apse. Four round arches at the crossing supported a dome. Unfortunately the arches fell and the south wall leant over so far that it could not be propped up. Later the entire church collapsed. For their preservation and security some of the icons were transferred to the church of Áyos Athanásios: a 17th-century icon of Christ in Majesty, a Virgin as Life-giving Spring and a St Demetrius with the saint enthroned.

14.1.5 Áyos Nikólaos (St Nicholas)

The Church of Áyos Nikólaos was old and had suffered the ravages of time. It was demolished in 1964 by the godfearing inhabitants in order to build the present modern church of Áyos Nikólaos, which is considered the central church of the island. From the ruins of the old church a marble slab 2.02 x 0.83 m and 12 cm thick was saved. It was the top of the altar, which had not been broken, despite the rather careless demolition of the building. The same fate befell the church of Áyos Pandeleímonas (St Panteleimon) which was joined to the church of Áyos Nikólaos. The two churches were of the same size, and both were in ruins.

Figure 14.2 Opening day of the new church of Ayía Paraskeví. *Courtesy of Fótis Tzortzátos.*

Figure 14.3 At the old church of Ayía Paraskeví, 1964 (it was later rebuilt).
Courtesy of Father Grigórios Tsamáris

Figure 14.4 Young women in traditional costume, Vótsi. *Courtesy of Ólga Tsoukaná.*

Figure 14.5 A feast day in Palió Chorió, 1956. *Courtesy of Ioánnis Frantzéskos.*

14.2 The Churches of Alónnisos: Outside the Old Village

14.2.1 Naós tou Evangelismoú (Church of the Annunciation)

The church of the Evangelismós is a small single-aisled basilica, which must have been built in the 18th century. The old icons have, however, been transferred to other churches inside Palió Chorió, and those that are there now are relatively new. The original iconostasis has been replaced by a modern one in a simple style.

14.2.2 Profítis Ilías (Prophet Elijah)

Profítis Ilías is a small wooden-roofed basilica beside the road up to Palió Chorió. It is more recent than the churches within Kástro and has no old icons. The Chapel of Áï Lías, as it is known locally, has recently been restored. The external wall plaster has been removed, revealing reused architectural members of considerable antiquity. In times of drought the locals resort to the chapel. The Liturgy (the Orthodox Mass) is performed and they pray to the Prophet Elijah, imploring him to send rain to save them.

Figure 14.6 The Church of Profítis Ilías.

14.2.3 Áyos Ioánnis (St John), Áyos Taxiárchis (Holy Archangel) and Kímisis tis Theotókou (Dormition of the Virgin)

These are all modern buildings, small chapels at various spots around the old village, and they contain very few old icons. In former times popular festivals were held at them. They are all well maintained and frequently visited. At Áyos Taxiárchis there is an ossuary containing three skeletons, probably of monks. Apostólis Vláikos, who was saved from the firing-squad in 1944 on the Feast of the Dormition of Virgin,[5] celebrated on 15 August, has made himself responsible for seeing that the Liturgy is performed in the church of the Dormition every year on that date.

Figure 14.7 At Mourteró, 1957. *Courtesy of Kóstas and Máchi Efstathíou.*

14.2.4 Áyos Yeóryos (St George) and Áyos Konstandínos (St Constantine)

Apart from the monastic churches described below, and a few country chapels, such as Áyos Yeóryos at Kardhámi and Áyos Konstandínos at Splirάchi, there are no other old churches on Alónnisos.[6] Áyos Yeóryos and Áyos Konstandínos were built in the 19th century, and served the needs of the faithful who lived in remote corners of the island (Yérakas, Mourteró, Koumarórachi). Later various small churches sprung up all over Alónnisos. They were built to fulfil vows or as offerings to saints, chiefly by elderly people, and out of deep religious feeling.

14.3 The Monasteries of Alónnisos

14.3.1 Monastery of the Áyi Anáryiri

Áyi Anáryiri is located on the west side of the island, on the edge of a dangerous cliff above the bay of Megáli Ámmos. Nearby is a mine which came into operation at the beginning of the 19th century. A story is told about the building of the monastery. Popular tradition always expects the saints themselves to play a part in choosing the place where their churches are to be built. When the faithful of Alónnisos set about building the church of the Áyi Anáryiri, the icon of the saints disappeared in the night and was found on the edge of a precipitous cliff.

This happened night after night until the people realised they would have to build the church by the cliff. And there it stands today. Similar traditions are found all over Greece and indicate the intense devotion of the people in such matters. Once the church of the Áyi Anáryiri had been built a monastic complex sprang up around it. Next to the church there are traces of cells and other ancillary buildings. The monks were under the authority of the Great Lávra Monastery on Mount Athos.[7] The Áyi Anáryiri monastery, like most of those in our region, must have been abandoned in the early 19th century.

Figure 14.8 The Monastery of the Áyi Anáryiri.

Figure 14.9 Feast day of the Áyi Anáryiri, 1956. *Courtesy of E. and D. Dhiómas.*

Figure 14.10 Feast day of the Áyi Anáryiri, 1961(a). *Courtesy of Valándis Vláikos.*

Figure 14.11 Feast day of the Áyi Anáryiri, 1961(b). *Courtesy of Valándis Vláikos.*

The church is a single-aisled basilica with a dome. At each of the four corners large ceramic jars have been built into the inner faces of the walls to improve the acoustics. After the earthquake it went out of use, and a new church was built next to it. Later on, certain persons who thought there was a hoard of money hidden inside the old church wrecked the interior. A restoration was begun in 1996 with funds collected by the French philhellene Maude Gallance to repair and maintain this historic monastery, so that it could function once more as a place of worship. Mme Gallance's actions were inspired by purely personal feelings. The restoration of the church is now complete.

14.3.2 Monastery of the Kímisis tis Theotókou (Dormition of the Virgin) at Vounó

The Monastery of the Kímisis tis Theotókou was built on Vounó, the hill to the north of Palió Chorió. Its position was chosen for a number of reasons. Even today there is a spring with good water nearby, the land around is fertile, and the place was not exposed to pirates. It was built in the 16th or 17th century and abandoned by the monks in the middle of the eighteenth, for reasons unknown. It was the most important monastic centre on the island, and the largest. The church, 7.2 m long and 4.3 m wide, is another single-aisled basilica with a dome. The church was visited in the 1920s by I. Sarrís, who was enthusiastic about the wall paintings and the carved wooden doors. (The latter no longer exist.) In the National Archives there are 14 documents that refer to this monastery.[8]

The church has many wall paintings. Most of them are covered by a layer of whitewash, but several are still visible today, including a Virgin (in the sanctuary) and a Christ in Majesty with Archangels (in the dome). In the outer zone of the dome you can see a John the Baptist; lower down, around the drum, the Twelve Prophets; and below them, in the triangular squinches, the four Evangelists. In the prothesis[9] there is a painting of considerable artistic merit of the Vision of Peter of ALEXANDRIA.

Figure 14.12 Monastery of the Dormition of the Virgin at Vounó, 1978. *Courtesy of Athanásios Páppos.*

In the 1965 earthquake cracks appeared in the building and repairs were necessary. Unfortunately these were not undertaken until many years later. The icons were transferred to more secure places but have since disappeared. The wooden iconostasis was old; it rotted and has been replaced.[10] A marble cross was removed from the church by Greek and German art thieves. They arrived at Vótsi in a yacht, as tourists. In the course of a walk across the island they saw the cross and stole it. They put it in a sack and took it aboard their yacht in broad daylight. Y. Efstathíou saw the cross sticking out of the sack and shouted at them. They took fright and made a hasty departure, exchanging insults with the locals. The authorities were informed but didn't have the means to pursue them, and thus the cross was lost forever from the island.

The British Lord Noel-Baker, well known as a major landowner in Évvia, visited the church in the 1960s. He noticed the damaged wooden cross on the iconostasis and sent it to Mount Athos for restoration. Following the intervention of some inhabitants of Alónnisos, Lady Noel-Baker returned it to the island. It was handed over to Father Grigórios and is now kept in the large modern church of Ayía Paraskeví in Patitíri.

14.3.3 The Monastery of the Análipsis (Ascension)

The monastery of the Análipsis is the true expression of the monastic spirit, built halfway down a steep cliff on the west side of a barren promontory at the north end of Alónnisos. It was probably built in the 17th century by monks who must have had great patience and determination. A path from above, which probably once led to the monastery, is now almost completely overgrown and impassable. The only approach now is from the sea. The church is very simple and austere, as befits this wild and inaccessible place. It was carefully located next to a spring, out of view from the sea (so as not to attract the attention of pirates), and in a position where there is no danger of landslides.

Next to the church there are remains of the monks' cells, and a little further away a cave converted into a stable. Patiently and with great labour the monks managed to transform the barren rocky site into cultivable land. Where there was a little soil they built terraces and cleared and seeded them. The visitor will be amazed at the courage of the monks who tamed the earth and survived bodily and spiritually in this little Golgotha. If an animal pulling the plough slipped, it could fall 100 metres on to the sharp rocks below; but even in such a place they tried to tame nature. There can have been no more than two monks living there.

Figure 14.13 The monastery of the Análypsis (Ascension).

Figure 14.14 Ascension Day, 1933. *Courtesy of Angelikí Florouís.*

The church, which has a small yard beside it, is roofed with stone slates. It is well looked after and has a fresh coat of whitewash. There are two icons from the 19th century but they are being ruined by the damp. A characteristic story about this little church concerns a woman who, in fulfilment of a vow, set out every Sunday from Patitíri to light the candles there.[11]

Figure 14.15 Ascension Day celebrations, 1933. *Courtesy of Angelikí Floroús.*

Figure 14.16 Ascension Day, 1966. *Courtesy of Father Grigórios Tsamáris.*

Figure 14.17 The priest Father Dhiómas, 1925. *Courtesy of E. and D. Dhiómas.*

14.4 Monasteries on the Other Islands

Important monastic structures erected during the period of Ottoman rule remain on a number of the uninhabited islands. Many monks sought refuge there and rebuilt or repaired the old monasteries. The best monastic centres are those on Kirá Panayá and Skántzoura. Built on fertile land, both have strong connections with the monastery of the Great Lávra on Mount Athos. After the period of intense unrest in the 16th century the uninhabited islands were flooded by great numbers of monks. The monasteries developed rapidly, not only in terms of the numbers of monks, but also economically. They were granted autonomy and received a number of important monastic personages.

14.4.1 Kirá Panayá: Monastery of the Yénnisis tis Theotókou (Nativity of the Virgin)

The monastery on Kirá Panayá once played a leading role. Refounded in the 16th century in an ideal, well-watered spot, it grew and came to be recognised as the chief monastery of the region. It was able to receive many men who chose the way of God. It became autonomous and had its own olive press, flour mill, vineyard and orchard. Hundreds of olive trees were planted. Two huge fields were enclosed and sown. The new monastery itself was built like a fortress, on the Athonite pattern, with buildings around a central courtyard. There were cells and guest rooms, storehouses, forges, two large ovens, a kitchen and toilet arrangements which were rather advanced for the time and included a sceptic tank.

Figure 14.18 A monk at the Kirá Panayá monastery, 1964. *Courtesy of Thomas Vestrum.*

Figure 14.19 The monastery on Kirá Panayá, 1968. *Courtesy of Thomas Vestrum.*

Figure 14.20 Taking in the view from the guest quarters of the monastery on Kirá Panayá, 1948. *Courtesy of N. Anagnóstou.*

Figure 14.21 Monks and shepherds at the monastery on Kirá Panayá. *Courtesy of Thomas Vestrum.*

Outside the walls they built stables for animals and a cistern. At first they had to climb up to it from the shore, but later they constructed steps. The growing needs of this large agricultural enterprise drew many lay people to the region around the monastery. They were given animals and land in return for a certain percentage of their produce which was sent to the mother house of the Great Lávra. They built their own ossuary in a small building near the cliff. There too they constructed their own meeting place, where they could enjoy their wine or a coffee together in the evenings.

On Mount Athos there is a great deal of information about this dependent monastery on 'Yimnopelayísia' (Kirá Panayá), including a list of all the monks who learned the monastic life there. Often there were lay people living in the monastery who helped with the running and maintenance of the building or with the agricultural economy of the island. Besides, the gates were always open to travellers who were greeted first with *tsípouro* (grappa) and *loukoúmi* (Turkish delight). The monks provided travellers with food and drink and, when they left, gave them bread for the journey. Hence the need for the two large ovens and the many guest rooms. Local people travelling by boat would often make a stop in the bay below the monastery, and climb up the hundreds of steps, to spend the night there and continue their journey refreshed.

The last monk there was Nektários, a well-educated old man who was thirsty for knowledge and very welcoming. With great determination he maintained the enormous complex of buildings. As long as he was there, burdened by years, he looked after the place with what little strength remained to him, whitewashing, digging and pruning the grapes. Nevertheless, the monastery fell into disrepair. Exhausted and without the strength to continue, he was recalled to Mount Athos for medical attention.

Figure 14.22 Father Nektários, Kirá Panayá, 1979. *Courtesy of Holger Reichhart.*

Figure 14.23 Kitchen of the monastery on Kirá Panayá, 1967. *Courtesy of Holger Reichhart.*

Figure 14.24 The author at a young age with Father Nektários at the monastery on Kirá Panayá.

Figure 14.25 Easter at the monastery on Kirá Panayá, 1953.

Figure 14.26 The hospitality of Father Artérmios at the monastery on Kirá Panayá.

When Father Nektários left, what was once one of the most flourishing and imposing buildings in the northern Aegean knew the decay that inevitably follows abandonment. The vine in the courtyard was uprooted, animals got inside, water began to penetrate the walls, the windows and the roof timbers rotted. Everything was in a wretched state, until the shipowner, Andhréas Potamiános, undertook to restore it, and in 1994 managed to get things going again. Potamiános appointed a warden, the building was restored and is being maintained so that it will withstand the passage of time.

The old people all recall with nostalgia the splendour of the community and the grandeur of the celebrations that took place there at Easter. Others remember their life alongside the monks and the heavy labour of oil production, harvesting and wood cutting.

In the 1950s oil production reached 6,000 *okádhes* (7.7 tonnes), wheat 10,000 (12.8 tonnes). The monastery took 25 per cent, the remaining 75 per cent belonged to the farmers. (Later the proportions were reversed in favour of the monastery on orders from Mount Athos.) The monastery had to pay the monastic servants (about thirty in number) and send to Mount Athos every year 3,500 *okádhes* (4.5 tonnes) of hard cheese, 200 *mizíthres* (soft cheeses) and 200 male kids. Today the island is leased to private persons who exploit it for farming.

The church of the monastery on Kirá Panayá, which is in the centre of the courtyard, as in all the monasteries of Athos, has recently been restored. The icons and books had already been transferred to the Great Lávra monastery for safekeeping.

14.4.2 Skántzoura: Monastery of the Evangelismós tis Theotókou (Annunciation of the Virgin)

The original monastery on Skántzoura was abandoned in Byzantine times[12] and a new one was built on the high point of the island. In Patriarchal deeds and synodical decisions which were inscribed on parchments in 1798, the then Patriarch of Constantinople, Gabriel, states that the monastery on the island of Skántzoura was dedicated in sanctity and piety to the Annunciation of our Most Holy Lady. The monastery was *stavropiyakó*, that is to say, it belonged to, was controlled by, and was directly accountable to, the Patriarch of Constantinople.

There were large numbers of monks who made Skántzoura into a great monastic centre. It is said that because of the number of boys who joined the former monastic community at a very young age, Skántzoura became known as the 'island of young men'. From Patriarchal documents, we see that, for a number of reasons, the monastery was suddenly abandoned and began to fall into decay. For many years it remained empty, until Serafím, the energetic Bishop of Pisidhía, a region of southern Asia Minor (the PISIDIA of the New Testament), went to the island and with the help of other monks re-established the monastic functions. Before he was appointed to the task, Serafím had been responsible for the church in Ankara (now the capital of Turkey).[13]

With his energetic spirit he came to Skántzoura, renewed contacts with the Patriarchate, and by means of this sought the Christian protection of the Voyvoda,[14] Nikólaos Mavroyénis, who was first admiral, or Kapudan Paşa, in the Sultan's

Navy. With financial assistance he began to rebuild the monastery, which, following its abandonment, had been pulled down, and instigated a general renewal. For some reason, though, he gave up this enterprising project and left the island.

Fortunately, the *igoúmenos* (abbot) of the monastery, who was called Isaías, took over. Isaías was a monk from the Great Lávra monastery, who, with great determination and hard work completed Serafím's half-finished project. He finished rebuilding the monastery and the ancillary buildings, planted vines and olives, cultivated the fallow fields, and generally set things in order. The monastery thrived again and began to produce an income, and was thus able to pay accumulated back taxes amounting to 1,500 piastres.

In September 1815, the Patriarchal Synod in Istanbul decreed, with the authority of the Patriarchal Seal, that no public official, lay or ecclesiastical, could demand anything whatever from the monastery on Skántzoura. It was to be independent and self-governing and subject only to the Patriarchal throne. The same synod established a sisterly relationship between the monastery on Skántzoura and the Monastery of the Great Lávra on Athos, probably on the initiative of the Lavriot Abbot, Isaías. The close economic links between the Great Lávra and the island, which persist even today, date from this time. The same sacred ordinance decreed that the abbot of Skántzoura should be chosen democratically by the monastic community on the basis of the deeds and virtues of the candidates. The then Patriarch, Kírillos, presided over this synod, which consisted of himself and 12 other reverend fathers.

It appears, however, from later documentary evidence, that the monastery was not maintained for long. By 1840 its books had been transferred to the bishopric of Skópelos. The parish church of Áyos Pandeleímonas (St Panteleimon) and a priest called Melétios were equally interested in buying them. A further patriarchal edict of 1840 determined the value of the books of the disused monastery so that they could be sold to those who were interested.

Until 1837 the island of Skántzoura was national territory, but from 1838 it was considered to be an ecclesiastical possession. In 1838 the only lay inhabitant of the island was a farmer from Mitzéla in Pílio.[15] In a document addressed to the authorities in Skópelos, this man complains about the exorbitant rent imposed on him. He had 250 animals and was obliged to pay 1,043 drachmas for three years. The monastery continued leasing the island to herdsmen.

Later the monastery of the Great Lávra took over the management. The Skántzoura monastery was maintained either by the lay inhabitants or by the monks when there were any living on the island. During the Second World War there was only a single monk there; for a while afterwards there were two. They had cattle, and with the help of servants (mainly from Alónnisos) they cultivated the land. The olive grove was ploughed and cleared. The plain was cultivated and grain was planted. Artichokes were produced in such quantities that they were taken to Alónnisos and sold by the sackload.

A story is told that one of the monks went down to the shore one day with a mule, to the spot known as Tarsanás (meaning 'shipyard'), to bring up some goods that had arrived for the monastery. When he got there he saw a seal sleeping among the rocks. At that time seals were much sought after for their skin. The skin was stretched on a frame and rubbed with ashes. Then it was cut into strips to make shoes. Sealskin has a special quality, being both flexible and durable.

The monk had no axe with which to kill the seal, and decided on the following strategy. He made a lasso out of rope, tied it to the mule's saddle and passed the loop round the neck of the seal. The seal woke up, terrified, and plunged into the sea. The monk, taken by surprise, chased after the mule which was being pulled into the sea by the seal. Luckily for the mule the saddle strap broke. The mule was saved but the monk bemoaned the loss of his saddle.

Later, under the Junta (the military dictatorship that ruled Greece from 1967 to 1974), eight opponents of the regime were sent to the monastery. They repaired the monastery and were obliged to report to the police on Alónnisos once a month. The leader of the group was Dhorótheos, a very energetic and resourceful man. They repaired both the main monastery building and the church, and introduced hens and rabbits and new crops such as potatoes.

Figure 14.27 The monastery on Skántzoura.

At the same time quarrying was started, to extract the rare type of marble that is found on the east side of the island. This stopped after a year because of the great distances involved in transport. In 1974, when the Junta fell from power, the monks as well as the exiled dissidents departed, and the island was left empty. The monastery, following its fate, was abandoned, and today the only person who stays there occasionally is the herdsman, Dh. Agállou.

The building is in urgent need of repair, since it is crumbling. The once imposing house of the Virgin is slowly dying. It is a fine piece of architecture and a rare example of a human construction in complete harmony with the environment .

14.4.3 Yoúra: Monastery of the Zoodhóchos Piyí (Life-giving Spring) or Kímisis tis Theotókou (Dormition of the Virgin)

On the remote and rugged island of Yoúra there was a small monastic foundation. The remains of cells, stables, cisterns and other ancillary buildings can still be seen. According to tradition, the community consisted of nine monks, who were either killed by pirates or, in another version of the story, consumed by a thunderbolt.[16] Their bones were still there until 1953. Then they were destroyed by the cows that the game-wardens kept.

An extraordinary feature of the church is that stalactites from the nearby cave were used in its construction. To collect water the monks had dug cisterns in the earth, which they lined with lime and clay. In summer they could also get water from the Cave of Márkos, better known as the Cyclops' Cave. The monks planted olive trees in a gully that was full of stones. Around the monastery itself they cleared the rocks and sowed seeds.

This humble monastery on Yoúra had the honour to be the home of Ierótheos the Morean[17] (1686–1745). Stéfanos Dhapóndes[18] founded a very important school on Skópelos, which during its early years was under the direction of Ierótheos the Morean. Ierótheos left the Ivíron Monastery on Mount Athos and, at the urging of Neófitos Mavromátis, took charge of the newly founded school.

He was a man of considerable learning for those days. He knew both ancient Greek and Latin, and had studied philosophy and pedagogy. With his knowledge and authority he raised the school on Skópelos to the level of the famous school of Pátmos. After a successful ten years he returned to Mount Athos, and later retired to the small monastery on Yoúra, there to live out the rest of his life. He died and was buried there in 1745. The Orthodox Church venerates him as a saint, St Ierótheos the Iviríte (that is, a member of the Ivíron monastery), or St Ierótheos of Kalamáta (his birthplace). His feast day is 13 September. This small peaceful monastery was the ideal place for the wise old man. In the image of an old man studying and writing in a small cell, with a candle burning, we see enlightened monasticism in its highest form.

Unfortunately the monastery was dissolved prior to 1840. The manuscripts of the venerable saint were transferred elsewhere or destroyed. The icons and the iconostasis that are there today are relatively recent. Like Skántzoura, the island of Yoúra was considered national territory until 1837, but from 1838 it was included among ecclesiastical possessions. In 1838 the only inhabitant of the island was the herdsman, Emmanouíl Triandafíllou. A document dated 10 June 1841 states that

Figure 14.28 Tourists in the Cave of the Cyclops, Yoúra, 1972.
Courtesy of Athanasíou Kiriazís.

Figure 14.29 The chapel on Yoúra. Its architectural peculiarity is that stalactites and stalagmites from the nearby cave were used in its construction.

> the title to the uninhabited island of Yoúra belongs incontestably to the General Ecclesiastical Treasury. [...] According to those from whom I have gathered information concerning the occupancy of this island in previous years, a herdsman, Emmanouíl Triandafillou, in the year 1838 kept, as he himself admitted in my presence, twenty-five sheep on the island, and in 1839, eighty, without paying pasturage tax to anyone, and in 1840, being unable to maintain the sheep on this island for the duration of the year, transferred them to another uninhabited island and paid his pasturage tax to the tenant there.

The document is signed by the Deputy Governor of Skiáthos, A. Th. Edhipídhis, and the Secretary, I. Papadhópoulos.[19]

Fifty years later the island was leased to a timber merchant who brought in Koulouriot muleteers and woodcutters.[20] Their first task was to make paths down the cliffs and in other places where access was difficult. Then they converted all the caves into houses and stables. They built furnaces and began to cut down the trees, even on the most precipitous slopes. Many mules lost their footing on the mountain paths and fell into the ravines. Two of the woodcutters lost their lives in the same way. One elderly man was injured in such a fall and died later of his wounds. The other, Manólis, who has given his name to a part of the island, was killed in the following manner.

> He was about to enter a small cave, but some startled goats charged out of the cave and knocked him off the cliff. He fell into a holm-oak tree and his body remained there for many years. No one knew where Manólis had gone and his disappearance was variously attributed to drowning, abduction by water nymphs, and suicide. It was only after the First World War that an Alonnisiot, hunting on the island, came across the tree. He spotted a bone in the lower branches, looked up and saw the rest of the skeleton and the man's gun. Thus the mystery of Manólis' disappearance was solved. Even today the place still bears his name.

14.4.4 Pipéri: Monastery of the Zoodhóchos Piyí (Life-giving Spring)

Pipéri regained its old Byzantine glory during the period of Ottoman rule. Next to the Byzantine church several entirely new ancillary buildings were constructed. the fields were cleared and new trees planted. The famous monastery on Pipéri is remote and impressive, on the summit of this harbourless island. Surprisingly, on the summit, a spring of fresh water gushes out. Many monks found a spiritual refuge in this peaceful spot, and practised there a kind of life perfectly adapted to this remote and rocky place. According to the story told by the old people of Alónnisos, a certain Kesários came ashore on Pipéri after being shipwrecked in a terrible storm. There had been other people, including some small children, with him in the boat, but he had been unable to save them. Kesários devoted his life from then on to God and became a monk.

Figure 14.30 The Wardens' houses, Yoúra, 1964. *Courtesy of Thomas Vestrum.*

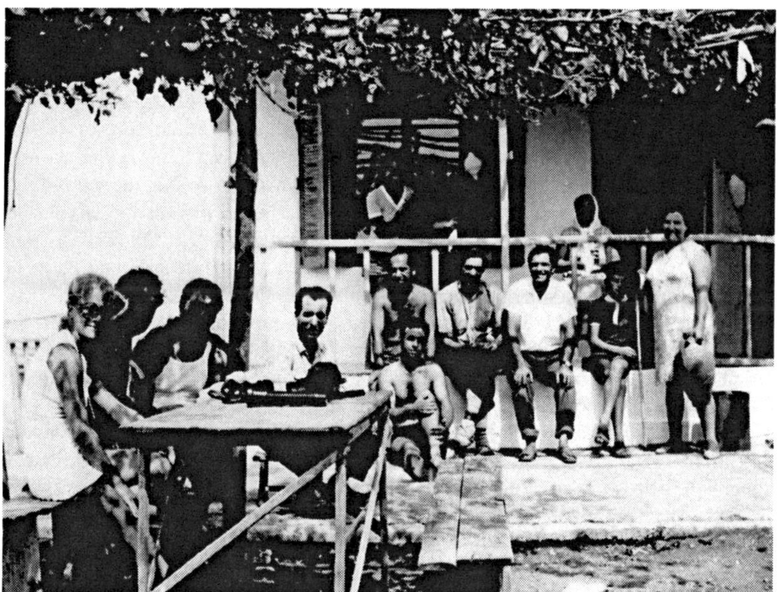

Figure 14.31 The first tourists on Yoúra, 1962. *Courtesy of Athanasíou Kiriazís.*

The story has some basis in truth, since a certain Kesários Dhapóndes (1713–1784), the son of Stéfanos Dhapóndes referred to above, did indeed live as a monk in the monastery on the island. Kesários Dhapóndes was one of the most significant and prolific writers of his period. A well-educated man with a restless nature, he held various important positions but was also imprisoned for a time, before seeking refuge on the tiny island of Chálki, off the west coast of Rhodes.[21] In 1749 he got married on Chálki and lived there peacefully for two years. His fate pursued him, however. His wife died and he turned against the world and set out for Pipéri. There he assumed the monastic garb, took the name Kesários. He lived on Pipéri for three years, and it was there that he received his baptism as a writer; and it is thus, in a sense, to Pipéri that we owe the important body of work he bequeathed to us.

From an eye-witness we learn that there was a large library in the monastery, created by Kesários. The library building was six metres long and two metres wide, crammed with old books and rare manuscripts. The manuscripts, of which many belonged to Dhapóndes, were written some on parchment and some on paper. After the war a literary scholar named Glikós, who came originally from Kími in Évvia, but was teaching in the secondary school in Skópelos, went to Pipéri and took away four sacks of manuscripts and old books. A mule carried the sacks down to the shore and Glikós took them by caïque to Skópelos. In the sacks there was indeed a veritable treasury from the first stage in the great writer's career.

There are also 197 later manuscripts, from the period 1834–55, which make clear that the monastery on Pipéri (called Pepárinthos) was a daughter house of the Moní Evangelismoú (Monastery of the Annunciation) on Skiáthos. Fiedler, a German traveller who visited Pipéri in 1834, encountered a powerfully built but insolent monk.[22] This was probably Laríon, who, according to tradition was a man of immense strength. There is a huge marble block there even today which no one but Laríon has ever been able to lift unaided. He had his own vine in the monastery, still known as Larion's vine. Like his predecessors in the monastery Laríon had good relations with the pirates, who respected him for his strength. On one occasion he ordered a new rowing boat in Skópelos, and when he went to collect it the boat was ready but his friend, the shipwright, wasn't there. For a joke he picked the boat up and carried it a considerable distance from the boatyard. When the shipwright came back he couldn't understand where the boat had gone and he didn't know how he was going to explain its disappearance to the monk. When he eventually spotted the boat he couldn't believe that Laríon had carried it so far on his own.

On 19 September 1841 King Otto visited the monastery on Pipéri and found four monks there, one of whom was very old and almost blind. These monks had bought the island as a hermitage, and their right to it dated back to the previous century. The community had acquired the whole island and appointed the best educated monk among them to look after their dealings with the outside world. This monk, in the boat that they had brought to the monastic boatyard (destroyed in a terrible southerly gale in 1943) used to go to Skópelos for provisions. There he picked up salt, pulses, wine, sugar, flour, nails and various other goods which the monks needed to get through the hard winters, when rough seas confined them to their island for long periods of time.

Figure 14.32 One of the special breed of oxen, Pipéri (see p. 293).

On one occasion, in the early years of the 20th century, the monk appointed to the task of collecting provisions made a trip to Skópelos. He selected more goods than he was able to pay for, but a cunning Skopelite was eager to lend him some money. He got the unsuspecting monk to sign a promissory note which purportedly described his debt. In fact, the paper that the monk signed certified the sale of the island to the wily Skopelite. Still suspecting nothing, the monk went back to the island in peace. The following spring a caïque arrived at Pipéri bringing the policeman and the creditor. At first the monks thought they had simply come to visit, but when they were presented with an eviction order they became extremely angry.

The young confidence trickster had brought along his adopted daughter who heard the furious monk say that he would kill the man who had deceived him. She told her father, who was too frightened to go ashore, and decided to give the monks a year's grace in which to prepare for their departure. Apart from anything else, he wanted to avoid becoming the object of public outrage and condemnation. In less than a year the disillusioned monks left the island, except for the unfortunate monk who had signed the paper. He could not endure the criticisms of his fellow monks and died of despair on the island. When the monks left the island, the monastery remained empty except when it was used by herdsmen.

In 1950, when systematic resin collection on a large scale began, there were some 16,000 pine trees on Pipéri; and by now there must surely be twice that number.

The monastic church is still in sound condition. The iconostasis is old, and particularly noteworthy is an icon of the Virgin, which has great vitality. The books have disappeared bit by bit and the ground has been dug up by treasure seekers. The island today remains the property of a family in Skópelos. No one can visit it any more. It has been designated a seal sanctuary for the rare Mediterranean seal and it is illegal for boats to approach its shores.

14.4.5 Pappoús: Monastery of the Yénnisis tis Theotókou (Nativity of the Virgin)

This island bears the nickname of St Athanásios the Athonite who from childhood was as virtuous and serene as a grandfather (*pappoús* in Greek). The small church of the Virgin was once the centre of a small monastery. The monks had a vineyard and cultivated half of the island.

Figure 14.33 The monastery church of the Nativity of the Virgin, Pappoús. From Dh. Alexíou, *Architecture of the Post-Byzantine Monuments.*

They fenced off the other half and used it for raising animals. Their water was collected in two cisterns which they built. There was also a windmill which may well have served neighbouring islands as well. They planted vegetables on an adjacent rocky islet, some of which are still growing today. They had a small boat which enabled them to communicate with both Kirá Panayá and Yoúra. The monastery couldn't have housed more than two or three monks on account of its restricted size.

14.5 Other Buildings

14.5.1 The Old Junior School in Palió Chorió

Another important building, perhaps the most important building on Alónnisos, is the Primary School (*Dhimotikó Scholío*) in Palió Chorió. This was built at the end of the 19th century with a gift from the banker and philanthropist Andhréas Singrós. In its original form it was a very beautiful neo-classical building. In 1956, however, the school needed to be enlarged, and the new additions have unfortunately spoiled its appearance and completely obscured the well thought out design of the original building.

Figure 14.34 School photograph, 1958. *Courtesy of Ioánna Tzórtzi.*

Figure 14.35 School photograph, 1965. *Courtesy of Kóstas and Karen Kaloyánnis.*

Figure 14.36 School photograph, 1971. *Courtesy of Kóstas and Karen Kaloyánnis.*

Figure 14.37 School photograph with the children in traditional costumes, Patitíri, 1972. *Courtesy of M. and D. Papavasilíou.*

Figure 14.38 Women on Psathoúra. The remoteness of the island necessitates hard work.

14.5.2 The Psathoúra Lighthouse

In the last quarter of the 19th century, a steel-hulled Danish cargo vessel, which had lost its way in the fog, ran aground and broke up on the treacherous rocks of the island of Psathoúra. Its steel plates can still be seen scattered in the sea. On board was an agent of King George I, who was king of Greece from 1863 to 1913, and of Danish origin. Afterwards the king issued a decree requiring a lighthouse to be built on Psathoúra. The building was undertaken in 1895 by masons from Skópelos, following a French design, and assisted by a craftsman from Alónnisos by the name of Athanasíou. The tower of the lighthouse is four metres in diameter at the base, reducing as it rises. It was constructed out of local stone, using locally produced mortar. Only the architectural members in marble were imported. The Psathoúra lighthouse is considered one of the finest in Greece.

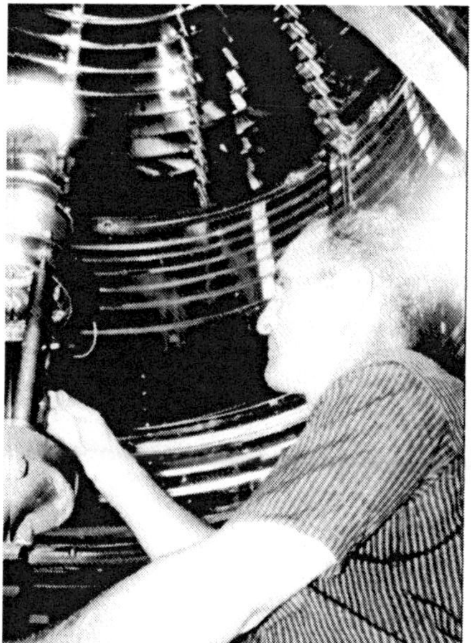

Figure 14.39 Lighthouse keeper, Yeóryos Alexíou, lights the lamp.

Figure 14.40 Wife of lighthouse keeper, Yeóryos Alexíou, on terrace of lighthouse.

Figure 14.41 The tallest lighthouse in the Aegean, Psathoúra, 1999.
Courtesy of Anthony Hirst.

Notes

1. The single-aisled basilica is the simplest form of church building, being rectangular in plan without major subdivision. Larger basilican churches have three or even five aisles. [Translator]
2. The narthex is a porch or antechamber extending across the full width of the west end of a church. In this small church the narthex is separated from the nave only by the posts supporting the gallery above. [Translator]
3. The iconostasis is the screen that separates the nave of the church from the sanctuary. There are doors in the centre (and at each side as well in larger churches), and icons are attached to the screen or painted directly onto its panels. [Translator]
4. This icon, as well as smaller ones of the *Dodekaórtos*, were stolen by art thieves and have not been recovered. (The *Dodekaórtos* is a row of 12 small icons across the top of an iconostasis depicting the 12 apostles, St Paul taking the place of Judas Isacariot. [Translator])
5. See pp. 233 and 236.
6. Kardhámi is a hill in the centre of the island. The church of Áyos Yeóryos is on its eastern side, close to the main road. Áyos Konstandínos is in a gorge near the coast due west of Áyos Yeóryos. [Translator]
7. Sampsón (1973).
8. *Yeniká Archía tou Krátous* (General Archives of the State), in the collection of *Monastiriaká éngrafa Évvías ke V. Sporádhon* (Monastic documents from Évvia and the Northern Sporades).
9. The niche on the left hand (or north) side of the altar. [Translator]
10. See the October 1972 issue of *Efimerís Vorión Sporádhon (Journal of the Northern Sporades).*
11. The story is told on p. 184.
12. See p. 165.
13. Lavriótis (n.d.).
14. An Ottoman title used by the Princes of Walachia, Moldavia and Transylvania. [Translator]
15. Síros (1987).
16. For the accounts of the monks' death, see pp. 182–3.
17. That is, a man from the Moréa, as the Peloponnese used to be called. [Translator]
18. The name derives from the Italian, Da Ponte. The family were originally from Venice. Stéfanos Dhapóndes was at one time the British representative on Skópelos. [Information provided by the author]
19. Síros (1987).
20. 'Koulouriots' means people from the island of Sálamis, popularly known as Kouloúri. [Translator]
21. Tomanás (1960).
22. For Fiedler's brief account of this meeting see p. 445.

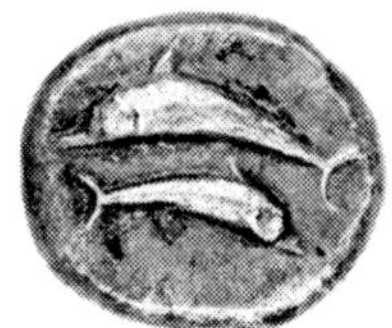

15

SHIPWRECKS AND MARINE ARCHAEOLOGY

Figure 15.1 Arriving at the harbour on the ferryboat *Paschális*.
Courtesy of Holger Reichhart.

THE SEA-BED around Alónnisos and the lesser Northern Sporades, to a distance of about 10 nautical miles offshore, is littered with every kind of submarine treasure. It is no exaggeration to say that in any descent in this region a diver will uncover some archaeological find. It may be only a fragment of an amphora, or, if he is lucky, something more substantial, such as an anchor, a heap of storage jars, the wooden hull of some ship sunk in recent times, or any of a range of objects that men have used at one time or another and which for various reasons have ended up at the bottom of the sea. The known wrecks in the area number more than a hundred, but the sites where there is reason to suspect the existence of a sunken vessel run into thousands, all patiently awaiting investigation which will expose to the glare of publicity their tranquillity, and their well-kept secrets, and, hopefully, reveal the dates at which time stopped for them, as well as their ports of origin and the objects of their ill-fated journeys. The secrets of the deep and the questions posed by the ships together create a complex riddle which we would all dearly love to solve.

Figure 15.2 The ferryboat *Kíknos* (*Swan*), 1967.

But why are there so many sunken ships in this particular area? The answer is simple. Alónnisos and the surrounding islands are at the centre of a sea route which has been in continual use throughout history by craft of all kinds, from simple canoes to the galleys, triremes and *dromones*[1] of antiquity; from sailing ships of all sizes to steel-hulled ships of huge displacement in modern times. Conditions were not always rosy for this ceaseless traffic. There were sudden storms, fires and other nautical disasters. Piracy was the cause of many shipwrecks.

Here we must recall that at most times from prehistory to the Greek Revolution of 1821, our islands served as a base for ruthless pirates. In the Minoan period, though, there was no danger from pirates for the sailors who crossed the Aegean. In those days an organised navy succeeded in driving out the Carian, Dolopian and other pirates. There was another brief period of security at the beginning of the classical period, when Cimon of ATHENS subdued the pirates. And in the Roman period Pompey rid the Aegean of this scourge of sailors, with somewhat more lasting effect. In all other prehistoric and historical periods every kind of piracy afflicted our region. Pirates found perfect hideouts on the smaller islands, from which to surprise passing ships, taking money and part of the cargo and then sinking the ships and killing or enslaving the crews. The problem of piracy was finally solved under Kapodhístrias, the first President of independent Greece (1828–31), when Miaoúlis, the heroic naval leader of the Greek Revolution, cleared the Aegean of pirates.

Storms have been a headache for Aegean sailors of all periods. Changeable and unpredictable winds are a constant problem in this region. Sailing vessels have to deal with changes in the direction and strength of the wind with each new island that they pass. The particular morphology of each island affects the direction of the wind. The mountainous mass of Yoúra, for example, affects the wind more than low-lying Skántzoura. It is clear that one needs the skill and knowledge of an experienced sailor to avoid running aground and to keep a vessel on course.

Figure 15.3 Repairing the lighthouse keeper's boat, Psathoúra, 1957.
Courtesy of Holger Reichhart.

Figure 15.4 A trip to the uninhabited islands, 1957.
Courtesy of Holger Reichhart.

Even this was often not enough, for in the days of sail heavily laden cargo vessels were difficult to manoeuvre and could not easily be propelled by oars. Their great displacement did not allow them any solution except to use their anchors to prevent collisions with the shore. This is one of the reasons why in many places the sea-bed is littered with anchors. Today, corroded anchors encrusted with marine organisms are eloquent testimony to the struggles with the elements of sailors of all periods. Besides, the geography of our islands is such that sailors are deceived into a false sense of security in what are, in reality, dangerous harbours.

In bad weather sailors may find themselves stretched to the limit, for some supposedly secure harbours have such sandy bottoms that anchors will not hold, while the morphology of the surrounding land may whip up the winds to a frenzy. The depths of these 'secure havens' on the smaller islands (Planítis and Áyos Pétros on Kirá Panayá, Vasilikós on Peristéra) are host to innumerable sunken vessels. These are the silent exhibits in a vast underwater museum, where ships of every type and every period form a unique mosaic; and when you come to visit that museum you have the strange impression of being an unwanted intruder.

From historical evidence we can easily confirm that almost all the significant naval events of Greek history had some connection with the nautical crossroads of the Northern Sporades. Though Jason's ships and those of the heroes of the Trojan War never met they followed, in their different epochs, exactly the same route. At Vasilikós the anchors of a Roman fleet, anchors from the fleet of the Byzantine emperor Nicephorus Phocas, and from the galleys of the pirate Barbarossa lie close together on the sea-bed. Merchandise, armies, slaves, booty have all passed this way in every kind of sailing vessel. The wrecks of such vessels, to their misfortune in their own time, but to our good fortune today, have become an inestimable heritage, which awaits the advance of science for its proper study and interpretation.

Let us now consider historical events in order, so we may see what an important role our islands have played in maritime history by virtue of their geographical and geopolitical position. Until today very little has been written about the northern outposts of the Sporades. Every inhabitant and lover of these islands has a quarrel with our forbears who have left us in the dark about some of our islands' greatest secrets.

15.1 A Short Maritime History

Let us begin with the vast span of prehistory in which man gradually developed his navigational skills. As the need for cultural and mercantile exchanges increased he sought new routes. His restless spirit overcame the barrier of the sea and he ventured out in home-made boats, whose design, in time, he perfected. A new material appeared, associated the most important technological developments of its time: obsidian, a crystalline mineral quarried on the island of Mílos in the Cyclades. The blades made from this dense material brought what was arguably the greatest technological revolution of any period. Obsidian was sought after by everyone, and particularly in the rich centres of civilisation in Asia Minor.

But let us look at the routes of the first vessels that sailed the Aegean, taking Mílos is our starting point. There, a rich trade developed through the system of barter. Sailors tended to avoid the passage from the Cyclades to the Dodecanese, because of the high winds and storms which still dominate that area today. Many voyages started out from the important prehistoric centre of LERNA in the Peloponnese, and proceeded via the island of Ídhra to Lávrio, on the east coast of Attica, and from there the ships sailed through the straits of Chalkídha (ancient MANICA) that separate Évvia from the mainland, or, passing to the seaward side of Évvia, made for Skíros. In either case they had then to pass along the chain of islands of the Northern Sporades, before proceeding via the island of Áyos Efstrátios, POLYOCHNI (on the east coast of Límnos) and TROY to Asia Minor. On their return they would follow the same route in reverse.

The existence of this route explains the foundation of flourishing prehistoric centres on the now uninhabited islands of the Northern Sporades, where exchanges, as much cultural as mercantile, took place. The crews of foreign ships that anchored in our region exchanged valuable knowledge with our remote ancestors. The exchange value of goods and the continual movement of rich merchandise encouraged the growth of piracy, and eventually the Minoan war fleet was obliged to hunt down and exterminate the pirates. Merchants could then breathe again and trade reached a peak under Minoan control. The Minoans established colonies and bases in the Northern Sporades, and pursued trade in the region with unremitting energy. Unfortunately most of the boats that must have been sunk, either by pirates or as the result of other causes, during this period have not been preserved, or, if some of them do still exist, have not yet ben located.

Figure 15.5 The small harbour at Mandráki, Psathoúra.

The centuries passed and the restless Greek tribes sought for richer regions. Their restlessness is reflected in the voyage of the Argonauts, the first organised expedition of discovery, mythologised as the search of the hero, Jason, for the Golden Fleece. The point of departure of this expedition was IOLCUS (present-day Vólos) and its destination, COLCHIS, at the far side of the Black Sea. Through this pioneering mission rich areas were discovered and the impetus given for further commercial and colonising endeavours. The lure of easy gain brought innumerable boats to Alónnisos, Skántzoura and Kirá Panayá. In the harbours of Vasilikós and Planítis, where the original Argonauts must have called on their voyage to the unknown, later sailors strove to get the best prices for their merchandise in these new markets.

The wealth of the new regions led the Greeks into the Trojan War, for which they assembled, according to Homer, an enormous fleet of 1,186 ships. The Mycenaeans and their allies gathered at AULIS (modern Avlídha, on the mainland opposite Évvia, just south of Chalkídha) – it would have made no sense to take the far longer route through the Cyclades – and from Aulis, via the Northern Sporades, they sailed to Límnos, Ténedhos[2] and thus finally to TROY. The only harbours in the immediate vicinity of Alónnisos large enough for so many boats were those at Áyos Pétros and Planítis on Kirá Panayá. For ten years this bridge of islands between IOLCUS and TROY constituted a line of communication vital to the successful outcome of the war.

After the decline of the Mycenaean civilisation our islands fell into oblivion and pirates reappeared in greater numbers than before. The situation changed in the 8th century BC when the people of Chalkídha used the Northern Sporades as a stepping stone in their colonisation of Chalkidhikí. From then on, a great variety of ships plied the sea that surrounds our islands. Thousands of trading vessels, warships and pirate ships came and went without ceasing on their journeys north and south.

If we make the rather macabre assumption that 0.5 per cent of all these ships sank for one reason or another in the seas around these islands, we can begin to get some idea of the extent of the wealth that has been left to us on the sea-bed. In the subsequent Archaic Period, the economic advancement of the city states was extremely favourable to the development of sea trade. However, the pirates, who were by then firmly established, were a major obstacle to trade. We have no information as to whether, during the Persian Wars (490–479 BC), the war ships, which for greater security accompanied the land-based expeditionary force, stopped at or passed through our region. In 475 BC, the Athenians sent the general Cimon with a large fleet to put an end to the destructive activities of the pirates. However the results of Cimon's successful campaign were short-lived, since our islands were too far from Athenian centre of influence.

The years rolled by and all the major events of Greek history left their marks on our region. The Peloponnesian Wars, the victory of SPARTA and the ascendancy of the Spartan fleet in the northern Aegean, and the eventual reconquest of the Northern Sporades by the Athenian fleet are the most important naval events before the rise of Macedonia. Commercial activity was sometimes in decline, sometimes on the increase. But throughout all such fluctuations the strategic and commercial importance of the passage through our islands remained constant.

The Macedonians exploited the rivalry between the great cities of the south, and as they became stronger they began to exert a stranglehold on Greece. Naval bases were of vital importance to them, and the island of Kirá Panayá offers the best harbour in the northern Aegean. Many ancient authors refer to the recurrent struggles between Philip II of Macedon and the Athenians for possession of our island chain. In the end, after the battle of CHAERONIA (338 BC), Philip seized all the islands of the Northern Sporades.

The contemporary Athenian orator Demosthenes praised the harbours of our region, and both the Athenians and the Macedonians after them used them as winter naval bases. When Philip's son and successor, Alexander the Great, infused new life into the whole of the then known world, our islands formed an integral part of his immense empire, and enjoyed the many advantages of their position. Their ports became vibrant centres of seaborne trade. There the two great civilisations of Greece and the Orient came into contact. Situated between the two our islands profited from these momentous changes.

In the period after Alexander, Greek civilisation continued to flourish. Thousands of ships from all the Hellenistic kingdoms passed this way en route to or from Macedonia, the heartland of Alexander's now divided empire. Alónnisos and the lesser Northern Sporades were busy places. Their seaports developed rapidly in order to supply the needs (water, timber, provisions) of the countless ships that called there. Little by little, though, Greek power began to decline and in the 2nd century BC the Romans were able to conquer our region without encountering much resistance. Polybius states that in 200 BC the Roman fleet made a brief stop at the island of Icos (Alónnisos).

Life on our islands carried on peacefully under the Romans, except for occasional pirate incursions, until Archelaus and Metrophanes, commanders of the fleets of Mithridates VI, King of Pontus, conquered the Northern Sporades. With these island as a base their forces attacked, despoiled and overran Magnisía and Évvia. A few years later the Romans undertook the reconquest of the region under Sulla, who defeated Metrophanes' fleet.

At about this period a serious thorn in the side of Rome developed, afflicting our islands too. Cilician pirates with a thousand swift ships captured all the strategic harbours of the Aegean, naturally including ours, and with these as bases terrorised merchant ships and maritime settlements. So well organised were these Cilician pirates that it took the Roman fleet eleven years of stupendous effort (78–67 BC) to destroy them. It was Pompey who delivered the final blow. In repeated naval battles and assaults, he saved the unfortunate islanders from the dreadful scourge of the ruthless pirates. For a while the Romans controlled the Aegean. But civil strife ensued, ended only by Octavian's defeat of Antony and Cleopatra in 30 BC.

In the resulting anarchy the pirates reorganised themselves. Trade continued, but on every cape the pirates were ready to pounce on their prey. Life became very difficult for the inhabitants of the islands. It was at this time that the city at Kokkinókastro on Alónnisos was completely abandoned.

In the next centuries anarchy ruled in the Aegean, until the power of the newly constituted Byzantine Empire extended everywhere. Then our islands served as the naval bases of this vast empire. Maritime trade revived, though the fear of piracy remained. Every Byzantine fleet that undertook campaigns in the southern Aegean, Crete or the Peloponnese anchored en route at Kirá Panayá or Peristéra.

The consolidation of Christianity in all the islands was characterised by the creation of monastic centres, which were at the same time naval stations offering information and provisions. Byzantine ships and merchant vessels from all over stopped at our islands. The sea-bed throughout this region is studded with Byzantine jars, dishes and cups, for reasons that we shall see below.

Because of their geographical position the islands were considered a crossroads and supply centre essential to the protection and development of Byzantium. They were the umbilical cord uniting all the parts of the empire. Our supposedly fellow-Christian Crusaders used it too when they carried away the plunder from the churches of the 'Ruling City' as Constantinople (Byzantium) was often called. The route through our islands retained its importance even after the fall of Byzantium. The conquering Turks were quick to realise the importance of the region.

Merchant vessels from every region of the world have passed through Alónnisos and the lesser Northern Sporades, carrying oranges from Malta, coffee and spices from Arabia, rice from Egypt, grapes from Zákinthos and the Moréa (as the Peloponnese was called in Byzantine times), oil from Italy, dates from Asia Minor, artwork from Venice, wool and more recently tobacco from Vólos, honey from Attica, grain from Thessalonica and much else besides.

Savary de Brèves, a diplomat who served under Henri IV and Louis XIII and was for fifteen years the French ambassador in Constantinople, confirmed the importance of our geographical position. Wishing to exploit the desire of western powers to expel the Turks from Constantinople and appropriate the wealth of the city, in 1605 de Breves outlined a plan in which he stated that

> it is well known that the greater part of the provisions destined for Constantinople come from the region known as Vólos, which is beyond the Holy Mountain [Athos] and close to Avlóna [Thessaly]. If this region were to be captured, Constantinople would be destroyed by hunger. No ship would risk transporting rice, sugar and other necessities from Egypt if the passage of the Aegean were forbidden it. If a sailor wishes to make the passage from Vólos to Constantinople he must of necessity pass through these parts.

Piracy evolved into a gainful and almost respectable profession, due as much to the decline of the Byzantine navy under the Emperor Manuel Comnenus (1143–1180), as, later, to the collective inability of the maritime states to secure the much used routes between Western Europe and the East. Franks, English, Genoese, Venetians, Maltese appeared on the scene, most of them knights, the sons of noble families.

On the pretext of attacking the infidels, they plundered the islands and tyrannised the population throughout the Aegean. The Aegean summer, the easy spoils, the wine, the women of our islands, attracted like magnets all these high-born scum. Besides, pirates established on the islands attacked their co-religionists and despoiled them of whatever they found. They took hostages and demanded ransom, they dragged off to the slave markets those inhabitants who would fetch a good price, the rest they killed or mutilated.

This state of affairs persisted throughout the late medieval and post-medieval period, right up to the Greek Revolution of the 1820s. All of the most notorious pirates despoiled the Northern Sporades, which offered them good harbours in which to hide or to rest in their journeys, and from which to ravage the local population. At the time of the Revolution there was great movement of warships, Russian, Greek, Turkish and Western.

When the situation was resolved and our islands became Greek once more, Miaoúlis came to the ‘Devil’s Islands’ (or ‘Thieves’ Nests’) to flush out the ‘devils’, that is, the pirates. After that, apart from the passage of part of the Greek fleet after 1910, and the bombardment of a convoy of German transports in 1944, there were no other naval events of great moment in the area. Today, the passage through the Northern Sporades is as important as ever, frequented by ocean-going steel-hulled freighters, tourist boats and fishing caïques.

In concluding this general survey of maritime history, we must mention, as a tribute to victims of shipwrecks, the countless graves around our shores. These are found chiefly where the soil is soft and easy to dig. There the drowned were brought by respectful local inhabitants and buried so that they would not become carrion for birds of prey or rats. Often enough it was the surviving relatives of the drowned who performed this arduous work in the midst of their grief. As the elderly people recall, almost every beach had its body. Bones would be brought to light by pounding waves, heavy rain, or dogs.

In the 20th century new graves by the sea have been dug on several islands: on Psathoúra; on Yoúra at Cape Pnigménos (the name means 'drowned man'); on Kirá Panayá by the monastery, in the bay of Áyos Pétros and at Planítis; on Peristéra at Livadhákia; on Alónnisos at Áyos Dhimítrios and Áyos Pétros (near Stení Vála) and by the monastery of the Análipsis (Ascension), and at various other spots.

There are also graves from earlier periods: a Byzantine grave on the islet of Áyos Pétros, probably one of the crew of the ship with the plates (see section 15.5.3 below); and graves of the classical period on the islet of Megálo Polemikó west of the northern tip of Skántzoura, on Lechoúsa, at Pethaménos (on the coast of Peristéra) and also on the southern shore of the bay of Tsoukaliás on Alónnisos. Many locations on the shore line now bear the names of those drowned there.

Figure 15.6 One of the first large fishing caïques.

Figure 15.7 The *Fridheríki* which used to run between Skópelos and Alónnisos.

Figure 15.8 An Alónnisos-type hull.

There are four main types of underwater sites to be described: sunken settlements, ancient wrecks in shallow water, modern wrecks in shallow water, and wrecks of all dates in depths of over 100 m. Wrecks in the last category lie in a peripheral zone around our islands. There is, however, little to be said about them, since in most cases there is only indirect evidence of their existence and location, and none has been investigated. They are discussed in general terms in section 15.11 at the end of this chapter.

There are several localities in our region where areas of what was once dry land have, at one time or another, sunk below the waves; and in three of these there is clear evidence that they were once habitation sites: a Neolithic settlement in the bay of Áyos Pétros on Kirá Panayá (section 15.5.1 below), and classical remains under water close to the shores of Psathoúra (section 15.2.1) and Alónnisos (section 15.6.1). These are described below along with four wreck sites of classical date (sections 15.2.2, 15.5.2, 15.7.1 and 15.7.2), three from Byzantine times (sections 15.5.3, 15.5.9 and 15.7.3), and one from the early Ottoman period (section 15.5.6). There are also some thirty accounts of shipwrecks that have taken place during the last hundred years. All four classical wrecks and two of the Byzantine wrecks (sections 15.5.9 and section 15.7.3) were first reported to the appropriate archaeological *Eforía* by my father, Dhimítrios K. Mavríkis.

Figure 15.9 Dh. Mavríkis (the author's father), who discovered the classical wreck at Pethaménos, inspecting the finds.

The modern shipwrecks are described in some detail for two reasons. The first is that, since they all happened in the course of a single century, they can provide a rough guide for the frequency with which ships may have sunk in earlier periods. The second reason is that they may help us to understand earlier disasters. They happened at key points, and we know the causes of their sinking, their routes, their cargoes, the lives lost and how the survivors were saved. The study of all these modern nautical accidents, has filled many gaps in my own understanding of earlier shipwrecks.

At first I couldn't imagine why a Byzantine ship should have sunk inside a harbour. Now, it seems to me quite obvious. Learning from eye-witnesses the manner in which ships have sunk in recent times, you can, by making comparisons, uncover the ancient hidden secrets of the undersea world. The accounts are organised geographically, beginning with sites around Psathoúra, and working from north to south through the chain of islands.

15.2 A Settlement Site and Wrecks around Psathoúra

15.2.1 The Sunken Settlement

Off the southeastern tip of Psathoúra, the most northerly of our islands, there is a submerged settlement, which is visible from the surface, the water being in places only 2 m deep. A paved road with the remains of buildings on either side of it can be clearly made out. At a slightly greater depth one can see a circular building. These days, to attract the tourists, everyone speaks of a 'sunken city'. The tourists come expecting something spectacular, and are disappointed to find only the indistinct outlines of buildings.

The island of Psathoúra is volcanic and the changes in land level were the result of an eruption. There are many different opinions about the nature of this sunken settlement. Ch. Athanasíou thinks it is nothing more than a fishing village, while I. Sarrís maintains that it is the ancient city of HALONNESOS. Perhaps the views of the French investigator, Jacques-Yves Cousteau, who visited the site three times in 1974, might have enlightened us, but Cousteau never expressed an opinion (he died in 1997). A party from the *Eforía* of Marine Antiquities also visited the area in 1994. My own view is that it is a large temple site of some importance in the ancient world. Around the temple are ancillary buildings and perhaps a small village, sustained by fishing, stock rearing and the offerings of visitors to the shrine.

There is some evidence to support my view. First there is the evidence of the 'sunken city' itself, in which a paved road leads to an unusually large building with two concentric circular surrounding walls. Secondly there is the view of the geographer Pausanias, generally a reliable guide to the ancient world. According to Pausanias the island of CHRYSE, with its famous temple of Athena, disappeared beneath the waves. Pausanias says that CHRYSE was not far from LEMNOS, that is, the modern Límnos, which lies to the northeast of Psathoúra. It is possible that an island consisting of Psathoúra, Psathonísi (the smaller island to the south) and the now submerged area in between them was the ancient CHRYSE, and that in actuality only a part of the island, the part where the temple stood, sank into the sea.[3]

The large part played by chance in the finding of the cities is shown by the following. The island of CHRYSE lay close to Límnos. It is said that on CHRYSE, Philoctetes met with his misfortune.[4] The whole island has since been covered by the waves. CHRYSE sank and disappeared into the deep. Another island named IERA, which did not exist at that time, later rose from the sea.

I also believe that in antiquity, before the land was submerged, hemlock, which we now call *mangoúta*, was another source of income for the islanders or their priests. If the plant grew there in antiquity they would surely have exploited it to produce the famous poison.

15.2.2 A Classical Wreck

Close to the sunken settlement that lies to the east of the island of Psathoúra, there are fragments of pottery of the classical period on the seabed, dated approximately to the 4th century BC. The density of these sherds and their concentration at a particular depth, suggests that they are from a wreck.

Some trading ship of the period had probably struck a reef in storm or fog. Even today Psathoúra is notorious for its shallows and reefs. The depth at this spot is only nine to ten metres. Consequently, those amphorae that weren't smashed at the time of the collision would have been broken up by the effects of bad weather and the currents which are very strong here. The few that remained were easy prey to archaeologists and tourists on the lookout for a souvenir.

The wreck was located by Cousteau in 1974. According to the lighthouse keeper at that time, Cousteau visited the sunken settlement and the wreck on three separate occasions. (In order to project a better image abroad, Greece had invited the great French scientist to make a series of documentary films.)

In 1994 the wreck was visited by a party from the *Eforía* for Marine Antiquities. In the course of their inspection they brought up a small classical amphora which was still in good condition. Unfortunately, time and the rocky sea-bed had almost completely destroyed the ship itself.

15.2.3 A German Bomber

From an interview with Yeóryos Agállou at Stení Vála, 2 June 1996 (Yeóryos Agállou was born in 1916 and was 26 at the time of the plane crash):

> During the Second World War I lived on Psathoúra with my father and mother. My father was a lighthouse keeper. There were only two events in those days that disturbed the peace and solitude of our life there. The first happened on 27 May 1942.
>
> It was a calm spring night with a full moon. We heard the sound of an aeroplane engine flying low right above our heads. A plane was making circles round the lighthouse. The lighthouse wasn't lit because of the war. It was only lit when needed and in response to a government order. Afraid that we were going to be bombed – in those days you never knew where they were coming from – we went outside and hid in the bushes. It was two o'clock in the morning and there was no wind. Above us we could make out quite clearly a large aeroplane going round in circles.

> Suddenly the engine cut out. As we learned later, it had run out of fuel. The warplane came down on the sea northwest of the island near a submerged rock known as Xéra, travelled a certain distance, giving the crew time to get away in a life raft, and then sank. My father, Agállos Agállou, and I shouted to them from the land and showed them the place where they could come ashore. My father was a smoker and he lit several matches together to guide them to a particular spot on the shore.
>
> When they got ashore, they beached the life raft and thanked us, and we went into the lighthouse. We asked them if they wanted some food but the said 'No' and ate raw onions from our garden for fear that we might poison them. Then they washed, pouring water over one another with the watering can from the cistern. Finally they went to sleep, but there was always one of the four on guard, change and change about.
>
> In the morning they asked us nervously where they were, whether there were any partisans and if they could join up with the other Germans. One of the crew was Austrian and spoke Italian. My father knew that language because he had been in the Greek Royal Navy. So we learned the story of the plane.
>
> It was a Junkers bomber en route from Tobruk to Sicily, but it had been pursued by allied planes and changed course for the German-held airport at Athens. But the chase continued and it headed instead for the northern Aegean. Over Psathoúra the fuel ran out and it came down in the sea. The life raft they'd used to save themselves turned out to be a godsend for us. From its tough rubber we made many pairs of rough and ready shoes, for ourselves and our relatives.
>
> Once I'd managed to synchronise the Germans' rowing of the small two-oared boat that was the only means of escape from our remote island, and with the calm spring weather in our favour, I took them to the monastery on Kirá Panayá. There they were welcomed by the monks Veniamín and Athanásios who were rather scared because they'd stolen and sunk a boat.[5] The next day we went on to Alónnisos where they stayed with Dr Tsoukanás, and the day after we rowed to Skiáthos where the guests were united with the German guards. One of them, grateful to me and my family for our help, gave me his photograph. Later on, when the Germans arrested me during a massive search operation in the Northern Sporades, I showed this photograph to the prison warden and it saved me. When he saw the photograph he stood to attention.

In July 1991, my friends the sponge-fishers, Y. Dhrosákis from Alónnisos and Leftéris Glinátsis from Kálimnos, discovered the Junkers referred to above at a depth of 30 m. The plane had sunk at a considerable distance from the point where it came down on the sea. Generally it was in a good condition except for a few parts that had become detached and were scattered around.

After my own investigation, the Greek Air Force was informed and they immediately sent a diving party. They went to Psathoúra and searched with their own boat in the spot the sponge-fishers had described to them, but found nothing and went away. They came back later, and, guided this time by the two men themselves, they hit on the exact spot right above the bomber.

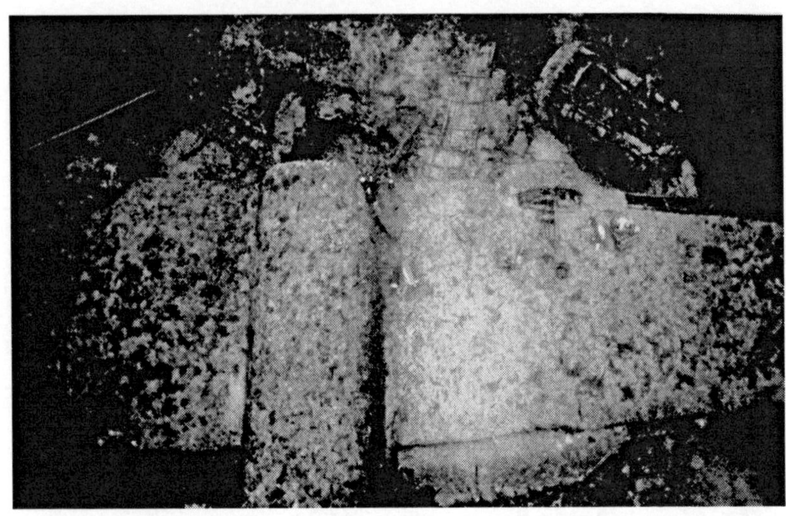

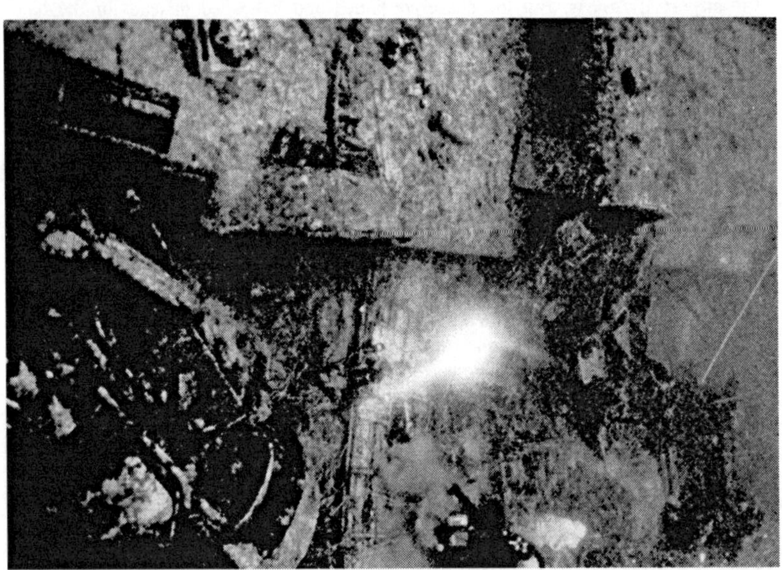

Figures 15.10 and **15.11** Parts of an aeroplane on the seabed, Psathoúra (a) and (b).
Photo by V. Mendoyánnis, from the periodical Thálassa (Sea), *No. 41.*

Figures 15.12 and 15.13 Parts of an aeroplane on the seabed, Psathoúra (c) and (d).
Photo by V. Mendoyánnis, from the periodical Thálassa (Sea), *No. 41.*

For forty-nine years the wreck had enjoyed the peace of the deep, becoming one with its environment. It had become the home of fish, large and small, according to the testimony of the two men who first disturbed the peace of the blackfish which had taken the place of the Luftwaffe pilots.

When Glinátsis, the one who first discovered the plane tried to get inside, six blackfish darted away from this intruder from another world. In our area there are five other sunken aeroplanes. In co-operation with Panayótis Agállou we pointed out their positions to the Air Force General Staff (*Yenikó Epitelío Aeroporías*) so that they might be officially recorded.

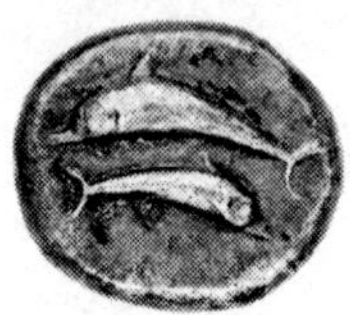

15.2.4 The German Ship the *Hüberman*[6]

From an interview with Yeóryos Agállou at Stení Vála, 2 June 1996:

> It was 8 October 1944. A cargo vessel laden with munitions and German soldiers, five hundred of them, was sailing past Komós on Psathoúra. We were following it, because we had noticed the furtive movements of one Greek and two foreign warships.
>
> The Greek vessel was the destroyer *Themistoklís* and the other two were British destroyers. They had received a signal from Allied Counter-Intelligence that a German ship, the *Hüberman*, was transporting men and material from the Dodecanese to Thessalonica, and had set a trap for it. First the *Themistoklís* approached and signalled to the *Hüberman* to surrender.
>
> The Germans refused and turned the prow of their ship towards the open sea. The three destroyers gave chase and with a total of five shots sank the German ship that was trying to escape
>
> With my boat I tried to get near to rescue the shipwrecked men, but from the *Themistoklís* they shouted angrily, 'Fisherman, don't go near or we'll sink you.' So we went back to the island. The destroyers picked up the survivors and departed. Later various items from the cargo of the sunken ship began to float to the surface. Some of these were 'manna from heaven' to us. We found a lot of spermaceti candles shaped like mushrooms, timber, chests full of fire-fighting equipment and life jackets (which were actually of Greek manufacture), barrels of fuel and many boxes of Hamburg butter. We were eating the butter for a long time and when it went rancid we made soap from it.
>
> With these 'godsends' a more sinister cargo came ashore. The body of a tall fair-haired soldier was caught among the rocks. He was a German officer and we buried him on the island. He'd been clutching a briefcase which contained his whole life history.

> There were photographs of his girlfriend and his family, his school-leaving certificate and various other personal effects. From other private documents it was evident that he came from Hamburg and that his name was August Pier. After the war I got to know a man called Christofidhis, who had studied medicine in Germany. With Christofidhis' help we sent the briefcase to the city authorities in Hamburg to be returned, as was proper, to the relatives of the dead man. Eventually we received a reply from the Mayor of Hamburg, thanking us, and informing us that there were no relatives to whom he could return the case. In the merciless bombing of the military harbour at Hamburg his whole family had been killed. It was a hard war.

The *Hüberman* lies in the volcanic depths off Psathoúra and only a very few fishermen know its position. Large numbers of fish, chiefly sea-bream, make their homes in its carcass.

15.2.5 A Copper-plated Wreck

From an interview with Yeóryos Agállou at Stení Vála, 2 June 1996:

> There were no other big events during the war except when a wooden cargo boat ran aground. But with our help and the rising tide the unfortunate sailors escaped the horror of shipwreck.
>
> There's another wreck which was found near the cape of Psathonísi. When we used to go fishing with my father, I thought of it as sunken gold, but it must have been a wooden boat which had sunk long before the war. In those days they used to cover wooden boats with copper below the waterline so they lasted longer. The copper was gradually polished when storms stirred up the sea-bed and began to glisten. When the weather was calm and we looked down from the surface we could see the shape of the wreck quite clearly.

15.2.6 A Modern Wreck near Psathonísi

(Information provided by Yeóryos Alexíou)

In the 1950s a trading vessel came from 'Capo d'Oro',[7] making for Mount Athos. There it was going to unload and go on to Thessalonica. It was carrying petrol in jerry cans. The sea was calm but visibility was zero, since a dense fog had come down. When, at the last moment, they saw Psathonísi, it was too late.

The boat was holed and began to take in water. It had crashed into the rocks and was stuck there. They crew got out onto the low-lying island and unloaded the cargo. By the time they'd finished unloading the fog had cleared and the lighthouse keepers saw them from across the water and came to pick them up. In the next few days there were storms and the boat broke up. Even today rotting planks and ribs can still be seen on the island.

15.2.7 A Liberty Ship with a Cargo of Ore

(Information provided by Yeóryos Alexíou and Kóstas Athanasíou)

A liberty ship carrying mineral ores was trying to cross the northern Aegean. It had been loaded the day before in Chalkidhikí in good weather. But when it was out in the open sea a strong north wind got up. In the high seas its heavy cargo shifted and the ship began to list. The captain sent out an SOS and several merchant vessels came to his aid. The liberty ship was listing more and was in danger of sinking. The sea was still high. The crew jumped into the sea and were picked up by the other ships, but those who couldn't swim drowned.

The ship's radio operator, who was wearing a life-jacket, wasn't spotted by the other ships. It was dark and the wind was blowing a gale, force seven or eight. The waves and wind brought him to the island of Psathoúra. With his last remaining strength the wretched sailor managed to climb the ladder up to the lighthouse, and just outside the gate of the forecourt he struggled free of his life-jacket and collapsed on the ground. Luckily for him he'd thrown his life-jacket on to a bush.

Because of the weather the lighthouse keepers had not been aware of what was happening in the lonely waters around their island. In the late afternoon of the following day, one of them went up to turn on the light. He was surprised to see something red by the gate and when he'd finished with the light he went down to see what it was.

There he found the shipwrecked mariner who had been unconscious for a whole day. They took him in and revived him. When a boat called a few days later they sent him to Alónnisos. Later he drowned when the *Iráklio* went down at Falkonéra (a small island in Cyclades west-northwest of Mílos).

15.2.8 The Wreck of the *Panayía Tínou*

In August 1991 the tourist ship *Panayía Tínou* ('Virgin of Tínos') was sailing down through the northern Aegean to the Cyclades. The *Panayía Tínou* was one of the last of the *karavóskara* (single-masted sailing ships with rounded stern) operating in our waters. She was 42 m long and 11 m wide, with a heavy-duty Skoda engine and two auxiliaries.

The ship had been chartered by a group of eight foreigners. The captain, thinking to delight his passengers, was heading for Psathoúra, since it is such an extraordinary island, unique in the Aegean, resembling a tropical coral island, and there is nothing like it anywhere in the Mediterranean. Consulting the charts, which give inaccurate information about the eastern side of the island, the captain passed too close to the shore. Suddenly someone looking down at the sea-bed saw that the depth was nothing like the 8 m shown on the nautical chart and the captain turned seaward.

With diabolical precision the ship ran straight on to two small reefs. They are only just below the surface of the sea and have been the cause of other shipwrecks. An SOS was sent out and a Greek Navy frigate which was within range received the signal and rescued the crew and the tourists.

Figure 15.14 The wreck of the *Panayía Tínou,* Psathoúra.

The sea was calm, and the following day the crew returned with a tug to try and pull the boat off the two rocks where it had settled. The way in which it was resting on the rocks was such that the couldn't get it free It had run on to the first reef at a speed of about seven knots. It carried on until the boat, balanced with its midpoint on the reef, was brought to a halt by a second reef in front. One tug wasn't enough and the crew therefore decided to get a second, larger tug. But Psathoúra is unforgiving – it is the fear and terror of local fishermen; during the night there was a northwesterly gale and in the morning the island was littered with flotsam and jetsam and ship's timbers.

In the dark the raging wind had smashed up the splendid vessel. When the wind died down and we went to see the disaster, we were seized by grief and despair. On the surface of the water we could see timbers, sheets, ropes, life jackets, bottles and various other utensils and equipment. Everyone was down on the beach picking up what they could. Later the crew brought a boat with a crane and took away the heavier items, such as anchors and engines. Afterwards we heard that an insurance company had paid out 40,000,000 drachmas in compensation. Today visitors to Psathoúra can still see the engine from the *Panayía Tínou* and many timbers from the wreck.

15.3 Wrecks near Yoúra

15.3.1 Wrecks in the Channel between Yoúra and Grámeza

(Information provided by V. Kaloyánnis)

Off the cape of Grámeza, fishermen from Alónnisos used to pull up, from a depth of 30 m, bits of timber and copper sheet. They could tell that the timbers were from a large cargo vessel. It had probably been trying to get through the Grámeza–Yoúra channel in a storm, and had struck some rocks and sunk. A few hundred metres away, at Cape Kassavétis on Yoúra, at a depth of 35 fathoms, there are timbers from another large wreck.

The channel is treacherous and must be full of the wreckage of boats. There are high cliffs on both sides of the channel, which give you the illusion of passing through deep, calm waters. But there are hidden dangers: on the one hand the tall masses of the islands which can cause sudden changes in the direction of the wind; and on the other the treacherous low-lying islets waiting for some unlucky boat.

Figure 15.15 A small fishing caïque, Yóura, 1964. *Courtesy of Thomas Vestrum.*

15.3.2 The Wreck of a Sponge Boat

(Information provided by Y. Kiriazís)

Captain Vangélis Fourtoúnas had been fishing around Chalkidhikí, and his 'machine' was heading for Tríkeri. (They used to call the sponge boats 'machines' because of the compressors mounted on the prow to provide the divers with oxygen.) The crew consisted of five divers ('mechanics'), four young apprentices (rowers) and the captain.

From Pórto Koufós on the tip of Sithonía (the middle of the three fingers of Chalkidhikí) they sailed to Psathoúra. There the sea was dead calm and they did some diving to supplement their cargo before heading back to Tríkeri. In the evening, after a hard day, they went up to the lighthouse for coffee. It was summer, the middle of June, 1961, but it suddenly looked as though a north wind was blowing up and the lighthouse keeper, Yeóryos Alexíou, turned them out, knowing Psathoúra is no place for a boat to shelter in a strong wind. So they set off for Planítis on Kirá Panayá.

On the way the weather got worse. There was a thick 'smoke' as the locals say. It was unprecedented to have high seas and rain in the month of June. Visibility was down to zero before they had even reached Cape Tambourás on Yoúra. They ran before the wind and tried to hold a course parallel to the land, but well out to sea. But the Devil must have been sent to sink this unlucky ship.

As though things weren't already bad enough, one of the divers fell against the flywheel and stopped the engine. Inevitably, in the pandemonium that ensued the men lost all sense of direction. They couldn't see the land at Tambourás which was lurking there, justifying its name (in local dialect a *tambourás* is someone who waits to ambush you), and threatening to destroy the fully laden sponge boat. When the land appeared out of the fog it was too late. Despite the desperate situation, the captain managed to run the boat up on to the rock ledge which ran along the shoreline at this point, and they all leapt ashore.

Suddenly the treacherous sea went quiet for a few minutes, without waves or gusts of wind. The divers, feeling secure now they were ashore, but fearing they might completely lose their livelihood, jumped back into the caïque intending to throw as many sacks of sponges as they could on to the rocks. The sponges represented many months' exhausting labour, and they couldn't stand by and see them lost in a moment. (In those days they worked for a share of profit.) Thus it was they let themselves be tricked by the brief pause in the storm and began to untie the sponges from the rails in the hope of saving them.

They were so preoccupied that they never saw the next wave coming. It struck with tremendous force, capsizing the boat and carrying off the five divers in its disastrous progress. The young assistants had remained safely on dry land, since they had no direct interest in the loss or otherwise of the sponges. The five experienced divers were battered by the sea and lost in its depths. But Captain Fourtoúnas, only lightly wounded and in shock, was dragged up on to the rocks by the young men and survived.

One of the young men had matches in his pocket and lit a fire over by the cliffs. They were able to warm themselves a bit and dry out while they waited, hoping to hear the voice of one of their companions. Tragically, though, the sea, on which they had lived since they were children and which had nourished them, had suddenly taken them to herself for ever.

At dawn on the following day the devastated captain and the four young assistants set out for the game warden's cabin on the other side of the island. For a long time there had been wardens on Yoúra whose job was to protect the species of wild goats that lived there.

But since Yoúra has some of the roughest terrain in the Mediterranean the barefoot sailors had trouble walking. They weren't familiar with the paths and kept having to retrace their steps. They didn't know that they needed to get out onto the spine of the island in order to find the route across. When you are by the sea, the mass of the cliffs is deceptive and you think that you are hemmed in on all sides.

Towards evening, by now in a truly wretched state, they reached Valsámia in the interior of the island. There they found water to drink and the two strongest went on towards the monastery. The captain was mentally and physically exhausted. On the mountainside one of the youths ran into a poacher. He explained that they were shipwrecked, but the poacher was scared that they would take him to the game-warden and wouldn't listen but ran off to his boat.

In the end the two young men reached the houses or the monastery and informed the warden, Y. Kiriazís, who got a torch and some pairs of shoes and set out to fetch the others. They stayed about a week in the monastery while the bad weather held. When the sea was calm again the caïque with the food supplies arrived and the shipwrecked men were taken to Alónnisos, and from there went back to Tríkeri.

Captain Fourtoúnas came back later with two trawlers. He dived down and found the sunken boat. By attaching floats he brought it to the surface, and towed it to Rousoúm where there was a *váza* and a slipway to enable them to get the boat out of the water.[8] As they pumped it out they found the bodies of two of the divers. According to the evidence of fishermen, the body of another of the missing divers was washed up on the tip of Grámeza. At Rousoúm they did some rough repairs and fixed the boat up, and then headed off for Tríkeri.

On the way one of the rowing boats they used for odd jobs (adjusting the tyres on the side of the sponge boat, collecting wood for cooking etc.) broke loose and was blown by the wind as far as Stení Vála. In the little harbour at Stení Vála there were several men from Tríkeri who recognised the boat and guessed that something bad had happened. They brought this herald of the tragedy into the harbour, and later it was returned to Captain Fourtoúnas.

15.4 Wrecks around Pipéri

15.4.1 Sailors from Lésvos

(Information provided by Y. Kiriazís)

By early 1941, the food shortages due to the war were beginning to have a serious affect on our island. The inhabitants resorted to exchanging goods. Islands that produced oil and wine took their products to Thessalonica where they exchanged them for wheat, barley and pulses. On one such dangerous voyage, a boat set out from Lésvos in clear weather, carrying oil to be exchanged for barley.

The barley was loaded in the estuary of the river Loudhía, just west of Thessalonica, and the boat headed straight back to Lésvos, where the crew hoped to sell the cargo at a premium. Near Pipéri, however, they were caught up in a terrible storm and after an unequal battle with the furious elements the ship went down.

The adjacent shore was not too precipitous and the three members of the crew were able to scramble on to the rocks. These unfortunate men didn't know that there was a monastery and several cabins on the island. And they never went up to explore.

They made themselves a crude shelter among the pines, and for twenty-eight days they lived off barley and limpets, and drank water from a stone trough. For warmth they had only the old clothes and rags they had saved from the ship. After twenty-eight days they were found by an Alonnisiot fisherman who brought them to Patitíri. They stayed there a while until they found a boat that was going to Límnos.

15.4.2 The Wreck of Andónis Malamaténios' Caïque

(Information provided by Dhimítrios Malamaténios)

Shortly after the war, old Andónis Malamaténios, who lived on Peristéra, had in his possession a large quantity of charcoal, which he was determined to sell for a good price, but not to the local merchants, since he knew they wouldn't pay very much. So he bought a caïque, a large one for those days, and loaded it up with charcoal. He decided to head for Límnos, where the market was good, taking his son along as crew. But his maiden voyage was doomed. Near Pipéri he ran out of fuel. He'd set off in a hurry and brought no extra petrol with him. The caïque was defenceless against the anger of the sea. At Sikiá on Pipéri, the boat was driven towards the rocks. The two men used poles to avoid the fateful collision, but their efforts were in vain, and the boat was smashed on the rocks.

The men went up to the monastery to seek shelter. The buildings were deserted. No one was there. They broke down a door and inside they found some lentils. With these and some cabbages they managed to survive. After seventeen days they were in a weakened state and in danger of starving to death, and the weather was still bad. But then a caïque equipped with dynamite paid a visit to Pipéri for some illegal fishing under cover of the bad weather. Malamaténios' son, Mítsos (my informant), who was only eight at the time, waved his arms, not having the strength to shout. The unknown caïque came in close and the boy told his story. The captain sent two sailors to bring the father, who was on the point of death, down to the shore. Having fed them, they took them to the monastery on Kirá Panayá.

15.4.3 Wreckage from Zisemís' Caïque

(Information provided by V. Paliaroútis)

In the 1950s Zisemís, who had a rather large caïque for those days, used to fish for eels in the shallows around Pipéri, and sell them in Skópelos. Pipéri has a bad reputation and there are many shrines on the shore set up by sailors and fishermen who had close shaves with death. Three shrines in a hundred-metre stretch of shore indicate the dread with which fishermen regard this treacherous and harbourless island. On one occasion, when everyone knew that Zisemís and his two sons were fishing as usual at Pipéri, the weather changed suddenly and a storm blew up. The other fishermen were all very worried for the unlucky Zisemís. He never returned and no one ever knew what happened. Certain objects from his boat were the only, and silent, witnesses to the tragedy. It was many years later that a drifter pulled up the tiller of his boat (the 'crow' as it's called in Greek). It had an unusual shape and was recognised by the local people.

15.5 A Neolithic Site and Wrecks around Kirá Panayá

15.5.1 The Neolithic Settlement at Áyos Pétros

Over the centuries a substantial area of land around the small island of Áyos Pétros, in the bay of the same name, has sunk into the sea. In the Neolithic Period, Áyos Pétros was not a separate island, but was joined to Kirá Panayá. The Neolithic settlement extended on to the isthmus which is now covered by the sea. The sandy seabed is full of sherds of pottery which date from the Neolithic occupation of the site. There has been no official systematic investigation, only the dives undertaken at their own expense by N. Efstratíou and his foreign colleagues, in order to make a preliminary survey. Despite the limited methods at their disposal some significant results emerged from their work. It is clear that we have here an important submerged settlement which certainly deserves systematic, time-consuming and exhaustive investigation by appropriately qualified scientists. Excavation would surely result in significant discoveries and important finds. We fervently hope that this will be undertaken very soon.

15.5.2 The Classical Wreck near Fangroú

Fangroú is an island that guards the approach to the large natural harbour of Áyos Pétros. The classical wreck at Fangroú and another (Byzantine) wreck nearby within the bay were both discovered in the same way in the early 1900s. Áyos Pétros is sheltered from the weather and the sea around is rich in the yellowish seaweed which often conceals sponges. In October when the sea is clear all the sponge fishers make for this area. At the appropriate depth the diver pushes aside the strands of seaweed to reveal a pale yellow object, which he removes with a special knife.

In 1989 I was in Athens as a sailor, doing my military service. One day when I was at IENAE,[9] the Institute for Marine Research, someone told me that there were still a large number of plates on the Byzantine ship and that it ought to be re-examined. Being an enthusiast for all things ancient, I decided to have a look myself. The next time I went home on leave I asked my father to take me to Kirá Panayá. On our last day there, combining fishing and research, we went to Áyos Pétros.

'You'll be disappointed with the Byzantine wreck,' my father told me. 'You'll see nothing but broken pottery lying in the sand. The plates you heard about are under the sea-bed. But there's another small wreck at Fangroú, you know.' Gripped by curiosity I went to see it.

At first it didn't make much impression on me, because the standard of comparison I had in my mind was the massive wreck at Peristéra (see section 15.7.1 below). Observing it more carefully, however, I gradually realised that it had its own appeal even though it was smaller. I eventually learned that this was the oldest ship that I have had the good fortune to visit. Later, making an examination of the area from the surface I noticed near the wreck in the shallows of Fangroú some 10–15 Byzantine amphorae concentrated in one spot. There was no trace of another wreck. Perhaps these were defective or superfluous amphorae which had been jettisoned by Byzantine sailors so as to make space.

The following details about the wreck at Fangroú are derived from the papers presented by Dh. Chaniótis and Dh. Caziánis to the archaeological conference that took place on Alónnisos in October 1996. Their first visit to the site was made in May 1994, in the company of my father, Dhimítrios Mavríkis. Their party, from the *Eforía* of Marine Antiquities, were enthusiastic about the new discovery. Dh. Chaniótis, who was in charge, with his years of experience realised the importance of this ship. It is the oldest wreck of classical date that has been discovered and excavated.

The first photographs and videos of this new treasure, hidden in the depths of the sea at Kirá Panayá, caused great excitement in the scientific world. Dh. Kaziánis promptly gave highest priority to the investigation of the wreck that began in September of the same year, 1994. The initial survey lasted two weeks and was based on my father's 12-metre caïque, the *Íkaros*. First they photographed and recorded the wreck exactly as it had been found. By photogrammetry, carried out by V. Koniórdhos, the length of the ship was found to be 80.2 m. It is lying on rocks at a depth of 28 metres at one end, going down to a sandy sea-bed 36 metres deep at the other. Most of the amphorae are concentrated in the intact section of the ship, which is 15 metres long and 11 metres wide, at a depth of 35 metres. Dh. Kaziánis and Dh. Chaniótis included the excavation of this wreck in the *Eforía's* summer research programme in 1995. The results of the excavation certainly justified their decision.

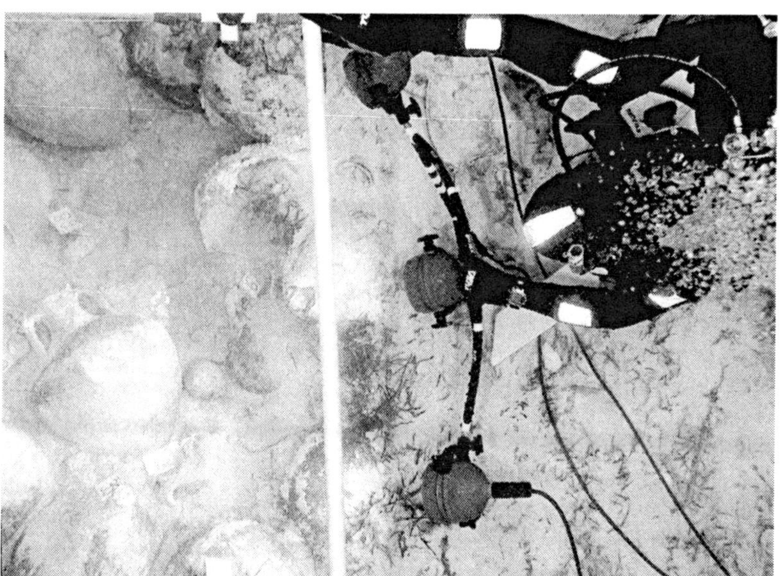

Figure 15.16 The archaeologist D. Chaniótis at work on the classical wreck near Fangroú, Kirá Panayá.

Work began in June 1995, after preparations by the *Eforía's* technical group, well known for its methodical approach and the excellent results it produces. The investigation was conducted from the *Panayía Kamaríou*, a trawler belonging to K. Chatziandoníou. It was this trawler whose nets had hauled up from the waters of the Dodecanese the famous bronze female statue of the Hellenistic period, which is now in the Archaeological Museum in Athens. The expedition was based at Stení Vála, though they also set up a camp on Fangroú itself.

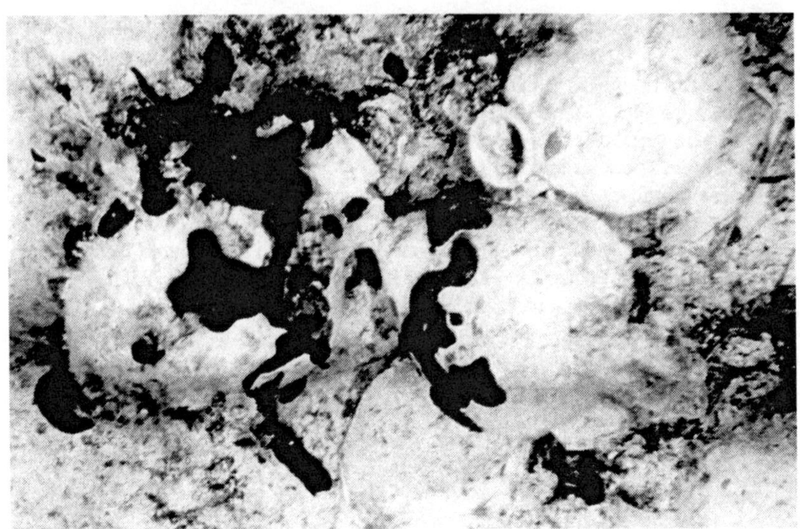

Figure 15.17 The classical wreck near Fangroú blending with nature.

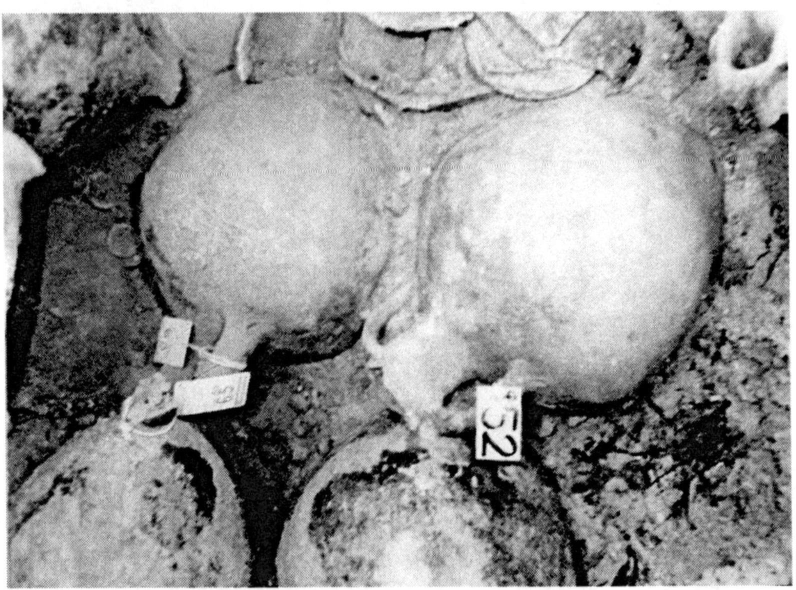

Figure 15.18 The classical wreck near Fangroú:
a clear view of the shape of the Mendian amphorae.

Figure 15.19 The classical wreck near Fangroú, showing clearly the way in which the amphorae were arranged in transit.

Investigations lasted about a month and were successfully completed without any unpleasant surprises. I mention this because the island of Fangroú is in a remote part of the northern Aegean. The nearest inhabited spot is 14 nautical miles from the wreck. The unstable climatic conditions at the depth of the wreck (28–36 m) made investigation difficult.

The excavation, which was carried out with the participation, and under the direction, of Dh. Chaniótis with the co-operation of Dh. Kaziánis, brought important finds to light. They began by laying out an aluminium grid divided into two metre squares over the entire surface of the wreck. They printed a layout plan and began the excavation of the first two squares.

First they removed the seaweed and sand from the surface, to reveal fairly regular rows of amphorae which they drew up to the surface. Underneath the layer of amphorae they found various other artefacts: a metal bowl, a mould for casting a double axe head with the letters 'NIK', various vessels of daily use, including an *oenochoe* (a jug used for ladling wine from the mixing bowl into the cups), a small *scyphos* (a two-handled cup), and a number of other items, all of which helped to date the wreck.

The most outstanding find was the ship's unusual anchor. Nothing like it has been found in other underwater excavations. It is in two parts, weighing 33.95 kg and 37.65 kg. Of almost equal significance was the finding of a piece of the ship's timbers, 70 x 17 cm, indicating that in the lower levels of the excavation the framework of the ship may still be preserved. Its eventual exposure will be a major event in the study of classical shipbuilding.

Excavations were resumed in 1996. The finds are being studied and we anxiously await the results. It has already been established that the ship sank at the time when the Athenian general, Cimon, was campaigning against the Persians who had seized Thrace. The Athenians' objective was to reopen the arterial route that linked them with the rich Black Sea region.

At the same time Cimon wiped out the pirates who had been long established in their hideouts in the Northern Sporades, and thus made the sea routes to the north of the archipelago viable once more. The ship at Fangroú would have been one of the first to resume the lucrative trade in wine.

The unfortunate captain, intent on supplying the Athenians with the 'Mendian wine' (the wine of MENDE in Chalkidhikí) of which they had for some time been deprived, fell victim to his own greed. His ship sank in a treacherous spot, for reasons which, let us hope, the patient excavations of the marine *Eforía* will uncover.

15.5.3 The Byzantine Wreck at Áyos Pétros

This wreck, which lies close to the shore within the bay of Áyos Pétros, has been an easy target for greedy and shameless dealers in illegal antiquities. It was the misfortune of the 'wreck with the plates', as it is known among Alonnisiots, to have been well known since the early 1900s.

Figure 15.20 Alonnisiot vessel in Vólos.

It was discovered because Kirá Panayá is an excellent sponge-fishing ground sheltered from the worst of the weather, and sponge fishermen, chiefly from Tríkeri and Kálimnos, were the first to learn the secrets of the deeps here. But they didn't keep them secret. In September and October, when the sea is clearest, the fishermen dive for sponges. In the course of their work they discovered the wreck and naively revealed its position to the rabid antiquities dealers. I deliberately refrain from naming the fishermen, because I believe they were not aware of the significance of what they did.

Our story begins in the 1950s with the influx of tourists into the Vólos bay area. At that time many tourists came to Greece to marvel at its ancient treasures, but many of them were not innocent visitors to archaeological sites. Influenced by the charlatans and thieves who came before them (the Marquis de Nointel, Sir Richard Worsley, Lord Elgin, Clarke, Stackelberg)[10] they wanted to acquire our treasures for themselves. The combination of their affluent ways, the naivety, the gullibility of naive local people, and the chaos that reigned in Greece in the aftermath of the Civil War (1946–49) resulted in the plundering of our islands.

It was in the 1950s that 'Max' first appeared in Vólos. Max is a modern vandal, an Austrian, well financed, who started his career in the bay of Vólos. Transporting his rudimentary diving gear (cylinders, a compressor) by car, he set about his illegal work. The Pagasitic Gulf (the bay of Vólos) was, as the old sponge fishers were happy to relate, full of amphorae, wrecks and anchors; and the art thieves had little trouble emptying it, though they might meet with problems at the border. Max and his gang, who were then going for small objects of high value, exploited the gullibility of the sponge divers.

These men, welcoming and pleasure loving, were seduced by unusual gifts (usually diving equipment), food and drink and parties with beautiful Austrian women, and gave away all the secrets of the deeps.

Figure 15.21 A bowl from the Byzantine wreck at Áyos Pétros. Thousands like this were exported for sale in all the great markets.

In any case, to the sponge divers the things that came out of the wrecks were nothing but 'old jars'. Most of them had no idea of the value of our archaeological treasures. Unwittingly they gave Max extremely valuable information, and he began to mark on his charts all the wrecks he heard about. He started visiting the wrecks and looting all sorts of objects.

He came to Kirá Panayá and stole Byzantine plates and Byzantine and classical amphorae. But Max was mainly interested in the Byzantine wreck with its plates, marvellous works of art, many of them unaffected by time and well preserved, which would fetch a good price with little risk. There was no harbour master at Alónnisos and the locals were co-operative. After about a year, Max gathered up his finds and transferred them to Vólos. From there he went on to Austria without encountering any problems.

At that time, a day's pay for an ordinary person in Greece was 20–30 drachmas, while a single plate from the wreck could fetch 60,000–70,000 drachmas in a private sale, and its value on the open market was over 100,000. Thus, from the sale of a couple of items Max could pay for his trip to Greece, and from the rest he amassed a considerable fortune. It was not long before this formidable art thief returned to Alónnisos with new plans. This time he chartered some local fishing boats. The owners of the boats, who also captained them for him, were willing to help the 'mad Austrian who throws his money around just to drag up some old junk'.

The Austrian made Stení Vála his base. He stayed there every summer for one month (usually August) for several years. Every morning he would set off from Stení Vála for the site of the wreck at Áyos Pétros, where he had even had the effrontery to fix a permanent buoy. The whole group would dive from the ship. They put the plates in baskets or nets to haul them to the surface, using larger ones whose shape was distorted as containers for other, smaller ones so that they would not break.

At the end of each day they would toss the broken plates, and any others they thought would have little commercial value, into the sea like so much rubbish. One summer my grandfather, Thodhorís, was in charge of their transport. He told me he used to throw the unwanted plates into the sea by the dozen. He took some of them home, though, and used them for feeding the hens. Completely oblivious of what he was doing, he also supplied his neighbours with these beautiful troughs for their hencoops. Every so often, when they'd collected several hundred good plates, the Austrians were brazen enough to bring them to Patitíri (where they had left their cars) in broad daylight.

In other years, of course, they engaged boat owners from Patitíri. For many years Max and his gang continued their systematic looting of the wreck, until Max was killed in a road accident in the 1960s. Some members of his gang came back to the island after his death but their activities were not so systematic. By then the wreck had become known to other, chiefly German, art thieves. The German group had been based on the island of Tríkeri in the bay of Vólos. When they had stolen everything that was to be had in the bay of Vólos, they turned their attention to our area. Using the same tricks as the Austrian gang, they learned about all the wrecks from the sponge fishermen, and were told of the particular interest that their predecessors had taken in the wreck with the plates at Kirá Panayá.

The Germans, based at Vótsi worked very intensively, and were better organised, with their own boat and crew. They even set up a line of metal posts in the seabed leading from the island of Áyos Pétros down to the wreck.

In the course of two decades they removed so many items that the mound formed by the cargo of plates disappeared completely. In the early years they found enough loot in the exposed layers, but later they used an airlift. An airlift is a simple but effective device. Two flexible tubes of different diameters are lowered to the seabed. The narrow tube is connected to a compressor on the ship, and air under high pressure is forced down it.

The jet of air is directed at the seabed immediately under the open end of the wider tube. Sand and small particles stirred up by the jet are carried up the wider tube by stream created by the ascending air bubbles. On the ship this tube discharges its contents into a sieve. Until recently parts of the airlift used by this gang could still be seen at Kalamákia, the place where the Germans had stayed to be nearer the wreck. In the final years the excavation with the airlift was highly profitable, since it enabled them to bring up plates, which are much sought after on the foreign markets, in perfect condition.

Figure 15.22 Shallow bowl from the Byzantine wreck at Áyos Pétros, Kirá Panayá (Papanikóla-Bakírtzi, 1999).

When the wreck became well known in Austria, another group of seven Austrians came to our island and employed a local boat owner. In the first year they didn't find many plates, because they were rather ill prepared for the work. They were more organised when they came back the next year, with a car and better equipment. This time they got up lots of plates which, without the slightest compunction they washed and spread out to dry on the shore of the bay or on the islet of Áyos Pétros. At the end of their stay they took away a total of twenty crates each measuring about 40 x 40 x 50 cm. They gave some good plates to the fishermen whose boat they'd chartered, which were used as serving dishes or flower pots. The activity of the art thieves diminished as rivalry broke out between the gangs. The plates that Max had accumulated were stolen by the other gang. Bitter and angry, Max went back to Austria, where he brought a case against one of his rivals with the object of preventing the new plates flooding the market and drastically reducing the value of his own stocks. Soon after, the police arrived unannounced at Stení Vála and arrested my grandfather when they found plates from the wreck in his hencoop. Naturally he was found innocent, on account of his ignorance. In fact the whole island knew about the activities of the shameless gang, but no one was prepared to talk. It was the fighting between the gangs that finally made the Greek government wake up and take an interest. Like Max, the German doctor was also killed in a crash, in a helicopter in his case. The two gangs had lost their leaders and the situation got very nasty, and police were installed on the island.

Every important art collection in the world has a plate from this wreck. They were sold in the famous auction houses of London, Tokyo, New York, Paris, Monaco and Australia. Here a rare example of sensitivity must be recorded. The Museum of Perth, Western Australia, had purchased 29 of the plates. When they identified their origin they voluntarily undertook to return them to Greece. In the end the Greek government was forced to take some action, and in the summer of 1970 the General Directorate of Antiquities and Restoration took on the responsibility.[11] This was the first instance of any significant investigation of the wreck. The primary objective was to raise the wreck and save it from the art thieves. The whole endeavour was funded by the Psíchas Institute. Peter Throckmorton was appointed technical director of the team, and his wife also made an important contribution.[12] The research expedition arrived at Kirá Panayá in Peter's boat *Stormie Seas*, which also carried all the necessary equipment. The Archaeological service was represented at first by Mrs A. Romiopoúlou and later by Ch. Kritzás. There were also Greek and foreign volunteers, including N. Tsoúchlos. This mixed group worked very well together and overcame all the problems. The first research was undertaken in June 1970, and the main operation lasted from 14 August to 29 September of the same year.

The preliminary research included photographing and drawing plans of the wreck, which lay in 34 m of water and was 20 m long and 10 m wide. The second stage involved raising the entire cargo, not only the plates and amphorae, to the surface. A total of 1490 objects were found, including a bronze handle, lamps and some glass bottles. Once removed from the wreck, however, they were put into store without any prior conservation work, and they are now in a poor condition. The plates are engraved and have some enamelling, They are of different sizes with a great variety of decoration. Some show scenes from the animal kingdom, and there are many different patterns. They were produced in a workshop near Constantinople around the 12th century.[13] From various technical differences it has been established that they are the work of three or four master craftsmen, one of whom had an exceptionally steady hand. We do not know whether the amphorae were filled with anything or were just for sale as such. Many questions remain which can only be answered by further research. The wreck was the original reason for the founding of the Institute of Marine Archaeological Research, which many years later applied for permission to proceed with a second excavation. Unfortunately this has not been forthcoming.

15.5.4 The *Fanoúrios* at Áyos Pétros

During the 1950s Matzitákias' cargo boat, the *Fanoúrios*, transported charcoal and firewood from Planítis, Kirá Panayá's northern harbour. On one occasion, coming to take on a new load, it dropped anchor offshore at Kókkina, on the northwest side of the bay of Áyos Pétros, and the captain and crew went ashore to visit their fellow islanders, the herdsmen on the plateau. While they were eating there, they noticed that the dog was getting restless and they guessed that something must have happened. They went back and were amazed and horrified to see that despite its two anchors the wind had caught the boat and driven it against the promontory by the old monastery, where it had broken up. In the bay there, there are two opposing currents which can affect the wind, giving it a catastrophic power. The ship could not endure Aeolus' rage[14] and sank immediately.

15.5.5 A Sailing Ship at Áyos Pétros

(Information provided by Y. Alexíou)

A trading *karavóskaro* (a sailing ship with a rounded stern) was approaching Áyos Pétros from the west. It was sailing close to the shore in order to shelter from the northwesterly and reach the harbour, but it ran aground on the north shore of the tiny island of Fangroú in the entrance to the bay, and began to ship water. It sank somewhere in the bay of Áyos Pétros. The crew were saved.

15.5.6 A Post-Byzantine Wreck at Psári

Near the promontory at Psári on the east coast of Kirá Panayá there is the wreck of a boat from the early Ottoman period, which had been transporting some very fine bowls, with beautiful enamelling. Almost all the houses of the local fishermen are decorated with them. They call them 'dishes from the *tsanakádhiko*' ('bowl shop'), because their shape is very similar to a common type of earthenware bowl called a *tsanáka*.

Despite the great depth of the wreck (65–68 m) two people have dived down to it. From their evidence we learn that the wreck consists of a large mass of heaped up bowls and small amphorae. The wreck appears to have rolled down the rocky slope and come to rest on the sandy seabed. The rock around the sand is full of fissures, where many of the plates were trapped. Some are sticking our at odd angles are and get caught in nets.

The ship probably ran into the steep shore of the island or, perhaps more likely ran into the islet of Mélissa ('Bee') which faces Psári. In that case, the sailors would have tried to run the sinking ship onto the shore for their own safety, like those involved in the recent accident at the exact same spot (see section 15.5.7 below). The wreck is of considerable size but half buried in the sand. Up till now the depth at which it lies has prevented systematic investigation, but perhaps, with technological progress, future generations will learn its secrets.

15.5.7 A Resistance Caïque near Mélissa

V. Kónstas tells the tale:

> In the course of the partisan struggle, an ELAN caïque was sailing north.[15] In the dark it was passing to the east of Kirá Panayá. When the sailors saw

the large rock known as Mélissa, they mistook it for a ship. They reckoned that with the speed they were making they would overtake it comfortably. But this ship was a solid little island and naturally it was not moving. To the crew's amazement they crashed into it. Some of the planking was loosened and the caïque began to take in water. In desperation the men turned towards Kirá Panayá to get as close as they could to the island. Near Psári their boat sank, but they swam to the shore. They walked to where our house was and took our little boat. Later we learned that the two sailors were from Tríkeri and that they had left our boat at Agnóndas on Skópelos. We were in no hurry to get it back, and it remained there for many years.

15.5.8 The Wreck of a Steamship near the Monastery

(Information provided by N. Floroús)

In the early years of the 20th century, a steamship called in at the bay by the monastery on the eastern side of Kirá Panayá, and there – for what reason it is not known (a fire perhaps) – it sank. It is said that the ship, which was Turkish and carrying a cargo of eggs, anchored in the bay to shelter from the weather and was capsized by the wind while riding at anchor. Anyone visiting that spot today can see the vast hulk of the steamship on the right side of the bay at a depth of 7 m.

15.5.9 A Byzantine Wreck near Planítis

In the northern part of Kirá Panayá there is a Byzantine wreck of the 11th century. It lies near the headland of Kátergo on the east side of the narrow entrance to the large natural harbour of Planítis. It probably sank here after striking a rock, while attempting to enter the harbour in bad weather or at night. This is suggested by the fact that only a part and of the cargo remains on the ship which lies in of 25–27 m of water.

The rest is scattered on the sea bed between the wreck and the shore (fishermen have often pulled up amphorae and other artefacts in their nets), and near one small heap of Byzantine amphorae there are three Y-shaped anchors, typical of the Byzantine period. It would appear that the crew of the Byzantine ship did not have time to use them before the ship was damaged. They may have jettisoned them with some of the cargo to try and prevent it sinking.

15.5.10 A Modern Shipwreck at Planítis

(Information provided by V. Kónstas)

This incident occurred after the war. A boat carrying wine and brandy was on its way from Mílos in the Cyclades. Its cargo was in 100- and 200-litre barrels. It must have been trying to enter the harbour at Planítis, but failed to make the narrow entrance (always difficult in bad weather) and crashed into the rocks.

The ship was propelled only by sail and couldn't manoeuvre easily, and the inexperienced captain came to grief. The shepherds, who came down from the hills above, found neither survivors nor bodies. The shore, though, was littered with broken barrels. Unluckily for them, though, they didn't find a single one intact.

15.6 A Sunken City and Wrecks around Alónnisos

15.6.1 The Sunken City at Kokkinókastro

Three factors played a part in the disappearance of the greatest city of ancient ICOS: its partial submergence in the sea, the instability of the soil, and its abandonment by its inhabitants for fear of pirates. The first two are still evident to the visitor today. The large well-built wall that encircled the city ran down on both sides towards the sea and disappeared when the city sank. After every storm ancient artefacts are washed up on coast to the south of the city, and chiefly on the beach of Kokkinókastro, where large quantities are now buried in the sand. The area needs specialised and intensive investigation to unearth the secrets of a city well known in the ancient world as a trading port. In 1991 the marine archaeologists Elpídha Chatzidháki and Ilías Spondhílis came to make a surface examination. They did indeed discover traces of the sunken city, but these were not extensively visible because they had been covered by landslides caused by the erosion of the coastline during storms. However, the archaeological deposits remaining on the land are no less rich than those under the sea. Quite impressive results have already emerged from this surface examination and a limited amount of excavation.

15.6.2 A Cargo of Ore at Áyos Dhimítrios

From ancient times till today ores have been one of the basic commodities transported by sea. At Achladhiá, at the northern end of the splendid beach of Áyos Dhimítrios on the east coast of Alónnisos, in only 5 m of water, there is a wreck from fairly recent times (the beginning of the 20th century) of a boat carrying unprocessed ore.

The older people remember pieces of wood, clearly from a boat, and quite a large one at that, being caught in trawl nets. No doubt the boat was travelling from the mines of Chalkidhikí to the industrialised regions further south, and it probably sank after running aground. The sailors may have been unaware of the strange tongue of land jutting out into the bay, and, sailing at night or in bad weather, had run into it. Fire on board is another possible cause of its sinking. One can see the wreck with nothing but a face mask and it is perhaps the most convenient wreck to visit for someone who doesn't go in for diving.

15.6.3 A Wreck at Kaloyírou to Éma ('Monk's Blood')

(Information provided by A. Athanasíou)

Immediately after the Second World War a large and brand new mechanically powered cargo boat set off from Thessalonica, bound for Piraeus. It was carrying a cargo of wheat, which is produced in large quantities in the plains around Greece's northern capital. At sea west of Alónnisos, the pin that holds the bottom of the rudder broke and the crew were unable to steer the ship. They kept lowering first the port and then the starboard anchor to try and steady the vessel.

In the course of their manoeuvres one of the anchor chains caught on the propeller and got hopelessly entangled. Sails were hoisted in an attempt to avoid collision with the land. But the wind picked up and drove the ship towards the spot known as 'Monk's Blood'. This name refers to a rock with a bright red band running through it.

The traditional explanation is that a monk was murdered here by pirates and his blood ran down the rock. It was near here that the cargo boat, out of control, struck a submerged rock and sank in 60–65 m of water. Three of the crew were drowned, while the more cool-headed got into the life boat and by rowing hard the poor wretches managed to get away from the rocky shore, and reached Megáli Vála (a bay on the west coast of Alónnisos) where the shepherds took care of them.

15.6.4 The *Bonus* at Vrisítsa

(Information provided by K. Efstathíou)

After the war a large cargo boat, the *Bonus*, loaded with local products ran aground at Vrisítsa, a narrow bay due north of Palió Chorió. It was making a round trip from Kími in Évvia to Thessalonica, and was now on its way home, with a crew of three. From Kími it had brought wine, which had been sold in Thessalonica to buy sugar, macaroni and *manéstra* (pasta in the shape of grains of barley, also known as *kritharáki*). On the return trip, with these products packed in bulk in large sacks, they ran into bad weather off the west coast of Alónnisos.

The wind was against them and in the stormy conditions the captain lost his bearings. Intending to pass through the Kókkinos Channel, between Alónnisos and Skópelos, he was deceived by the hills either side of Vrisítsa Bay and sailed into the bay. When he saw that he was trapped with no time to turn the boat round and get back to the open sea, he decided to run the boat on to the sand.

He beached the boat sideways and the sailors set about unloading the cargo and other useful items. Within a day the boat itself was destroyed by the diabolical force of the northwest wind. The foodstuff was stored on Alónnisos and the men returned home to Kími in another boat, taking with them the reusable parts of the wreck.

15.6.5 An Unidentified Wreck at Yérakas

(Information provided by D. Mavríkis)

There is the wreck of a ship in Yérakas bay. Its hulk can be seen at a depth of about 14 m. It was probably wrecked by violent waves, having sailed into the narrow entrance to the bay under the impression that this was the channel between Alónnisos and Peristéra.

Being a sailing ship and difficult to manoeuvre, it had not been able to respond in time and sank. None of the old people on the island can remember it sinking. Most likely it was not a local boat and sank suddenly before any of the islanders were even aware of it. It is easily accessible to the skin-diver.

15.6.6 A Wreck with Apples at Vótsi

In the 1940s a caïque going under sail from Pílio to Límnos passed by the bay of Vótsi on Alónnisos. Pílio was an apple-producing region and Límnos one of its markets. The weather was fine and the caïque anchored in the bay at Vótsi so that the captain and crew could have a rest. But in the bay, near the caves, there is a reef. The hull of the boat from Pílio was torn open by the top of the reef. It rolled and was balanced on its timbers, but they didn't hold.

Water poured into the boat and it began to sink. The sailors were taken by surprise, and before they knew what was happening, they found themselves swimming for the shore. The surface of the sea was covered with *firíkia* (the particular kind of apples the boat was carrying), and the schoolchildren came down to the shore to gather them up. The sailors were given hospitality on the island until they found a boat going back to Pílio.

15.6.7 Apples from Parkéta

(Information provided by Y. Karakatsánis)

A similar disaster had occurred before the war, when another boat on its way to Límnos ran into the reef known as Parkéta, which lies between Peristéra and Dhío Adhérfia, and covered the sea with apples. The current carried the apples to the shores of Alónnisos. The inhabitants of the island came and began, with great delight, to pick up the fruit from the shore. Unfortunately, though, by then the apples had absorbed seawater and were inedible.

15.7 Wrecks around Peristéra

15.7.1 The Classical Wreck at Pethaménos

The great and miraculous marine jewel of our region has been known since the beginning of the 20th century, when sponge fishermen in diving suits linked to a hand-operated compressor discovered 'the jars'. Naturally they did not immediately realise the significance of the discovery, for 'the jars' did not seem to them particularly unusual.

Of course they were surprised by the sheer quantity of jars, but the sponges around them were far more valuable to the divers, and they didn't bother to report the find. Before the war some of them brought up a few jars and sold them at two drachmas apiece; and after the war the war the rumour got around that there was a sunken ship full of jars in the bay of Kokkaliás on Peristéra.

Certain retired sponge divers knew its silent secret, but because of all the furore about the rush of illicit antiquities dealers to Kirá Panayá they had kept their mouths shut. The rumour about the size of the wreck persisted even after the old sponge divers had all died. In the 1960s foreign dealers visited Alónnisos and set up camp at Kávos ('Cape'), the southern headland of Patitíri bay. Making daily excursions from this base they tried to find the spot, where, according to their informants in the Pagasitic Gulf, a great treasure was concealed.

There were five of these art thieves altogether, four men and one woman, all experienced skin-divers. Their leader was an Austrian. For their regular expeditions they used a local man with his own caïque. They had left their van in Vólos, and they eventually went back there in a larger Alonnisiot boat, wanting to avoid travelling on the *Kíknos* ('Swan'), the regular ferry boat of those days, in case they aroused the suspicion of the authorities.

They took away about ten amphorae concealed in large sacks. On the trip back to Vólos they stopped at Cape Leftéris on Skiáthos to photograph a ship, the *Normandy*,[16] which had sunk there during the Second World War. This suggests they were generally well informed. When these people had gone, others came. This time they were Germans, again well informed, and it was obvious there was some connection between them and the other gang. They found the wreck immediately and set about their work undisturbed. According to a local witness, whom they employed to help them, they brought up jars and also some small black-painted objects. This accounts for the hollow that now exists in the heap of jars. The Alonnisiot suspected that their business was illegal, and voiced his suspicions in the village cafe.

When the policeman and the customs officer heard what the foreigners were up to, they set off in a caïque to arrest them. The Germans had been tipped off, and when the authorities approached to search their boat, they got into inflatables to make their escape. The authorities hailed them in Greek, demanding they surrender. The Germans coolly pulled out army pistols and starting firing, but only to scare them off. Then they made off at speed in the direction of Skíros. Our officials didn't have their service revolvers with them and were pretty scared. When they got back to Patitíri they were too badly shaken to take any further action.

In the 1970s scuba diving equipment first appeared in Alónnisos, and my father, who already fished with a harpoon, learnt to dive. The old rumour that there was an enormous wreck at a certain spot drew him into a lengthy search which eventually brought the wreck at Peristéra to light. In 1984 the civil engineer, K. Stávrakas, a friend of my family, came to Alónnisos. When he was told about the wreck nearby, he immediately went with my father to the *Eforía* of Marine Antiquities, and they pointed out on the charts the position of this and other wrecks they knew of. The officials of the *Eforía* received them politely, but the *Eforía* had neither the finance nor the organisation to carry out a proper investigation. The report that the two men made went into the archives, and it was six years before any further action was taken.

Between 1982 and 1990 I myself dived many times to see this enchanting and at the same time tragic memorial. On the first occasion I was only 14. In those days we used to go down with makeshift equipment for underwater fishing. I was always hearing about the strange ship and I was very excited by the idea and impatience to see it. From a depth of about 15 metres I first made out its great bulk, and as I went deeper the image gradually got clearer. When I got near, it took my breath away. It was a frightening sight, a fantastic spectacle. I felt my stomach tighten and my limbs were paralysed. It was the feeling you have when you're in love and your love first meets with a response. Completely absorbed I began to examine the wreck from end to end. I felt that I had before my eyes a silent, living giant. The amphorae gave me the impression that they were a contented group of living beings. Some seemed to be playing, others sleeping, others lined up like soldiers.

I had the sense that in a moment they would begin to speak to me, that they would tell me their story. Instinctively I touched them, expecting a response, expecting them to express their irritation at their strange visitor. I felt like an intruder, like some strange alien, next to these sleeping witnesses to a tragedy two-and-a-half-millennia old. But the oxygen was beginning to run out and I was brought back to reality. I had to go up, the dream was over. My imagination ceased its wild activity, and I rose to the surface. Yet it was as though a silent siren was reluctant to release me. We got back to land, but for the rest of the day I was overwhelmed by a kind of excitement I'd never experienced before.

Our visits to this beautiful part of the sea-bed continued and the fascination it held for me remained undiminished. The wreck was my secret retreat. Whenever I came home on leave during my military service in the navy, I was impatient to see my undersea lover again. It was not until 1991 that the Greek government took any real interest in the wreck. Four years earlier the German conservationist, Peter Winterstein, a regular visitor to our island and a founder member of DEGUWA[17] (a German non-profit-making organisation for the promotion and study of underwater archaeology throughout the world), started asking local fishermen for information about the wrecks in the area. Not surprisingly they were rather guarded, and entertained doubts about the intentions of this foreigner, who in fact was interested in the wreck from a purely scientific perspective.

Figure 15.23 The author making the first dive to the classical wreck at Pethaménos, 1984.

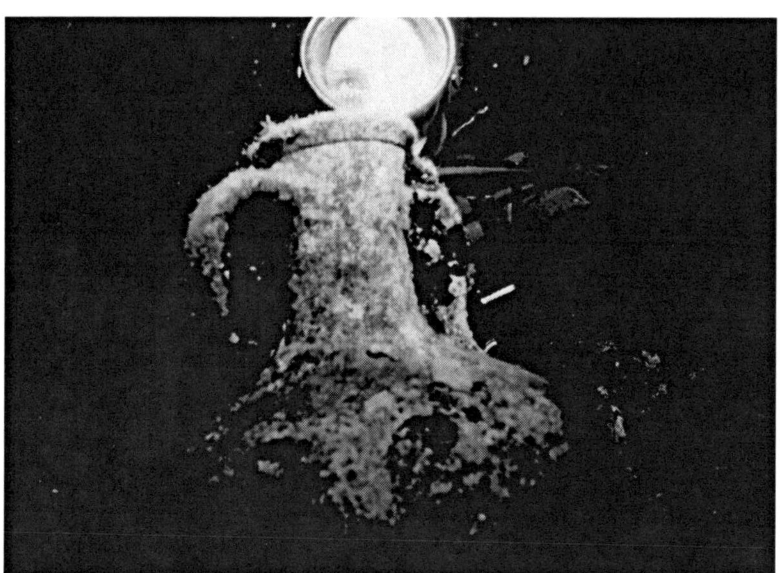

Figure 15.24 The author diving at the classical wreck at Pethaménos, 1987.

Figure 15.25 The author diving at the classical wreck at Pethaménos, 1986.

Figure 15.26 The classical wreck at Pethaménos (a).

Figure 15.27 The classical wreck at Pethaménos (b).

Figure 15.28 Partial view of the classical wreck at Pethaménos.

Figure 15.29 The classical wreck at Pethaménos. The end of the ship.

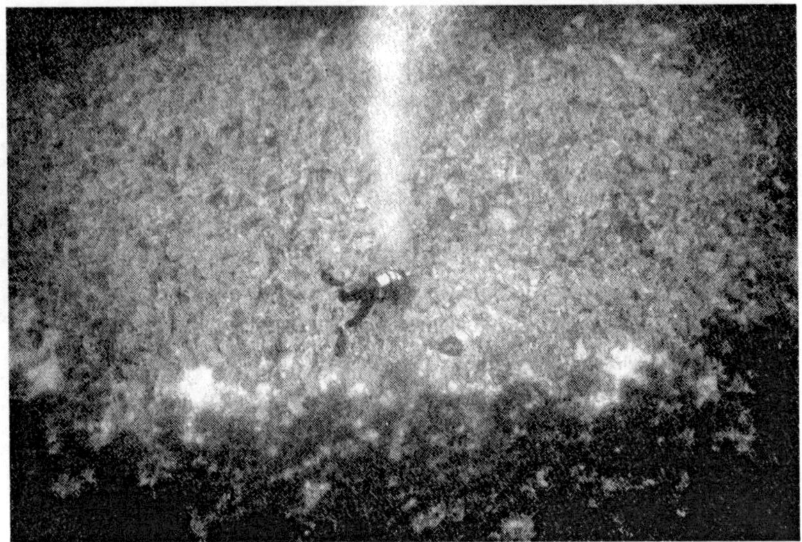

Figure 15.30 The classical wreck at Pethaménos. One of the first dives, with limited equipment.

Figure 15.31 The classical wreck at Pethaménos (c).

Figure 15.32 The classical wreck at Pethaménos. Peter Sala, a devotee of the wreck.

Figure 15.33 The classical wreck at Pethaménos (d).

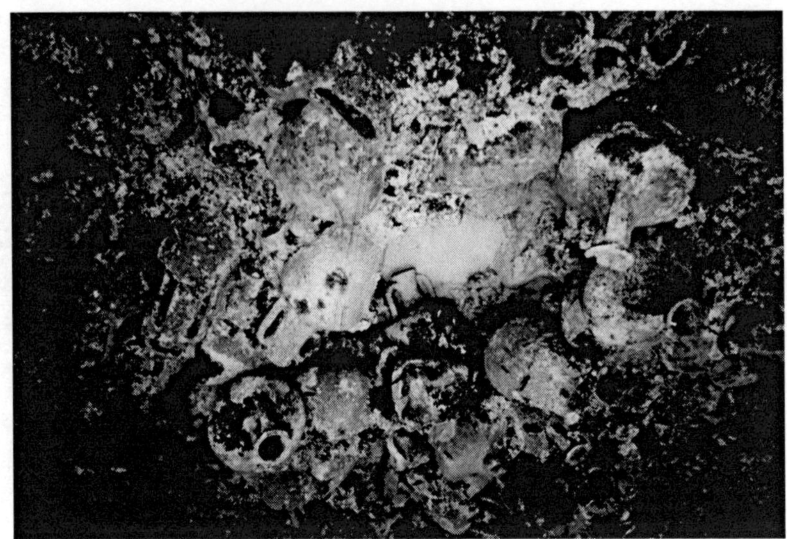

Figure 15.34 At the centre of the classical wreck at Pethaménos.

Figure 15.35 The classical wreck at Pethaménos. Peter Sala, a devotee of the wreck, making rough measurements of the surface of the mass of amphorae for the benefit of the local *Eforía* (archaeological adminstration).

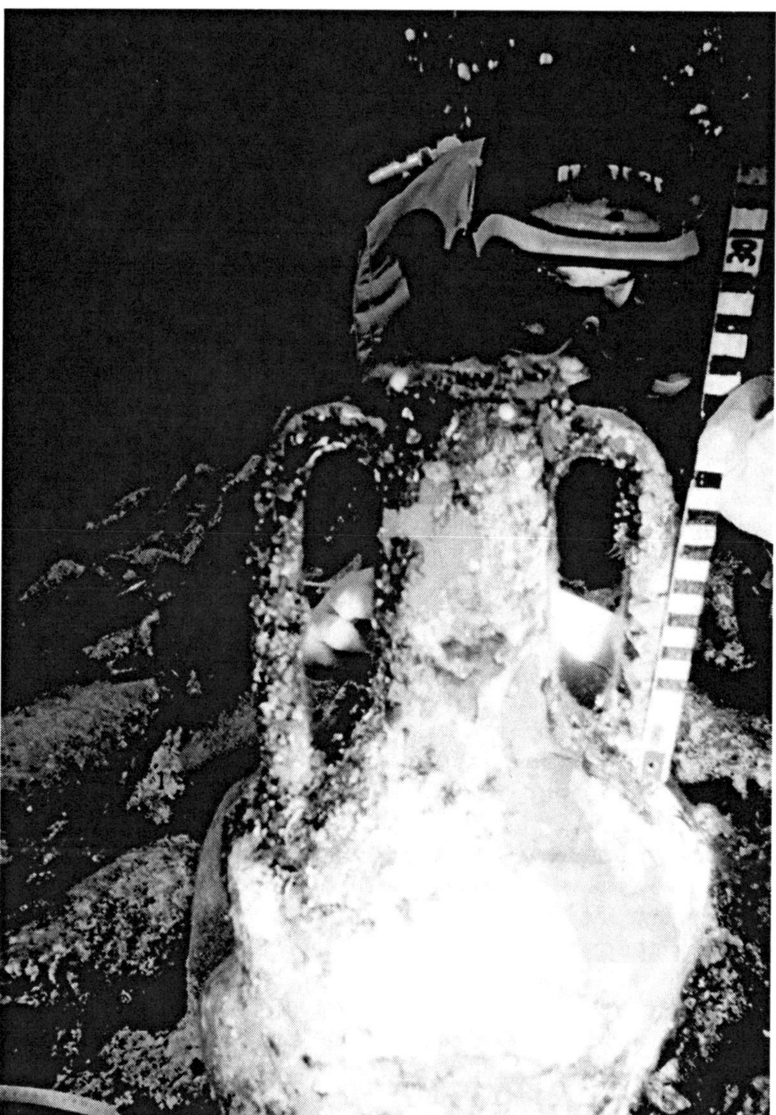

Figure 15.36 The classical wreck at Pethaménos. The author making initial measurements of the amphorae for the benefit of the *Eforía* (a).

Figure 15.37 The classical wreck at Pethaménos. The author making initial measurements of the amphorae for the benefit of the *Eforía* (b).

It was their enthusiastic determination to promote research on the one hand, and the indifference of the Greek government on the other, which led Peter Winterstein and his colleagues into a join venture with us. As a combined group we carried out the first investigation of the wreck at Peristéra, taking photographs, recording it on video, and carrying out a survey of the visible amphorae. We counted them, measured them, noted their orientation and plotted their shapes with a planimeter.

When the survey was completed, along with the video-recording and photography of M. Haust, we agreed to advance on two fronts. We would present the Greek state with the new evidence in the hope that it would provoke some interest, while the Germans would present this magnificent marine treasure store to the international media. The whole process took place in the summer of 1987, and then we split up to await the results.

One of the team, Peter Sala was suffering from an incurable illness. The doctor had given him four or five months to live. Often when people find themselves at the gates of death they are anxious about those they are going to leave, or about something they have not managed to complete. Peter Sala was no exception. His greatest desire was to be involved in the survey and excavation of the wreck. His friends vowed to help him realise his dream. Though facing death, he was calm and despite his physical weakness he made a firm and moving decision to come to our island and dive again. His will proved stronger than the insidious illness and this determined man managed to get to Stení Vála, in the company of a nurse, in the spring of 1988.

Sala begged us to take him for one last dive. He was a living skeleton, weighing no more than 45 kilos, but his eyes were so alive and sparkling that we were deeply moved. We couldn't possibly refuse. So, at midday on 19 May, we began the descent. He was so weak that he couldn't dive alone. Holding on to him, we led him down to the great spread of amphorae. There, under the sea, Peter Sala began to weep, as he marvelled at the glorious insentient spectacle, which in his eyes was a living friend. Weeping the whole time, 28 metres down, he continued to stare at this unique vision. Silently I signalled to him that we should go up, because they would be getting anxious on the surface. With a nod Peter acquiesced and we began our ascent. With great effort we got him back on board the boat and headed back to our base, happy that we had been able to fulfil the wish of a dying man. He himself was especially happy, and tearful at the same time. After that he returned to his homeland where he died some months later, on 9 September 1988.

But not even death could separate him from his undersea love. He had decided to be cremated and had asked his friends to scatter his ashes on the sea above the wreck. They collected the little sack containing the ashes of this lover of antiquity and brought it to Alónnisos. About fifteen people held an unlikely party, with great quantities of beer, as a libation to the dead. After the party, we put out to sea in a large local caïque, and scattered the ashes with loud applause over the place where the wreck lies.

In October 1991 there was a preliminary underwater investigation directed by Elpídha Chatzidháki.[18] Along with her and the divers and archaeologists, Vasílis Koniórdhos and Ilías Kondhílis, we dived on the wreck. When we came back up to our caïque, I saw the other divers faces shining. Even these experienced people had been amazed by the sight of the ship. They returned to Athens and all winter were absorbed in the study of Peristéra, to which they returned in the spring, better organised.

The advance party put up four prefabricated huts to live and work in, two ancillary buildings (a toilet and a store) and a small cistern from which to fill their bottles. They constructed a jetty and diving platforms on the stony shore, and everything was ready for the arrival of the scientific personnel from the *Eforía*. The *Dhímos* of Alónnisos offered space to help with the research programme, which began in August. I was very pleased to see that the man in charge of diving was Theofánis Matanás, who had been my commanding officer for two years during my national service, and was also a friend.

Since many scientists were now involved in the project, the Greek navy had sent experienced frogmen to see to the safe conduct of the diving. A navy decompression chamber was brought to the site of the wreck, but fortunately this was not needed. In order to facilitate detailed inspection and accurate recording, Theofánis Matanás, with the help of skilled craftsmen, constructed a diving platform out of barrels, which was positioned directly over the wreck, about 100 metres from the shore. The archaeologists stayed at Stení Vála and went across every day in two inflatable boats to dive on the wreck.

Figure 15.38 The harbour at Stení Vála in the 1960s.

The experienced archaeologist, Elpídha Chatzidháki, and her colleagues studied the wreck and measured it with great precision. The area outlined on the sea-bed by the amphorae is 25 m long and 10 m wide. The depth varies from 22 m to 30 m, and there are several hundred amphorae that together define the shape of the ship. The amphorae are in three layers. At the bottom of the ship's hold the first layer were set up on wooden stands or in sand. On top of these they stacked the remaining amphorae fitting their pointed bases into the gaps between those below. The amphorae had contained wine from MENDE (on the western 'finger' of Chalkidhikí) and PEPARETHOS (i.e. Skópelos). These two city states were among the most important wine-producing areas in the ancient world. Their delicious wines were exported to the whole of the then known world, from Egypt to the Black Sea. The amphorae at Peristéra date from around 400 BC.

Figure 15.39 The shape of the amphora can be clearly made out. This type was used for the transport of wine.

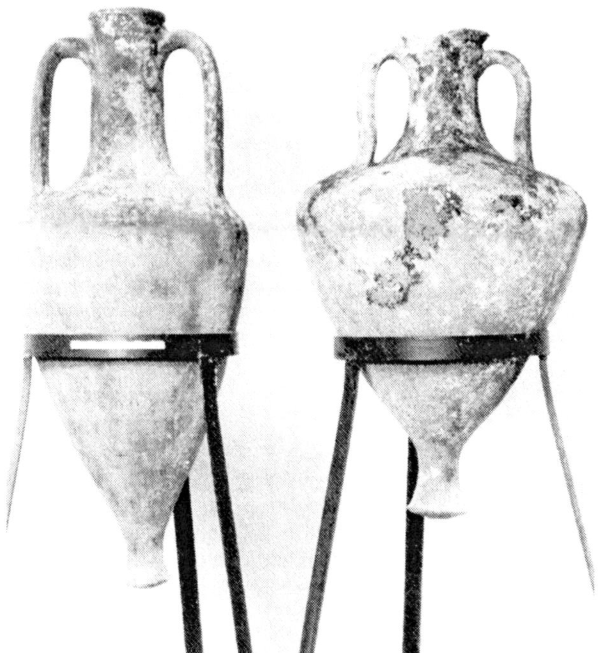

Figure 15.40 Amphorae from the classical wreck at Pethaménos.

The wreck was photographed in its original state and the preliminary survey completed. Next it was necessary to draw and record the wreck as it was, before starting the intrusive work of archaeological excavation. This was a difficult undertaking that required specialist knowledge. The first step was to lay down a rope grid dividing the whole site into 72 squares measuring 2 x 2 m. This was done by highly skilled topographers with the assistance of young men, who participated with delight and enthusiasm in this important work.

All the amphorae visible on the surface of the wreck were then counted, as well as all those lying around it to a considerable distance. In the central area a total of 976 amphorae, of two different types, were recorded, with 33 others scattered around. Each one was given a numerical identity. The archaeologists attached to each one a numbered plastic tag. Other important surface finds included a portion of a lead anchor, at some distance from the ship, and some items of black-painted pottery. These finds particularly delighted the people at the base camp and encouraged them to persevere with the difficult investigation.

Figure 15.41 A black-painted jug from the classical wreck at Pethaménos.

They now proceeded to the stage everyone had been waiting for: the trial section of one of the 2 x 2 m squares. For the excavation of this 1/72 of the wreck an airlift was used (see section 15.5.2 above). The amphorae within the square were detached (some with a saw) and raised to the surface. Within this small area a total of 40 amphorae were found. The airlift was then brought back into action and everyone was amazed by the finds that were then uncovered.

The experience and instinct of Mrs Chatzidháki, who chose the point at which to begin the excavation were justified once more. As the sand was cleared away, almost immediately some black spots appeared, and soon ten black-painted cups were uncovered, of the type the ancients drank wine from.[19] Among them were also found bowls, plates, a wine pourer and cooking pot, all in perfect condition having been buried in sand. But how is it that they had not been broken by the weight of the amphorae above them? This puzzle was eventually solved by Mrs Chatzidháki herself, as she explained at the archaeological conference on Alónnisos. The black-painted vessels were part of the ship's cargo and the sailors had stowed them in well sealed wooden boxes for their protection. When the ship went down, they were underneath the amphorae, but the sand got inside the cases and prevented the cups and other pottery from being crushed.

In the same season they found a bronze ladle which probably belonged to the crew, and the handles of a bronze vessel, the rest of which had unfortunately corroded and disintegrated. The second season, in 1992, involved ten technicians from the Ministry of Culture and 35 divers from the *Eforía* of Marine Antiquities, with different areas of specialisation. Many of them were young scientists and the wreck at Peristéra was their baptism into marine archaeology. Their work lasted two months, after which the finds were transferred to Athens for conservation and safekeeping. Two officials were appointed to guard the wreck over the winter and everything looked promising for the following year. The results of the investigations were made known throughout the world and aroused intense interest for the second year running. The international scientific community was particularly interested in the study of the timbers. Unfortunately, though, they had not quite reached the point of excavating the hull itself at the end of the 1992 season.

Investigations were resumed in 1993. The skilled craftsman came first to rebuild the jetty, which had been destroyed by southerly gales, repair the huts and build a new platform with barrels and large timbers. This time K. Thoktarídhis was responsible for co-ordination and supervision, a man of great experience who had an accident-free record in more than 800 dives.

Although many members of the expedition were beginners, the third excavation was not short of young specialists of various kinds. Another 2 x 2 m square was excavated, and yielded important finds in good condition. In the 1993 season the official Greek divers were joined by an American diver and photographer sent by the *National Geographic Magazine*. In all, there were 49 divers working that season, specialists in every branch of science relevant to marine archaeology. Again the work lasted for two months, and it was financed by LOTTO (the Greek national lottery) and the European Union who provided 60 million and 150 million drachmas respectively.

Suddenly, when everything was going well, the investigation of the wreck itself was cut short in order to study the finds. Certain disciplinary measures were taken against Mrs Chatzidháki because she had allowed the *National Geographic Magazine* to photograph the site without first seeking the permission of the Central Archaeological Committee in Athens.[20] Consequently, the journal with the widest circulation in the world was not able to publish the wreck at Peristéra, and our island and the Greek cultural heritage in general lost a unique opportunity for international publicity. In Turkey, on the other hand, an article was published which insisted that the wrecks in Turkish waters were far more important than the Greek ones.

Although it was not completed, the investigation was of great significance, involving many significant discoveries. Most importantly, the conclusions that emerged changed all previously held views of ancient shipbuilding. Before the excavation of the Peristéra wreck, all the scholars, with rare exceptions (such as Carson), maintained that large cargo vessels in excess of 100 tonnes displacement were not built by the ancient Greeks, but only later by the Romans. The Peristéra ship shows the Greek to have been the pioneers in this. It confirms that in shipbuilding as in so many other areas the Romans were not originators, but adapted Greek things to their measure.

Figure 15.42 The three different types of amphorae from the classical wreck at Pethaménos.

There have been occasional efforts to revive the project; the subject has been discussed in the *Voulí* (the Greek Parliament); scientists throughout the world have voiced their criticisms; but all to no avail. Several years have already past without permission being granted to resume the investigations. The whole population of Alónnisos hopes that the bureaucratic problems can be solved and that this unique underwater treasure can be fully revealed.

Peter Winterstein came back to the island in the summer of 1995, and, when he heard that the excavation had made no progress for two years and saw the results of official indifference, he began to weep like a child. Elpídha Chatzidháki, who also thinks of the wreck as a living organism to which she is deeply attached, is equally concerned. The silent calm of this wreck enthrals us and summons us to learn its secrets, the secrets of our ancestral heritage.

15.7.2 A Classical Wreck at Cape Tsélios

This wreck was located before the war by sponge divers, who discovered its beautiful elongated jars and, regrettably, sold some of them in Skiáthos for trivial sums of money. According to rumours and the recollections of the old people, a lot of finds were carried off and found their way on to the black market. I came across the wreck myself quite by chance in 1985, at a depth of 25 m.

At first I thought it was just a matter of some scattered amphorae. I didn't attach much importance to it and carried on fishing. Later, when I went back to the place with my father and the officials from the *Eforía* of Marine Antiquities, I recognised more clearly the image of a sunken ship. From the position of the remaining amphorae it appeared that the ship, sailing close to the shore, had run into the projecting tip of Cape Tsélios, been holed on the rocks and sunk. Its cargo had then rolled away from shore, down the submerged rock slope, and ended up on the sandy seabed. The amphorae were from Chíos and would certainly have contained wine. The wreck has been roughly dated to the 4th century BC. The submerged part of Cape Tsélios was probably the cause of many accidents. In addition to the sunken ship, three anchors on the seabed bear witness to the treacherous nature of the place.

15.7.3 A Byzantine Wreck at Vasilikós

Near Vasilikós lies the largest Byzantine ship found anywhere in the world. Its depth (50–56 m) and awkward position do not allow thorough investigation. The wreck was discovered more than twenty years ago by my father, after fishermen had told him of the round-bodied amphorae which they found in their nets.

It is a rather strange wreck. There are two large heaps of unbroken amphorae. The number of amphorae must be in excess of 4,000. The heap nearer to the shore measures 16 x 5 m with its long access oriented northeast/southwest. The other, only slightly smaller heap, 15.5 x 5 m, differs slightly in its orientation, which is east-northeast/west-southwest. Because of the great size of the two mounds of amphorae, which lie about 5 m apart, it has been assumed that there are two separate wrecks here. My personal opinion is that the two piles belong to the same ship that split in two as it went down.

The seabed at this point is pure sand and will surely have preserved the hull more or less entire. The amphorae are Byzantine, 12th-century, and of a local type, and almost all are in good condition. In the northern corner of the larger heap there are also some spherical clay vessels, 15 cm in diameter. What they contained is not known.

Once, when I was spear-fishing at a depth of 40–45 m off the cape at one side of the bay of Vasilikós, and before I knew about this particular wreck, I spotted two large Byzantine anchors on the seabed. I didn't pay much attention, because the straits between Alónnisos and Peristéra are littered with such things.

When I learned that there was a wreck nearby I immediately made the connection. I imagined an enormous Byzantine cargo vessel anchored in the bay, sheltering from the weather. The strong winds so common in this region could have exerted sufficient force on the tall and bulky ship to break its anchor chains. The crew would have been unable to hoist sail in time to control this lumbering vessel before it ran aground, its timbers split, water poured in and they had to start jettisoning the cargo. I could see their panic as they started to hurl the amphorae and other heavy objects – a metal water barrel was found – into the sea, in an attempt to lighten the boat and prevent it sinking.

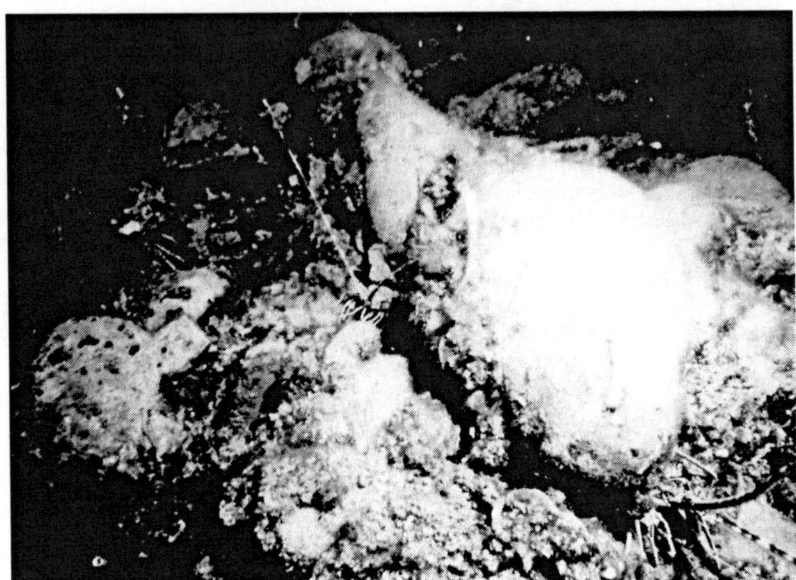

Figure 15.43 Byzantine wreck at Vasilikós, Peristéra. Lobsters are the wreck's only guards.

Such efforts evidently proved futile and the ship sank with all hands, but they explain how a part of the amphorae came to settle at a depth of 25 m, that is, some 25–30 m higher than the wreck itself.

All this is, of course, speculation that I offer only as a suggestion. Fire or a pirate attack could have been the real cause of sinking. However, the size of the ship has created a great impression in international scientific circles, who are anxiously awaiting some investigation. So far, this has not been possible.

Let us hope that with new technology we shall be able to overcome the problems of working at such a depth (50–56 m) and thus uncover the secrets of this wreck. The wreck was reported to the marine *Eforía*, together with the classical wreck at Pethaménos. An official inspection was carried out in 1994 by a party from the *Eforía* led by Dh. Chaniótis.

When I first dived there at Easter 1986, the area between the two deposits of amphorae was full of lobsters. It was delightful to see some 10–15 of these small creatures guarding this memorial to the ancient dead. When you first get close to them, dread can grip you, the fear of a strange encounter in the deeps. Very quickly, though, the playful waving of their horns and the peculiar movements of the surprised lobsters give you the reassuring feeling that you are in a friendly environment.

Up till now the wreck has not been plundered, either by sponge divers or by dealers in antiquities. The depth is its guardian angel. Fishermen from Alónnisos casting lobster nets sometimes have brought up 'jugs', which now decorate their houses.

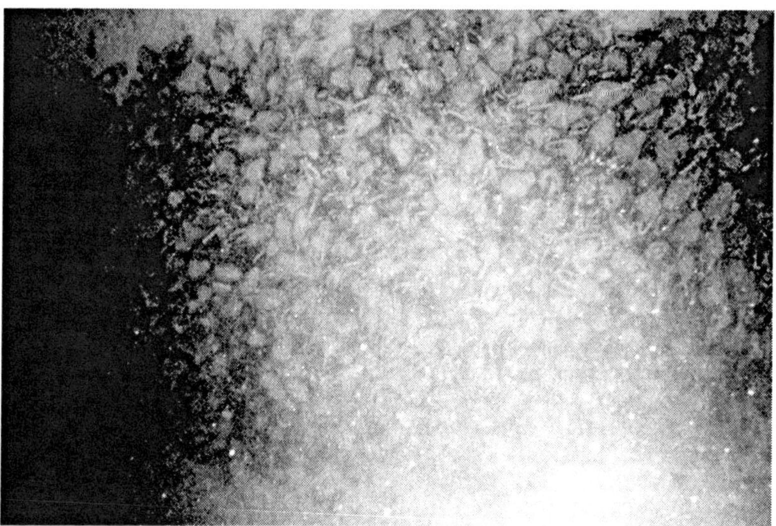

Figure 15.44 General view of the Byzantine wreck at Vasilikós.

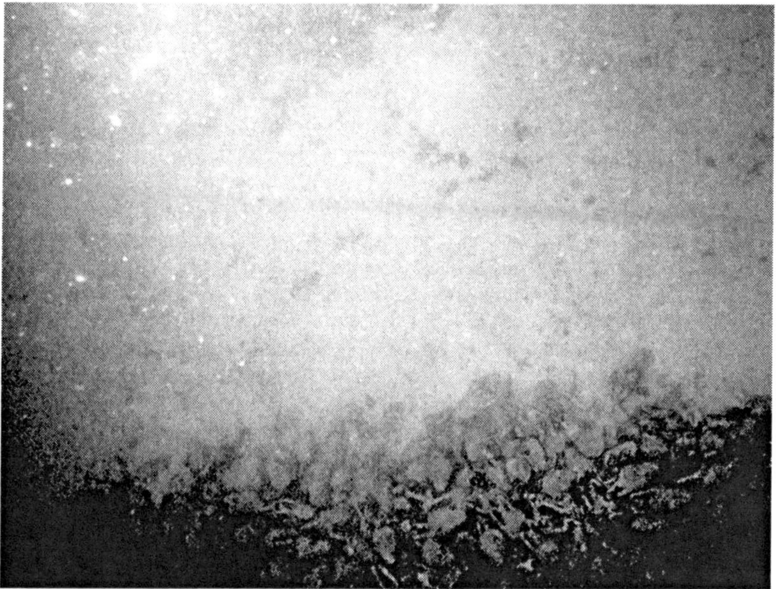

Figure 15.45 One side of the Byzantine wreck at Vasilikós.

15.7.4 A Caïque Full of Bricks at Vasilikós

(Information provided by I. Agállou)

Around 1922 a fairly big trading caïque had taken on a cargo of bricks and straw at Almirós in the bay of Vólos, and was bound for Límnos. The crew decided to go through the straits between Alónnisos and Peristéra, intending to anchor overnight at Vasilikós on Peristéra and carry on to Límnos the following day. Unfortunately, though, while they were still in the open sea outside the bay of Vasilikós, the bales of straw, which they'd put inside the hold and on top of the hatches, caught fire from the engine exhaust.

The crew tried frantically to put the fire out, but failed, since the material was so inflammable. They got into the lifeboat and made their escape to the promontory just beyond Kalámi from where, mortified, they watched their property vanish. Later they came back and retrieved the engine, for in those days they were difficult to find and expensive. (There were four factories in Magnisía making such engines: Rodhíti, Axílou, Papathanási and Malkótsi.)

After that, the locals used the unlucky sunken boat as a source of bricks. Another, folkloric, explanation for the fire has got around. It is said that on the land opposite where the boat sank there was an old woman who was permanently afflicted with the evil eye, and she had no sooner expressed her admiration ('My, what a load that boat has!') than the caïque caught fire and sank.

15.7.5 A Caïque with Tiles at Kanoúta in the Bay of Klíma

(Information provided by Kóstas Malamaténios, also known as Kóstas Athanasíou)

In the 1920s a heavily laden caïque was on its way from Chíos to Thessalonica. Its hold was full of roof tiles from the Eléfas ('Elephant') tile factory in Chíos. In the course of the voyage it ran into a fierce storm, of the type known to the fishermen of Alónnisos as 'smoke'. The name refers to the conditions of reduced of visibility in which ships can lose their bearings. The slow-moving boat couldn't contend with such conditions and tried to enter the Peristéra channel (the huge natural harbour between Alónnisos and Peristéra) to get some protection from the tempestuous weather. The boat was moving slowly because of its heavy load, and because it was a sailing ship with no engine.

From the sea they could just make out the mountains either side of the bay of Klíma, on the east side of Peristéra. The view resembles the entrance to the Peristéra channel, and in their confusion they entered the bay. To those who know the island the captain's fateful error is understandable, given the appalling weather conditions.

So they sailed into the bay and by the time they saw the steep cliffs of Peristéra emerge from the fog right in front of them it was too late. Manoeuvring is difficult with sails and the storm winds were driving the boat towards the rocks. They tried to get the boat out of the bay, but this would have been difficult enough even with an engine. Disaster was inevitable. The crew, who struggled to the last minute to prevent it, were still on board when the ship ran aground at the spot known as Kanoúta.

Three of the men were killed when the waves hurled them on to the rocks. The fourth was wounded, but with superhuman effort managed to climb higher up, where, exhausted and battered, he died.

Kóstas Malamaténios was there at the time and remembers the disaster:

> Five or six days later when the rain and wind had died down, I went down with my father to the bay where the accident had happened. We were standing in front of the sheepfold and from there we could see the hulk of a wrecked ship. I was only a child then. One of the men had reached the bushes and was lying there.
>
> The pounding sea had forced the others into fissures in the rocks. There was nothing to be seen but some hands and patches of human skin sticking out. But this wreck was 'manna from heaven' for the poor herdsmen of the island. They got up the tiles with grappling irons to roof their huts. Almost old the old huts on Peristéra have roofs whose tiles have 'Eléfas', the name of the tile factory in Chíos, stamped on them.
>
> Before we got those European-style roof tiles, which were difficult to get in those days, the local people built their roofs as follows: the first layer was made of timbers and small branches. On top of this they put sea weed with well kneaded mud made from red clay. There were some small cabins with this older type of roof which had tile roofs added on top, with tiles from the ill-fated boat.

15.7.6 A Wreck at Paliofánaro

In 1990, when I was diving near Cape Paliofánaro on the northern tip of Peristéra, I discovered the remains of a wooden boat at a depth of 30 m. I could see clearly the wooden frame, some metal fixings and the rowlocks. It was lying right by the narrow neck of land that links the promontory of Paliofánaro to the island.

This suggests that the boat, which couldn't have been very big, had been trying to get into the channel to shelter from the weather, and had crashed into the rocks and sunk. It was a sailing boat and such boats could not easily escape collisions. I asked an old man who lived on Peristéra (Kónstas, aged 86) about it, and this is what he told me:

> Our fathers recalled that a boat once foundered at Paliofánaro in high wind, when it was trying to get past the cape to find shelter. For years timbers used to come loose and float to the surface where they get broken up by the sea. The men who were sailing the boat were killed when the waves threw them onto the rocks. Only one was saved.

Later I leaned from Dh. Athanasíou that old Thodhorís Athanasíou saved the lone survivor. He found him frozen and covered with a tarpaulin. He carried him on his back to his hut, where he revived him.[21]

15.7.7 A Wreck at Cape Malámis

(Information provided by D. Agállou)

This is a pre-war wreck, from the time when Meladhiótis (well-known as a timber merchant to the people of Alónnisos) was busy felling timber for charcoal. The kilns were near the harbour of Yérakas, at the northern end of Alónnisos. On one occasion, in response to a request the previous day, a boat came from Chalkídha in Évvia to collect the stockpiled charcoal for transport back to Chalkídha. The sea got up and it was forced to anchor in the bay of Vasilikós. Even there the wind was very strong and all day long the crew, who were inexperienced, struggled to hold the ship with two anchors. The anchor chains were not very long with the result that the boat kept dragging itself free.

If they had run a mooring line from the front of the boat to the shore they would have had no problem and been safe. In the evening, they made a final desperate attempt, raising the anchors and dropping them yet again. The exhausted sailors then went ashore. Unfortunately, though, the wind driving the current in the bay was strong and violent, and little by little the caïque dragged its anchors out of the sand.

Before they could react, the boat had drifted out to sea, its anchors useless in the sandy seabed, given the strength of the winds. The wind carried it across the bay where it smashed into the rocks between Xílo and Cape Malámis. Later they came and removed the engine, but they could do nothing with the damaged hull. Today its outline is clearly visible, since it lies in only 3 m of water.

15.7.8 A Wreck at Ladhádhiko

(Information provided by Em. Tsaparíkos)

Ladhádhiko is in the southern part of Peristéra. There in the yearly years of the 20th century a boat carrying olive oil in wooden barrels was wrecked in bad weather. The barrels disintegrated and the whole area was covered with oil. This is why the bay is known as Ladhádhiko (meaning 'oil factory'). The wreck is in the shallows that extend about 100 m out into the bay.

15.7.9 A Wreck at Livadhákia

(Information provided by K. Athanasíou)

During the First World War a large wooden sailing ship was coming from the region of Istanbul, headed for Vólos. It was winter and the weather was bad. At dusk the ship emerged from the strait between Alónnisos and Kirá Panayá, and was approaching Paliofánaro, the northern tip of Peristéra, intending to pass to the right of it, between Peristéra and Alónnisos. All sailors prefer this route since you can lay up and rest at Vasilikós, in a safe harbour out of the wind. The captain of the ship had been this way before, but on this occasion he made a mistake, passing to the left of Paliofánaro into the channel between Peristéra and the small island of Lechoúsa, and entered the bay of Livadhákia.

Anyone visiting the area will understand how the ill-fated captain made his mistake. Which ever side of Paliofánaro you pass you have land on both sides. The experienced crew responded immediately when the mistake was realised and dropped anchor. But Poseidon's curse was upon them. They anchored out in the middle of the bay, but, as it happened, very close to a reef. For a while everything was fine and the crew, feeling reassured, decided to rest and relax. But then the direction of the wind changed, gradually shifting the ship towards the reef. A sudden jolt, quickly followed by a second, galvanised the crew into action. They ran to haul up the anchor and get away from the reef.

The hold was full of blocks of marble (commercial marble, not just ballast). The four or five blows that the ship had received were fatal. The heavy marble blocks acted like hammers, widening the holes in the hull. The sea flooded in and that was that, the ship broke up and sank on the spot. The crew had just time to abandon ship and escape in the lifeboat. Local people retrieved the marble blocks and used them for building. If you go to Livadhákia now, you will see one of these blocks in the stone wall around a garden.

Another, much smaller, wooden cargo boat was lost in the same way in the same area, among the rocks on the right hand shore of the bay.

15.8 Wrecks around Skántzoura

15.8.1 The Wreck of a Trawler at Skántzoura

(Information provided by Dh. Agállou)

Captain Yórgos Efstathíou, from Skíros, with years of experience behind him, bought a trawler. A shrewd man and a good sailor, he had transported patriots and allies to Asia Minor during the war and acquired considerable experience of the sea. One day he was on his way to drop his nets in the open sea off Skántzoura. He was tired and left the tiller to one of the crew and went to sleep. While the other man was steering the boat ran over a rock ledge at full speed. It was balanced there for a moment and then plunged back into the sea with some of its planking torn loose. The helmsman lost his head, the captain and the other fishermen woke up but it was too late. In several places water was pouring in. Soon the boat sank and the engine was left there to rust. The crew got to the monastery on Skántzoura and from there back to Skíros.

15.8.2 A Wreck with Timber near Kórakas

(Information provided by N. Kiriazís)

Some time in the 1920s a *karavóskaro* (see p. 402) was on its way from Thessalonica in a calm sea. Near Skántzoura at the islet of Kórakas, it hit a rock and began to sink. The crew were taken by surprise, since they were not expecting an accident in such fine weather. Some started to bale while others threw the cargo into the sea. But in vain. The ship went down with all hands a few metres further on. The sea was filled with baulks of timber and the Alonnisiots all came out to collect them.

15.9 Some Comparisons

I have discussed at some length the importance of our islands as a nautical crossroads, and described wrecks from different historical periods that lie in our waters. Now I shall consider the connections between the ancient wrecks and the wrecks from recent times. It is surprising how many similarities there are in their location, and in the cause and manner of their sinking. One example is to be found at Peristéra, where an ancient ship sank, so the archaeologists think, as a result of a fire at Pethaménos (see section 15.7.1). A similar tragic event took place 2,500 years later, when a ship sank following a fire just two nautical miles away at Vasilikós (see section 15.7.4).

Another characteristic indication that the trade routes remained the same from antiquity to today is offered by the wrecks in the southern part of Peristéra. Near Cape Tsélios there is a the wreck of an ancient Greek ship which was carrying wine from Chíos to the northern markets (section 15.7.2). In more recent times, a large wooden sailing ship carrying European type roofing tiles, also from Chíos, from the Eléfas tile factory, sank nearby (section 15.7.5). Thus we see that the same trade routes were used continuously throughout history. In any period the master of a merchant ship just adapted himself to the current needs of the market in order to maximise profit. Besides, the sailors of all periods encountered the same problems (storms, low visibility, difficult channels). Another parallel can be drawn between the Byzantine wreck at Vasilikós, Peristéra (section 15.7.3), and the modern one at Cape Malámis (section 15.7.7). The two wrecks are only about one nautical mile apart, and were sunk in the same bay by the force of the wind. There is a further parallel in the case of the *Panayía Tínou* (section 15.2.8) which sank at Psathoúra in exactly the same spot as the classical wreck (section 15.2.2).

The concealed entrance to the harbour of Planítis has been a headache for sailors in every period. At night or in bad weather it is difficult to make out, and the area around remains a watery grave for many vessels. The fierce winds of the Aegean have been the cause of many accidents, such as those that befell the Byzantine ship with the cargo of plates (section 15.5.9) and the caïque carrying charcoal which sank in 1948 (section 15.5.10). Many ships have struck the small island of Mélissa and the crews have then made frantic efforts to reach Kirá Panayá, where there was habitation, before the ship sank. The post-Byzantine ship with the enamelled bowls (section 15.5.6) and the caïque commandeered by ELAN (section 15.5.7) were probably both victims of this low rock which seems to pop up unexpectedly from nowhere in the middle of the sea.

15.10 Unreported Wrecks

Around the Northern Sporades there are many more wrecks than are generally known about. Up till now these have not been investigated. All Alonnisiots must ask themselves whether it is not better that the government be kept in ignorance. Once they become known, these wrecks will be prey to the art thieves, like those that have already been reported. After the government's abandonment of a wreck as important as the one at Peristéra (see section 15.7.1), or the equally important one at Fangroú (section 15.5.2), what can we expect for the smaller or more recent ones?

The positions of those two wrecks are well known and yet they are left unguarded during the winter. According to the estimates of G. Bass, there may be as many as 10,000 ancient wrecks in the eastern Mediterranean. From this one can deduce that the Marine Park of Alónnisos must be host to a very large number of wrecks. This largely uninhabited and remote region cannot be controlled by wardens. The only possibly method of control is satellite surveillance, with specialists based on the island to monitor the equipment. (Throughout the world today airports, army camps and some remote archaeological sites are protected by satellites.)

If we want to create an archaeological park we must use the most advanced methods to protect what is there. The international community needs to be reassured that the archaeological park will not become a paradise for art thieves. It would also be necessary to enlarge the *Eforía* of Marine Antiquities and to obtain the assistance of the Greek state and the European Union. There are many scientists who would be only too willing to involve themselves in this marine research if they were given the opportunity. If at some point the administration were to be decentralised and local departments of underwater archaeology created, it would be logical for the Northern Sporades to have its own department. A flexible and well-organised local archaeological administration would help to protect the sites from looting, promote the publication of research and the conservation of finds.

The archaeological material of the region is unique in its richness and variety. There are 18 known ancient or medieval wrecks in the waters around Alónnisos and the lesser Northern Sporades. Psathoúra, Yoúra, Lechoúsa and Peristéra each have one; Alónnisos, Skántzoura and Pipéri have two each; while Kirá Panayá has no fewer than eight. In addition, there are four such wrecks around the shores of Skópelos. The telltale signs are everywhere among these islands: anchors of every period have been found throughout the region. We hope that very soon there will be a conservation office and a marine museum. This will make the need for further developments more pressing, and in particular the introduction of measures to prevent the repetition of incidents such as the following:

1. A German set up a tent on Pipéri where he spent a month diving on a wreck known to local people. At the end of the stay a large boat came to collect him and his extensive 'luggage'.

2. Seven foreigners spent two weeks diving in the same spot near Yoúra. They had their own boat, to which they hauled up sacks from the sea. There can be little doubt about the contents of those sacks.

15.11 Wrecks in Deep Water

In the seas around the Northern Sporades there is a large number of wrecks at depths of more than 100 m. These are all well preserved, because of the depth and the generally sandy nature of the seabed. The wrecks are dotted about all over the place and come from many periods. The remote islands have pride of place since the bulk of the wrecks lie in the zones around them. Most of the wrecks are modern, but the Byzantine and other medieval wrecks are more important. Fishermen are constantly pulling up Byzantine amphorae and other kinds of pots in their nets. The pots are of various kinds and some have coloured glazes. Most are small and, unfortunately, many break in the nets or when they are tipped out on to the decks of caïques.

The amphorae are also of many different types. There are those that the fishermen call 'balloons' and the round-bottomed ones. Wrecks with similar amphorae and other artefacts have been found out at sea off Pipéri, Skántzoura, Dhío Adhérfia and Skópelos. Amphorae from the wreck near Skópelos were full of resin which is now very dark in colour. Of course there must be a number of classical wrecks, like the one out at sea off Psathoúra with the splendid amphorae from Chíos (see section 15.2.2). Many other kinds of objects are dragged up daily from the depths: anchors of all types, wooden and metal components of sunken ships, as well as mines, shells and aeroplane parts. Most are smashed up by the crews or thrown back into the sea far from the fishing grounds so that they won't get caught in the nets again. 'If we hand them over to the harbour-master,' say the local fishermen, 'there'll be no end of trouble for us.'

Apart from the wrecks already referred to there are innumerable modern wrecks scattered throughout the region. These have been noted on charts and captains avoid them so as not to get their nets entangled. The future progress of technology will overcome the problems of the great depth and man will be able to study them exhaustively.

The wrecks in the various categories discussed above amount to a considerable number. We all hope that they will be the subject of thorough investigation using proper archaeological techniques. As an enthusiast for the undersea world, it is my conviction that they will provide the answers to many historical questions. And they will help us to realise how fortunate we are to live in a place such as Alónnisos, with its rich cultural heritage. An inheritance going back 100,000 years, an occasion for jealousy or admiration on the part of others.

Alónnisos holds the prize for the oldest human presence in the whole of the Aegean region. A number of Palaeolithic and Neolithic sites in the Sporades archipelago have shed new light on the remote beginnings of human history. Important finds have overturned the theory that culture was brought here and was not indigenous. Entirely new evidence has come to light which indicates the advanced culture of the prehistoric population of these islands in navigation and fishing, pottery making, stonework and the carving of figurines. It is evident that in other periods too man inhabited this region in order not only to survive but also to express his unquenchable spirit. All vestiges of the past, whether under the sea or on land, come down to us as our greatest cultural property. It is we who must reveal them and study them and develop them.

An important step towards achieving this would be the establishment of an archaeological institution on Alónnisos. The communication of knowledge and the exchange of views under the auspices of such a body would provide an impetus for further progress. A conference, which I hope will prove the first step towards the establishment of such an institution, was held on Alónnisos in October 1996.

Notes

1. *Dromones* were light, fast-moving cargo vessels, propelled by many oars.
2. Ténedhos is the original, Greek name for the now Turkish island of Bozcaada, close to the mainland of Turkey, south of the entrance to the Dardanelles. [Translator]
3. On this issue see also pp.50–1.
4. In Greek mythology, Philoctetes, who is among the leaders of the Trojan campaign, inherited the bow of Heracles. According to Sophocles' play *Philoctetes*, he was bitten by a poisonous snake at the shrine of CHRYSE on the island of that name (= LEMNOS), while they were on their way to TROY. The wound festered and the smell was intolerable to his companions, who left him behind on the island. After ten years of suffering, Philoctetes was rescued when Odysseus and others returned to LEMNOS, following a prophecy that without the bow of Heracles TROY could not be conquered (see also pp. 50–1). [Editors]
5. See p. 272.
6. The name of the German cargo vessel is given only in Greek transliteration, yielding the pronunciation *ooverman*. The German name is likely to be *Hüberman*, or something similar: there are a number of variations on this not uncommon German surname (with or without the *umlaut*, with or without the initial H, with single or double N at the end). It has proved impossible to find in other sources any positive identification of the ship referred to. [Translator]
7. The sailors' name for Cape Kafiréas on the southern tip of Évvia. [Translator]
8. For the operation of the *váza* see pp. 308–9.
9. IENAE is the acronym formed from the Greek name: *Institoúto Enallíon Erevnón*.
10. These are all people who removed significant quantities of antiquities from Greece in the Ottoman period. Charles François Ollier, Marquis de Nointel (d. 1685) visited Greece in the 1670s. Sir Richard Worsley (1751–1805) was a collector of antiquities who travelled in Greece in the 1780s. The British diplomat Lord Elgin (1766–1841) is well known as the man who obtained the elements of the Parthenon frieze now in the British Museum, the so-called 'Elgin Marbles', that remain a bone of contention between Britain and Greece. Edward Daniel Clarke (1769–1822), was mineralogist, traveller and collector who removed more than 1000 small items from Greece. Otto Magnus Baron von Stackelberg (1786–1837) was an early German archaeologist who travelled and excavated extensively in Greece. [Translator]
11. Kritzás (1971).
12. See Throckmorton (1977).
13. Ioannidaki-Dostoglou (1989).
14. In Greek mythology Aeolus was given control of the winds. [Translator]
15. For more on the resistance organisation ELAN see pp. 229ff.
16. The name of the ship is given in Greek as *Normandhía*. It is not clear what country this ship belonged to. If German or French, the name would be *Normandie*, if Italian *Normandia*, if British *Normandy*. It has not been possible to positively identify the wreck from other sources. [Translator]
17. Deutsche Gesellschaft zur Förderung der Unterwasserarchäologie.
18. Reported in *Enália* 4, 1/2 (1992) published by IENAE.
19. Hadjidaki (1995).
20. See Chatzidhákis (1997).
21. See p. 205 for a slightly more detailed account of this incident, and pp. 202–5 for the life history of Theódhoros Athanasíou.

EPILOGUE

When I completed this book, I felt great joy and great relief, for I had succeeded in fulfilling my obligations towards my own homeland, to my ancestors and to my fellow islanders of today and tomorrow. As one generation gave way to another, I had watched an epoch being lost. The old people, departing one by one, were taking with them their traditions and their irreplaceable knowledge of the turbulent historical events they had lived through. With such skills as I had, I determined to gather together and to preserve this rich heritage which was in danger of disappearing for ever. And with the generous co-operation of many people who confided in me, I brought to a conclusion this summary of the history of Alónnisos and the surrounding islands.

The ancient Greeks, whose wisdom and institutions, and works of art and architecture formed the foundations of the entire modern world, always maintained the importance of posthumous reputation. The imposing reputations of three uncles of mine who were executed by the Germans, and the reputations of other heroic persons, impelled me to record their bravery and self-sacrifice.

While I was searching for material, I was often moved by the eager and unselfish willingness to help on the part of all my fellow islanders. I did not find a single person who refused to share with me what they knew. They were all delighted to respond to my insistent and exhausting questioning. They have all played a part in the writing of this book, and I thank them once again for their co-operation, which has moved me deeply.

I also received a great deal of help from Alonnisiots living outside the island, in many different parts of Greece, people who love their island and who willingly offered me every assistance. I thank all of them too, and especially Dhimítris Athanasíou and Tákis Vláikos.

Finally, I would beg once more for your lenience in judging this book, for, as I have said already, I am not a historian. What compelled me to write about the island's progress through history was deep devotion to my incomparable homeland, Alónnisos.

APPENDIX 1

THE ISLANDS THROUGH THE EYES OF FOREIGN TRAVELLERS

Many travellers, both Greek and foreign, have passed through our islands at various times and for various purposes. Most of the foreigners came to the Northern Sporades in the service of their own countries, as spies or cartographers, to conclude treaties or to seek for mineral deposits. Some came for personal reasons – a passion for travel and discovery, a fascination with our islands – or out of necessity, seeking a safe anchorage in bad weather or needing to replenish supplies. Many came to steal antiquities and, with the necessary permissions (which were easily obtained in the Ottoman period), they seized whatever they came across.

For our islands, which became something of a backwater from the dissolution of the Pax Byzantina until their liberation from the Turks, the written accounts of travellers have a special importance. They are the only rays of light that pierce the cloud of historical obscurity that lay over the islands almost continuously from the fourteenth to the 19th century. Foreign travellers were numerous, and I shall present extracts from the writings of a only a few of them, sufficient to indicate the nature of their work and the reasons for their visits.

The earliest foreign travellers were the Italians who in their isolari *(books of islands) and their* portolani *(pilot books) gave some not very accurate descriptions of our islands. Their chief interest was to show the harbours of each island, and on their maps these appear enormous. There work was, however, of use to the sailors of the time, enabling them to locate their position within the labyrinth of the Greek archipelago. If one takes into account the limited means that these first cartographers had at their disposal, their work appears worthy of admiration. Their information was chiefly geographical, and rarely do any other details appear on their maps. Many of them never went ashore, but sketched the outline of each island from their ships. Others did not even make a voyage, but simply copied the maps of older geographers in order to pass them off as their own work. But they made mistakes and the names of the islands got mixed up.*

A1.1 Cristoforo Buondelmonte

The first of the Italian travellers was the Florentine Chief Ambassador, Cristoforo Buondelmonte, who came to Greece in the first quarter of the 15th century to collect manuscripts, and for six years travelled around the Greek islands. He was one of the first true cartographers. Here is what he has to say about Alónnisos (which he calls Dromo) as it appears in the 1897 edition of his isolario, *the* Book of the Islands of the Archipelago:[1]

> Next comes the island called Dromo. Ships making the passage from east to west consider it an important reference point. Often, and even when they come this way by night, once they reach this landmark, they are able to set their course.

A1.2 Benedetto Bordone

Bordone was a cartographer from Padua who had studied both astronomy and geography. In 1528 he published his Book of All the Islands of the World.[2] *Bordone provides the information required by those who are navigating amongst our islands, and at the same time makes some historical observations. This is what he says about some of our islands:*

> The northern harbour of Pelagisi [Kirá Panayá] is good and large, but it is dangerous to enter since the mouth is very narrow. It is rich in fish. Pelagisi is about forty miles in circumference. Not far from there lies a rock named Iura [Yoúra] which is very steep, and another named Piperi [Pipéri].

After his brief references to these uninhabited islands (and to Psathoúra, which he calls Larsura), Bordone turns to Alónnisos and Peristéra. He visited Alónnisos before the slaughter perpetrated by Barbarossa.

> When the bad weather ceased we came to Dromo [Alónnisos], which in Latin is called Corto. It is a long and narrow island. The island where the fleet of King Antiochus I of Syria was destroyed by the Romans is called Sarachino [Peristéra]. Dromo has good water, but Sarachino has the harbour. Both are suitable for habitation, good islands without great heights. The former is about forty miles in circumference, the latter about thirty.

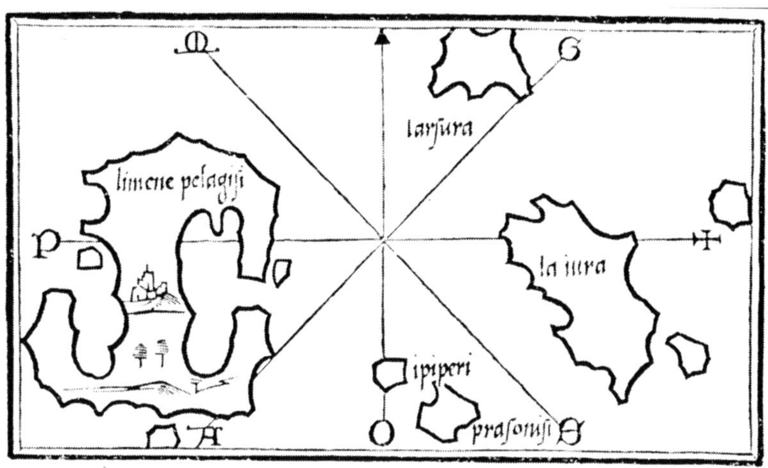

Map 11 B. Bordone, 1547 (Kirá Panayá, Yoúra, Pipéri).
Source: Kóstas and Angéla Mavríkis' collection of old maps.

Map 12 B. Bordone, 1547 (Alónnisos and Peristéra).
Source: Kóstas and Angéla Mavríkis' collection of old maps.

A1.3 The Dhimitriís

In 1791 a book by 'the Dhimitriís' entitled A New Geography *was published in Vienna. 'The Dhimitriís' took their name from their home town of Dhimitriádha (now known as Vólos). Their real names were Daniíl Filippídhis and Grigórios Konstandás. Their work was characteristic of the Greek Enlightenment. In* A New Geography *they refer to Alónnisos and some of the neighbouring islands:*

> Lidhrómia or Chiliodhrómia [Alónnisos], some three or four miles distant from Skópelos, is an island consisting of little more than a rocky spine with a some pines, olives and cedars, and a few fruit trees. There is a village high up with sixty or seventy houses enclosed within a defensive wall, which is in a very weakened and wretched state.
>
> To the east of Lidhrómia there are some other reasonably large islands, but they are uninhabited with the exception of those in which there is a small monastery, such as Yoúra, Kirá Panayá, Skántzoura and Pipéri. These uninhabited islands are full of wild goats. [. . .] On Yoúra and Skántzoura there are beehives whose honey is better even than that of Imittós.[3] In these and many other islands, anyone intending to make a separate treatise on the Aegean Sea, will be able to examine many things worthy of note.

A1.4 Karl Fiedler

One of the most renowned travellers was Karl Fiedler, a mineralogist in the service of the Greek government. He came to Alónnisos in 1834 to carry out excavations which he described in his book published in Leipzig in 1841, Voyage through all Parts of the Kingdom of Greece. *Fiedler had been appointed by the government of King Otto to oversee the exploration and exploitation of mineral deposits, and on Alónnisos he was particularly interested in the mines at Áyi Anáryiri, where lignite had been extracted. Included here are his detailed descriptions of the ancient Greek tombs he investigated at Kokkinókastro.*

A1.4.1 The Village of Alónnisos[4]

> We had disembarked in a bay on the south side of Alónnisos. From here one can see, in the distance, among the rocks at the summit of a hill, a village, the only one on the island. Up there, at one of the most advantageous spots on the island, the inhabitants have chosen to establish their dwellings, for fear of the pirates who still dominate the Aegean, though not many years ago the inhabitants themselves were involved in this profession.
>
> The village consists, as is the general rule in these parts, of simple, irregular houses built close together, and separated by narrow, twisting and ill-kept alleyways. The village is encircled by a wall, and one enters through a wooden gate. In several places the houses are built into the wall. On the north and west sides it rise from precipitous rock-faces; nor is the south side easy of approach. On the east side, however, there is some more or less level ground below the wall, and it is here that the gate is located. From here, too, one can watch for the first signs of an attack. On the east side,

outside the wall, there are a number of houses, built in recent times, and in one of these I myself was given hospitality. The village has no central point of interest, nor any cafe. In total some fifty families inhabit the village, including those in the houses outside the wall on the east. The people are for the most part fair-skinned with thick jet-black hair; and the women have fine faces.

On the east side, behind the houses built outside the wall, rises a steep hillside, on the lower slopes of which are located a pair of ancient wells. It is from these that the villagers must draw their water. There is no water within the village itself, and any assailant would immediately gain control of the water supply.

To the north of the village stands a windmill.

Walking northeast from the village, one comes first upon clay schist, with varying inclination, and then a small deposit of lime marl, overlain with fine-grained limestone. To the south of the road is a terraced slope, planted with vines. Here and there stand small groups of olive trees. Viewed from the sea, this part of the island has the appearance of a large vineyard.

A1.4.2 Lignite on Alónnisos

After about an hour the road descends northwards towards the sea [at Áyi Anáryiri] and the visitor is confronted by a hillside densely planted with pines. As he proceeds he comes to a small knoll on which stand the walls of a building, a small abandoned monastery. To the northeast of this building there is a steep cliff of white limestone in which a deposit of lignite is visible. Samples of the lignite were submitted during the presidency of Count Kapodhístrias, and the lignite was mined by the French Expedition under Colonel Bory de St Vincent. The valuable work, *Expedition scientifique de Morée etc.* [*Scientific Expedition to the Peloponnese. . .*] contains a report on the mining.[5]

This mine was worked again after the war, in 1948. During the opening of the galleries, however, the coal-miners broke into an underground watercourse which completely destroyed the galleries. For months it poured out into the sea and dried up all the underground water reserves in the area.

Fiedler now devotes several pages to describing the lignite and other mineral deposits, before resuming his more general geographical descriptions:

A1.4.3 The Harbours of Vasilikós and Áyos Dhimítrios

Between the islands of Peristéra and Alónnisos (lying next to each other, the two create a broad channel in the shape of a half-moon, and at the north and south ends approach each other closely), a great harbour is outlined, in which, in any weather, one can make a landing or set sail. Whichever way you go from one side to the other, you are protected from all winds. The anchorage, in short, is very good; it has a depth of 45–55 m. The bay on the island of Peristéra is the larger and for this reason it is called Vasilikós, that is to say 'Royal',[6] while that on Alónnisos is called *Dhimítri*, that is, the harbour of St Demetrius.

On the Peristéra side there is no water supply or clear land for building. The Alónnisos side has space for at least a hundred buildings, and, besides, there is fresh water. Furthermore, there are several houses here, which have been laid waste by pirates. The great harbour offers protection to more than a hundred ships and shelters sailing ships from the winds. Chiefly these are en route from Constantinople or Smyrna to Vólos or Thessalonica.

On the south side of the rocky projection, where the ancient castle stands, I was shown a greyish-white spot about the size of a ninety-six-pound cannon ball. This was half embedded in the rock and was in fact made of lead.

Towards evening we managed to return to Alónnisos. The following day was a feast day which even the pirates observed. Thus we managed, though with some difficulty, to set off in two sailing boats, and around three in the afternoon we reached the harbour of Skópelos. We sailed into the harbour beneath the continual firing of guns which delighted the assembled populace.

Later, an official of high standing in Athens was unwilling to believe that the pirates had had the intention of making a surprise attack on us. But one week afterwards, news reached Athens that pirates had made a surprise attack on a felucca, murdering fifteen men before they paid a visit to the poor inhabitants of Alónnisos. The pirates returned with a small amount of booty to their accustomed haven in the bay of Kassándhra, but there the fate that they deserved overtook them: a frightful storm drove them ashore, where the Turks were waiting for them. The boats foundered and those who reached the shore were shot; there can have been no more than two or three who saved themselves by hiding in the bushes.

The pirates of these seas are not for the most part seamen themselves, but use the services of the most able seamen from captured ships, who are compelled to serve them for a period of time, during which they are well treated. When other sailors are captured the earlier ones are released without any ransom being required. The pirates detain only those people of some standing for whom they can demand ransom. If this is not received, a second letter follows, in which one of the hostage's ears is enclosed. If land-bound thieves are scarcely human, these pirates are even more fiendish. A wild beast rends its victim and afterwards is docile, but these devils in human form sport to the last extreme with their prisoners, and amuse themselves in the most inhuman fashion. I should provoke indignation if I were to describe their sadistic acts.

From the 7th to the 10th the storm was blowing strong. On the 11th it was calmer and on the 12th we sailed to the north coast of Alónnisos. The worthy local elder Nikólas welcomed us and escorted us, for he was in hope of his island being revitalised.

The north and northwest shores are nothing but steep cliffs, and here one meets the fiercest storms. Only to the north of the village is there one small cove where a very few boats anchor, or are pulled up on the beach. Further to the northeast, though, there is no bay that could offer shelter to a boat. We sailed almost as far as the northern tip of the island and dropped anchor there. A debate flared up about where the iron ore was situated. In the upper, broken strata of the rocks there was no deposit visible, in fact nothing to be seen but a few wild goats clinging to the steep slope. The local people maintained that high up on the cliffs there was indeed iron, but they thought I would have to content myself with viewing the place from the sea, since the cliffs were insurmountable and often overhanging. I had stepped back to see if I could make out a place where we could clamber up on to the island, when my companion suddenly seized his gun, jumped from the boat on to the rocks, and, calling to a sapper to follow him, made off at a run towards the cliff. Without pausing to reflect, I too seized my rifle and leapt on to the rocks. We had picked a bad spot to climb, for it was enough for a piece of rock or a plant to break loose for one to be pitched into the deep waters of the sea. A little further on, though, we found a path which lead upwards.

With considerable effort we managed to get near the summit. We scrambled with difficulty up the final incline and reached a plateau where everything had been burned and cleared by the shepherds (they burn the forest so that grass for grazing will grow). There we met a family of shepherds. The man had neither nose nor palate and could speak only hoarsely. I was amazed when they all maintained that this was a natural deformity, but the man later explained that he had been wounded in the navy. His wife and an adult son were working in a small field. The man led us back towards a steep cliff, the very one below which our ship was anchored, and at that point everything became clear.[7]

Fiedler now recounts how they climbed down the cliff and found the deposit, which he describes in great detail, before concluding his account of their descent:

It was dark and we had to hurry to get back. We had to traverse, in the dark, an appalling route over sharp rocks. In the bushes our clothes got torn, especially those worn by the interpreter, who now saw the advantages of European dress over the Roumeliot or Macedonian. His beautiful *foustanéla* was completely ruined that evening. Finally we reached a ravine leading down to a small cove. There we had supposed we would find the boats. For a considerable time we shouted in vain. Eventually, however, we heard a gunshot and replied immediately. Now in the darkness of the ravine we had to descend the precipitous rocks with ropes. We reached the boat completely exhausted. The sailors had been obliged to use their oars continually to keep the swaying boat off the rocks, and they were very worried that we had not returned earlier. They were delighted now to be rowing seawards. The moon was bright. Finally at five in the morning and still dark we reached Skópelos, where the first customers were already in the cafe.

As regards natural history, I have the following remarks to make about Alónnisos. In the rough, almost inaccessible northern part of the island there are wild goats. Among the limestone rocks, close to the deposit of coal, one occasionally meets golden eagles. Here, and on Skópelos, there are more blackbirds than anywhere else.

Near the ancient palace, there is a wild and dense pine forest, where wild rabbits live. They are greyish brown and smaller than the domestic sort. The local people say that they come in thousands in the spring when the vines are budding in the vineyards. They eat the new grapes and cause widespread devastation. It is not possible to catch them alive in those labyrinths unless they get trapped in some empty pit. From such a pit I obtained a charming little animal of this type.

The shores of Alónnisos and the uninhabited islands are especially rich in fish. By this I mean that there are more fish there than in many parts of the Mediterranean, which, generally, though, is not as rich in fish as the northern seas.

As an epilogue to this description of the island of Alónnisos, there follows an account of its antiquities.

A1.4.4 Ancient Greek Tombs on Alónnisos

Before we disturb the dead who have been resting for more than 2,000 years in their final dwelling place, let us first visit the city [at Kokkinókastro] which they once inhabited and filled with life.

Starting from the mine [at Áyi Anáryiri] and following the marl deposit towards the south [i.e. crossing the island] one soon comes to the old castle, near which lay the island's most ancient city. At the edge of the rocks, which fall steeply towards the sea, it is said that there once stood a marble statue of the king, or war lord, of this northern island, who with extended hand pointed towards Évvia, towards his palaces. The rock on which the statue stood collapsed into the sea taking the statue with it. It is said that the king still lies in the sea, at no great depth, trying to make out the spot where he once stood. The remains of the collapsed rock fall smoothly down to the sea which is indeed shallow at this point. Next to the old city, on a prominent rock, was the built the fortress of the city, its acropolis, which was eventually destroyed. Only some sections of the outer wall remain to be seen, and these are constructed of small rectangular blocks. A large part of the rock has been eroded by the sea. This ancient fortress included many buildings within its inner circuit. The area is rich in shards of pottery and amphorae.

The ground on which the city was built and also the rock of the acropolis is limestone. On the rock of the acropolis one finds, here and there, traces of old copper objects in the grooves worn by the rain. On this occasion I found a thin fragment of copper, completely oxidised and with two holes in it, which might have been used to secure something. The interpreter was more fortunate. He found a glass bead with blue and white decoration, about the size of a pea.

Behind the ancient city there are several ancient graves. Those that were visible have been opened and destroyed. The stone slabs that covered them, and broken vessels, are scattered left and right, and in many graves not even the bones of the occupant remain. The wreckers hoped that they would find objects of value, but they were mistaken, for the people who lived here were poor. Apart from a few copper coins and a few small round copper mirrors, there was nothing metallic. There was very little work of artistic value on the island. In the vessels of unrefined clay, which had in a few cases a little black or red decoration, but no pictorial representations, only the shape was pleasing.

The Greek whom I had engaged to work with the others in the mine had opened a number of tombs in the past, in search of objects of value and had been very disappointed, having gained no profit from his labours.

Indeed, he remarked that they must have been very poor people. It was this man who led me to the tomb which I shall now describe.[8]

The tomb was covered by two large slabs of limestone. It was full of soil which had been washed in by the rain, and for this reason the bones were completely decayed.

On the right, next to the skull, was a small black cup, like the one that I found later in the mouth of a jug. Next to the right hand of the skeleton were two small copper coins, too corroded to be legible. Next to the left foot was a shallow black plate 6 cm in diameter.[9] This skeleton (of a male) was lying on a thin bed of sand.

Internally this tomb had a length of 2.15 m and a width and depth of about 65 cm. The walls were constructed from very closely jointed courses of limestone blocks. At the two short sides were vertically set slabs of limestone. The mountainside descends smoothly in a southerly direction towards the sea, and the grave too is slightly inclined towards the south, enabling the corpse to see the storage chamber with its provisions at its feet. Immediately adjacent to the tomb my eye fell upon a vertically set stone slab and, having the idea that it indicated a second tomb, I gave the order to begin excavation. The Greek who was nearby looking for other tombs came over and told me that it was a storage chamber for provisions.

We lifted the three slabs that covered it and it became clear that it really was immediately adjacent to the tomb, at the foot end, and perpendicular to it, oriented, that is to say, east–west. It was a constructed chamber, 1.4 m long and 55 cm wide, which had, however, filled up with soil brought in by rainwater.

On the east side was a water pitcher with a height of 65 cm. Its diameter was 25 cm in the middle and it had two handles. Its mouth was fairly large, 10 cm in diameter. Its base was round and smooth. Apart from the base, which in these days has become, for no apparent reason, broader, this pitcher resembles very closely most of the pitchers which are used today in the Northern Sporades and particularly those used in Alónnisos. It was placed on its side in the same manner as women returning from the well or spring will rest their pitchers, one handle down and the other up, so that they can pick them up again more easily. So as not to spill the water, nowadays they stop the mouth with a piece of sponge or a lemon.

Next to the jar, on the south side, were two jugs, each with a single handle and a broad mouth, and an oil jug with a round body. On the west side there were two more water pitchers like the first. All these vessels were of red fired clay and the uppermost side of the first pitcher was covered with a calcareous lichen-like deposit.

On the southwestern side there was a black lamp, 10 cm in length; and on the northwestern side a black bowl with a diameter of 17 cm, in which was placed a smaller bowl of red fired clay.

In the middle of the chamber there was a dish for offerings, 26 cm in diameter. On the outside it was black; inside it had a red band around the lip, and the centre was also coloured red. The lip, which was turned down 2.5 cm, had been damaged before it was placed in the tomb.

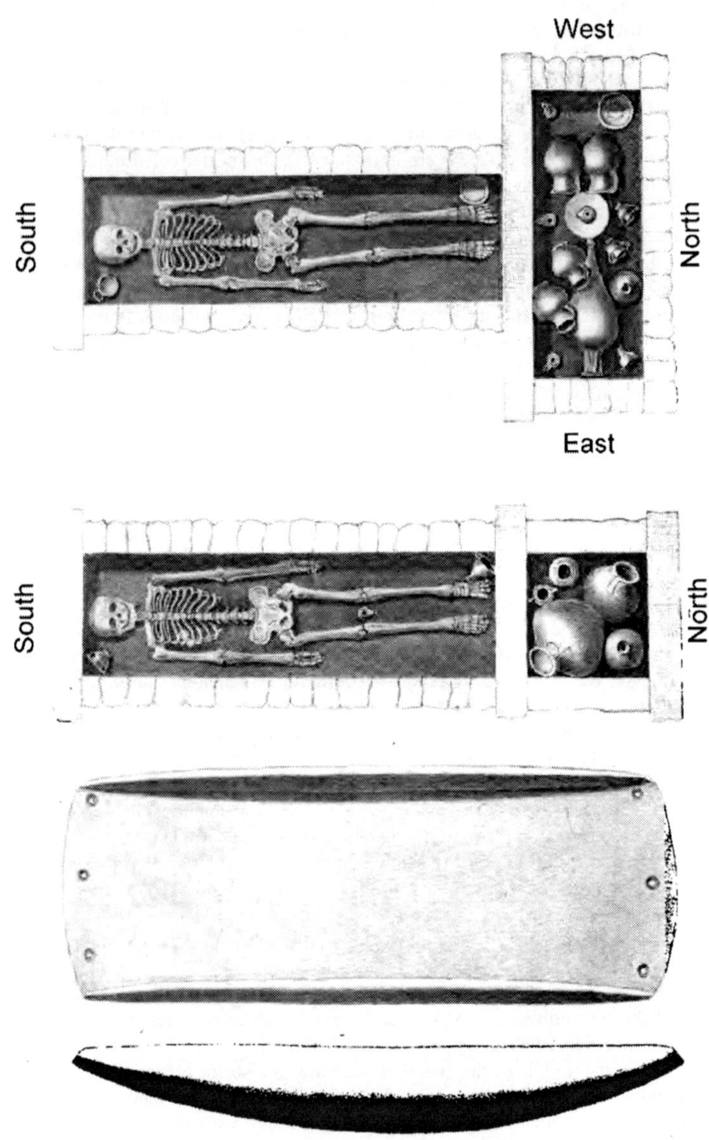

Figure A1.1 Graves at Kokkinókastro (from Fiedler, 1841).

Below this dish was a circular copper mirror, 12 cm in diameter and 3 mm thick. On one side the edge was raised, and a line in relief ran around the circumference 6 mm from the edge; the centre point was slightly depressed, and at distances of 12 and 18 mm from the centre there were two irregular concentric circles in relief. The other side was completely smooth and polished to provide a reflective surface.

On top of the dish lay a round clay lamp, 7.5 cm in diameter. At the point where the wick would have emerged there was some soot, and the lamp must, surely, have been alight when the corpse was buried. To the south of the dish was another lamp which was blackened on the outside. Its handle, like that of the lamp that was found on the northwest, was broken. This suggests that it had been in use for some considerable time. On the north side of the dish were two small cups similar to the one on the north side of the large pitcher.

This tomb was nearer to the fortress than those found further north, and more impressive, as were two others beside it.

Since none of the other graves was undisturbed, I gave orders that several of those that had already been opened should be re-examined, having heard while I was in Skópelos that they had only been examined before in a very cursory fashion.

In the first tomb there was a small graceful cup of fired clay with only the merest suggestions of handles.

The second grave had an especially large covering slab. The interior was completely empty, 2.3 m in length and 45 cm wide.

The third tomb was 2.2 m long and 65 cm wide. In the soil filling the tomb we found a small cup, and at the north end of the tomb there was a small storage chamber, 65 cm square. In this we found a long-handled pitcher, crushed by the pressure of the soil washed in by the rain. A clay lamp and a shallow bowl were found intact.

The fourth tomb was largely destroyed by soil pressure. The storage chamber at the north end of the tomb was square, 65 x 65 cm, and contained a large broken pitcher, two large dishes for offerings and another smaller one, two lamps and a vessel for oil.

It soon became evident that the further a tomb lay from the old city the less carefully it had been constructed, and accordingly I moved closer to the city.

The fifth tomb. In the soil a broken lamp and a small cup were found, and in the middle of the tomb a small round mirror with a diameter of 9 cm. It was made of copper and 2.5 mm thick. One side was slightly recessed inside the rim, while the other was completely flat, but covered with a patina. In one spot that was free of patina it was bronze coloured and highly polished. The storage chamber was 65 cm square, and contained a large pitcher, a vessel for oil and a small cup. On the west side, standing up, was a large red and black dish for offerings, and on the south side a lamp and a small dish for offerings.

The sixth tomb contained the remains of a large skeleton, but there were no vessels.

The seventh tomb. On the slab that covered it an axe was engraved. Probably it was carved at a later date, since the ancient Greek axes were attached to their handles in the middle and had two blades. Perhaps the carpenter of some passing ship had been laid to rest here. The slab was found in its proper place and my men moved it. In the earth we found two skulls, a small copper mirror, two defaced coins and a button made of bone like those we use today. The mirror had a diameter of 10 cm, and was exactly like the one in the first tomb at the rim, and in the middle there were two circles. It was covered with a thick layer of verdigris, and had come to resemble Malachite, especially on the reflective side, on which had been impressed the clothing of the deceased person, so that the fine weave was still entirely distinct.

The eighth tomb was of the usual size, but at the north end were two skulls, one in each corner, facing each other.

The ninth tomb. In one corner was a shallow bowl or drinking cup.

When I returned to Skópelos dreadful storms broke out. As soon as I had finished my excavations I made my departure, but the weather forced our small vessel to seek shelter in a cove on the southeast coast of Alónnisos. From there, I ran with two men and my servant to the tombs that are situated about an hour away. As all the tombs that I had found before were filled with soil, I was very keen to find a well-sealed tomb, in which the skeleton might be intact. This thought had occupied me so much in the nights that I had imagined many spots where it would be possible for a tomb to have remained undiscovered. I hurried now to the spot that seemed to me most probable, and started to dig.

Once we had removed a bed of soil some 40 cm thick, to the great amazement of my men, who did not know the reason for digging in this particular spot, we came upon a stone slab. And a few minutes later one of the men called out that he had found a second slab ten paces beyond the first.

By our joint efforts we cleared away the soil, but we were unable to lift the slab. We got branches from a nearby pine to make levers. The interior of the tomb was free of soil, because the slab had sealed it hermetically. The skeleton of the dead man was undisturbed. My wish had been fulfilled.

On the right side of the head (which was at the south end) was a small cup, and next to the left foot a second cup which was very delicately worked. Between the legs was a lamp, which was black on the outside.

As we were trying to remove the slab completely, a rock which we were using as a fulcrum fell into the tomb and crushed the jaw of the skull. The skull was large and male, with a crooked nose and a strong sense of individuality. Unfortunately my servant left it in Skíros, being unable to pack it. The larger bones were still firm, but the smaller ones disintegrated as soon as one touched them. We found no metal objects, and no coins. The skeleton lay on a thin bed of sand, consisting of tiny particles of quartz (which can be found in a neighbouring bay). The tomb was constructed in the same fashion as the one I described first. At the feet of the skeleton, at the north end in the square storage chamber, was a pitcher, the largest we had found up till then (as I concluded from the sherds I had seen), being 95 cm high and 35 cm across; and it was almost full of water. But we had to break it, not only because it was too heavy for us to lift, but also because it was tightly wedged and we couldn't reach the other vessels. Stuck in the wide mouth of the pitcher was a shallow vessel with a handle.

Next to the large pitcher was a small one (height 52 cm, diameter 25 cm). The dead man must have drunk prodigious quantities of water, or so the custom here suggests.

In the other corner was a vessel for oil with a handle. There were also a few small broken cups.

The second tomb was a few paces further. It was, however, half full of soil brought in by the rain. Here the effect of damp soil was clearly evident. In these conditions the bones themselves very quickly turn to soil; and in this tomb we did not find bones apart from a few fragments and the skull, whereas the skeleton in the first tomb was almost complete. The skull in the second tomb belonged to a woman, and the bone structure suggests she had a small turned-up nose.

Next to this skull, on the west side, was another, with the face turned towards the ground, but the features were indistinct.

In the other corner, on the east side, was a small drinking vessel. In the middle of the tomb was a shallow bowl, and at the feet of the skeleton, on the left side, a small cup, and on the northeast side a small vessel for oil. There were no coins, nor anything else metallic. On the base there was only a light covering of sand, as in the previous tomb.

In the northeast corner of the square storage chamber there was a pitcher with two handles. In the northwest corner stood a bulb-shaped thick-walled jug with a handle, 13 cm high with a rounded base, on the southeast side a small cup, and on the southwest side a dish for offerings with a diameter of 18 cm, and a turned-down lip, and a lamp, black on the outside.

I set my men to work to rebury the bones of the dead, and I took away only the vessels which, one way or another, had not been used for a long time by their owners.

Here Fiedler adds a revealing footnote:

Through a letter from the Ministry of Culture, His Majesty King Otto permitted objects that could be described as antique to be taken abroad. The objects we found were dispatched as ordinary freight, but eleven of the more delicate pieces were smashed due to careless packing and unpacking. It is no use lamenting this. However, every traveller should be advised always to be present when sending any natural, historical or ancient objects, or to entrust them to the care of a very reliable agent.

Fiedler then draws some conclusions about the results of his excavations:

These excavations constitute a rich contribution to archaeology.

(1) Graves with a special storage chamber, a hitherto unknown type as far as I am aware, are not found anywhere else in Greece. In all the other Greek, as well as Roman and Egyptian tombs, all the objects offered to the dead are in the same chamber as the body. Indeed, they often surround and cover the corpse, as though to prevent it moving. On this island the inhabitants provided their dead with a more comfortable space. The storage

chambers are usually square (65 x 65 cm), and only the first was of double size. The reason for this exception is not as yet known.

(2) All the mirrors that were found were of copper, which is malleable, while usually mirrors are of bronze; and no other mirrors of pure copper have been found. Besides, they are round and uniform, without a handle by which to hold them.

The following summary observations may also be made:

In each storage chamber there was at least one amphora, and either in that chamber or in the tomb itself there was a vessel for oil and at least one lamp. Each of the dead had more than one cup.

As for metallic objects, there were only copper mirrors and small unidentified copper coins, though certainly not in all the tombs.

The dead were all placed with the head to the south and the storage chamber was always at their feet, that is, towards the north. The base of the tomb was covered with very fine sand so that the dead would not lie directly on the bare ground. The dead were for the most part large bodied but not excessively so.

The tombs are all built of limestone slabs, 2.5–5 cm thick, and are 65 cm deep, and at the head and foot the space is bounded by an upright limestone slab. So far no sarcophagi have been found on the island, a fact that probably reflects the lack of suitable rock or the poverty of the inhabitants of the island.

The handles of most of the vessels, and especially those of the larger ones were bent towards the left near the bottom. This was not done deliberately (so that they could be held with greater ease); it appears, rather, that they had warped during firing, a thing that still happens fairly often today even with good quality porcelain.

In the evening the wind died down and we went back with our ancient spoils to our little ship in the bay.[10]

Here Fiedler sets out 'what became known to [him] about the rest of the Northern Sporades'. Most of this information is very basic, and much of it derived from books. Fiedler's meeting with a monk from Pipéri is of interest:

On Alónnisos I spoke with a young monk from Pipéri. He was shunned by the people of Alónnisos, since he was extraordinarily short tempered and impulsive in speech and movement. On Pipéri, though, he found space and time to calm himself. Perhaps he had been sent there by a wise superior.[11]

After his notes about the smaller islands, Fiedler gives an account of his voyage from Alónnisos to Skíros:

The following morning (15 February) we put to sea with a moderate wind (the Levante). At midday we came to a halt for lack of wind and the captain wanted to turn and spend the night at Skántzoura, which was, however, some way behind us. This made us all suspicious, for in Skópelos my men had overheard our crew having a heated debate with some other sailors, in which they said they would stay a night in Skántzoura. The day before, in Alónnisos, the crew had suggested going to Skántzoura for the night, and now the captain made the same proposal. On the coast of Tríkeri I had had a similar experience, and for this reason I rejected his plan. The captain, however, did not obey and demanded to know who would pay for repairs if we spent the night at sea and the boat suffered damage. One of the most experienced sailors, who had been a year in Vienna and spoke some German, gestured to me. He pointed out to me two ships in the harbour at Skántzoura, and said. 'We must go to Skíros for the night, and if no one objects, I myself will direct the ship. Don't go to Skántzoura.' So I went back to the captain, who was sitting by the tiller and asked him what kind of ships those were in the distant harbour of Skántzoura, and whether they did not, perhaps, belong to his brothers or some acquaintances of his. He stood his ground, saying he could not sail to Skíros today, even though we were already one third of the way between Skántzoura and Skirópoulo.[12] So I told him exactly what I would do as soon as the first hostilities commenced in Skántzoura. His face became distorted and he cursed, but he turned the ship around, and with a gradually improving wind we sailed on into the darkness. Finally, at nine o'clock in the evening we reached the harbour of Linariá on Skíros. When we had dropped anchor, the sailor whispered to me 'Was I not right?'

In the harbour there was a gunboat, with twenty-four soldiers on board.[13]

A1.5 Ludwig Ross

The German, Ludwig Ross, was the first professor of Archaeology and Philology at the University of Athens. His book Wanderungen in Griechenland (Travels in Greece), *published in 1851, was inspired by his tour of the islands with King Otto in 1841. The king took with him a large number of Bavarian and Greek functionaries. The captain of the steamship* Óthon *(named after the king) was Papanikolís, the former commander of a fire ship. Other members of the company included General Tzavéllas and the Colonels Gardhikiótis and Grívas, Baron von Stengel and the Professors Voúros and Váris, as well, of course, as Professor Ross himself. One reason for the voyage was that Otto's wife, Queen Amalia, was spending a long summer holiday in Oldenburg, visiting her parents. In those days the Northern Sporades were at the outer limits of the newly constituted Greek State. Turkish waters began just six nautical miles north of Psathoúra.*[14]

On 19 September at dawn we were below the west side of the steep rocky island of Pipéri, whose almost vertical cliffs rise to a considerable height above the sea, and which is to a large extent pine-clad, as the green-forested heights of the Northern Sporades and northern Évvia generally are, reflecting the effects of their relatively cool and damp climate, in contrast to the sun-baked and for the most part barren Cyclades. The sea was like a mirror, and as this made it possible for us to disembark on the rock, against whose sides any skiff would be dashed to pieces if the sea were only moderately rough, the king decided to make the ascent of this rocky island. High up among the trees there is a secluded monastery, whose few monks are the island's only inhabitants. One of these monks was summoned by a cannon shot to guide us to a suitable landing place; but it was some considerable time before we saw him approaching. When he finally arrived, he pointed out to us a place where the boats could lie close inshore; and after an hour's exhausting and dangerous scrambling we reached the summit. During the ascent we had the opportunity to make some instructive observations on the peculiar inflexibility of preconceived opinions.

A few months before, a number of pirate ships had disturbed the security of these waters. Several Greek warships, along with the steamship *Óthon*, had been sent to harry them and had cleared the seas. Now one of the German officers in the king's entourage had got it into his head that the monastery on Pipéri must have been one of their hideouts, and that the monks must have been their accomplices. It was in vain that we tried to make him understand that it was only in one or two places on this rocky island, and then only on a completely windless day, that it was possible to disembark; that in the whole circuit of this rocky island there was no bay capable of sheltering even the smallest boat from wind and weather; that, in consequence, the monks did not have in their possession so much as a little fishing boat, and for whole months together were cut off from all communication with the rest of the world, until by chance some ship approached the island; that there was not a single piece of evidence to suggest a connection between them and the pirates; and other similar arguments likely to convince almost any unprejudiced mind. But all to no avail. The more he failed to grasp the counter arguments, especially those of the monk, the more entrenched became his fixed idea: he was determined to see these uncouth and long-haired, but peaceable, brothers from the monastery as nothing less than assassins; and he was almost beside himself when he was unable to persuade the rest of the company to share his prejudice. How difficult it is for many minds to acknowledge what is true and right, even when it stares them in the face. What would have happened if this man, reasonable and well informed in other matters, had been sent alone to decide whether the poor priests were innocent or guilty?

The highest peak of Pipéri is, perhaps, the best vantage point from which to survey this northerly archipelago. Unfortunately, to the north and northwest visibility was not good. Thessalian Olympus and Thracian Athos[15] we recognised only through the massing clouds, heralds of the north wind that was approaching. Of the Turkish islands to the northeast we saw only Áyos Efstrátios (NEA or HIERA).[16] From here, though, we had a perfectly clear view of the Greek islands: to the northwest of Pipéri, the completely flat island of Psathoúra or Psathonísi;[17] to the west, Youra, rocky and barren except for a few strips of pine forest, and to the south of Yoúra, Kirá Panayá; to the east of Kirá Panayá lies the little island of Prasonísi [Prásso] and to the west Peristeronísi[18] and the large imposing island of Chiliodhrómia [Alónnisos], and, finally, lying beside it, Xeronísi [Peristéra]. These are the better known of these uninhabited islands, apart from Skópelos and Skiáthos. In the course of our descent the king visited the humble monastery, where a mere four monks are living; it lies among the trees in a small hollow on the southeast side of the peak. The worthy monks attended to their honoured guest with bread, cheese, honey and fruit, produced by their own efforts on this rock, and wine from Skópelos. The extremely aged and almost blind abbot of the monastery, stood before the king and said, 'May you live long, my child, and may the grace of the

Panayía be with you!' So simple and direct are the ways of these supposed pirates.

Our onward journey towards Skópelos brought us among the small islands referred to above. We passed by the southern tip of Yoúra whose only inhabitants are a monk and a shepherd family. We passed on our left, to the south, Kirá Panayá which is reasonably large, green and suitable for cultivation. Next, on the northeast side of the large island of Alónnisos, the steamer stopped for a while, without dropping anchor, because Captain Papanikolís wanted to show the king a certain narrow inlet penetrating deep into the land. As larger vessels could not enter it, it had been a favourite hideout of the pirates. We got into the boats and were rowed to the farthest corner of this narrow bay.[19]

The island is of considerable size, mountainous, and covered with pine forest. There is a single village of about forty houses on the side of the mountain near its southern peak.[20]

A1.6 Alfred Philippson

Philippson was a geographer of German origin, who travelled widely throughout the Greek lands and gave extensive descriptions of many regions. He describes in some detail life on Alónnisos and the lesser Northern Sporades at the beginning of the 20th century. He described his experiences and observations in his book, Contributions to the Knowledge of the Greek Islands *(1901).*

A1.6.1 Philippson's Itinerary

In the channel (4 km wide and up to 100 m deep) between Skópelos and Alónnisos, and closer to the former, stand two small islands: the steep sugar loaf mountain Áyos Yeóryos and the smaller and lower Mikrós Áyos Yeóryos, which together form the continuation of the mountains of Skópelos. A small, now abandoned, monastery lies high up on the southern slopes of the larger island, in amongst small gardens and olive groves. On our return journey from the sparsely inhabited islands, we were forced by the wind and current to rest up there. As a rule, the steamers from Piraeus to Thessalonica, which sail around Évvia, use the channel between Áyos Yeóryos and Skópelos, keeping close to the imposing cliffs of the latter island.

All the straits in the Magnesian Archipelago are affected by strong and variable currents which, according to the *Mediterranean Pilot*, are strongly influenced by the wind. My boatmen, however, assured me that the currents changed every six hours. This would make them tidal currents. Both views appear to be correct. My own experience with regard to this is as follows. On 6 July between 6.30 and 9.15 in the morning, I travelled, together with two sailors, in a small boat capable of being propelled by sail or oars, from the town of Skópelos to the landing place on Alónnisos. The weather was hot and there was no breeze, so that we were obliged to row; there was no appreciable current.

In the evening, after I had explored a part of the island's interior, we spent the night at a spot called Áyos Dhimítrios on the southern shore – the boatmen in the boat that lay anchored a little way off from the shore, and I myself out in the open on the lonely beach. Soon after 10 p.m., I was awoken by a great gale blowing from the north. It had become rather chilly, a few drops of rain were falling – elsewhere nearby it was raining quite hard – and, despite the enclosed nature of the channel between Alónnisos and Peristéra, the heavy breakers washed right up to my encampment, so that I had to move further inland. I could hear the boatmen talking excitedly, but couldn't see the boat in the pitch dark. I discovered the following morning that they had weighed anchor because of the menacing waves and had moved further out to sea, where they had spent a far from pleasant night. At midnight the wind lessened and I was able to get back to sleep, although I was very uneasy about the boat's disappearance. A sailing boat, which had left Skópelos at the same time as us, only narrowly escaped disaster that night off the coast of Kirá Panayá, due to the sudden onset of the squall.

At 5 in the morning on 7 July we set sail for Kirá Panayá. There was still quite a heavy swell and a strong current from the north in the channel between this island and Alónnisos. Though the wind had decreased to a light northerly, it still it carried us quickly across the 7 km strait, and at 6.30 a.m. we passed the western end of Kirá Panayá; but sailing around the southern point of this island up to the landing place on the eastern side took us a further two hours or more of tacking against the current and the now very light wind, which were both coming from the north. In the afternoon, from 2.30 to 4.00, we sailed from Kirá Panayá to Yoúra, and made the return journey between 5.15 and 6.45. The wind was by then a light southeasterly and the current was from the south. Nevertheless, the northerly swell resulting from the night's storm persisted until evening.

At 4.45 in the morning of 8 July we set off from Kirá Panayá in order to return by a direct route to Skópelos, and after an hour we passed the southwestern tip of the island. Crossing the channel to Alónnisos turned out to be a rather precarious enterprise in our open boat, as a fresh *meltémi* was blowing from the north-northwest, while a strong southeasterly current – from the opposite direction, that is to say – was doing battle against it. This resulted in a pretty tempestuous crossing, and we were very glad to reach the shelter of Alónnisos after no more than an hour. The following wind allowed us to sail the whole 20 km length of the island's southeastern coast in two and a half hours (excluding a half-hour stop). Then, at 10 a.m. we again encountered a strong current from the north accompanied by an increasingly fresh northerly wind.

For three hours we laboured with sail and oar against the wind and current in an attempt to cross the strait between [Alónnisos] and Skópelos.[21] Again and again we were driven back. Finally, at 1 p.m., we reached Áyos Yeóryos and, exhausted, rested there until 2.30. By this time the northerly wind had died down and was followed by almost complete calm, so we had only the current to contend with. Nevertheless it took us two and a half hours of rowing to reach the town [Skópelos] which was only 6 km away. At 7 a.m. the following day I set off in the same boat from Skópelos to Skiáthos. It was calm and very hot and we had to row most of the way. Consequently, we only reached the northern tip of Skópelos at noon; we were aided by a light southeasterly in the channel between Skópelos and Skiáthos, where we arrived at 3.15 p.m., having thus taken over eight hours to travel 30 km. No current was in evidence.

These observations seem to confirm the boatmen's statement that, whilst the currents in these straits are, naturally, affected by the winds, the basic pattern is that they change direction every six hours.

A1.6.2 Alónnisos

Alónnisos extends for 21 km, but at its widest is only 5.5km from south-southwest to north-northeast The western third is narrower still, 2–3 km; its contours contrast sharply with the broader part and it is also considerably lower. Seen from a distance the island appears as a single extended mountain ridge. The northwestern coast extends in broad sweeps, and only towards the western end are there a few bays opening to the northwest and some small narrow inlets. At the northeastern end of the island there is a larger inlet at Yérakas, a safe haven for small boats. The western part of the southern coast has several deep inlets, which are sheltered from the north wind; besides, a large part of this coast is protected by Peristéra, and it is here that a small triangular plain called Áyos Dhimítrios juts out into the sea. Thus Alónnisos does not possess any actual harbours, but a large number of safe landing places which can be used in certain weather conditions. The majority of these small bays are backed by sandy beaches. A few rocky islets lie around the island.

I explored Alónnisos from a point close to its western end as far as Áyos Dhimítrios, roughly two-thirds of its length; and I saw the entire southeast coast from the boat.

The western end of Alónnisos is dominated by Kalóvoulo, a limestone hill about 300 m high, which descends very steeply to the coast. To the east the limestone is covered by a thin layer of slate. This forms a saddle which extends southwards down to a small bay, the landing place of the only village on the island. The village lies just over 1 km from the western end, on the island's ridge, just above the steep northern coast. In fact it stands on a layer of limestone which towers up like a cliff. Built on a stormy, easily defended height, and recognisable from afar by its tall windmill, it is one of the poorest, most isolated hamlets in the archipelago, deprived of any regular communication with the outside world whether by steamer or telegraph. And apart from this hamlet there is not a single house on this long island. The population in 1879 was around 400; and in 1896 it was 594. The people live by crop farming and more especially from livestock. They no longer go to sea, although in the past, it is said, they were pirates.

Immediately to the east of the village the area of Tertiary rocks begins, and it makes up most of the rest of the narrower part of the island. Along the northern coast the chalk rock emerges, forming in parts quite a high ridge and every now and again little outcrops of chalk slate appear within the Tertiary region. The Tertiary itself is a landscape of gentle hills which has been well cultivated with vines, cereals and olive trees; here I also noticed some remarkably attractive cattle. Above the second bay on the northern coast, at the top of a steep cliff lies the spot where Virlet and Fiedler examined the lignite deposits.

The props have collapsed, the whole terrain has subsided and been partly washed away, so that I was unable to discover where the deposit reached the surface. More or less opposite this spot, on the southern coast, stand the remains of the old town of ICOS, which, because of the red colour of the conglomerate and the fairly massive earth layer lying on it, is now called Kokkinókastro ('Red Castle'). The remains occupy the end of a low, flat peninsula with, a very steep coastline; and a small island lies in front of it between two bays which could serve as landing places. A small fertile valley runs down to the eastern and larger bay. Immediately to the east, just within the region of the limestone rocks, lies another bay called Lefkós Yalós, at the end of a long valley.

At the point where the island suddenly doubles in width towards the northwest, the Tertiary is cut off by higher limestone mountains. Here practically all cultivation ceases. Only a few goatherds, resembling Red Indians in their leather trousers, some charcoal burners and woodcutters roam through this extensive isolated mountain region. Towards the steep northwest coast these mountains rise to a range of high ridges and peaks (the highest is 477 m according to the hydrographic chart); towards the east it forms a broad plateau, 200–250 m in height, which then drops quite steeply to the coast and is transected by a number of narrow valleys.

Further to the north the high mountains carry on right up to the east coast. As far as Áyos Dhimítrios, the mountains are covered by magnificent pine forests with maquis undergrowth and occasional wild olive trees. By contrast, the northern part of the island is nothing but a maquis wasteland, now that the charcoal burners and ship builders have devastated the area.

Only on the eastern coast, around Áyos Dhimítrios, can one find a few cultivated slopes and a few fields on the small plain itself. The beach on the triangular promontory at Áyos Dhimítrios consists of coarse pebbles (beach detritus); and the promontory itself has clearly been produced by the action of the sea, for the little valley that reaches the sea here is no larger than several others which have not formed any promontory. It is made up of drifting coastal debris deposited by the waves at that point in the channel between Alónnisos and Peristéra where the waves from the north meet those from the south. The shore offers tolerable anchorage here, as it is protected by the aforementioned island. (That the shelter is not perfect has been indicated above.) This is where the wood and charcoal destined for Skópelos and Skiáthos are normally loaded. It is also where the Skopelites build their small sailing craft. We came across some people busy with the construction of a caïque. They were camping nearby in huts built of brushwood.

Alónnisos is undoubtedly the most significant of the sparsely populated islands. Even though it does not possess a real harbour, it is today the only island with a settlement.

A1.6.3 Peristéra and Dhío Adhérfia

Not far from the southeastern coast of Alónnisos lies Peristéra. It really is a very lonely island, for it is only visited by goatherds. It consists entirely of relatively flat and featureless limestone rock and is almost completely covered by maquis. I have only seen its western side while sailing past. The limestone appears to form a folded basin facing north.

The outline of the island is fairly ragged. Its northern tip approaches to within 400 m of Alónnisos, the southern part is 1.2 km distant; in between the coast recedes and so forms a splendid harbour protected on all sides, with yet smaller, narrow inlets within it. This is the 'royal harbour', Vasilikós. It reduces the island in the middle to a very narrow, rocky isthmus. There are further narrow inlets which cut into the island, one of which goes by the name of Peristéri.

The southern continuation of Peristéra, on a line jutting out 200 m, is formed by the adjacent islands of Dhío Adhérfia ('Two Brothers') and several small reefs in line with these. According to the hydrographic chart the larger of the two islands is 159 m high. I have only seen them from the sea. They are uninhabited.

A1.6.4 Kirá Panayá

Beyond Alónnisos the main chain of islands is continued by Kirá Panayá.

This island lies 7 km northeast of Alónnisos. Overall it has more or less rectangular outline, but is deeply indented by bays. In the north, besides a few smaller bays, the remarkable harbour of Planítis opens up behind its narrow entrance. This is only 100 m wide, and no more than 8 m deep, and leads into a broad basin which culminates in two small coves. Another larger, branching bay [Áyos Pétros] extends deep into the island from the southwest. Both serve as refuges during the frequent and sudden northerly storms; and they used to be pirates' lairs. The western coast has yet another narrow inlet. The eastern side, by contrast, is steep and closed off. Only one small bay in the form of a three quarter circle opens up in the cliff face. This is the landing place (only for small boats, however) for the monastery that lies above the bay and is the island's only building.

This is where we too landed.

A deep depression traverses the island between the two large bays mentioned above. Adjoining Planítis Bay is a plain of arable land which is only separated from the southwestern harbour and the narrow inlet on the west coast by low hills.

To the northwest of this depression a higher ridge rises and runs north-northeast. It includes the island's highest peak (320 m hydrographic chart; my estimate from a distance being 380 m). A very similar broad ridge flanks the central valley in the southeast. Adjoining this ridge and occupying the southern part of the island is a low, gently undulating chalky plateau. This broad stretch of wilderness, covered by maquis and wild olive trees, and serving as a feeding ground for the monastery's considerable herds of goats, is interrupted only occasionally by cultivated fields. Numerous rock pigeons and turtle doves provide welcome game (there are no hares, rabbits or partridges).

The monastery, to which the whole island belongs, lies directly south of the small inlet on the east coast, on the terrace formed in the mountainside by a band of slate. It looks out over the sea, with a view of precipitous Yoúra and the solid mass of Pipéri. Its design is that typical of the Greek monasteries – a square building, showing only a few embrasures in its exterior walls; the inner rooms open on to a wooden balcony which runs right round the inner courtyard and is reached by ladder-like steps. The entrance to this courtyard is through a massive gate guarded by powerful dogs. At its centre stands a little church. A few minutes' walk to the north, in a little valley behind the bay, is a spring where the monks have established a small garden.

The monastery, a *metóchion* (daughter house) of the large, wealthy monastery of the Great Lávra on Mount Athos, is run by a young, relatively well educated Spetsiot,[22] assisted by two or three older, serving monks. Also accommodated here, when they are not camping out in the open to be near their herds and fields, are the farm labourers and the goatherds, and a poor young imbecile from Évvia, who lost his mind as a result of an unhappy love affair, and who, it is hoped, will recover in this isolation. The entire population of the island in 1896 was only 16, of whom two were women. This little colony leads a very lonely existence. Their only link with the outside world is a small open boat down in the harbour. They are almost totally self-sufficient; the abundant income from the young cattle and the cheese goes into the monastery's treasury. Day after day, apart from work, there is nothing but the eternal sound of the sea!

Monks are said to have lived on the island for a very long time. There are widespread signs of old terracing, indicating former cultivation in the now overgrown terrain.

Besides the few islets around the coast of Kirá Panayá, there are, in the channel between this island and Yoúra to the east, the small flat island of Pappoús, with its little church and the ruins of a windmill, the reef Stróngilo, and the larger and higher island of Grámeza, all three of them limestone, the last with a steep cliff facing east.

A1.6.5 Yoúra

Unfortunately my time was limited – I still had to investigate Skiáthos, and there were only four days to go before the departure of the weekly steamer, which was going to take me to Skíros – and I was only able to spend a little over one hour on the interesting island Yoúra. The island, which is 8 km long from north to south and 3 km wide, rises out of the water, 4 km northeast of Kirá Panayá, a wild barren mountainous rock. Its height has not yet been measured, but may well reach 500 m. The jagged ridge drops almost vertically to the east coast where there are no bays at all. To the west it declines more gently, and is transected by some steep gorges, and the west coast is indented by little inlets which can only be used for landing boats in good weather.

The whole island appears to consist of light grey limestone, which, judging by the surface formations, runs north and falls off to the west. The last remaining Holly Oak bushes (*Quercus coccifera*) have been decimated by the charcoal burners; the bare rock is covered almost exclusively by phrygana and in places by the caper bush, common on all these islands. A type of wild goat can be found on the almost inaccessible slopes on the eastern side of the island.

I landed in the tiny inlet on the south coast and climbed up the steep cliff to the top of the projecting peninsula-like southwest tip of the island. The white, semi-dense, massive limestone contains fragments of sea shells and snail shells that have coalesced with the rock. Several large caves have, as elsewhere, been transformed by fences of prickly phrygana into dung-filled goat stables, which the animals use for shelter during severe winter weather. Up on the heights a young goatherd was sitting, watching me. He took me to the dwelling of a goatherd family from Skópelos, who were pasturing their flock here. They live in a small disused monastery at the top of the peninsula, with a little garden and a cistern of wonderfully cool water. An old woman sat spinning in the doorway, together with a young woman with an infant at her breast, and soon two men came from their herds nearby to join them. But soon I had to take my leave of these friendly people, after I had sketched the visible part of the island, for the sun was already going down.

The island belongs to the state and the hunting of wild goats has, thankfully, been prohibited. Apart from goatherds only charcoal burners occasionally visit this solitary island. According to the census in 1896, it had a population of 13.

A1.6.6 Psathoúra, Pipéri and Skántzoura

To the northeast of Yoúra lies a rocky bank, at a depth of 18 m, undoubtedly the remains of an eroded island; and in a direct line north at a distance of 6 km the island of Míga [Psathonísi], and 1 km beyond that is Psathoúra, the last of the islands of the Magnesian Archipelago. I saw Psathoúra only from a distance; this strange formation appears to be floating on the water like a flat disk. It is roughly 2 km long and 1 km wide and very low-lying. A lighthouse was built on it a few years ago; 14 people (4 of them women) have been living there since 1896.

I also only saw from afar the two islands which emerge from the deeper sea to the east of the main archipelago.

Pipéri ('Peppercorn') lies 12 km east of Yoúra, has a simple oval outline and steep cliffs on all sides, though it levels off at the top to a broad ridge, almost giving the impression of a plateau. The high areas are uncharted. The island has beautiful pine forests; and there is a monastery, apparently inhabited by a few monks. The island is not mentioned, however, in the 1896 census.

Skántzoura is a flat island deeply indented by bays and surrounded by a swarm of little islands. It lies east-southeast of Dhío Adhérfia and Alónnisos, close to the shipping route between Skíros and Skópelos. It also possesses a monastery. Its population in 1896 was 16. I was told that white marble has been quarried there in recent times.[23]

Notes

1. Buondelmonte (1420/1897). The 1897 (Paris) edition includes a Greek translation which the author quotes here. [Translator]
2. Bordone (1528).
3. Imittós (HYMETTUS) is a mountain on the east side of Athens, famous for its honey since antiquity. [Translator]
4. In the original German of these extracts from Fiedler, and of those from Ross and Philippson that follow, Alónnisos is almost always referred to as 'Chiliodromia' or some variant of this name. In the translations 'Alónnisos' has been substituted throughout. Obsolete

names of other islands have also been replaced by the names in common use today. There are many unsignalled omissions, some minor and some quite extensive, in these extracts (so many that it would have been unsightly to mark them with ellipses). The omitted material is mainly of a technical nature, including extended geological descriptions. [Translator]

5. Fiedler (1841), pp. 32–4.
6. Fiedler's explanation of the name is erroneous. See p. 61. [Translator]
7. Fiedler (1841), pp. 44-8.
8. Fiedler's description of the graves and their contents should be read in conjunction with his drawings reproduced on pp. 130 and 446.
9. Fiedler gives the dimensions in *Ellen* and *Zoll*. An *Elle* is about 25 ins, or about 65 cm, and a *Zoll* is an inch, or about 2.5 cm. All dimensions have been converted to metres, centimetres or millimetres, and the larger dimensions have in most cases been rounded to the nearest 5 cm to reflect the evident approximate nature of some of Fiedler's measurements. [Translator]
10. Fiedler (1841), pp. 49–61.
11. Fiedler (1841), p. 62.
12. A small island due west of Linariá (the harbour on Skíros to which they were headed). [Translator]
13. Fiedler (1841), pp. 64–5.
14. Deyánnis (1960).
15. Mount Athos is actually in Macedonia, not Thrace. [Translator]
16. Ross's parenthesis is evidently giving its possible ancient names. [Translator]
17. 'Psathonísi' is now the name of a separate very small island to the south of Psathoúra, but it is possible that it has in the past been used as an alternative name for Psathoúra itself. [Translator]
18. It is not clear which island Ross is referring to as 'Peristeronísi' (which he gives in Greek characters as well as in transliteration). It sounds like Peristéra, but he clearly refers to this just below as Xeronísi, and Peristéra is not, in any case, to the west of Kirá Panayá. The only island which might be described in this way is Fangroú: it guards the west side of the bay of Áyos Pétros, and is also known as Pelérissa. This might take the form 'Pelerissonísi' (the suffix -nísi meaning island), which Ross could then have confused with 'Peristeronísi' (for Peristéra), which he may also have heard. [Translator]
19. Ross is presumably referring to Yérakas. [Translator]
20. Ross (1851), vol. 2, pp. 36–40.
21. Philippson actually says 'zwischen Geórgios und Skópelos' ('between Áyos Yeóryos and Skópelos'), but this makes no sense in the context, and 'Geórgios' is probably an error for 'Chiliodromia' ('Alónnisos'). [Translator]
22. A Spetsiot is a person from the island of Spétses, in the Argolic Gulf (Peloponnese). [Translator]
23. Philippson (1901), pp. 134–41.

BIBLIOGRAPHY

In addition to all the works cited in the text or notes, this bibliography also includes other works consulted by the author or translator. English translations are provided for titles in transliterated Greek.

Anagnóstou, Evángelos Y. (1978), *Imerolóyon* (*Journal*), Athens.

Athanasíou, Ch. Y. (1964), *I nísos Alónnisos* (*The Island of Alónnisos*), Alónnisos.

Baudrand, Michel Antoine (1682), *Geographia ordine literarum disposita,* Paris.

Baudrand, Michel Antoine (1688), *La Grèce,* Paris.

Benoist, Michel (1827) *Asia and Europe*; first published 1775, Peking.

Bordone, Benedetto (1528), *Libro de tutte l'isole del mondo*, Venice.

Boschini, Marco (1658), *L'Archipelago*, Venice.

Brownson, Carleton L. (tr.) (1918), *Xenophon: Hellenica, Books I–V*, London & Cambridge MA (Loeb Classical Library).

Buondelmonte, Cristoforo (1420), *Liber insularum Archipelagi* (manuscript).

Buondelmonte, Cristoforo (1897), *Description des îles de l'Archipel*, tr. (Greek) anon., ed. and tr. (French) E. Legrand, Paris.

Bursian, Conrad (1862–72) *Geographie von Griechenland*, 2 vols, Leipzig.

Chatzidhákis, E. (1997), article in *Némesis*, January 1997.

Choiseul-Gouffier, Marie Gabriel Auguste Florent de (1782), *Voyage pittoresque de la Grèce*, 3 vols, (1782–1824), vol. 1, Paris.

Christopoulos, George A. & John C. Bastias (eds) (1974–), *History of the Hellenic World*, various translators under the direction of Philip Sherrard, London.

Coronelli, Vincenzo (1696), *Isolario*, Venice.

d'Anville, Jean-Baptiste Bourgignon (1756). 'Détroit des Dardanelles', in *Memoires de l'Académie Royale des Inscriptions et Belles-Lettres* 28, 318–46, Paris.

da Vignola, Giacomo Cantelli (1685) *Mercurio geografico*, Modena.

Dakin, Douglas (1966), *The Greek Struggle in Macedonia 1897–1913*, Thessalonica.

Dapper, Olfert (1688), *Naukeurige beschryving der eilanden, de Archipel der Middelantsche Zee*, Amsterdam.

Dapper, Olfert (1703), *Description exacte des isles de l'archipel, et de quelques autres adjacentes*, Amsterdam (French translation of Dapper (1688)).

Delisle, Guillaume (1733), *Atlas nouveau*, Paris; first published 1730.

Deyánnis, Yórgos I. (1960), 'Vasiliká taxídhia stin Évvia ke tis V. Sporádhes ópos ta periégrapsen o L. Ross' ('Royal Travels in Évvia and the Northern Sporades as described by L. Ross'), in *Archío Eviïkón meletón (Archive of Evvian Studies)* 7, 283–311.

Dhapóndes, Konstandínos (1994), *I skopelítes: míthi, nisiotiká diiyímata* (*The People of Skópelos: Myths, Island Tales*), ed. Vasílis Tomanás, Skopelos.

Doulgéri-Intzessiloglou, Argyroula & Yvon Garlan (1990) 'Vin et amphores de Péparéthos et d'Ikos', *Bulletin de correspondance hellénique* 11(4/1), 361–89.

Efstratíou, Níkos (1985) *Agios Petros: A Neolithic Site in the Northern Sporades: Aegean Relationships during the Neolithic of the 5th Millennium*, Oxford (British Archaeological Reports, International Series 241).

Fairbanks, Arthur (tr.) (1931), *Philostratus: Imagines; Callistratus: Descriptions*, London & Cambridge MA (Loeb Classical Library).

Fiedler, Karl (1841), *Reise durch alle Theile des königreiches Griechenland*, vol. 2, Leipzig.

Fredrich, Carl (1906) 'Skiathos und Peparethos', in *Mitteilungen des kaiserlich deutschen archäologische Instituts athenische Abteilung* 21, 99–128.

Gastaldi, Giacomo (c. 1575), *Europe*; first published 1559, Venice.

Grace, Virginia R. (1961), *Amphoras and the Ancient Wine Trade*, Princeton (American School of Classical Studies at Athens: Excavations of the Athenian Agora: Picture Book No. 6).

Graindor, Paul (1906), *Histoire de l'île de Skyros jusqu'en 1538,* Liège.

Greek Government (1992), *Stichía sistáseos ki exelíxeos ton dímon ke kinotíton, Ar. 48: Nómos Magnesías (Statistics for the Composition and Development of Municipalities and [Rural] Communites, No. 48: the Nómos of Magnesía)*, Athens.

Hadjidaki, Elpida (1995), 'Ein Schiffswrack aus klassischer Zeit vor der Insel Alonnisos, Griechenland', in *In Poseidons Reich: Archäologie unter Wasser* (*Antike Welt: Zeitschrift für Archäologie und Kulturgeschichte*, Year 26, Special Number).

Hourmouziadis, G., P. Asimakopoulou-Atzaka & K.A. Makris (1982), *Magnesia: The Story of a Civilization*, tr. H. Zigada & C.N.W. Klint, Athens.

Ikonómos, S.A. (1883), *I nísos Pepárithos* (*The Island of Pepárithos*), Jena.

Imhoof-Blumer, Friedrich (1883), *Monnaies grecques*, Paris.

Ioannidaki-Dostoglou, Évangélia (1989) 'Les vases de l'épave byzantine de Pélagonnèse-Halonnèse', in *Recherches sur la céramique byzantine*, ed. V. Déroche & J.-M. Spieser, Athens (*Bulletin de correspondance hellénique* Supplément 18).

Jones, Horace Leonard (tr.) (1917–32), *The Geography of Strabo*, 8 vols, London & Cambridge MA (Loeb Classical Library).

Jones, W.H.S. (tr.) (1918–35), *Pausanias: Description of Greece*, 5 vols, London & Cambridge MA (Loeb Classical Library).

Karkatzélou, María (1995), article in *Thessalía (Thessaly)*, 26 September.

Kefalliniádhis, N.A. (1984), *Piratía: Koursári sto Eyéo* (*Piracy: Corsairs in the Aegean*), Athens.

Konstandinídhis, Kostís Anastásios 1988, *I listía ke i piratía sti Skíro, Skiátho ke Skópelo katá ti dhiárkia tis epanástasis tou 1821 méchri ke tis andivasilías tou Óthona: Istorikí meléti vasisméni apoklistiká epí engráfon* (*Looting and Piracy in Skíros, Skiáthos and Skópelos during the Revolution of 1821 and up to the Regency of Otto: A Historical Study Based Exclusively on Documents*), vol. 1, Athens.

Kritzás, Ch. (1971), 'To vizandinón naváyon Pelagonnísou–Alonnísou' ('The Byzantine Wrecks of Pelagónnisos-Alónnisos'), *Archeoloyiká análekta ex Athinón* (*Archeological Gleanings from Athens*) 4/2, 176–82.

Lapie, Pierre (1838), *Atlas universel de géographie ancienne et moderne*, Paris.

Lauremberg, Johannes Wilhelm (1638), *Graecia Antiqua,* Amsterdam; first published 1656.

Lauremberg, Johannes Wilhelm (1638), *Sea Atlas of Greece and the Aegean*, Amsterdam.

Lavriótis, Kallístratos (n.d.), *Istorikón proskinitárion Ierás Monís Meyístis Lávras* (*A Historic Icon Stand from the Holy Monastery of the Great Lávra*).

Lazarídhis, Pávlos (1966), 'Meseoniká Thessalías ke Sporádhon Níson' ('Medieval remains in Thessaly and the Sporades Islands'), in *Archeoloyikón dheltíon* (*Archaeological Bulletin*) 21/B2, 258–64.

Lolling, H.G. (1889), 'Landeskunde und Topographie', in *Geographie und politische Geschichte des klassischen Altertums*, ed. Iwan Müller, Nördlingen (vol. 3 of *Handbuch der klassischen Altertums-Wissenschaft*).

Maclean, Jennifer K. Berenson & Ellen Bradshaw Aitken (trs) (n.d. [*circa* 2002]), Philostratus, *On Heroes*, Atlanta GA.

Mallet, Alain Manesson (1683), *Description de l'univers*, 5 vols, Paris.

Mercator, Gerhard (1590), *Italiae, Sclavoniae et Graeciae tabulae geographicae*, Duisburg.

Miller, Frank Justus (tr.) (1977–84), *Ovid: Metamorphoses*, 3rd edn. (vol. 1), 2nd edn. (vol. 2), rev. G.P. Goold, 2 vols, London & Cambridge MA (Loeb Classical Library).

Moutsópoulos, Nikolas C. (1982), *Skiathos–Scopelos: Essai d'une étude de l'écologie-sociale des écosystèmes insulaires des Sporades Septentrionales*, Thessalonica.

Nasoúlis, Dh. (1950), *Skópelos: I archéa Pepárithos* (*Skópelos: The Ancient Pepárithos*).

Nikitídhis, N. (1995), article in *Adhésmeftos típos* (*Free Press*), 21 Sept, 49.

Nikonános, Níkos (1972) 'Vizandiná ke meseoniká mnimía Thessalías' ('Byzantine and Medieal Monuments of Thessaly'), *Archeoloyikón dheltíon* (*Archaeological Bulletin*) 27/B2, 420–32 (esp. 424–5).

Papadhiamándis, Aléxandhros (1981–88), *Ápanda* (*Complete Works*), 5 vols, ed. N. Dh. Triandafillópoulos, Athens.

Papadiamantis, Alexandros (1987), *Tales from a Greek Island*, tr. Elizabeth Constantinides, Baltimore & London.

Papanikóla-Bakírtzi, Dhímitra (1999), *Vizandiná emfialoména keramiká* (*Byzantine ceramic wine containers*), Athens.

Paton, R.E. (tr.) (1916–18), *The Greek Anthology*, 5 vols, London & Cambridge MA (Loeb Classical Library).

Philippson, Alfred (1901), *Beiträge zur Kenntnis der griechischen Inselwelt*, Gotha.

Porcacchi, Tommaso (1572) *L'isole più famose del mondo*, Venice.

Rackham, H., W.H.S. Jones & D.E. Eichholz (trs) (1938–63), *Pliny: Natural History*, 10 vols, London & Cambridge MA (Loeb Classical Library).

Rangabé, A.R. (1842 & 1855) *Antiquités helléniques, ou Répertoire d'inscriptions et d'autres antiquités découvertes depuis l'affranchissement de la Grèce*, 2 vols, Athens.

Rangavís, Iákovos Rízos (1853–54), *Ta Elliniká* (*Greek Antiquities*), 3 vols, Athens.

Robijn, Jacob (1683), *Zee Atlas*, Amsterdam.

Rogers, E. (1932), *The Copper Coinage of Thessaly*, London.

Rohmer, F.E. (tr.) (1998), *Pomponius Mela's Description of the World*, Ann Arbor, MI.

Ross, Ludwig (1851), *Wanderungen in Griechenland im Gefolge des Königs Otto und der Königin Amalie*, Halle.

Roux, Joseph (1764), *Carte de la Mediterranée*, Marseilles.

Roux, Joseph (1764), *Nouveau recueil des plans des ports et rades de la mer Mediterranée*, Marseilles.

Sampsón, Adhamándios (1968), *I nísos Skópelos: Istorikí ke archeoloyikí meléti* (*The Island of Skópelos: A Historical and Archaeological Study*), Athens.

Sampsón, Adhamándios (1970) 'Íkos–Alónnisos ke e érimi nisídhes ton V. Sporádhon katá tin archeótita' ('Íkos–Alónnisos and the uninhabited islands of the Northern

Sporades in antiquity'), in *Archío Eviïkón meletón* (*Archive of Evvian Studies*) 16, 349–70.

Sampsón, A. (1973) *Alónnisos—Erimónisa: Touristikós odhigós (Alónnisos [and] the Unihabited Islands: A Tourist Guide)*, published by the newspaper *Vóries Sporádhes* (*Northern Sporades*).

Sampsón, Adhamándios (ed.) (1995), *Praktiká anichtoú seminaríou aïfórou anáptixis ke ikotourismoú, Alónnisos apó 21 éos 23 Septemvríou 1995* (*Proceedings of an open seminar on sustainable development and ecotourism, Alónnisos, 21–23 September 1995*).

Sarrís, Ioánnis (1925), 'Tís i archéa Alónnisos?' ('Which was Ancient Alónnisos?'), in *Athiná* 36, 214–22.

Seller, John (1675), *Atlas Maritimus*, London.

Simópoulos, Kiriákos (1970), *Xéni taxidhiótes stin Elládha 333 m.Ch.–1700* (*Foreign Travellers in Greece* AD *333–1700*), Athens.

Simópoulos, Kiriákos (n.d.), *Xéni taxidhiótes stin Elládha 1700-1800* (*Foreign Travellers in Greece 1700–1800*), Athens.

Skavéntzos, Ioánnis M. (1854), *Ékthesi archeoloyikí perí tis nísou Skopélou* (*An Archaeological Exhibition about the Island of Skópelos*), Athens.

Theocháris, Dhimítrios R. (1970a), 'Anaskafi epí tis nisídhos tou Ayíou Pétrou (Kirá-Panayás)' ('Excavation on the islet of Áyos Pétros'), *Archeoloyikón dheltíon* (*Archaeological Bulletin*) 25/B2, 271–6.

Theocháris, Dhimítrios R. (1970b), 'Paleolithiká evrímata en Alonníso' ('Palaeolithic finds on Alónnisos'), *Archeoloyikón dheltíon* (*Archaeological Bulletin*) 25/B2, 276–9.

Theocháris, Dhimítrios (n.d.), *I Skíros katá tin epanástasi tou 1821 (Skíros during the Revolution of 1821)*.

Throckmorton, Peter (1971) 'Explorations of the Byzantine Wreck at Pelagos Island near Alonnisos', *Archeoloyiká análekta ex Athinón* (*Archeological Gleanings from Athens*) 4/2, 183–5.

Throckmorton, Peter (1977), *Diving for Treasure*, London.

Tomanás, Vasílis (1960), 'Skópelos', in *Archío Evviïkón meletón* (*Archive of Evvian Studies*) 6.

Tomanás, Vasílis (n.d.), *Skopelítes* (*The people of Skópelos*).

Tselíkas, Agamémnon (1985), *Martiríes apó ti Sandoríni (1573–1819): Ékthesi istorikón engráfon* (*Evidence from Sandoríni: An Exhibition of Historical Documents*), Athens.

Van der Aa, Pieter (1729), *La galerie agréable du monde*, 66 vols, Leyden.

Vince, J.H., A.T. Murray *et al.* (trs) (1926–49), *Demosthenes*, 7 vols, London & Cambridge MA (Loeb Classical Series).

Visscher, Claes Jansz III (1682), *Atlas minor*, Amsterdam.

Wace, A.J.B. (1906), 'Skiathos und Skopelos', *Mitteilungen des kaiserlich deutschen archäologische Instituts athenische Abteilung* 21, 129–33.

White, Horace (tr.) (1912–13), *Appian's Roman History*, 4 vols, London & Cambridge MA (Loeb Classical Library).

Yangákis, Yeóryos K. (1989), *Simvolí stin meléti tou archipelágous ton Vórion Sporádhon* (*Contribution to the study of the archipelago of the Northern Sporades*), Tínos.

INDEX

Note: *page numbers in italics refer to illustration captions.*

D

Lightning Source UK Ltd.
Milton Keynes UK
20 September 2010

160084UK00002B/2/P